THE INTERNATIONAL
SLIM GOURMET COOKBOOK

THE INTER NATIONAL SLIM GOURMET COOK BOOK

Barbara Gibbons

HARPER & ROW, PUBLISHERS

New York, Hagerstown,
San Francisco, London

ACKNOWLEDGMENTS

For inspiration, determination, perspiration, and sheer drudgery, I'd like to express my grateful appreciation to all the people who worked so hard to see that things came out right, or as right as we could make it. To my home economist Dot Fast, to editor Joe Vergara and all the people at Harper & Row, to editor Gael McCarthy at United Features Syndicate . . . so many their names could fill another book! I must also say thank you to all the readers and newspaper editors of my Slim Gourmet column who took the time to express comments, criticisms, and compliments over the past eight years. You are all editors of this book as well.

Some of the recipes in this book have appeared in Barbara Gibbons' newspaper column "The Slim Gourmet" distributed by United Feature Syndicate.

THE INTERNATIONAL SLIM GOURMET COOKBOOK. Copyright © 1978 by Barbara Gibbons. All rights reserved. Printed in the United States of America. No part of this book may be used or reproduced in any manner whatsoever without written permission except in the case of brief quotations embodied in critical articles and reviews. For information address Harper & Row, Publishers, Inc., 10 East 53rd Street, New York, N.Y. 10022. Published simultaneously in Canada by Fitzhenry & Whiteside Limited, Toronto.

Library of Congress Cataloging in Publication Data

Gibbons, Barbara.
    The international slim gourmet cookbook.
    Includes index.
    1. Cookery, International. 2. Low-calorie diet—
Recipes. I. Title.
TX725.A1G37 1978   641.5'635   78–2136
ISBN 0–06–011507–6

79 80 81 82 10 9 8 7 6 5 4 3

CONTENTS

INTRODUCTION: FABULOUS FOOD WITH A FOREIGN FLAIR ...

... Who says it has to be fattening?

Do you salivate for schnitzel, souvlaki or sukiyaki? Covet crêpes or cassata? Are you fond of flan, partial to pilaf, and hooked on hasenpfeffer? You say your favorite way of learning the language is to study the menu? Have we got news for you!

"Foreign" food doesn't have to be fattening. In fact, slimming down is extra easy if you cook with an ethnic flair. It's true that travel is broadening. Sometimes in the least desirable places, hips for example. But you *can* take a trip right in your own kitchen, and leave the excess calories behind, so to speak. After all, flavor is what food is all about . . . and flavor isn't necessarily fattening.

Consider spices and seasonings. The right combinations can give the most humdrum fare an unmistakable foreign accent. Yet most seasonings have no calories to speak of. Oil, on the other hand, has no flavor whatsoever, yet it's the most fattening ingredient of all!

YES, YOU CAN BE A FOOD ADVENTURER...WITHOUT BEING FAT

If you're poundage prone, you may be wary of expanding your culinary horizons, for fear of unwittingly widening your waistline. But think of it this way: those of us with weight problems are the very people who need to have the broadest possible spectrum of foods to choose from. If you routinely

1

restrict your food choices to a familiar few, what alternatives are left after all the high-calorie goodies are ruled out? The more ways you know to cook fish (or any other nonfattening food) the more likely you are to like it!

HOW THE FATTEST GIRL IN NEWARK, N.J., BECAME "THE SLIM GOURMET"

Maybe I *wasn't* the fattest kid in Newark. But as a 208-pound 12-year old, it certainly seemed that way. I was a fat baby, fat toddler, fat teenager, and finally a fat housewife and mother, whose every effort to slim down resulted in failure.

One thing I was *not* was a gourmet cook. Oh, I enjoyed cooking and eating, especially eating, but back then my favorites were steak and potatoes, bread and butter, cake and ice cream in any flavor so long as it was chocolate. My favorite "spices" were salt and sugar. Now I'm the kind of person who is normally inclined to try new things. But not food. Like lots of overweights, I would have told you that I wasn't really interested in food (but my size 20½ girth betrayed otherwise.) Of course I was interested, *intensely* interested. But kidding myself into a pose of indifference seemed the best course of action. I had enough trouble resisting the foods I was already familiar with. Better stay out of the kitchen, I thought; who needs new temptations?

Then a funny thing happened. In my thirty-second year I took up cooking. And stripped off eighty pounds! After a lifetime of trying and failing at every conceivable slim-down plan, I stumbled onto the secret of slimming *right in my own kitchen*. I found out that

• foods don't have to be as fattening as they usually are

• recipes aren't carved in stone. (Who says spaghetti sauce needs half a cup of oil! Or any oil at all!)

• most cookbooks—and most commercial food products—are "calorie contaminated," full of extra calories they don't really need.

• unneeded calories are America's most dangerous food additive!

Cooking became my hobby, *creative* cooking. Not slavish, follow-the-directions, mindless recipe reproducing . . . what fun is that? But a do-your-own thing, self-pleasing, personalized expression of my own culinary creativity . . . geared to my own nutritional needs and limitations. To hell with Julia and Craig!

MY "CALORIE ALLERGY"

You see, I had finally come around to thinking of myself as the blameless victim of an inherited food allergy. (As a point of fact, that's what *most* of us could-be fatties are—victims of genetics!) Like both my parents and everyone else in my family, *I am uniquely sensitive to certain substances widely existing in most "ordinary" foods.* Those substances are excess calories, and they make me break out in excess fat all over my body. (If *you* have a weight problem, don't let the smug skinnies of this world make you feel like a weak-willed glutton. You are not suffering from a character defect. You are simply biologically programmed to fatten easier on fewer calories than others do. *You* are calorie allergic.)

Now lots of people have other food allergies and learn to live with them, either by limiting themselves to a few simple foods or learning to cook their own thing with the offending substances omitted. You've got the same choices. You can limit yourself to a few simple foods (strict dieting) or you can cook your own thing with the unneeded extra calories omitted. I chose the latter path. After all, diets never did work for me.

EDITING OUT THE UNNEEDED CALORIES

What *are* the main sources of unneeded calories that make foods fattening? For us poundage-prone types with calorie allergies, the "offending substances" are basically fats and fatty ingredients, plus the overprocessed, nutritionally-neutered starches and sugars. (Fat and sugar are pure calories. Fat and sugar are what's left after they've processed out everything of any nutritional value.)

Though widely found in "ordinary" foods, most fats and sugar have no real flavor. All they add to food is oiliness (greasiness) or otherwise flavorless sweetness. Now, since they contribute nothing of value—and no real flavor—to foods, I set out to reproduce my favorite foods without them—or using them as little as possible.

THE JOY OF COOKING SLIM

Cooking without unneeded calories became such an absorbing challenge—with such delicious results—that I had no awareness that I was dieting, no sense of deprivation. For the first time in my life I was on a weight-loss program in which I *didn't* count the days or months until reaching my "goal." After all, my only goal was to make each meal as delightfully filling and nonfattening as possible—*without* sacrificing the joy of eating. (You see, I think enjoyment is a necessary ingredient in food, a little like vitamins. If you don't get your quota of enjoyment from the food you eat, you're likely to keep on eating until your daily requirement of joy is satisfied. That's what's wrong with diets!)

To my astonishment, my lifelong legacy of excess flab painlessly melted away. Slowly, to be sure . . . but I wasn't counting the months. Perhaps it took some 18 months for those 80 pounds to disappear (but then I had spent years acquiring them). I'm not sure *how* long it took, because the scale plateaued at 128 for days and weeks, and finally months. And finally I realized that 128 is the weight I was meant to be.

It's now a dozen years later, and I'm still 128!

I never went *off* my "diet," because I never went on one to begin with. I never went back to my old way of eating and cooking, because I enjoy eating now more than I ever did when I was fat.

Today I'm a food adventurer, and I delight in trying all the new, unusual and exotic combinations that never would have occurred to me when I limited my menus to a few fattening favorites.

HOW THIS BOOK CAME TO BE

Since I was an ex-fatty *and* a professional journalist, it was only natural that I would eventually want to share my decalorized recipes with others. After teaching low-calorie cooking classes in the Y's and adult schools in my home state, I began writing a food column for my local daily newspaper, the Elizabeth (New Jersey) *Daily Journal.* Reader response was so enormous that it quickly became syndicated and now appears in newspapers all over the country.

This book is a collection of all my foreign favorites, including some of the most popular recipes that have appeared in my Slim Gourmet newspaper columns over the past seven years. Many recipes were inspired by readers from a variety of ethnic backgrounds who applied their newly-learned "decalorization" skills to their family favorites. A lot of recipes are the happy outcome of my travels. I'm an insatiable traveler who never neglects the opportunity to taste something new, even—*especially*—if it's fattening! (A taste will never make you fat, and you don't need to eat it *all* to find out what it tastes like.) I collect recipe ideas the way other tourists pick up souvenirs. Then I head straight for the kitchen and unpack a suitcaseful of inspiration to see if I can recapture that foreign flavor—with local ingredients and as few calories as possible.

YES, BUT ARE THESE RECIPES AUTHENTIC?

Of course not! How could they be? *Authentic* ethnic food is fattening because the recipes originated in times or places where lots of calories were the main requirement of food. Long ago and far away people lived and worked a lot differently than we do today. (I work hard, but I sit down. What about you?)

The truth is that here and now most of us just can't afford all those calories, but we can still selectively borrow inspiration from the way other people in other places combine foods and flavors. We can blend the best of their ideas with the best of what we have. And come up with a delightful adaptation rather than a literal translation.

The best of what *we* have needn't be discounted! We've got park-and-shop supermarkets with a bounty of fresh foods from everywhere, *regardless* of the season. And when fresh isn't convenient, there's frozen, dried, packaged, processed, evaporated, canned, or condensed. Everything convenient isn't necessarily junk. "Instant" may not be better than fresh, but "instant" garlic is better than *no* garlic if no garlic is what you happen to have. I'd rather have frozen asparagus tonight than wait for fresh next April!

We also have a kitchenful of gadgets to simplify every task. Of course, we need them. Unlike our foreign forebears, few of us have all day to spend in the kitchen. Which brings me to another point about authenticity: calories aren't all I've cut from these recipes. I've also tried to cut the time and trouble, to make them more workable for the busy way we live today . . . in your kitchen, using *your* appliances and the foods easily available in your supermarket. Why not? Would Ling Wong have stir-fried in a wok with a pint of oil if she could have used only a tablespoonful in a nonstick skillet? If you're weight wary, you probably already have nonstick skillets; why go out and buy a wok? Why search out expensive imported dried mushrooms in a gourmet shoppe or Chinese grocery, just because an "authentic" recipe calls for them. The originator of the authentic recipe used dried mushrooms because she didn't have a corner Acme with fresh white button mushrooms available for the picking.

In the final analysis, a good recipe represents the best a caring cook can create in a given set of circumstances, making the best use of what's available, using skill and imagination as substitutes for what's not available.

If you have to be weight wary, the *only* thing that's *not* available is excess calories!

1
APPETIZERS
AND
PARTY TREATS

Today nearly every party includes "mixed company": dieters and nondieters. The thoughtful hostess sees to it that the waistline watchers don't have to keep their hands in their pockets because everything on her table is liberally larded with calories.

So reserve a corner of your cocktail table for calorie-wise nibbles: crunchy raw vegetables in place of greasy chips, dips based on yogurt or cottage cheese instead of sour cream, all prettily arranged on trays decorated with bows fashioned from a tape measure.

You'll also need some filling fare (lots of people skip dinner, knowing there'll be plenty to eat at a party). Chilled shrimp, sliced roast beef, and cold turkey are high-protein appetite appeasers. Here are two other protein-rich partygoers, done the decalorized way with low-cal diet mayonnaise (available in most supermarkets.)

Taking the Fat Calories Out of Party Dip Recipes

Once upon a time a harried hostess stirred an envelope of dry onion soup into a carton of sour cream and started the social phenomenon known as the "party dip." Hostesses have been stirring and guests have been dipping ever since.

Sour-cream dips were fattening enough, but soon somebody discovered cream cheese as a dip base. It's even more fattening! In fact, fat accounts for more than half the calories in cream cheese.

Then the food industry came along with "nondairy" dressings and dips, which only served to give diet-wise partygoers a false sense of security. Many are made with coconut oil, twice as saturated as butterfat!

But things are looking up. During 1973, a number of food firms introduced low-fat sour dressings and cream-cheese replacements that really are lower in calories, by as much as one-third to one-half. Look for them in your supermarket dairy case, but read the fine print for the calorie count.

"SOUR HALF-AND-HALF." In some areas it's still possible to buy "sour half-and-half," real sour cream but with a reduced butterfat content. If you can't find it, make your own, by combining real sour cream with an equal measure of either skim or whole milk. Leave the mixture, covered, at room temperature overnight. Then stir and refrigerate.

PLAIN (UNSWEETENED) YOGURT AND ORDINARY BUTTER-MILK. The consistency of these sour-cream substitutes is just right for most dip recipes.

LOW-FAT COTTAGE CHEESE. This protein-rich food can be turned into a low-calorie cholesterol-shy sour-cream substitute that defies detection —if you have a blender. Simply add ¼ cup or more skim milk or buttermilk for each cup of cottage cheese, then blend smooth. A tablespoon of lemon juice will heighten the sour-cream illusion.

CREAM CHEESE SUBSTITUTES. These include Neufchâtel cheese, the part-skim version of cream cheese; new "imitations" with reduced fat content; and farmer cheese, which has the texture of cream cheese but a flavor more like cottage cheese. All can be thinned with skim milk for use in dip recipes. Check this chart for calorie comparisons:

HOW DIP BASES COMPARE

Eight Ounces	*Calories*
Dairy Sour Cream	500
Sour Half-and-Half	320
Nondairy Sour Cream	380
Low-Fat Sour Cream	210
Buttermilk	88
Plain Low-Fat Yogurt	130
Low-Fat Cottage Cheese	180
Cream Cheese	840
Neufchâtel Cheese	550
Low-Fat "Imitation" Cream Cheese	430
Farmer Cheese	305

NEUFCHÂTEL CLAM DIP

   8-ounce package Neufchâtel cheese
   7- or 8-ounce can minced clams
1 tablespoon lemon juice
1 teaspoon Worcestershire Sauce
½ teaspoon garlic salt
   Dash of Tabasco

Drain clams, reserving liquid. Combine cheese with remaining ingredients, adding just enough of the liquid to create the desired consistency. *About 1½ cups, 20 calories per tablespoon.*

NEUFCHÂTEL TUNA DIP

   8-ounce package Neufchâtel cheese or low-calorie cream cheese
   3-ounce can water-packed tuna
2 tablespoons skim milk
2 envelopes chicken bouillon
2 tablespoons chopped fresh or freeze-dried chives

Blend and chill. *About 1¼ cups, under 30 calories per tablespoon.*

ROQUEFORT DIP

½ cup crumbled bleu cheese or Roquefort
2 cups low-fat cottage cheese
1 teaspoon dried onion flakes

Beat smooth and chill. *About 2¼ cups, 15 calories per tablespoon.*

NEUFCHÂTEL NIPPY DIP

   8-ounce package low-calorie cream cheese, Neufchâtel cheese, or farmer
     cheese
3 tablespoons skim milk
1 tablespoon lemon juice
8 radishes
1 tablespoon chopped chives
   Salt and freshly ground pepper

Beat cream cheese, milk, and lemon juice smooth. Put radishes through a vegetable shredder; squeeze out moisture. Stir in radishes and chives. Season to taste with salt and pepper. *About 1⅓ cups, 20 calories per tablespoon.*

BRAUNSCHWEIGER DIP

¼ pound Braunschweiger sausage
1 cup low-fat creamed cottage cheese
2 tablespoons dill-pickle relish
½ small onion, minced, or 2 teaspoons dried onion flakes
1 teaspoon Worcestershire sauce
2 or 3 tablespoons skim milk

Combine all ingredients in blender, cover, and process smooth, adding just enough milk to make a thick dip. Chill. *About 1½ cups, about 25 calories per tablespoon.*

GORGONZOLA DIP

Gorgonzola is Italian blue cheese, sold in some supermarkets and in Italian groceries.

1 cup low-fat cottage cheese
½ cup plain low-fat yogurt
4 ounces crumbled Gorgonzola or other blue cheese
¼ teaspoon salt
1 clove garlic, minced
  Dash of Worcestershire sauce
1 tablespoon lemon juice
1 tablespoon chopped fresh or freeze-dried chives

Combine all ingredients except chives in blender, cover, and blend smooth. Stir in chives. Serve with green pepper strips or sliced raw zucchini "chips." *About 2 cups, 20 calories per tablespoon.*

LOW-CAL ONION-SOUP DIP

1 cup low-fat tangy-style cottage cheese
¼ cup buttermilk or skim milk
1 tablespoon lemon juice
2 envelopes (2 tablespoons) beef bouillon
2 tablespoons dried onion flakes

In your blender, combine the cottage cheese, buttermilk, lemon juice, and beef bouillon. Blend until smooth, then stir in the onion flakes and refrigerate until serving time. *About 1½ cups, 10 calories per tablespoon.*

"CREAM CHEESE" AND CHIVE DIP

    8-ounce package low-fat imitation cream cheese
 1 teaspoon garlic salt
½ cup skim milk
    Chopped fresh or freeze-dried chives to taste

In your blender, combine the imitation cream cheese, garlic salt, and skim milk. Blend until smooth, then stir in the chives. Chill until ready to serve. *About 1½ cups, 25 calories per tablespoon.*

RAW CAULIFLOWER WITH CHEDDAR DIP

 1 head raw cauliflower
 1 pound low-fat cottage cheese
    Skim milk
1½ cups (6 ounces) coarsely shredded extra-sharp Cheddar or American
       cheese
 1 tablespoon grated onion or 1 teaspoon dried onion flakes
 1 tablespoon prepared mustard
    Few drops each Worcestershire sauce and Tabasco
 2 teaspoons celery salt

Wash cauliflower and break into florets. In a covered blender, beat cottage cheese smooth, adding just enough skim milk for a thick-sour-cream density. Add Cheddar and blend smooth. Blend in onion and seasonings to taste. Spoon into a bowl on a large platter and surround with cauliflower. *Three cups, about 16 calories per tablespoon.*

SLIMMER'S GUACAMOLE

 1 cup low-fat cottage cheese
 1 tablespoon grated onion or 1½ teaspoons dried onion flakes
 1 clove garlic, minced, or ⅛ teaspoon garlic powder
 1 teaspoon salt
    Pinch of cayenne pepper
 2 teaspoons lemon or lime juice
 1 ripe avocado, peeled and cut in chunks
 1 tomato, peeled and chopped

Combine all ingredients in blender except avocado and tomato. Cover and blend smooth. Add avocado chunks a few at a time. Cover and blend smooth. Stir in tomato. Serve with corn chips or celery scoopers. *About 2 cups, 15 calories per tablespoon.*

BROCCOLI GUACAMOLE

    10-ounce package frozen broccoli in cheese sauce
3 tablespoons low-fat sour dressing
2 tablespoons grated Parmesan or Romano cheese
2 tablespoons lemon juice
2 teaspoons dried onion flakes
    Pinch of instant garlic
¼ teaspoon chili powder

Cook broccoli until tender; allow to cool. Combine with remaining ingredients in blender, cover, and blend smooth. Chill. Serve with raw pepper strips or corn chips. *One and one-half cups, about 15 calories per tablespoon.*

LOW-CAL APPLE-CURRY PARTY DIP

1½ cups low-fat cottage cheese
1 cup unsweetened applesauce
1 envelope onion-soup mix
3 tablespoons sugar (optional)
2 teaspoons curry powder, or to taste

In a covered blender, beat cottage cheese and applesauce smooth. Stir in soup mix; season to taste with sugar, if desired, and curry powder. Serve with raw vegetables, fresh fruit, or cubes of lean cooked cold meat on picks. *About 2⅔ cups, 15 calories per tablespoon.*

TURKEY CURRY SPREAD

2 cups cooked minced turkey
1 tablespoon minced onion
5 tablespoons plain low-fat yogurt
5 tablespoons low-fat mayonnaise
1 teaspoon lemon juice
1 teaspoon curry powder
    Salt and freshly ground pepper to taste

Combine all ingredients; cover and chill. *Two cups, under 25 calories per tablespoon.*

COMRADE'S "CAVIAR"

1 large eggplant
1 large onion, minced
1 clove garlic, minced
1 large ripe tomato, peeled and minced
1 tablespoon olive oil
1 tablespoon vinegar
  Salt and freshly ground pepper to taste
1 tablespoon olive juice, from jar
  Black olives, pitted and sliced (optional)

Bake the eggplant whole in a 350-degree oven until soft, about 30 minutes. When cool, peel and finely dice the eggplant meat. Combine with remaining ingredients, except sliced olives, and chill several hours. Serve, garnished with olives, as a spread or dip. *Two and one-half cups, under 15 calories per tablespoon; 1 large olive is 10 calories.*

Spreads from Your Food Processor or Blender

Here's how to process your own skinny cheese spreads—without a crockful of unwanted calories. Begin with nearly no-fat pot cheese (that's cottage cheese without a lot of cream calories or liquid added). Then whip it up in a blender or food processor with flavor adders like garlic, onion, pepper, mustard, Worcestershire, Tabasco, and zesty seasonings.

Serve your skinny spreads in small brown crocks, the kind left over from the fattening spreads. Low-fat pot cheese is 99 percent fat free (check the label) while most processed cheese spreads are 20 percent fat or more, and about 50 calories a tablespoon.

A food processor can make short work of spreads. It used to be that only well-heeled cooks could afford to tinker around with food processors, but now there are affordable American versions that do the job just as well as the fancy imports for far fewer dollars. A food processor's steel chopping blade can mince ingredients in a few seconds flat, then whip pot cheese into "cream cheese" almost as fast as you can turn it on and off.

Lacking a food processor, you can still make these spreads in a blender. Chop, shred, or grate the solid ingredients by hand. Whip the pot cheese smooth in the blender and then add the minced ingredients last. Blend only till combined. (Thick mixtures are more difficult to remove from a blender than from a food processor.)

GARDEN CHEESE SPREAD I

1 cup low-fat pot cheese or dry cottage cheese
½ teaspoon salt or garlic salt
1 teaspoon Worcestershire sauce
2 radishes
½ small onion
¼ green bell pepper, seeded

IN BLENDER: Blend cheese, salt, and Worcestershire smooth. Mince or chop vegetables *by hand* and blend into cheese.

IN FOOD PROCESSOR: Chop vegetables, using metal chopping blade. Add remaining ingredients and blend just until mixed. Spoon into a small crock or covered refrigerator bowl. Keep chilled. *Makes about 1⅓ cups, under 10 calories per tablespoon.*

GARDEN CHEESE SPREAD II*

2 cups low-fat pot cheese or dry cottage cheese
½ teaspoon dry mustard or 1 teaspoon prepared
½ teaspoon salt or celery salt, or to taste
  Pinch of freshly ground pepper
2 large radishes, quartered
½ small cucumber or zucchini, in 1-inch lengths
½ small green bell pepper, seeded
1 small onion, quartered
4 pimiento-stuffed green Spanish olives, halved

IN BLENDER: Blend cottage cheese, mustard, salt, and pepper smooth. *By hand* mince or chop vegetables fine, then add to blender. Process only till mixed.

IN FOOD PROCESSOR: Chop vegetables, using steel chopping blade. Add remaining ingredients and process only until smooth. Store in small crocks or a covered bowl in the refrigerator. *About 2½ cups, 10 calories per tablespoon.*

MOCK BOURSIN

1 cup low-fat pot cheese or dry cottage cheese
½ teaspoon salt, or to taste
2 or 3 sprigs parsley
1 clove garlic, peeled

*Adapted from the Farberware® *Food Processor Use and Recipe Guide.*

IN BLENDER: Beat cheese and salt smooth (will be thick). Mince parsley and garlic, and blend into cheese.

IN FOOD PROCESSOR: Chop garlic and parsley, using steel chopping blade. Add cottage cheese and salt, and blend smooth. Store in a covered crock in refrigerator. *One cup, about 10 calories per tablespoon.*

INDIAN CHEESE SPREAD

½ cucumber, peeled
½ teaspoon cumin seeds
½ teaspoon salt or garlic salt, or to taste
  Pinch of freshly ground black pepper
  Pinch of cayenne pepper
1 cup low-fat pot cheese or dry cottage cheese

IN BLENDER: First shred the cucumber, using a hand shredder. Set aside in a bowl for 10 to 20 minutes, then pour off any accumulated moisture. Combine remaining ingredients in blender and blend smooth. Add cucumber and blend only until mixed.

IN FOOD PROCESSOR: Shred cucumber, using the fine shredding disk. Remove and set aside 10 to 20 minutes. Meanwhile, replace shredding disk with steel chopping blade. Put remaining ingredients in processor and whip smooth. Drain shredded cucumber. Add to cheese and blend only till mixed.

Store in covered dish in refrigerator. Good with tortilla chips. *About 1½ cups, about 7 calories per tablespoon.*

GREEK EGGPLANT SPREAD OR DIP

1 eggplant, peeled and diced
½ cup water
1 clove garlic or ⅛ teaspoon instant garlic
3 tablespoons chopped fresh parsley
2 teaspoons lemon juice or white vinegar
2 teaspoons olive oil
½ teaspoon oregano or Italian seasoning
  Salt and freshly ground pepper to taste
  Fresh parsley for garnish

Combine eggplant and water in a covered saucepan; simmer 10 minutes. Drain well. Combine the cooked eggplant, the garlic, chopped parsley, lemon juice, oil, oregano, salt, and pepper in food processor or blender. Blend smooth. Chill in covered container. Use as a spread or dip, garnished with fresh parsley. *Two cups, 6 calories per tablespoon.*

LOW-CALORIE LIVER PÂTÉ

1 pound beef liver
2 tablespoons diet margarine
1 onion, sliced
1 stalk celery, trimmed
1 clove garlic, peeled
2 tablespoons lemon juice
  Salt and freshly ground pepper

Cook liver in diet margarine in a nonstick skillet over low heat. (Don't overcook. The liver should be slightly pink in the middle.) Cool.

Put liver, onion, celery, and garlic through a food mill, processor, or blender. Add lemon juice and salt and pepper to taste. Blend to a smooth paste. Chill thoroughly before serving. *Six appetizer servings, 135 calories each.*

TURKEY PÂTÉ

2 cups ground cooked turkey meat
2 eggs, hard-cooked and shredded
1 tablespoon white wine
  Salt and freshly ground pepper to taste
  Pinch of cayenne pepper or chili powder, or to taste
2 tablespoons chopped fresh parsley
3 or 4 tablespoons low-fat mayonnaise

Combine all ingredients, adding just enough mayonnaise to make a paste. Chill until serving time. Serve with saltines or other crackers. *Six appetizer servings, about 130 calories each.*

VEGETABLES À LA GRECQUE

20 ounces (2 boxes or 1 bag) vegetables, either whole green beans, artichoke hearts, asparagus, Brussels sprouts, Belgian carrots, cauliflower, or sliced zucchini
 1 cup water
 2 tablespoons olive oil
   Salt and freshly ground pepper to taste
½ bay leaf
 1 clove garlic, minced, or ⅛ teaspoon instant garlic
½ teaspoon thyme
   Other herbs to taste: tarragon, rosemary, basil, dill, or chopped fresh parsley
 3 tablespoons lemon juice

Combine all ingredients except lemon juice in a saucepan. Simmer vegetables just until thawed but still crisp. Remove from heat and stir in lemon juice. Chill and serve in the sauce. *Eight servings, about 50 calories each.*

VEGETABLE APPETIZER OREGANATA

20 ounces (2 boxes or 1 bag) frozen vegetables (see list above)
2 tablespoons chopped onion
1 cup water
½ teaspoon oregano or Italian seasoning
½ cup low-fat Italian salad dressing

Combine all ingredients except salad dressing in a saucepan. Simmer vegetables just until thawed but still crisp. Add salad dressing and chill in sauce. *Eight servings, about 30 calories each.*

ITALIAN MELON APPETIZERS

1 large honeydew melon
4 ounces baked Virginia ham or Canadian bacon, very thinly sliced
2 limes, cut in wedges

Cut melon in half and scoop out seeds. Cut each half into 6 wedges. With a sharp knife, cut away the melon rind. Slice the ham into 12 thin strips. Wrap a strip of ham around each melon wedge and secure with a toothpick. Impale a lime wedge on each toothpick. *Twelve wedges, about 35 calories each.*

JAFFA ORANGE COCKTAIL

4 oranges
1 tomato, diced
4-ounce jar cocktail pearl onions, drained
3 eggs, hard-cooked and chopped
1½ tablespoons low-fat mayonnaise
1 tablespoon horseradish

Halve the oranges; scoop out the fruit, leaving the shells intact. Dice the fruit. Mix with all other ingredients. Heap mixture in orange shells. *Eight servings, about 80 calories each.*

STUFFED GRAPE LEAVES À LA GRECQUE

　2　cups water
　1　cup long-grain rice
　2　teaspoons salt
　　　8-ounce jar grape leaves, drained
1½　pounds lean, ground fat-trimmed lamb
　1　cup finely chopped onion
　2　tablespoons finely chopped pine nuts (optional)
　½　teaspoon oregano or Italian seasoning
　¼　teaspoon freshly ground pepper
　1　cup hot water

Bring water to a boil in a covered 2-quart saucepan. Stir rice and 1 teaspoon salt into water; cover and cook over low heat 20 minutes. Cool slightly.

Meanwhile, rinse grape leaves under a running spray of water. Drain well. Separate leaves carefully on a cutting board and trim away stems. Allow to stand until needed.

Combine lamb, onion, nuts, oregano, pepper, and remaining teaspoon salt. Add rice, tossing together lightly with a fork. Place a rounded tablespoonful of lamb mixture on each grape leaf near stem end, fold sides of leaf inward to enclose filling and roll up. Arrange stuffed leaves open edges down in Dutch oven or 3-quart sauce pot. Add hot water; cover and simmer 1 hour, adding a little more hot water, if necessary. *Eight servings, about 180 calories each; or sixteen appetizer servings, 90 calories each.*

INDIAN TWICE-SPICED BROILED SHRIMP

　1　pound large raw shrimp, cleaned and shelled
　2　tablespoons mixed pickling spices
　1　tablespoon dried onion flakes
　1　teaspoon salt or garlic salt
　½　cup water
　2　tablespoons melted butter or soft diet margarine
　½　teaspoon ground cumin
　1　teaspoon turmeric
　1　tablespoon lime juice
　　　Paprika
　　　Lime wedges

Combine shrimp, pickling spices, onion, salt, and water in a saucepan. Simmer 2 minutes; drain. Return shrimp to empty saucepan. Add butter, cumin, turmeric, and lime juice. Stir to coat shrimp well with seasonings.

Spread in a single layer on a shallow flameproof broiling pan. Sprinkle with paprika and broil 5 minutes. Serve with lime wedges. *Four dinner servings, under 160 calories each; eight appetizer servings, under 80 calories each, with butter. Under 135 calories per dinner serving, and under 70 calories each per appetizer serving, with diet margarine.*

Pretty Party Meatballs
Needn't Be Calorie Rich

During the social season even the lowly hamburger takes on party dress, emerging as glamorous party meatballs, elegantly at the ready in a pretty chafing dish.

Unfortunately, most party meatballs are off limits for calorie counters and cholesterol watchers. Fatty meat, bready fillers, and super-rich sauces combine to tempt the uncautious nibbler. What an incredible number of calories can be crammed onto one tiny toothpick!

If you're a Slim Gourmet hostess, however, you can create spicy, savory party meatballs without those unglamorous extra calories, and nobody will be the wiser.

Here are a couple of festive party meatball dishes that start with lean beef round, trimmed of fat and chopped to your order. (Don't use ordinary hamburger; it's 30 percent fat and sometimes more!)

POLYNESIAN PARTY MEATBALLS

3 pounds lean, fat-trimmed ground beef round
½ cup Japanese-style soy sauce
1 teaspoon monosodium glutamate (optional)
2 eggs or 4 egg whites, beaten
3 sixteen-ounce cans juice-packed pineapple tidbits, undrained
2 teaspoons mixed pickling spices
2 green bell peppers, seeded and thinly sliced into strips
2 red bell peppers, seeded and thinly sliced into strips
1 tablespoon cornstarch
¼ cup cold water

Combine meat, ¼ cup soy sauce, monosodium glutamate, eggs, and toss lightly. Shape into 1-inch meatballs. Arrange in a single layer on cookie tins or large shallow broiling pans. Broil, turning once, until brown.

In a large nonstick frying pan or electric skillet, combine pineapple, spices, peppers, and remaining soy sauce. Cover and simmer 2 minutes. Combine cornstarch and water and stir into skillet; cook and stir until sauce thickens and bubbles. Stir in meatballs and heat through. Keep warm in skillet or chafing dish. *About fifty party servings, under 60 calories each.*

BAVARIAN MEATBALLS IN CREAM SAUCE

1 cup water
6 slices dry protein or high-fiber bread
2 thirteen-ounce cans evaporated skim milk
3 pounds lean, fat-trimmed ground beef round
2 eggs or 4 egg whites
½ cup chopped fresh parsley
2 onions, finely minced
2 teaspoons caraway seeds
2 teaspoons salt or garlic salt
  Pinch of cayenne pepper
  8-ounce can mushrooms, including liquid
3 tablespoons all-purpose flour
  Butter-flavored salt or butter flavoring (optional)
  Paprika or chopped fresh parsley (optional)

Combine water and bread with ½ cup evaporated milk. Mash well, then add meat, eggs, parsley, onion, caraway, salt, and cayenne. Toss lightly and shape into 1-inch meatballs. Arrange in a single layer and brown under broiler, turning once.

Combine a little of the remaining evaporated milk with the flour and mix until smooth. Add this to the remaining evaporated milk in a saucepan and stir over low heat until free of any lumps. Add mushrooms and cook and stir until cream sauce thickens. Season to taste with butter-flavored salt.

Combine browned meatballs and cream sauce in an electric skillet or chafing dish and keep warm. Sprinkle with paprika or chopped parsley, if desired. *About fifty servings, 60 calories each.*

2
SOUPS

SLIM VICHYSSOISE

  3 cups cubed potatoes
1½ cups minced onion
  4 chicken bouillon cubes
     Dash of freshly ground pepper
½ cups water
  1 cup evaporated skim milk
  2 tablespoons chopped fresh or freeze-dried chives

In a tightly-covered large kettle or Dutch oven, cook potatoes, onion, bouillon cubes, and pepper in 2 cups water for 30 minutes, or until potatoes are tender.

Puree potatoes and liquid in an electric blender, or press through a food mill, or sieve until smooth. Stir in milk.

Chill; serve topped with chives. *Six servings, about 115 calories each.*

SEAFOOD MACARONI SOUP

One of the nice things about fall and winter months is the wider availability of oysters. If you're weight watching, oysters need never be avoided. They're very low calorie, only 316 calories per pound or pint of meat.

What about the old idea of avoiding oysters during months without an R in them? A superstition, according to our know-it-all food book, *The Wise Encyclopedia of Cookery.** The encyclopedia notes that quick spoilage during summer months may have given the idea some validity during the pre-refrigeration age.

Another old idea is that calorie counters should avoid macaroni and other pastas. Actually, macaroni is a nutritious low-calorie food offering some protein, iron, niacin, thiamin, and riboflavin—but very little fat (or sodium).

Here we combine macaroni with oysters and other seafood in a spicy gumbo with hardly any fat at all, and follow it with a chicken variation. Either is just the thing for a hearty fall lunch or supper.

2 cloves garlic, chopped
1 cup chopped onion
   28-ounce can tomatoes
1 quart water
1 pint (2 cups) clam juice
1 tablespoon salt
1 teaspoon oregano or Italian seasoning
2 bay leaves
   Dash of Tabasco, or to taste
8 ounces (2 cups) dry elbow macaroni
1 pint (1 pound) shucked oysters, drained
1 pound shrimp, cleaned and shelled
   7¾-ounce can crabmeat, drained

In a Dutch oven or large heavy saucepan, combine garlic, onion, tomatoes, water, clam juice, salt, oregano, bay leaves, and Tabasco. Simmer, covered, 40 minutes. Bring to a boil; gradually add macaroni. Cook, covered, 15 minutes or until macaroni is tender, stirring frequently. Stir in oysters, shrimp, and crabmeat. Cook 5 minutes longer. *Eight servings, 260 calories each.*

VARIATION

Turkey or Chicken Macaroni Soup . . . and a great way to recycle leftovers! Follow the preceding recipe, but make these substitutions.

• Substitute 2 cups fat-skimmed homemade or canned chicken or turkey broth for the clam juice (omit or reduce salt if using highly-salted canned broth).

• Substitute 4 cups cubed white meat of roast turkey or other poultry for the oysters, shrimp, and crabmeat. *Serves eight, 270 calories each.*

*New York: Grosset & Dunlap, 1971.

SEAFOOD CHOWDER

Chowder seems like a Yankee invention. But the word, like so many food words, is essentially French, after *chaudière,* for caldron. Unfortunately, many seafood soup recipes are also caldron size, with quantities more appropriate to an entire fishing village. The calories, too! Many chowder recipes are rich with cream, butter, lard, salt pork, or other fattening ingredients.

Here is a hearty seafood chowder that is scaled down to today's nutritional needs—very rich in protein but extremely low in fat and calories. It can easily be doubled for a company dinner. A tossed salad or coleslaw with diet dressing, some crackers, and a glass of dry white wine are all you need to turn this hearty soup into a full meal.

    1 tablespoon butter or margarine
    1 onion, thinly sliced
    1 pound fresh or defrosted haddock fillets or cod steaks
 3½ cups boiling water
    4 cups thinly sliced raw peeled potatoes
    2 stalks celery, minced
  ¼ cup cold water
    1 tablespoon all-purpose flour
      13-ounce can evaporated skim milk
      Salt and white pepper
      Paprika and minced fresh parsley

In a nonstick saucepan, heat the butter and onion until onion is soft but not brown. Cut the fish into bite-size pieces and add to the saucepan, along with the boiling water, potatoes, and celery.

Cover and simmer over very low heat until the potatoes are just tender, about 10 minutes. Combine cold water and flour into a paste and stir into the saucepan over low heat until mixture is thick. Stir in the milk and heat gently until the chowder is thick and bubbling. Season to taste. Pour into bowls and sprinkle with paprika and parsley. *Six servings, 210 calories each.*

TUNA BISQUE

      7-ounce can water-packed solid tuna
    1 tomato, peeled and chopped
    2 tablespoons minced onion
    1 stalk celery, minced
  ½ cup water
 1½ tablespoons all-purpose flour

13-ounce can evaporated skim milk
Salt, or butter-flavored salt, and freshly ground pepper
Paprika and chopped fresh parsley

Drain the liquid from the tuna into a saucepan. Add the tomato, onion, celery, and water. Cover and simmer until the celery is tender. Meanwhile flake the tuna coarsely and set aside. Beat flour and milk together and stir into the saucepan. Simmer uncovered until soup is thick and bubbly. Stir in tuna and heat through. Season to taste. Pour into 2 bowls and garnish with paprika and parsley. *Two servings, 295 calories each.*

Who Says Chicken Soup Isn't Glamorous!

SLIM CHICKEN-SOUP STOCK BASE

Although chicken necks are half bone (about 51 percent) the meat remaining in 1 pound of chicken necks is enough to make a meal for 2. At less than 20 cents a pound (or almost free, if you collect chicken necks in your freezer) that makes the chicken neck one of the best protein buys around. Neck meat is particularly flavorful, and the bones yield an especially savory broth.

If you're watching your weight as well as your pennies, it's easy to discard the excess fat calories along with the bones. I simmer the necks *before* adding other ingredients. Then I discard the fat, skin, and bones.

Two pounds of chicken necks will make about 2 cups of chicken meat (for chicken salad) and a deliciously defatted broth for soups, sauces, gravies, or for flavoring vegetables. Or combine the meat and broth in a meal-size soup, like the recipe that follows.

2 pounds chicken necks
6 cups cold water
½ cup dry white wine (optional)
2 teaspoons salt
2 teaspoons monosodium glutamate (optional)
1 bay leaf

Combine all ingredients in a large pot or pressure cooker and heat to boiling. Skim off foam. Lower heat to a simmer and cover tightly. Cook 1 hour, until very tender, or 20 minutes under pressure (follow manufacturer's directions). Remove chicken necks and allow to cool. Pour broth into a cool container and allow fat to rise to the surface.

When cool, strip meat from necks. Discard bones and skin. With a bulb-type baster, skim off and discard all fat from the surface of the broth. Use chicken meat and broth in the following recipe, which can be served with crusty French bread for a light meal.

FRENCH CHICKEN DINNER SOUP

Slim Chicken-soup Stock Base (see page 23), meat reserved
6 small onions, peeled and quartered
3 cups sliced carrots (fresh, frozen, or canned)
¼ pound sliced fresh mushrooms (or 4-ounce can sliced mushrooms)
¼ cup chopped fresh parsley or 1 tablespoon parsley flakes
Salt and pepper to taste

Reheat fat-skimmed chicken broth to boiling; add onions and carrots. Cover and simmer until tender, about 20 minutes. Add mushrooms and simmer 5 more minutes. Add reserved chicken meat, parsley, salt and pepper to taste. Simmer until heated through.

Four servings, about 215 calories each. Leftovers can be frozen or refrigerated, and reheated for another meal.

MEXICAN CHICKEN SOUP

Neck, back, wings, gizzard, and heart of 1 frying chicken
1 quart water
Salt and freshly ground pepper to taste
1 carrot, thinly sliced
2 stalks celery, in 2-inch lengths
1 small onion, chopped
1 clove garlic, chopped
½ small red or green bell pepper, diced
1 tablespoon raw rice
2 tablespoons chopped fresh parsley
Pinch each of oregano, ground cumin, and chili powder

Combine chicken, water, salt, and pepper in a soup pot. Cover and simmer 1 hour or more, until meat falls from bones. Strain liquid into a bowl and chill until fat rises to the surface and hardens. Remove and discard fat. Remove chicken meat from bones and discard bones.

Combine fat-skimmed broth with remaining ingredients in the soup pot. Simmer until vegetables are tender, about 20 to 30 minutes. Add chicken meat and heat through. *Four soup-course servings, 90 calories each.*

COCK-A-LEEKIE

2 whole chicken breasts
1½ teaspoons salt, or to taste
3 cups water
10-ounce can chicken broth
4 cups sliced leeks or 4 onions, sliced
18 pitted dried prunes
12 peppercorns

Trim all visible fat from chicken. Place chicken in a large pot with salt and water. Simmer, covered, about 1 hour, or until chicken is tender.

Remove chicken; set aside to cool. Skim canned and cooked broths of all fat. Combine.

Slice the white part of the leeks; add to chicken stock along with prunes and peppercorns. Cover, and continue simmering 20 minutes more.

Meanwhile, skin and bone chicken, and cut into strips. Add to soup and heat through. *Four main-dish servings, 235 calories each; or eight soup-course servings at 115 calories each.*

CHICKEN-RICE SOUP AVGOLEMONO

2 pounds cut-up frying chicken
2 quarts water
1 cup raw rice
Salt and freshly ground pepper to taste
3 eggs, separated
Juice of one lemon
1 teaspoon monosodium glutamate (optional)

Cover chicken with water in a soup pot. Simmer 50 minutes or more until meat can be removed easily from bones. Strain broth and chill until fat rises to the surface and can be removed. Separate chicken meat from bones and cut into chunks; discard bones and skin.

Reheat fat-skimmed chicken broth and add rice. Simmer until rice is cooked.

Add a pinch of salt to egg whites in a mixing bowl and beat with an electric mixer until stiff. Slowly beat in the egg yolks and lemon juice. Then beat in the hot chicken broth, a little at a time. Pour this mixture back into the soup pot and heat gently. Add the chicken chunks and heat through. Do not boil. Season to taste and add monosodium glutamate, if desired. *Eight lunch-size servings, about 170 calories each.*

EAST INDIAN CHICKEN CHOWDER

This spicy main course is a cross between a soup and a stew, a simplified main course inspired by mulligatawny. Chicken thighs are ideal for this dish, since each contains only one large bone. Serve the chowder in large shallow soup plates with knives and forks (for the chicken and vegetables) and soup spoons (for the spicy, savory broth).

8 chicken thighs
   Paprika
   10½-ounce can condensed fat-skimmed chicken broth
1 cup tomato juice
1 quart water
2 carrots, sliced
2 onions, sliced
2 stalks celery, thinly sliced
¼ cup chopped fresh parsley
4 tablespoons raw brown rice
1 bay leaf
¾ teaspoon curry powder, or to taste
⅛ teaspoon grated nutmeg
   Pinch of ground cloves
½ green bell pepper, in thin strips (optional)
2 small unpeeled red apples, diced

Spray a large nonstick skillet or chicken fryer with cooking spray for no-fat frying. Brown the chicken pieces skin side down until skin is crisp and well rendered of fat. Drain and discard fat. Turn chicken skin side up and sprinkle with paprika. Add remaining ingredients except apple. Cover and simmer until chicken is tender, about 40 minutes or more. Skim fat from surface of broth. Add diced apple and simmer only until heated through. Serve in large shallow soup plates with knife, fork, and soup spoon. *Four main-course servings, under 275 calories each.*

Meal-Size Minestrone with Seafood or Meat

Meal-size soups, Italian style! They needn't be multi-caloried if you're a Slim Gourmet cook. Here are two main-course inspirations, perfect for a hot lunch or hearthside supper. Each is a complete meal in itself since each combines meat or seafood with vegetables. (Red or white Chianti wine and some crunchy Italian breadsticks can add a festive note, but not a lot of calories.)

The seafood minestrone is made with canned tuna or shrimp—or both. In choosing tuna, be sure to pick the water-packed variety—only half the calories of tuna packed in oil. In making mini-meatballs for the beef version, it's important that the chopped meat be ground fat-trimmed round, not ordinary hamburger (which can be one-third fat).

For convenience's sake, both soups are based on canned broth, either chicken or beef. For true homemade flavor, substitute homemade stock, if you have it. In any case, be sure to skim off any fat globules from the surface before using. Also, since the salt content of broths varies, taste-test before adding more salt.

SKINNY MINESTRONE MARINARA

    8-ounce can tomatoes, chopped
2 cups tomato juice
    10½-ounce can condensed fat-skimmed chicken broth
1 onion, chopped
2 stalks celery, minced
1 clove garlic, minced
2 tablespoons chopped olives
1½ teaspoons oregano or Italian seasoning
    Pinch of thyme
2 seven-ounce cans water-packed tuna or small shrimp (or 1 of each)
    Dash of Tabasco (optional)
    Salt and freshly ground pepper

Combine all ingredients except canned seafood and seasonings in a covered saucepan. Simmer 10 minutes. Add canned seafood (including liquid). Reheat to simmering. Season to taste. Serve immediately. *Four servings, about 200 calories each.*

MINI-MEATBALL MINESTRONE

1 pound lean, fat-trimmed ground beef round
    Salt and freshly ground pepper
    16-ounce can Italian plum tomatoes, broken up
2 ten-ounce cans condensed fat-skimmed beef broth
4 ounces shredded cabbage or ½ eight-ounce package frozen coleslaw vegetables
1 stalk celery, minced
1 onion, chopped
2 tablespoons chopped fresh parsley
1 bay leaf
1 teaspoon oregano
½ teaspoon basil
¼ teaspoon thyme
    Cayenne pepper or Tabasco to taste

Sprinkle the chopped meat lightly with salt and pepper. Then use a melon-ball scoop (or your hands) to shape the meat into 20 tiny meatballs.

Combine remaining ingredients in a saucepan and heat to a simmer. Drop in the meatballs a few at a time. Simmer, covered, stirring occasionally, for 15 minutes.

Remove from heat. Skim fat, if any, from surface. Serve immediately. *Four servings, 230 calories each.*

TURKEY MINESTRONE

Nothing worse than a holiday visitor who's overstayed his welcome. Especially if he's a turkey.

Why not hide the remains (the turkey, that is) in something totally untraditional and non-Thanksgiving-like? Such as minestrone soup.

Of course, you could make turkey soup—you know, onions, celery, carrots —but that's so predictable. Minestrone, on the other hand, is a zesty Italian soup-stew that's a continent removed from the Pilgrims, turkey, or Thanksgiving leftovers. Except in this case. Here the meaty turkey frame is used as the base for a slimmed-down minestrone that's hearty and appetite appeasing.

There are probably as many variations of minestrone as there are Italians. Here's one more. This one is easy and nonfattening.

Meaty turkey frame
1 teaspoon salt
1 teaspoon monosodium glutamate (optional)
4 cups water
2 cups sliced potatoes (fresh, thawed, or canned)
3 onions, thinly sliced
   8-ounce bag shredded coleslaw
   cabbage
2 cups sliced celery
   16-ounce can kidney beans
6 pitted ripe medium olives, chopped
1 teaspoon oregano or Italian seasoning
3 cups tomato juice
   Salt and pepper
   Parmesan cheese (optional)
   Chopped fresh parsley (optional)

Combine turkey frame, salt, monosodium glutamate, and water in a soup pot or pressure cooker. Cover and simmer 2 hours over low heat—or 45 minutes in a pressure cooker (follow manufacturer's directions). Strain broth into a container. Set turkey frame aside to cool. When fat has risen to the surface of the turkey broth, skim with a bulb-type baster (or, if you're not in a hurry, chill until fat hardens, then lift off the fat).

Combine fat-skimmed broth with remaining ingredients, except cheese and parsley. Cover and simmer until vegetables are tender. Meanwhile, strip meat from turkey frame and chop into bite-size pieces. Add to the soup and heat through. Salt and pepper to taste. Season with Parmesan cheese and chopped fresh parsley, if you like. *Six meal-size servings, 245 calories each.*

Meal-Size Soups, Thrifty with the Calories

Rich with flavor, thick with barley and vegetables, these two Slim Gourmet soups are a meal in a bowl. Slim Scotch Broth is not only hearty but economical, because it recycles the meaty bones from leftover lamb (or any other meat). Must be one reason the Scots got their reputation for thriftiness!

The following soup is another meal-size barley and vegetable soup, Italian style.

SLIM SCOTCH BROTH

Generally, the word "broth" implies a thin soup, but the traditional Scotch broth is so thick and chunky it's more like stew than soup. However, this version is thin about calories.

That's because it's made a day ahead so that every greasy glob of fat can rise to the surface and be skimmed away.

Scotch broth is traditionally made with barley, a tasty, slow-cooking grain that's less fattening, more filling and fiber rich than rice or noodles. After 45 minutes of gentle simmering, barley cooks up soft and plump, and helps to thicken the soup.

Lamb is also traditional, but you can make this soup with the meaty bones from a leftover beef, veal, or fresh ham roast—even a meaty turkey frame, the meatier the better. (The actual calorie count depends, of course, on how much meat goes into your soup. The counts here are estimates only.)

    Meaty bones left over from a roast lamb (or other meat)
2 **quarts water**
2 **teaspoons salt**
½ **teaspoon monosodium glutamate (optional)**
3 **tablespoons medium pearl barley**
2 **onions, quartered**
3 **stalks celery, with leaves, in 1¼-inch lengths**
4 **carrots, sliced**
3 **or 4 sprigs fresh parsley, chopped**

A day ahead put the meaty lamb bones in a stockpot or pressure cooker. Add water, salt, and monosodium glutamate. Cover and simmer 1½ hours (just 30 minutes in a pressure cooker; follow manufacturer's instructions) until meat falls easily from the bones.

Allow to cool, then reserve meat and discard bones. Refrigerate soup and meat overnight.

Lift hardened fat from the surface of the soup and discard. Reheat. Add barley, vegetables, and parsley, then simmer until barley is soft, about 45 minutes. *Each meal-size serving (about 1 cup meat and vegetables plus 1 cup fat-skimmed broth) under 200 calories.*

BARLEYSTRONE ITALIANO

Meaty turkey frame or meaty bones from leftover veal roast
20-ounce can Italian tomatoes, broken up
5 cups water
2 teaspoons salt or garlic salt
½ teaspoon monosodium glutamate (optional)
1 teaspoon fennel seeds
1 teaspoon oregano or Italian seasoning
3 tablespoons medium pearl barley
4 onions, quartered
1 carrot, sliced
1 cup chopped raw cabbage
¼ cup chopped fresh parsley, preferably Italian parsley
Sprinkle of Parmesan cheese (optional)

Combine meaty bones, tomatoes, water, salt, monosodium glutamate, fennel seeds, and oregano. Cover and cook according to preceding recipe's directions. Cool; strip off meat; discard bones; chill.

Next day skim off fat and add remaining ingredients except cheese. Then simmer until barley is tender, about 45 minutes. Serve with a scant sprinkle of grated Parmesan cheese, if desired. *Each meal-size serving (1 cup meat and vegetables plus 1 cup fat-skimmed broth) under 200 calories.*

3
BEEF

STEAK AU POIVRE

If you can afford money more than calories, think "tenderloin." It's the most expensive cut there is, the tenderest and most flavorful. Of the "super steaks," it's also the leanest and least fattening.

Also known as *filet mignon,* tenderloin may turn out to be even less fattening than its calories indicate; because it's *so* expensive, few people can afford to overindulge.

Because it's boneless and waste free, a 5- or 6-ounce steak should be more than adequate for most dieters.

You can cut the cost somewhat by investing in a whole tenderloin. (And "invest" is the word! Still, whole tenderloins *do* sell at a lower price per pound than cut steaks.)

Trim away the outer coating of fat and slice the tenderloin evenly into steaks. Use a kitchen or postal scale for portion control. Wrap and freeze.

The tapered end of tenderloin can be cut into 1½-inch cubes that you can use in delicious low-cal skillet dishes.

[*continued*]

1 **tablespoon (or more) whole peppercorns**
4 **slices beef tenderloin, about 5 ounces each**
2 **teaspoons vegetable oil**
5 **tablespoons white wine**
1 **tablespoon Worcestershire sauce**
  Dash of Tabasco or hot sauce (optional)
  Minced fresh parsley
  Chopped chives

Coarsely crush the peppercorns by putting them between sheets of wax paper and pounding them with a kitchen mallet only until they are broken (don't use a peppermill; it grinds too fine). Press the crushed pepper into both sides of the steaks.

Heat 1 teaspoon oil in a nonstick skillet over high heat. Add the steaks and brown quickly on one side. Add second teaspoon oil; turn the steaks and cook the other side to desired doneness (preferably rare).

Remove steaks to a heated platter. Stir remaining ingredients into the hot skillet until simmering. Scrape the skillet well and pour the pan sauce over the steaks. Serve immediately. *Four servings, 255 calories each.*

POLYNESIAN TERIYAKI STEAK

Hawaiian "teriyaki" often means syrupy soy gravy served over hamburgers, steaks, or some other form of beef. Here's a less-fattening version:

1½ **pounds beef round or flank steak**
  Meat tenderizer (optional)
3 **tablespoons soy sauce**
  Garlic powder
¾ **teaspoon arrowroot or cornstarch**
  6-ounce can unsweetened pineapple juice

Trim away and discard all fat. If you wish, sprinkle steak with meat tenderizer an hour or so before cooking.

Put the steak in a very large nonstick skillet and sprinkle both sides liberally with soy sauce and garlic powder. Cover and cook over a moderate flame, turning once, until liquid evaporates and meat is well browned on both sides.

Combine arrowroot with pineapple juice. Pour into skillet. Turn steak frequently in simmering pineapple juice, until juice is thickened into a dark sauce. Remove steak to a platter and pour on sauce. Steak should be served as rare as possible. *Six servings, 185 calories each.*

·

ITALIAN-STYLE LEMON-BAKED ROUND STEAK

This is not quick-cooked pink-in-the-middle steak, but rather a slow-baked fork-tender dish that lends new meaning to the phrase "well done."

1½ **pounds fat-trimmed beef round steak,**
  ½ **teaspoon oregano or Italian seasoning**
  2 **teaspoons dried onion flakes**
  ¼ **teaspoon instant garlic**
  3 **or 4 tablespoons lemon juice**

Put the steak in a shallow baking pan just large enough to hold it. Sprinkle the surface with seasonings and lemon juice. Bake in a very slow (225-degree) oven for 3 hours or more, depending on the thickness, until very tender. *Six servings, about 215 calories each.*

CHINESE STEAK AND ONIONS WITH BEAN SPROUTS

Like onions? Good! A thick slice of onion may help minimize the cholesterol consequence of a hamburger or other fatty meat. At least that's the implication of a new medical study from New Delhi, India. A recent report in the *Indian Journal of Medical Science* points up the possibility that onions may have a cholesterol-lowering effect on humans.

According to the study, 15 healthy people were fed a high-cholesterol diet for 15 days—9,000 calories including 15 grams of fat. That's more than 5 ounces of fat, but some Americans routinely consume that much. Predictably, their blood cholesterol levels rose. Then the same people were fed the same diet for another 15 days, along with 10 grams of onions, and their cholesterol levels dropped.

So . . . don't "hold the onion"!

Luckily for calorie watchers, onions pack a lot of flavor punch for relatively few calories. A thick slice has less than 10 calories; a whole average onion only 37. Onions are also rich in valuable food fiber, that missing ingredient we hear so much about these days.

A pound of onions offers 2.5 grams of fiber for only 157 calories. It would take 220 calories' worth of bran-flakes breakfast cereal to net as much fiber. Two tips for those who don't like too much of a good thing: cooked onions are less "oniony" than raw ones; big sweet Spanish onions are less sharp than the everyday yellow variety. Here is an easy main course that uses lots of onions, and is low in fat, calories, and cholesterol but so delicious you won't think of it as "diet."

1 tablespoon salad oil
4 lean minute steaks (beef round), about 1 pound
2 beef bouillon cubes
½ cup boiling water
¼ cup soy sauce
2 tablespoons sherry
1 large Spanish onion, thinly sliced
1 cup fresh or canned bean sprouts, drained if canned
2 teaspoons finely chopped fresh ginger root (optional)

Use a large electric or range-top skillet with nonstick finish. Heat the oil. Add the minute steaks and sear quickly on both sides. Remove and set aside. Dissolve bouillon in water and add to the skillet. Stir in remaining ingredients. Simmer uncovered, stirring frequently, only till onions are tender but crisp.

Return the browned minute steaks to the skillet at the last minute and continue to cook and stir over moderate heat only until steak is heated through. *Four servings, 220 calories each.*

SPANISH SANGRÍA STEAK WITH FRUIT

2¼ pounds fat-trimmed beef "Swiss steak" (round steak or arm steak)
1½ cups white sangría
16-ounce can tomatoes, broken up
2 onions, chopped
1 clove garlic, minced
1 green bell pepper, seeded and diced
¼ cup white raisins
¼ cup dried apricots
10 stuffed green Spanish olives, sliced
1 large bay leaf
1 teaspoon basil
½ teaspoon thyme
Salt and freshly ground pepper to taste

Trim off all fat. Put the steak into a small shallow nonstick pan and bake uncovered in a very hot (450-degree) oven for 20 to 25 minutes, until brown. Pour off all melted fat.

Combine remaining ingredients and pour over meat. Cover the pan loosely with foil. Lower heat to 325 degrees and bake 2 hours or more, until meat is nearly tender. Remove foil and continue to bake, basting frequently, until liquid is reduced to a thick sauce. *Eight servings, about 250 calories each.*

Steak You Make Ahead

Make-ahead is a great idea, especially for summer cooks—prevents slaving over a hot stove during the day's peak heat period. For work-all-day cooks, do-ahead is often the only answer. But, even if you have no job and have air conditioning, make-ahead still makes sense for calorie watchers. If you make tomorrow's dinner tonight and chill it all day in the refrigerator, you'll find that all the fat (and fat calories) has conveniently congealed on the surface. Simply lift off those greasy globs and toss away your weight worries!

Almost any slow-simmered dish in which meat is cooked in liquid is a candidate for the make-ahead method. Or try these:

MEXICAN ROUND STEAK MAÑANA

1 pound fat-trimmed beef round or arm steak
1 tablespoon diet margarine
3 cups tomato juice
1 tablespoon red wine vinegar
3 tablespoons chopped onion
3 tablespoons minced celery
3 tablespoons minced green bell pepper
1 teaspoon garlic salt
1 teaspoon oregano or Italian seasoning
¼ teaspoon cumin
   Pinch of cayenne pepper, or to taste

AHEAD: Brown meat in diet margarine in a nonstick skillet, turning once. Add remaining ingredients; cover and simmer 1 hour or more over very low heat until tender. Cool and refrigerate, covered, all day or overnight.

BEFORE DINNER: Remove from refrigerator and lift off hardened fat. Reheat to simmering. Allow to simmer, uncovered, until liquid is reduced to a thick sauce. *Four servings, 210 calories each.*

SUNRISE STROGANOFF

Make it in the morning, serve it at sunset!

1 pound lean fat-trimmed beef round steak,
1 teaspoon prepared mustard
1 tablespoon diet margarine
1 cup tomato juice
3 tablespoons dry white wine
1 beef bouillon cube
2 onions, sliced
   4-ounce can sliced mushrooms
1 cup evaporated skim milk
2 tablespoons all-purpose flour
   Salt and freshly ground pepper

Cut beef into 2-inch strips and coat lightly with mustard. Heat diet margarine in a nonstick skillet. Add beef and brown lightly over moderate heat, stirring to brown evenly. Add tomato juice, wine, bouillon cube, and onions. Cover and simmer over very low heat about 30 minutes. Cool skillet and refrigerate, covered.

BEFORE DINNER: Remove from refrigerator and lift off hardened fat. Add canned mushrooms, including liquid, and reheat to boiling. Simmer, uncovered, until most of the liquid has evaporated. Stir evaporated milk and flour together and add slowly to simmering skillet, until mixture simmers and thickens. Season to taste. *Four servings, 265 calories each.*

Low-Cal Flank Steak—Quick Skillet, Oven Barbecue, or Pot Roast

With hardly any fat to speak of, beef flank steak is one of the leanest and least-fattening steaks there is—only 650 calories per pound, compared with 1,800 or more for boneless rib. For that reason, it is a frequent feature on my Slim Gourmet menus.

Flank steak can be quick-cooked and served rare, or slow-baked and offered well done; it can also be turned into a rolled roast, slow-simmered until tender and thinly sliced. All ways, if you follow my suggestions, it will be deliciously tender and flavorful.

For quick-cooked flank—to keep the steak flat as it cooks and to aid tenderness—your first step will be to score the steak on both sides with shallow criss-cross cuts. Be careful not to cut too deep; you don't want to cut through the meat, just "decorate" the surface on both sides with a diamond-shaped pattern, as you might with the fat on a ham.

SPEEDY SKILLET STEAK STROGANOFF

If you're a calorie-wise cook in a hurry, you'll like my favorite TV dinner. This dinner has nothing to do with the heat-and-serve kind; it's a meal I often make on camera, a sort of speedy beef stroganoff made in a skillet.

As the author of several low-cal cookbooks, I'm frequently invited to appear on TV talk shows. There's nothing more "short order" than TV cookery. Nor more inconvenient.

No matter how fancy and efficient those TV kitchens appear on the home screen, they're really all for show: Gleaming stainless sinks with faucets that pour nothing but air. (The nearest water is the drinking fountain upstairs. Guests get to wash their dirty dishes in the ladies' room!) Wall ovens that never need to self-clean because they're not hooked up. Fool-the-eye refrigerators that are really painted flats.

The countertop stove, if used at all, will be connected at the last minute, after the entire set is wheeled into camera range. Maybe it will work. The only utensils on hand were left behind by the last cookbook-author guest. In short, your average campsite is better equipped.

So authors on a "cook's tour" quickly learn to develop special recipes edited for TV—which means the fastest way possible, with the fewest dishes.

My stroganoff number fills the bill. A meal in one pan. With everything assembled beforehand, it can be tossed together on camera in 5 minutes, yet it tastes every bit as telegenic as it looks. It has a five-star rating with the stagehands, who always finish it off.

So, if you need a quickie on cue, try this.

1 small beef flank steak (about 1¼ pounds)
Meat tenderizer
Monosodium glutamate (optional)
Garlic powder
1 large Spanish onion, cut in half and thinly sliced
1 tablespoon diet margarine
2 cups thinly sliced peeled potatoes
1 cup fat-skimmed canned beef broth or 1 bouillon cube dissolved in water
2 tablespoons minced fresh parsley or 2 teaspoons parsley flakes
2 tablespoons catsup
½ teaspoon dry mustard or 1 teaspoon prepared mustard
2 tablespoons dry sherry
½ cup plain low-fat yogurt
2 tablespoons all-purpose flour

Put the flank steak on a cutting board and score it on both sides in a crisscross pattern. (This aids tenderness and keeps the steak flat as it browns. Don't score it too deeply.) Sprinkle with meat tenderizer, monosodium glutamate, and garlic powder. Slice onion and assemble all remaining ingredients near stove.

Heat margarine in a large nonstick skillet or electric frying pan. Add steak and sear quickly on both sides.

Remove browned steak to a cutting board and set aside. Into the skillet stir onion, potatoes, broth, parsley, catsup, mustard, and sherry. Stir well. Cover and cook until potatoes are tender (on camera, I use canned potatoes).

While the vegetables cook, slice the steak very thin against the grain on a cutting board. It should be very rare, almost raw, inside.

Stir yogurt and flour together. Uncover skillet and stir in yogurt combination to make a "sour cream" sauce. Stir in steak slices and heat through. Don't overcook; steak slices should still be rare.

Five servings, 275 calories each.

OVEN-BARBECUED FLANK STEAK

1 large beef flank steak (about 1½ pounds)
1 cup unsweetened pineapple juice
3 tablespoons lemon juice
  6-ounce can tomato paste
  Dash of Tabasco
1 bay leaf
¼ teaspoon coarsely ground pepper
1 onion, chopped
½ cup sliced stuffed green Spanish olives
1 teaspoon liquid-smoke seasoning
1 pound fresh mushrooms, sliced
¼ cup cold water
1 tablespoon arrowroot

Place the steak on a cutting board and score both sides.

Combine all ingredients except mushrooms, cold water, and arrowroot in a shallow nonmetallic baking dish. Cover with foil and refrigerate overnight. Next morning, turn the steak over in its marinating sauce; cover and refrigerate until cooking time. About 2 hours before dinner, add the mushrooms. Put the foil-covered baking dish into a 350-degree oven and bake, covered, until the meat is very tender, about 1½ hours. Remove the steak to a platter and keep warm. Use a bulb-type baster to skim fat from the liquid in the pan.

Pour the liquid into a saucepan and heat to boiling. Combine arrowroot and water and stir into the simmering sauce until thickened. If too thick, thin with a little boiling water. Slice the steak thin and pour the sauce over. *Six servings, 240 calories each.*

KOREAN SKILLET STEAK

1 large beef flank steak (1½ pounds)
1 clove garlic, finely minced, or instant garlic to taste
  Monosodium glutamate (optional)
  Meat tenderizer
5 tablespoons soy sauce
3 tablespoons dry white wine
2 teaspoons sugar
1 tablespoon sesame seeds
4 teaspoons safflower oil
4 scallions or green onions, sliced

Lay the flank steak on a cutting board and make shallow diagonal criss-cross slices on both sides. Then sprinkle both sides of the steak with instant garlic, monosodium glutamate, and meat tenderizer.

Put the steak into a shallow dish. Combine the soy sauce, wine, and sugar, and pour over the flank steak. Set aside for 30 minutes.

Meanwhile, in a shallow nonstick frying pan, brown the sesame seeds over high heat, shaking constantly so they don't burn. Remove from the skillet and set aside.

Lift up the flank steak with a fork and hold over the marinating dish so that most of the liquid drains off. Reserve liquid. Quick-cook the steak over moderate heat, using 2 teaspoons oil for each side. Make a shallow cut in the meat to check doneness; steak is best if served rare.

Remove the steak to a platter and slice thin against the grain. Add scallions to reserved marinade and heat quickly in skillet over high heat and pour over steak slices. Sprinkle with browned sesame seeds. *Six servings, 210 calories each.*

DIETER'S PARMESAN POT ROAST

Each serving is around 200 calories instead of the 400 calories or more that most pot roast cuts would be.

1½ **pounds beef flank steak**
3 **tablespoons grated Parmesan cheese**
1½ **teaspoons oregano or Italian seasoning**
1 **clove garlic, finely minced**
  Salt and freshly ground pepper
1 **tablespoon diet margarine**
  16-ounce can Italian tomatoes, broken up
¼ **cup Chianti wine**
¾ **cup water**
½ **cup chopped onions**

Lay flank steak flat and sprinkle with cheese, Italian seasoning, and minced garlic. Sprinkle lightly with salt and pepper. Roll the flank steak lengthwise; tie in several places with clean white kitchen string. Heat the diet margarine in a heavy nonstick Dutch oven or electric skillet. Brown the rolled steak slowly on all sides. Pour off any fat.

Add tomatoes, wine, water, and onions. Cover and cook very slowly over low heat about 2 hours, until very tender. Uncover during the last ½ hour, allowing liquid to evaporate into a thick sauce. Slice, top with sauce. *Six servings, 205 calories each.*

FLEMISH FLANK ROAST

1 beef flank steak (1½ pounds)
1 clove garlic, finely minced
½ teaspoon salt
  Pinch of freshly ground pepper
½ teaspoon poultry seasoning
1 tablespoon diet margarine
  Small bay leaf
¾ cup (½ twelve-ounce bottle) low-calorie, low-carbohydrate "light" beer
½ teaspoon brown sugar
1 onion, thinly sliced
  Chopped fresh parsley

Lay steak flat and sprinkle with garlic, salt, pepper, and ¼ teaspoon poultry seasoning. Roll up lengthwise and tie with string in several places. Brown rolled steak slowly on all sides in diet margarine. Add bay leaf, beer, and brown sugar, and remaining poultry seasoning. Cover and simmer 1½ hours. Add onion and simmer an additional 20 minutes. Uncover and continue to simmer until most of the liquid has evaporated. Stir in parsley. Slice and serve, topped with pan juices. *Six servings, 190 calories each.*

Slow-Baked Rolled Steaks, German or Italian Style

Imagine cooking minute steaks for an hour and a half. A great idea, if the dish you have in mind is roulade or braciole. The former is a German-style dish (*Rolladen* in German) in which pieces of beef are wrapped around pickles, then slow-simmered to a melt-in-the-mouth tenderness. The latter is an Italian-style version of slow-baked rolled steak, seasoned with cheese and herbs. In both cases, the dishes only taste fattening, if you follow our Slim Gourmet directions.

Both recipes use minute steaks cut from beef round, one of the leanest beef cuts there is. You can make your own by cutting up a round steak into six equal portions. Whack the steaks with a meat mallet, to make them as thin as possible, then slow-cook in a liquid which becomes the sauce.

ROULADE OF BEEF
German-Style Rolled Steak

6 minute steaks or 1½ pounds beef round, cut into steaks, trimmed of fat, and pounded thin
2 teaspoons hot mustard

3 dill pickles, cut in spears
1 cup beer (low-calorie beer can be used)
½ cup boiling water
2 tablespoons all-purpose flour
¼ cup cold water

Spread the meat lightly with mustard and wrap around the pickle spears, securing with toothpicks. Arrange close together in an ovenproof casserole, flameproof range-top pot, electric skillet, all-day cooker, or pressure cooker. Add beer and boiling water.

Cover and cook until tender: simmer on top of the range or bake in a 300-degree oven for about 1½ hours. Follow manufacturer's suggestions for electric skillet, all-day cooker, or pressure cooker.

When meat is tender, skim off surface fat with a bulb-type baster. Thicken the liquid with the flour and cold water combined into a paste, stirring it into the sauce over low heat. Cook gently until sauce is gravy thick. *Six servings, 185 calories each.*

BRACIOLE

Italian-Style Rolled Steak

6 minute steaks or 1½ pounds beef round, cut into steaks, trimmed of fat,
   and pounded thin
6 teaspoons grated extra-sharp Romano cheese
6 tablespoons chopped onion
   Oregano or Italian seasoning
   8-ounce can plain tomato sauce
¼ cup Chianti wine
½ cup water

Sprinkle each steak with cheese, onion, and oregano. Roll up and secure with toothpicks. Arrange close together in a pan. Combine remaining ingredients and pour over the steaks. Cover and simmer over very low heat or bake at 300 degrees until tender, about 1½ hours.

Uncover and continue cooking until sauce is gravy thick. Skim off fat, if any, with a bulb-type baster. *Six servings, 180 calories each.*

AUNT NADIA'S SPICY BEEF ROLL

Beef shoulder or chuck—as every pennypincher knows—is a less expensive, less tender cut that's ideal for stew or pot roast. But did you know that so-called shoulder or chuck can come from two different parts of the steer, and that the calories, and fat, are dramatically different? For a weight-wise cook and shopper, it pays to know the difference.

The upper—and more fattening—cut really is the "shoulder." Sometimes it's called the "blade" cut (as in shoulder blade!). You'll recognize it by the flat shoulder-blade bone.

The lower—and less-fattening—cut is part of the animal's foreleg and may be labeled "beef arm." You'll be able to recognize it because the bone is round . . . just as you might expect to find inside a steer's "arm."

Although the pieces of meat are adjacent, there's a considerable difference in fat and calories. Here's how they compare: One pound of boneless beef blade chuck is 30 percent fat, has 74 grams of protein and 1,597 calories, while one pound of boneless beef arm chuck is 14 percent fat, has 88 grams of protein and 1,012 calories.

In buying or preparing beef arm for cooking, further cut calories by meticulously trimming away as much remaining fat as possible. Then cook it in a manner that allows you to skim off any remaining melted fat. The separable lean meat is only 640 calories a pound.

Here's a savory slow-cooked pot roast that minimizes fat and calories—ideal for both calorie and cholesterol watchers.

4 **pounds fat-trimmed boneless beef arm roast, rolled and tied**
2 **tablespoons prepared mustard**
2 **teaspoons garlic salt**
1/2 **teaspoon sage**
Pinch of freshly ground black pepper
1 **cup chopped onion**
1 **cup chopped celery**
1/4 **cup chopped fresh parsley**
1/2 **cup boiling water**
2 **tablespoons red wine vinegar**
2 **tablespoons all-purpose flour**
1/2 **cup cold water**
2 **teaspoons (or more) prepared horseradish**
Salt, if needed

Choose lean beef and have it trimmed of all fringe fat before boning and tying. Spread the meat with prepared mustard and season well with garlic salt, sage, and pepper. Brown the meat well under your broiler, turning to brown evenly. Discard melted fat.

Put the browned meat into a heavy Dutch oven or flameproof casserole. Add the onion, celery, parsley, boiling water, and vinegar. Cover and simmer on top of the range over very low heat until tender, 3 hours or more. Or cover and bake in a 300-degree oven.

Drain pan liquid into a 2-cup measuring cup and chill in the freezer for 10 to 15 minutes, until the fat rises and hardens on the surface. Lift off and discard fat. Add enough water to make 2 cups and return to pot. Heat to simmering.

Combine flour and cold water and stir into simmering sauce until gravy thick. Stir in horseradish to taste. Add salt and additional pepper, if needed. *About twelve servings, 230 calories each.* Chill the leftovers for sandwiches.

ITALIAN POT ROAST WITH RIGATONI

Pot roast, Italian style. What a wonderful way to welcome your hungry tribe! The heady aroma of tomatoes, vegetables, and herbs combine to hint at fattening fare to come. But this inspired dish is anything but that.

The recipe combines slices of fork-tender beef with tubes of rigatoni pasta and a savory tomato sauce that's spiked with celery and Italian squash—a lot less fattening than its fragrant flavor indicates, and so filling and satisfying that a big tossed salad and some fresh fruit dessert are all you need to complete the meal.

Lean top or bottom beef round pot roast (about 3 pounds)
Salt and freshly ground pepper
2 **cups tomato puree**
4 **cups canned Italian tomatoes**
1 **large Spanish onion, chopped**
3 **stalks celery, sliced**
3 **cups diced zucchini**
1 **clove garlic, minced**
1 **bay leaf**
1 **teaspoon oregano or Italian seasoning**
¼ **teaspoon basil**
8 **ounces dry rigatoni or macaroni**

Trim all fat from meat. Season with salt and pepper and put in a heavy flameproof Dutch oven. To brown the meat with no fat added, put the Dutch oven in a preheated very hot oven (450 degrees), and bake uncovered for about 20 minutes, until the meat is well browned. Drain off fat.

Add all remaining ingredients to Dutch oven except rigatoni. Cover and return to oven for an additional 20 minutes at high heat.

Then lower heat to 325 degrees and bake, covered, for 3 to 4 hours, until the meat is very tender and the sauce has simmered down. At dinnertime, cook rigatoni or macaroni in boiling salted water until tender (see page 000). Drain. To serve, remove meat from sauce and slice thin against the grain. Top the rigatoni and meat with the sauce (skim off fat, if any). *Eight servings, 410 calories each.*

Beef in Cubes, for Tasty, Low-Cal Stews and Skillet Dishes

BEEF EN DAUBE

2 pounds lean boneless beef round, in 2-inch cubes
1 slice bacon, diced
1 cup water
½ cup dry white wine
1 tablespoon Worcestershire sauce
1 large tomato, peeled, or 1 cup canned tomatoes, broken up
2 carrots, chopped
2 onions, chopped
2 small white turnips, pared and chopped
6 cloves garlic, minced
3 bay leaves
¼ teaspoon thyme
¼ teaspoon oregano or Italian seasoning
   Salt and freshly ground pepper

Have all fat trimmed from beef before cutting into cubes. Combine the diced bacon and beef cubes in a nonstick heavy Dutch oven over moderate heat. Brown, stirring occasionally, until bacon is crisp and well rendered of fat and beef cubes are brown.

Add the water, heat to boiling, then drain off into a cup. Skim the fat from the surface and return the water to the pot. Add all remaining ingredients. Cover and cook over very low heat 2 hours or more until meat is very tender (add water, if needed). Uncover and continue cooking until liquid is reduced and sauce is thick. *Six servings, about 270 calories each.*

PRESSURE-COOKER BEEF BOURGUIGNONNE

2½ pounds lean, fat-trimmed bottom round, cut in cubes
1 cup Burgundy or other red wine
1 cup water
2 teaspoons salt or garlic salt
   Coarsely ground pepper to taste
1 bay leaf
¼ teaspoon poultry seasoning
1 pound carrots, in 3-inch lengths
   8-ounce can small boiled onions, drained
1 cup sliced mushrooms, fresh or canned
2 tablespoons chopped fresh parsley (optional)

Use a nonstick pressure cooker, or coat the interior with cooking spray for no-fat frying. Add the beef cubes and heat over moderate flame until the meat begins to brown. Stir to keep from sticking.

Add wine, water, salt, pepper, bay leaf, and poultry seasoning. Cover and cook under pressure 7 minutes, following manufacturer's instructions. Reduce pressure. Uncover. Stir in carrots, onions, and mushrooms. Cook, uncovered, stirring frequently until the liquid is reduced to a sauce. Stir in parsley at the last minute. *Eight servings, 225 calories each.*

ONE-POT GOULASH

Here's a savory goulash you can make on top of the range in a heavy pot or pressure cooker. This easy dish contains noodles, often considered off limits by calorie watchers . . . but you can see by the calorie total that it doesn't exceed your limit! This recipe is made with curly noodles, the kind with ruffled edges that keep them from sticking together.

Cooked carrots, a big tossed salad, some wine, and fruit could complete your meal.

> 2 **pounds fat-trimmed beef round, cut in cubes**
> 1 **tablespoon salad oil**
> 1½ **cups water**
> 2 **onions, chopped**
> 1½ **teaspoons salt**
> ¼ **teaspoon freshly ground pepper**
> 1 **tablespoon paprika**
> ¼ **teaspoon caraway seeds**
> **8-ounce can tomatoes**
> **8-ounce can tomato puree**
> **8-ounces (2 cups) dry curly egg noodles**

Brown the meat in the oil in a heavy nonstick Dutch oven or pressure cooker. Add the water and heat to boiling, then drain off. Set aside to allow the fat to rise to the surface. Skim off fat with a bulb-type baster, then return the liquid to the pot. Stir in all remaining ingredients except noodles. Cover and simmer over very low heat until tender, 1 hour or more. Or cook in a pressure cooker for 20 minutes, following manufacturer's directions.

Stir in uncooked noodles. Cover and cook an additional 10 to 12 minutes (or 5 minutes under pressure). Add more water, if needed. *Eight servings, 265 calories each.*

SKILLET CUBAN CHILI

Hot and spicy don't necessarily go together. Consider Cuban cookery. Spicy, sí! Hot, no!

Americans unfamiliar with Cuban food tend to mix it up with Mexican. And avoid it, if they tend to be tender-tongued. But Cuban cooks are much less aggressive with the hot peppers, though they still share the same language and love for seasonings and savory combinations. Though more tepid in temperature than Mexican, Cuban cuisine can hardly be considered tame.

Nor low calorie, unfortunately. Cuban cookery is too well lubricated with oil for weight-wary Yankees to duplicate faithfully. But if calorie watchers can't adopt Cuban cuisine, they can adapt it—particularly the dishes based on seafood and lean meats.

Here I've interpreted a Cuban favorite for Slim Gourmet kitchens, using ingredients available in any supermarket, and techniques that trim away unneeded calories.

This skillet stew is Cuban-style chili. It's made with the leanest beef . . . and olives instead of olive oil. This recipe serves 8, but you can cut the ingredients in half to serve 4. Or, better yet, freeze the extras for an easy heat-and-eat meal another day. It's that kind of recipe!

2 **pounds fat-trimmed boneless beef bottom round, cut in 1½ cubes**
1 **cup chopped onion**
2 **cloves garlic, minced**
1 **cup minced celery**
2 **cups canned tomatoes, broken up**
¼ **cup raisins**
1 **tablespoon vinegar**
   10-ounce can fat-skimmed beef broth
2 **teaspoons salt**
   Freshly ground pepper
¼ **teaspoon ground cloves**
½ **teaspoon chili powder, or to taste**
¼ **cup sliced stuffed green olives**
4 **cups cooked brown rice (optional)**

Put the beef cubes into a large nonstick skillet, with no fat added. Brown slowly over moderate heat, stirring constantly to keep from sticking. Add the remaining ingredients, except olives. Cover and simmer 1 hour or more, until meat is very tender. With a bulb-type baster, skim off fat, if any. Uncover and continue to simmer until most of the liquid is evaporated. Stir in olives. (Serve with cooked brown rice, if desired.) *Eight servings, 200 calories each without rice; 300 calories each with ½ cup serving rice.*

FIVE-MINUTE SKILLET STEAK CURRY

¾ pound lean, fat-trimmed beefsteak, cut in 1½-inch cubes
6-ounce can (¾ cup) tomato juice
6 ounce can (¾ cup) unsweetened apple or pineapple juice
1 large or 2 small onions, cut in half and sliced
1 medium zucchini, sliced in slender 3-inch strips
3 stalks celery, slit lengthwise and then sliced
1 red or green bell pepper, seeded and diced in 1-inch squares
3 tablespoons soy sauce
1 level teaspoon curry powder
2 unpeeled medium red apples, cored and diced
¾ cups green seedless grapes, sliced in half
¼ cup dry-roasted peanuts, broken up

Spray a large nonstick skillet or electric frying pan with cooking spray for no-fat frying. Brown the meat quickly over high heat, stirring constantly so that it doesn't stick. Add the tomato and fruit juices, onion, zucchini, celery, bell pepper, soy sauce, and curry powder. Lower heat to medium and simmer uncovered, stirring frequently, for 3 to 4 minutes, until celery is tender-crisp and most of the liquid has evaporated to a thick glaze. Stir in the apples and green grapes.

Cook and stir for 1 more minute. Sprinkle with nuts and serve immediately. *Four servings, 265 calories each.*

VARIATIONS

Turkey or chicken cutlets (skinless boneless breasts) cut into cubes could substitute for the steak. Yellow summer squash could stand in for zucchini. A yellow apple, diced pear, or ½ cup juice-packed pineapple chunks could replace the red apple. Try cashews instead of peanuts or ¼ cup raisins instead of grapes.

SKILLET STEAK BOURGUIGNONNE

In French cuisine, "Bourguignonne" means prepared in the cooking style of Burgundy, the region that gives its name to great wines as well as food. Burgundy-style dishes are generally slow-simmered in dry red wine and herbs, and served with tiny onions and plump mushrooms. Carrots are a great addition.

It's an ideal way to handle the leanest and least-fattening cuts of beef, making *boeuf bourguignonne* a Slim Gourmet's delight:

3 pounds lean, fat-trimmed beef round, cut in cubes
1 onion, finely chopped
2 cloves garlic, minced
2 cups dry Burgundy wine
1 bay leaf
1 pound small carrots, scrubbed
16 pearl onions, peeled (fresh or frozen)
1/2 pound small fresh mushrooms
1/3 cup cold water
1 tablespoon flour
1 tablespoon cornstarch
Salt and pepper
Chopped parsley (optional)
4 cups cooked brown rice or broad noodles (optional)

Use a nonstick Dutch oven or very large electric skillet. Spray well with cooking spray for no-fat frying. Add cubes of beef and brown well on all sides over high heat. Add chopped onion, garlic, wine, and bay leaf. Cover and simmer until tender, 2 hours or more. Use a bulb-type baster to skim fat from liquid. Add carrots. Cover and cook 20 minutes. Add pearl onions and mushrooms. Cover and cook 10 minutes. Mix cold water, flour, and cornstarch and stir into the simmering sauce. Salt and pepper to taste. Garnish with chopped parsley and serve with cooked brown rice or broad noodles, if desired. *Makes eight servings, 300 calories each without rice or noodles; 400 calories each with 1/2 cup rice or noodles.*

TENDERLOIN ROMANOFF

1½ pounds beef tenderloin (from end), cut into cubes
1 teaspoon Worcestershire sauce
1 tablespoon prepared mustard
2 teaspoons salad oil
1/4 cup dry white wine
1/2 pound fresh mushrooms, sliced
2 cups thinly sliced onion
1 clove garlic, minced
1 cup fat-skimmed beef broth
1/2 cup plain low-fat yogurt
2 tablespoons all-purpose flour
2 tablespoons grated extra-sharp Romano cheese
2 tablespoons minced fresh parsley
Salt and freshly ground pepper

Toss the steak cubes with Worcestershire, mustard, and 1 teaspoon oil. Then cook and stir in a large nonstick skillet over high heat, until meat is browned but still nearly raw in the middle. Remove from the skillet and set aside.

Add remaining teaspoon oil and 2 tablespoons wine to the skillet. Add the mushrooms. Quickly cook and stir over high heat until the liquid evaporates and the mushrooms brown. Remove and set aside.

Add the onion, garlic, beef broth, and remaining 2 tablespoons wine. Cook uncovered 5 minutes.

Stir the yogurt, flour, and Romano cheese together, then stir into the skillet. Cook and stir until sauce is thick and bubbling. At the last minute, stir in the browned mushrooms, steak cubes, and parsley. Season to taste. Cook only until heated through (steak should be rare). May be served with cooked brown rice, if desired.

Six servings, 260 calories each without rice; 1/2 cup cooked brown rice per serving would add 100 calories.

POLYNESIAN SKILLET (SWEET 'N' SOUR STEAK TIPS)

1 **pound lean beef top round, cut in 1½-inch cubes**
  Meat tenderizer (optional)
2 **tablespoons vinegar**
¼ **cup soy sauce**
  8-ounce can juice-packed pineapple chunks, juice reserved
2 **large onions, chopped**
2 **carrots, coarsely shredded**
2 **thinly sliced red or green bell peppers (or 1 of each)**
¼ **cup catsup**
¼ **teaspoon ground ginger**
3 **tablespoons brown sugar**

Trim fat, if any, from steak and discard. Cut the steaks into 1½-inch cubes, sprinkle with meat tenderizer, and set aside for 10 or 15 minutes. Combine meat with vinegar, soy sauce, and juice from the canned pineapple. Marinate 1 hour at room temperature or several hours in the refrigerator, covered.

Spray a large nonstick skillet or electric frying pan with cooking spray for no-fat frying (no added fat is needed). Drain the steak cubes (reserving the soy-vinegar-pineapple-juice mixture) and brown quickly over high heat. Stir in the onions, carrots, peppers, catsup, ginger and soy mixture. Cover and simmer 3 minutes. Uncover and continue to simmer only until vegetables are tender-crisp and liquid has evaporated to a thick glaze. Stir in the pineapple chunks at the last minute and heat through. Remove from heat and stir in brown sugar. *Four servings, under 300 calories each.*

Stews Slow-Cooked in the Oven or Crock Cooker

Put these on in the morning. At night come home to the fragrant aroma of a main course that's ready to serve. These beef dishes cook themselves to tender perfection in 8 to 10 hours, more or less. The timing's not critical; no problem if you're late.

The secret is the super-low temperature, only 200 degrees. You can do these dishes in an automatic crock cooker, if you have one, or in the oven if you don't. (But your oven must be untemperamental and reliable, able to maintain a trustworthy 200 degrees; check it with a thermometer and see.)

Differing from some slow-cooked recipes, these require no pre-browning. Pre-browning is not only extra time and work, it adds extra calories (in the form of fat) and makes more dirty dishes (the frying pan). Worse yet, it defeats the whole purpose of slow-cooking. The hot, high temperature of pre-browning only serves to toughen the meat. So being lazy pays off!

The best beef for these dishes is fat-trimmed bottom round. What luck! It's also the leanest and least fattening, the best buy for calorie and cholesterol watchers, and only 612 calories per pound.

You can double the quantity of these recipes, with no change in cooking time or temperature.

FRENCH-DRESSED BEEF

What could be easier! For Italian-dressed beef, use Italian dressing. For Russian-dressed beef, use . . . well, you get the idea! Be sure to use low-calorie dressing (which makes a sauce) and not regular dressing (which just separates out a lot of oil).

1 **pound fat-trimmed beef bottom round, cut in cubes**
⅓ **cup low-calorie French dressing**
3 **tablespoons dried onion flakes**
1 **teaspoon instant garlic (optional)**
  Salt and freshly ground pepper, if needed
2 **cups cooked rice or noodles**

Combine ingredients, except salt and pepper, in a crock cooker or ovenproof dish, and cover tightly with foil. Slow-cook at 200 degrees for 8 to 10 hours. Taste and add seasonings if needed. Serve over rice or noodles, if desired. *Serves 4, about 200 calories each, without rice or noodles; 1/2 cup rice adds 90 calories, 1/2 cup noodles, 100 calories.*

BEEF AU DIABLE

1 **pound fat-trimmed beef bottom round, cut in cubes**
3 **tablespoons prepared mustard (mild or hot)**
2 **tablespoons dried onion flakes**
¼ **teaspoon instant garlic (optional)**
2 **tablespoons Worcestershire sauce**
  Salt and freshly ground pepper

Stir all ingredients together to coat meat evenly. Cook in a crock cooker, covered, or bake in a warm oven, in a small pan tightly covered with foil. Cook 8 to 10 hours at 200 degrees. *Four servings, 235 calories each.*

STEAK AU SUISSE

1 pound fat-trimmed beef bottom round steak
1 onion, peeled and minced
2 tomatoes, peeled and chopped
Salt and freshly ground pepper

Cut steak in 4 equal pieces and smother with onion and tomato. Season with salt and pepper. (For Italian flavor, add a shake of oregano and a tablespoon of grated extra-sharp Romano cheese.) Slow-cook, covered, 8 to 10 hours at 200 degrees. *Four servings, 180 calories each.*

BEEF CUBANO

1 pound fat-trimmed beef bottom round, cut in strips
3 tablespoons low-calorie Italian salad dressing
2 tablespoons catsup
Dash of Tabasco, or to taste
2 tablespoons dried onion flakes
¼ teaspoon instant garlic
Pinch of cumin

Stir all ingredients well together to coat meat evenly. Slow-cook, covered, 8 to 10 hours at 200 degrees, in crock cooker or oven. *Four servings, 195 calories each.*

Turn Low-Cal Stew Beef into Steak on Skewers

Nothing beats beef-on-skewers for glamour. Or calories! Unfortunately, the cuts of steak best suited for skewer cooking are also the most fattening. Most expensive, too.

On the other hand, the leaner cuts usually need stewing or slow cooking to be tender. But you can save calories and money by using these leaner, less tender beef cubes for skewer cooking. My method is two steps. First, the meat is cut in cubes, threaded on skewers, wrapped, and slow-cooked in its own tenderizing marinade. Then it's unwrapped and quick-browned over the coals or under the broiler. You can use this method indoors or out, any time of year. Your beef-on-skewers will be well done, but tender and tasty, flavored through with the marinade. Here's how:

TENDER-COOKED LEAN BBQ BEEF
ON SKEWERS

1 pound fat-trimmed lean beef round steak or arm steak, cut in cubes
1 cup Tenderizing Marinade Baste (see below)

To Cook Outdoors: Thread meat onto skewers. Place on heavy-duty foil sheet. Lift foil up around skewers. Pour on the marinade. Double-wrap with foil, taking care not to puncture it with the skewers. Arrange the packet on your covered barbecue grill over hot coals. Cook 1½ hours or more, until tender. Turn the packet occasionally to insure even cooking. Unwrap carefully to check tenderness. When meat is tender, remove skewers from foil. Arrange the skewers on a grill over hot coals. Continue cooking until nicely browned. Turn frequently and baste with reserved marinade from packets.

To Cook Indoors: Arrange the meat-threaded skewers in a shallow baking dish. Pour on marinade. Cover dish with foil. Bake in a 325-degree oven until tender—about 90 minutes. When tender, remove the skewered meat from the baking dish. Finish cooking under the broiler. Turn to brown evenly and baste occasionally with reserved marinade. *Four servings, about 200 calories each.*

Tenderizing Marinade Baste: Any combination of slightly acid liquids can be used—tomato juice, citrus juice, dry wine diluted with water. One teaspoon commercial meat tenderizer may be stirred into the liquid. Season to taste with garlic powder, spices, or herbs, which add few or no extra calories. Absolutely no fat or oil is needed.

Here are some combinations to try:

Japanese Teriyaki Baste: ¼ cup dry sherry, ¼ cup soy sauce, ½ cup water, ¼ teaspoon ground ginger, ¼ teaspoon monosodium glutamate

Italian Baste I: 3 tablespoons lemon juice, 1½ teaspoons garlic salt, 1 teaspoon oregano or Italian seasoning, ¾ cup water.

Italian Baste II: ½ cup low-calorie Italian diet dressing, ½ cup water or, for variety, substitute any other type of diet salad dressing.

French Baste: ½ cup diet French dressing, ¼ cup dry white wine, ¼ cup water.

Polynesian Baste: ¾ cup unsweetened apricot juice, 2 tablespoons catsup, 2 teaspoons prepared mustard, 2 tablespoons soy sauce, 1 teaspoon vinegar, 1 teaspoon granulated sugar.

Hot 'n' Spicy Baste: 1 cup tomato juice, ½ envelope or more Bloody Mary mix, 1 teaspoon onion powder.

TURKISH-STYLE SLIM SKEWERED STEAK

Calorie-free flavor. If there's one ingredient that meets that definition, it must be the bay leaf. Its calories are next to nothing to begin with, but the leaves are not even eaten. Most times bay leaves are removed or set aside; only the flavor remains.

Bay (or laurel) is a widely-loved seasoning, starred frequently in many cultures, including African, Cuban, French, Greek, Italian, Jewish, Mexican, Polish, and Spanish. Because bay leaves are such potent flavor adders, most cooks use them with caution.

However, here is a dish in which bay leaves are added with abandon, permeating lean meat with flavor and perfuming the air with heavy fragrance.

1½ pounds boneless lean, fat-trimmed sirloin of beef
  5 tablespoons low-calorie Italian salad dressing
     Few drops liquid-smoke seasoning (optional)
 12 bay leaves
  2 lemons, thinly sliced
  2 large onions, cut in chunks
  3 green bell peppers, seeded and cut in 1-inch squares
  2 large tomatoes, cut in chunks, or 12 cherry tomatoes
  1 tablespoon olive oil

Trim off fat and cut meat into 1½-inch cubes. Combine meat with salad dressing and liquid-smoke seasoning. Marinate at room temperature 30 minutes. Drain meat and reserve marinade.

Thread the meat on metal skewers, alternating with bay leaves and lemon slices. Alternate onion chunks and pepper squares on another set of skewers. Assemble tomato chunks or cherry tomatoes on a third set of skewers. Combine the reserved marinade with 1 tablespoon olive oil and brush the marinade mixture over the vegetables.

Broil or barbecue the meat skewers and onion-pepper skewers about 4 to 5 inches from heat source for about 6 minutes, turning frequently. Add the tomato skewers during the last 2 or 3 minutes of cooking. Brush with reserved marinade mixture while skewers cook. *Six servings, 240 calories each.*

SKEWERED STEAK AND ONIONS ROMANO

1½ pounds lean, fat-trimmed top round, cut in 1½-inch cubes
 ¾ cup low-calorie Italian salad dressing
 12 cherry tomatoes
  6 yellow onions, quartered
  2 tablespoons grated extra-sharp Romano cheese (optional)

Put meat into a plastic bag or bowl and add salad dressing, so that meat is well coated. Cover and marinate all day or overnight in the refrigerator.

Thread meat on skewers, alternating with whole tomatoes and onion chunks. Broil about 12 minutes, turning frequently. Or barbecue over hot coals. Sprinkle each with 1 teaspoon cheese just before serving, if desired. *Six servings, 240 calories each without cheese; add 10 calories per serving with cheese.*

Easy Low-Calorie Ways to Glamorize Leftovers

No need to apologize for leftovers if you're an imaginative cook. Yesterday's roast or vegetables can make a grand comeback in fresh new form, without excess calories. Deftly seasoned for a return engagement, leftovers can be better than ever the second time around.

SCHNITZEL AUF WIEDERSEHEN

Recycle leftover lean steak or roast beef into a sour-creamy beef and mushroom dish.

1 cup sliced onion
1 cup sliced fresh mushrooms
1 tablespoon butter or margarine
2 tablespoons water
1 cup canned condensed fat-skimmed beef broth
1 teaspoon paprika, or to taste
1 teaspoon prepared mustard
1 pound leftover lean rare beef round steak or other lean steak
2 tablespoons all-purpose flour
½ cup plain low-fat yogurt
Few drops brown gravy coloring (optional)
Chopped fresh parsley
Salt and coarsely ground pepper to taste
2 cups cooked rice or noodles (optional)

In a nonstick skillet, combine onions, mushrooms, butter, and water over a moderate flame. Cook and stir until water evaporates and vegetables brown lightly. Stir in broth, paprika, and mustard. Simmer uncovered 5 minutes. Meanwhile, slice steak very thin against the grain into bite-size strips. Then set aside.

Stir flour into yogurt until smooth, then stir into simmering skillet until sauce is thick (stir in a little brown gravy coloring, if desired). Stir in steak strips at the last minute and heat until warmed through. Add chopped parsley, salt and pepper to taste. Serve over rice or noodles, if desired. *Four servings, about 295 calories each without rice or noodles; add 90 calories per ½ cup serving of rice and 100 for noodles.*

SWEET 'N' SOUR PINEAPPLE TERIYAKI

One man's (leftover) meat can be another man's teriyaki.

    Leftover steak or rare roast beef (see note below)
2 tablespoons Japanese-style soy sauce
2 tablespoons sherry
2 teaspoons vinegar
¼ teaspoon monosodium glutamate (optional)
    6-ounce can (¾ cup) unsweetened pineapple juice
    8-ounce can unsweetened pineapple chunks, undrained
1 large onion, cut in chunks
2 green bell peppers, seeded and sliced
¼ teaspoon fennel seeds or anise seeds
8 cherry tomatoes, halved

Combine thinly sliced leftover rare beef with soy sauce, sherry, vinegar, monosodium glutamate, and 2 tablespoons pineapple juice. Cover and marinate 30 minutes at room temperature or several hours in the refrigerator.

Spray a large nonstick skillet with cooking spray for no-fat frying. Add all remaining ingredients except tomatoes. Cover and simmer 3 minutes. Uncover and continue to simmer until nearly all the liquid is evaporated and vegetables are crunchy tender. At the last minute, stir in tomatoes and sliced beef (including marinade). Cook and stir until heated through and well coated with sauce. *Two servings, 360 calories each.*

NOTE: Use lean leftover flank or round steak or rare roast beef round, well trimmed of fat, sliced thin against the grain. For 2 servings you will need about 7 ounces.

STEAK AND PEPPERS WITH SPAGHETTI

¾ pound lean leftover broiled round steak or roast beef
1 large onion, thinly sliced
2 green bell peppers, seeded and cut in strips
1 or 2 cloves garlic, minced, or ⅛ to ¼ teaspoon instant garlic
    16-ounce can tomatoes, broken up
    8-ounce can plain tomato sauce
    Salt and freshly ground pepper to taste
¼ cup dry red wine
¾ cup water
½ teaspoon basil
½ teaspoon oregano
4 cups tender-cooked protein-enriched spaghetti (see page 245)

Slice cooked lean beef thin against the grain into strips. Trim and discard any fat. Combine meat with remaining ingredients, except spaghetti. Cover and simmer 45 minutes. Uncover and continue simmering until sauce is thick. Serve over hot cooked spaghetti. *Four servings, 380 calories each, including 1 cup tender-cooked spaghetti.*

ORIENTAL STEAK AND VEGETABLES

What do you do with barbecue leftovers if you're a Slim Gourmet cook? Most backyard hosts invariably cook more than their guests can eat, lest anyone have less than he wants. The result? Leftovers!

Don't be tempted to overeat rather than see those too-generous servings go to waste—or waist. Hotdogs, hamburgers, steak, and chicken can be recycled easily into next-day family meals. They'll be all the more calorie-wise, because most of the fat has been broiled away.

1 **pound leftover lean, boneless rare barbecued steak**
  6-ounce can (¾ cup) tomato juice
3 **tablespoons soy sauce**
  Dash of Tabasco
  10-ounce package frozen Chinese- (or Japanese-) style vegetables with sauce
1 **cup diagonally sliced celery**
4 **onions, sliced**

Put meat on a cutting board. With a sharp knife, slice against the grain into thin strips. Set aside.

Combine remaining ingredients in a large skillet with a cover. Cover and cook over moderate heat until frozen vegetables are defrosted. Uncover and continue cooking until vegetables are tender-crisp and sauce is thick; stir frequently.

At the last minute, stir in rare steak slices and cook only until heated through. When served, the meat still should be rare and the vegetables crisp. *Six servings, 245 calories each.*

How to Reclaim an Untender Beef Leftover

"Tough luck!"

Is that what you say when a picture-pretty roast beef turns out tough and chewy? No need to, if you're a Slim Gourmet cook. Those disappointing leftovers can be recycled into trim and tender reruns much more tempting than the original. Tonight's disaster can be tomorrow's success . . . and low-calorie, too.

How do you tenderize beef after the fact?

The same way you could have beforehand: with meat tenderizer or a tenderizing marinade.

Yes, post-roasting tenderization will work—with meat still quite rare and pink in the middle—meat that was cooked too quickly at too high a temperature, and wasn't very tender to begin with. On the other hand, if it's tough because it was cooked to death—gray and dry—posthumous first aid won't help.

To reclaim leftover roast beef with commercial tenderizer, slice the meat very thin against the grain and sprinkle lightly with the tenderizer. Wrap in plastic and refrigerate overnight. Next day, heat it very gently in some fat-skimmed beef broth, only till heated through.

Another trick is to marinate the thinly sliced beef in a little dry wine or some diluted low-calorie salad dressing or some diluted tomato or fruit juice. The acid liquid helps break down the fibers and adds interesting flavor.

Cover and refrigerate several hours, then reheat gently in the marinating liquid.

New beef-grading standards will put more lean beef on the market. This is good news for calorie—and cholesterol—watchers, but the leaner beef is less forgiving of hasty cooking techniques.

If it's your tough luck to be stuck with an untender roast, try this reclamation technique.

Here are some second-day recipes with reclaimed roast:

BEEF ENCORE, KOREAN STYLE

1 **pound leftover lean, rare roast top round beef**
6 **tablespoons Japanese-style soy sauce**
6 **tablespoons sauterne**
1 **teaspoon honey or sugar**
2 **tablespoons sesame seeds**
2 **cups cooked rice (optional)**

Slice beef thin against the grain, discarding fat. Then slice into strips. Stir well with remaining ingredients, except sesame seeds. Cover and marinate in the refrigerator all day or overnight.

Fifteen minutes before dinner, toast the sesame seeds in a nonstick skillet over high heat, with no fat added, watching carefully so they don't burn. Remove and set aside. Put the beef strips and marinade into the skillet. Cook and stir over high heat until the beef is heated through and the liquid is reduced to a thick glaze.

Stir in the sesame seeds at the last minute. Serve with cooked rice, if desired.
Four servings, 185 calories each without rice; 275 calories with 1/2 cup rice.

BEEF ENCORE MILANESE

1 pound leftover rare roast beef round
¼ cup low-calorie Italian salad dressing
7 tablespoons dry white wine
4 teaspoons grated Parmesan cheese (optional)
2 cups cooked rice (optional)

Slice beef as in preceding recipe, and marinate in the salad dressing and wine all day or overnight in the refrigerator. Reheat in the salad-dressing mixture. Serve over rice, if desired, sprinkled with cheese. *Four servings, 170 calories each without rice; 260 calories with 1/2 cup rice.*

RECYCLED ROAST BEEF ROMANOFF

1 pound leftover lean, rare roast beef round
  Meat tenderizer
2 teaspoons salad oil
2 tablespoons sherry
½ pound mushrooms, sliced
1 cup water
2 beef bouillon cubes
1 onion, thinly sliced
1 teaspoon dry mustard
2 tablespoons catsup
1 tablespoon all-purpose flour
½ cup plain low-fat yogurt
2 tablespoons grated Romano cheese
2 tablespoons chopped parsley
3 cups cooked noodles (optional)

Slice the meat very thin against the grain, into 1-by-4-inch strips. Trim off and discard any fat as you slice. Sprinkle meat lightly with meat tenderizer. Wrap in plastic and refrigerate all day or overnight.

At dinnertime, in a large nonstick skillet or electric fryer, combine the oil, sherry, and mushrooms. Cook and stir, uncovered, over high heat until liquid evaporates and mushrooms are lightly browned. Remove mushrooms with a slotted spoon and set aside.

Add water to skillet and heat to boiling. Stir in bouillon cubes until dissolved. Add sliced onion, mustard, and catsup. Cover and cook 5 minutes, until onions are tender-crisp.

Stir flour and yogurt together until smooth, then stir into skillet over moderate heat until sauce thickens slightly. Add sliced beef and browned mushrooms to skillet. Cook and stir until heated through. Season to taste and sprinkle with cheese and parsley. Serve over cooked noodles, if desired. *Six servings, 215 calories each without noodles; 1/2 cup of cooked noodles adds 100 calories.*

BEEF TIPS ALOHA

Say "hello" and "goodbye" to leftover roast beef.

1 pound leftover lean, rare roast beef round
6 tablespoons soy sauce
1 cup canned unsweetened crushed pineapple (including juice)
2 tablespoons vinegar
2 tablespoons finely minced onion
2 tablespoons finely minced green bell pepper

Slice the roast very thin against the grain, trimming off and discarding all fat. Cut the meat into strips 1 by 4 inches. Combine with soy sauce, pineapple, and vinegar in a nonmetal bowl; cover. Refrigerate 24 hours.

At dinnertime the next evening, empty the bowl into a nonstick skillet. Add the minced onion and green pepper. Cook and stir uncovered over moderate heat until sauce is hot and bubbling, but meat is still rare. Don't overcook. *Four servings, 265 calories each.*

SAYONARA SUPPER WITH ZUCCHINI

1/2 pound leftover lean, rare roast beef or broiled round steak (any low-fat leftover meat or poultry may be substituted)
3 tablespoons Japanese-style soy sauce
1 small zucchini
1 small onion
3 tablespoons white wine
3 tablespoons water, tomato juice, beef or chicken broth

Before cooking, slice the meat very thin against the grain into very thin strips; trim off and discard fat, if any. If using poultry, cut into bite-size chunks and discard skin. Toss lightly with soy sauce and set aside.

Cut the zucchini in half, then cut each half into 8 lengthwise strips. Peel and slice the onion thin.

Combine the zucchini, onion, wine, and remaining liquid in a shallow nonstick skillet. Cover and cook 5 minutes. Uncover and add the meat. Cook and stir over high heat, uncovered, until the meat is heated through and the liquid has evaporated into a sauce. Serve immediately. *Two servings, 260 calories each.*

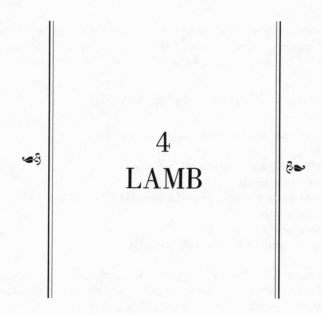

4
LAMB

Can you name a red meat that's always tender and tasty, even the leanest and least fattening cuts? The answer, lean-meat lovers, is lamb!

Differing from beef and veal—in which toughness or relative blandness is the price sometimes paid for leanness—even the leanest cuts of lamb are flavorful. And what is the leanest cut? A leg of lamb, at only 590 calories per pound (of lean boneless meat).

In texture and cooking technique, lamb is more akin to veal than it is to beef. Like veal, lamb is a young animal with no fatty marbling running through the meat.

Lamb has never achieved the popularity in the United States that it enjoys in other countries. However, as Americans become more interested in "ethnic" cuisines, perhaps those who have never cooked it will be more inclined to try. Unfortunately, lamb is sometimes difficult to find outside of metropolitan areas, often requiring special-order purchasing. I think it's well worth the effort.

And here's how to cook it, the leanest and least-fattening way:

HOW TO ROAST A LEG OF LAMB

LAMB COUNCIL RECOMMENDED METHOD. Defrost, if frozen. Season with salt, pepper, other seasonings. Place fat side up on a rack in an open roasting pan. Insert meat thermometer. Do not cover or add any liquid.

Place the pan in a preheated 325-degree oven and roast until desired doneness is reached, 170 degrees for medium rare. (Rare is 165 degrees, medium is 175, well done is 180.) Remove from oven and let stand for 10 minutes before carving.

SLOW-ROAST METHOD. Follow preceding directions, but use an oven temperature of 275 degrees.

HIGH-LOW FREEZER-TO-OVEN METHOD. Put frozen lamb on a rack in an open roasting pan, without seasoning or liquid. Do not cover.

Turn oven to high setting, about 475 degrees, and set a timer for 45 minutes. At the end of 45 minutes the fat will be seared and melted, the outside crisp and well browned, the juices sealed in. Set oven temperature at 250 degrees. After about an hour, insert a meat thermometer in the roast. Season the outside. Continue to roast until the meat thermometer registers the desired doneness. Remove from oven 10 minutes before carving.

HOW TO SEASON LAMB

GREEK LEMON LAMB. Crush or crumble fresh or dried mint leaves, mix with lemon juice, minced garlic or garlic powder, salt and pepper. Sprinkle liberally over lamb.

ROAST LAMB TARRAGON. Sprinkle roast liberally with lemon juice, dried tarragon, garlic or onion salt, pepper.

ROAST LAMB OREGANATO. Crush dried oregano or mixed Italian seasoning and mix with dry red wine, garlic salt, and pepper. Sprinkle over lamb.

ROAST LAMB MARJORAM. Coat a leg of lamb liberally with dried marjoram. Season with salt, freshly ground pepper, and garlic powder.

WHAT GOES WITH LAMB?

SALADS: A curried fruit salad made with diced unpeeled apples, chunks of seeded peeled orange, minced celery, and raisins, dressed with equal parts plain yogurt and low-fat mayonnaise seasoned with curry powder and soy sauce. Or cucumber and onion slices marinated in plain low-fat yogurt sprinkled with chopped parsley or mint. Or ripe tomato wedges marinated in low-calorie Italian dressing.

VEGETABLES. Sliced zucchini sautéed in a teaspoon of olive oil, seasoned with onion or garlic and Italian herbs. Or parsleyed fresh carrots simmered in a little white wine. Or cooked green beans dressed with diet margarine and a sprinkle of toasted slivered almonds.

SIDE DISHES. Baked potato topped with yogurt and chopped chives. Cooked brown rice seasoned with soy sauce. Hot drained noodles stirred with yogurt and a sprinkle of grated sharp cheese.

WINE. Any dry red wine.

DESSERT. There's nothing better than chilled fresh fruit. And with lamb, no fruit is better than chilled fresh pineapple.

GREEK LEMON LAMB ROAST

What's more luscious than a roast leg of lamb! Have you ever done it the Greek way?

A whole leg of lamb is about 6 or 7 pounds. If that's too much to roast at once, simply ask the butcher to divide it, and give you a pound of ground lamb for lamburger and a pound of boneless lamb cut in 1½-inch cubes. Wrap them in separate packages, and freeze them for later.

2 or 4 cloves garlic
  Whole or half leg of lamb
2 to 4 tablespoons lemon juice
1 to 2 teaspoons oregano or rosemary
  Pinch of dried mint (optional)
  Fresh parsley
  Salt and freshly ground pepper

Peel the garlic cloves and slice them lengthwise into slivers. With a sharp-pointed knife, insert the garlic slivers into the meat and push them in with the tip of the knife. Arrange the roast on a rack in a shallow roasting pan. Sprinkle the meat liberally with lemon juice, herbs, and seasonings. Insert a meat thermometer into the thickest part of the meat, not touching the bone.

Place the roast in a cold oven and set the temperature gauge at 300 degrees. Roast uncovered, basting occasionally, until the meat thermometer registers 170 (the cooking time will depend on the amount of lamb). Don't overcook. Allow to stand 10 to 20 minutes before carving. *Each 4-ounce serving, 150 calories.*

Lamb Is Lean and Luscious for Low-Cal Cookout Fans

When the barbecue season is upon us, it's time for us would-be skinnies to rediscover lamb. Lean and luscious, it is a favorite in nearly every cuisine in which cooking over the coals is popular. Lamb is the perfect "shish" for your "kebab."

Here are a group of calorie-wise cookout delights featuring lamb.

LAMB TERIYAKI

1½ pounds lamb cubes, cut from leg
 ½ teaspoon garlic powder
 ¼ teaspoon ground ginger
  1 teaspoon sugar
 ½ cup Japanese-style soy sauce
 ¼ cup sherry

Have meat cut in 2-inch cubes, trimmed of fat.

Combine with remaining ingredients in a plastic bag or bowl. Marinate at room temperature 2 hours or all day in refrigerator.

Thread meat on skewers. Barbecue about 4 inches from the coals for 10 to 12 minutes, turning and basting occasionally with reserved marinade. *Six servings, 255 calories each.*

LAMB À LA GRECQUE EN BROCHETTE

1 pound lean, fat-trimmed boneless lamb (from leg), in 1½-inch cubes
¼ cup lemon juice
1 clove garlic, minced, or ⅛ teaspoon instant garlic
1 teaspoon oregano or mint
⅛ teaspoon ground cinnamon
⅛ teaspoon grated nutmeg
2 teaspoons olive oil

Combine all ingredients except oil in a glass or plastic bowl. Cover and marinate 1 hour at room temperature, or several hours in the refrigerator.

Thread meat on skewers, reserving marinade. Add oil to remaining marinade, and brush meat.

Barbecue or broil about 10 minutes, turning occasionally. Brush meat with marinade each time you turn it. *Four servings, 175 calories each.*

SLIM SHISH KEBABS

1½ pounds lamb cubes, cut from leg
1½ teaspoons garlic salt
¼ teaspoon freshly ground pepper
¼ cup lemon juice
¼ cup water
2 bell peppers, seeded and cut in squares
12 cherry tomatoes
4 onions, quartered.

Combine lamb, garlic salt, pepper, lemon juice, and water in a plastic bag or nonmetallic bowl and marinate 2 hours at room temperature or all day in the refrigerator. Thread meat on skewers alternating with vegetables. Barbecue over hot coals, turning and basting occasionally with reserved marinade, about 15 minutes. *Six servings, 265 calories each.*

SKINNY BBQ RIBS

Lamb instead of pork.

3 pounds lamb breast, trimmed of fat and cut into ribs
16-ounce can plain tomato sauce
2 tablespoons vinegar
1 onion, minced
1 teaspoon garlic salt
⅛ teaspoon cayene pepper, or to taste

To oven barbecue, bake the ribs in a shallow pan in a hot (400-degree) oven for 45 minutes. Drain off fat in the pan. Combine remaining ingredients, pour over ribs, and bake at 325 degrees for 1 hour, basting occasionally. *Eight servings, 290 calories each.*

SOUVLAKIA

1½ pounds boneless fat-trimmed lamb, cut from leg, in 1-inch cubes
¼ cup vinegar
1 teaspoon oregano or Italian seasoning
2 cloves garlic, minced
6 green bell peppers, seeded and cut in 1-inch squares
6 small onions, halved
12 cherry tomatoes
1 tablespoon salad oil
Salt and freshly ground pepper

Combine meat, vinegar, oregano, and garlic in a plastic bag. Chill in refrigerator all day or overnight to marinate and tenderize. Thread meat on skewers, alternating with vegetables. Brush with remaining marinade plus the oil. Broil or barbecue 3 or 4 inches from heat source for 20 minutes, turning frequently. Salt and pepper after cooking. *Six servings, about 220 calories each.*

MARINATED LAMB CHOPS ROMANO

½ cup low-calorie Italian salad dressing
½ cup dry white wine or water
6 lean shoulder lamb chops, trimmed of fat
6 teaspoons shredded Romano cheese

Combine salad dressing and wine; pour over lamb chops in a nonmetallic dish. Cover and refrigerate all day or overnight.

Remove from marinade; barbecue or broil 4 inches from heat source 10 to 12 minutes on each side. Baste occasionally with reserved marinade. Sprinkle each chop lightly with a teaspoon of the cheese just before serving. *Six servings, 300 calories each.*

Trim and Tasty Lamb Stews and Skillet Dishes

ORIENTAL LAMB AND VEGETABLE SKILLET

2 lamb steaks, cut from leg (8 or 9 ounces each)
1 onion, sliced
1 green bell pepper, seeded and diced
1 cup diagonally sliced celery
½ cup dry white wine or water
  5-ounce can sliced bamboo shoots, drained
  16-ounce can bean sprouts, drained
1 tomato, diced
1 tablespoon cornstarch or arrowroot
3 tablespoons soy sauce

Cut lamb steaks into 1-inch cubes; trim off and discard fat and remove center round bone.

Spray a large nonstick skillet with cooking spray for no-fat frying. Add lamb and brown over high heat, turning frequently. Add onion, pepper, celery, and wine. Cover and simmer 5 minutes. Uncover and stir in bamboo shoots, bean sprouts, and tomato. Heat, uncovered, until simmering. Stir cornstarch into soy sauce to make a paste. Stir into simmering skillet until thick. *Four servings, 220 calories each.*

SLIM IRISH STEW

2 pounds lean, fat-trimmed boneless leg of lamb or beef round, cut in cubes
1 large onion, chopped
1 clove garlic, minced
3 beef bouillon cubes
3 cups boiling water
2 bay leaves
¼ teaspoon grated nutmeg
½ teaspoon thyme
2 pounds small carrots, peeled but left whole
2 pounds small white potatoes, peeled

If you wish, meat may be prebrowned under the broiler or by baking in a very hot (450-degree) oven for 10 to 12 minutes, but prebrowning the meat is not traditional.

Combine all ingredients except carrots and potatoes. Stir together in an ovenproof casserole or heavy Dutch oven. Cover and bake in a preheated 325-degree oven or simmer on top of the range until tender, about 2½ hours. Add water if needed.

Skim all fat from the pot.

Add vegetables, cover, and continue to cook until tender, about 20 minutes. *Eight servings, 275 calories each.*

CROCKED IRISH STEW

2 **pounds lean lamb, cut from leg, in 1-inch cubes**
2 **potatoes, peeled and diced**
2 **onions, sliced**
4 **carrots, sliced**
¼ **cup dry white wine (or water)**
2 **bay leaves**
   Salt and freshly ground pepper to taste

Combine all ingredients in a crockpot or slow-cooker. Cook on high heat 30 minutes, then lower to slow-cook setting. Cook, covered, 8 to 10 hours, according to manufacturer's directions. *Eight servings, 195 calories each.*

VARIATION

Thicken, if desired, by stirring 2 tablespoons flour into ¼ cup cold water to make a paste. Raise heat to simmering. Stir paste into stew. Cook, stirring occasionally, until gravy is thickened and bubbling. *Adds less than 10 calories each serving.*

INDIAN CURRIED LAMB

1½ **pounds lean, fat-trimmed boneless lamb shoulder, cut in ½-inch cubes**
   Garlic salt and freshly ground pepper
   10½-ounce can fat-skimmed beef or chicken broth
2 **tablespoons lemon juice**
1 **tablespoon soy sauce**
2 **tablespoons raisins**
1 **tablespoon curry powder**
1 **cup sliced onion**
3 **tablespoons all-purpose flour**
2 **unpeeled red apples, cored and diced**
2 **tablespoons dry-roasted peanuts**

Spray a nonstick skillet or pressure cooker with cooking spray for no-fat frying. Add lamb cubes and brown quickly over high heat. Pour off any fat. Season with garlic salt and pepper. Add 1 cup broth, lemon juice, soy sauce, raisins, and curry powder. Cover and simmer in skillet until tender, 1 hour or more. Or pressure cook, according to manufacturer's directions, for 20 minutes.

Skim fat, if any, from surface.

Add onion and simmer, uncovered, 5 minutes. Combine flour with remaining broth and stir into simmering liquid until thick. Stir in apples and peanuts at the last minute. *Six servings, about 260 calories each.*

5
VEAL

Veal may be expensive . . . but not in calories!

Succulent and subtly-flavored veal is an epicurean treat that also happens to be a calorie bargain. Veal chops are less than 600 calories a pound, compared with 1,600 or more for full-grown beef. Trouble is, they charge you for the full-grown steer the veal could have become!

Though veal is hardly a budget item, it is somewhat more plentiful and less crushingly expensive than it has been. And it's such a good buy—calorically speaking—that diet watchers can indulge more often.

HOW TO ROAST VEAL

Veal roasts can be subtly seasoned with herbs and a dash of white wine or lemon juice . . . or more dramatically spiced with garlic, oregano, and a baste of tomato juice. In either case, veal should always be slow-roasted at a relatively low temperature—300 to 325 degrees—and removed from the oven when a meat thermometer inserted in the middle reads 170 degrees. (Veal is tenderest when served still slightly pink.) Leftover roast veal is delicious and thrifty when combined with eggs and seasoning; see Low-Calorie Veal Frittata (page 209).

VEAL POT ROAST WITH EGGPLANT SAUCE

Lean boneless veal rump roast (3 pounds)
2 twelve-ounce cans tomato paste
1 cup water
2 cups canned fat-skimmed chicken broth
¼ cup dry white wine (optional)
2 cloves garlic, minced
1 green bell pepper, seeded and chopped
1 large onion, chopped
1 medium eggplant, peeled and finely diced
2 teaspoons oregano or Italian seasoning
Salt and freshly ground pepper
2 tablespoons chopped fresh parsley

Trim fat, if any, from veal. Brown briefly under a broiler. Combine remaining ingredients in a large Dutch oven and stir well after each addition. Put the browned veal on top of the mixture and sprinkle with additional salt, pepper, and oregano. Cover and simmer over lowest heat on top of the range, *or* bake, covered, in a 325-degree oven, until meat is very tender and sauce is thick (about 3 to 4 hours). Skim fat, if any, from sauce before serving.

To serve, slice meat thin and top with reserved sauce. *Eight servings, 315 calories each.*

VEAL POT ROAST PAPRIKASH

Among the heartiest and tastiest of all "ethnic" cuisines is Hungarian—but hardly low calorie, with all its sour cream and noodles. Luckily for calorie counters, veal is one of the leading main-course meats, always tender and flavorful.

Paprika is the national spice of Hungary. However, imported Hungarian sweet paprika has little relationship to the flavorless brownish powder so often sprinkled over fish and potato salad.

Here's a flavorful Hungarian-inspired pot roast with budget-priced veal shoulder. The paprika-powered "sour cream" sauce is made with low-fat yogurt.

    Lean boneless veal shoulder (about 3 pounds), rolled and tied
½ **cup dry white wine**
½ **cup water**
2 **onions**
2 **teaspoons Hungarian paprika**
1 **clove garlic, finely minced**
3 **tablespoons all-purpose flour**
1 **cup plain low-fat yogurt**
    Salt and freshly ground pepper
2 **teaspoons minced fresh parsley**
    Tender-cooked noodles (see page 245) (optional)

Put the pot roast into a heavy Dutch oven and pour on the wine and water. Peel the onions and cut in half. Add them to the pot, cut side up. Sprinkle the veal and onions with paprika and minced garlic. Cover closely. Simmer on top of the range, or slow-bake in a 300-degree oven until the meat is very tender, about 2 hours. Remove the meat and onions to a serving platter and keep warm.

Simmer down the pan juices until reduced to about ½ cupful. Blend the flour and yogurt together and stir into the simmering liquid with a whisk. Simmer until thickened (if sauce is lumpy, blend smooth with an electric mixer or whir in a blender).

Season to taste with salt and pepper and sprinkle with parsley. To serve, spoon the sauce over sliced veal. *Each serving—about 4 ounces of meat and ¼ cup sauce—under 300 calories. One-half cup tender-cooked noodles will add about 100 calories.*

Mastering the Art of Low-Cal French Cooking
. . . with Veal Cutlets and Chops

There's another French Revolution, this time in the kitchen. Complicated, calorie-laden, and cholesterol-rich, classic French cooking is giving way to *la cuisine expresse* (short order cooking) and *la cuisine minceur* (you guessed it, cooking the Slim Gourmet way—but with a French accent!). It had to happen. A country that loves food and fashion with equal fervor would eventually need creative ways to trim time and calories from a cuisine dependent on rich ingredients like butter, cream, and eggs. No frozen dinners or diet-meals-in-a-can for the food-loving French!

Here we offer two Slim Gourmet "translations" for veal cutlets that are surprisingly slim and easy, yet very Continental in flavor, followed by some veal chop recipes that keep the same slim profile but expand the cultural horizons.

SLIM GOURMET ESCALOPE BRILLAT-SAVARIN

1½ pounds lean veal cutlets
 6 tablespoons all-purpose flour
 2 tablespoons polyunsaturated oil
 3 tablespoons dry white wine
 ½ pound small fresh mushrooms, sliced
   13-ounce can evaporated skim milk
   Butter-flavored salt
   White pepper
 1 tablespoon chopped fresh parsley

Cut the veal into 6 equal pieces. Coat lightly with flour, about 3 tablespoons.
Heat the oil in a nonstick skillet. Add the cutlets and cook quickly over moderate heat, about 4 minutes on each side, only until cooked through. Remove to a hot platter. Put 2 tablespoons wine and the mushrooms into the skillet.

Cook and stir until all the wine evaporates and mushrooms are lightly browned. Put the mushrooms on top of the cutlets. Combine remaining 1 tablespoon wine, evaporated skim milk, and 3 tablespoons flour. Stir smooth. Pour into the skillet and cook and stir over moderate heat until sauce simmers and thickens. Season to taste with butter-flavored salt, white pepper, and parsley flakes. Pour over meat and mushrooms and serve. *Six servings, 285 calories each.*

VARIATIONS

Chicken or Turkey Cutlets Brillat-Savarin: Proceed with the recipe as described above, only substitute 1½ pounds boneless skinless chicken breasts, cut in half, or 6 slices of raw turkey-breast steaks (sold in some areas) for the veal.

QUICK VEAL, MARENGO STYLE

 ½ cup dry white wine
 2 teaspoons olive oil
 1 pound lean, fat-trimmed veal cutlet or leg steak
 1 large sweet onion, cut in chunks
 1 clove garlic, finely chopped
 1 cup thinly sliced fresh mushrooms
 4 ripe tomatoes, peeled and cut in wedges
   Salt and freshly ground pepper to taste

Spray a large nonstick skillet with cooking spray for low-fat frying. Add 2 tablespoons wine and the olive oil. Add the veal. Cook over high heat, uncovered, until wine evaporates and under side is brown. Turn and quickly brown the other side. Remove to a cutting board.

Put onion, garlic, and mushrooms into the skillet. Cook and stir over high heat, just until onion chunks are slightly seared. Add remaining wine and tomatoes. Salt and pepper to taste. Cook, stirring occasionally, over high heat until onions are tender-crunchy. Meanwhile, slice browned veal into slender strips (will be very rare in the middle). Stir meat into skillet. Continue to cook and stir until veal is just cooked through and sauce is reduced. *Four servings, about 230 calories each.*

VEAL CHOPS CREOLE

4 **lean fat-trimmed veal chops, cut ¾ inch thick**
1 **tablespoon salad oil**
1 **cup canned tomatoes, broken up**
½ **cup sliced onion**
1 **clove garlic, minced**
1 **teaspoon prepared mustard**
   Salt and freshly ground pepper
3 **tablespoons chopped fresh parsley**

Brown the chops in the oil in a hot nonstick skillet: remove from heat and drain off the oil. Mix together all remaining ingredients except parsley. Pour over chops and cover the skillet. Simmer over lowest heat 1 hour or more, until chops are very tender. Uncover and cook until sauce is gravy thick. Stir in parsley. Season to taste and serve. *Four servings, 205 calories each.*

HAWAIIAN VEAL CHOPS

4 **fat-trimmed lean, veal chops,**
   Garlic salt and freshly ground pepper
½ **cup sherry**
2 **tablespoons vinegar**
1 **red or green bell pepper, seeded and cut in chunks**
   8-ounce can unsweetened pineapple chunks
2 **tablespoons soy sauce**
2 **teaspoons arrowroot or cornstarch**
1 **tablespoon sugar**
3 **scallions or green onions, finely chopped**

Put chops in a single layer in a shallow baking dish just large enough to hold them. Season with garlic salt and pepper. Combine sherry, vinegar, bell pepper, and pineapple (including liquid) and pour over chops. Cover and bake 1 hour at 325 degrees, basting frequently, until chops are tender.

Combine soy sauce, arrowroot, and sugar, and stir well. Stir into the pan. Continue to bake until sauce is thick and simmering. Remove from the oven and sprinkle with finely chopped scallions. *Four servings, about 260 calories each.*

Try These Skinny Veal Stews and Ragouts

COUNTRY FRENCH VEAL RAGOUT

```
  1  tablespoon salad oil
1½  pounds lean veal, cut in cubes
  5  or 6 small peeled onions (or 16 ounces, canned)
 ½  cup dry white wine
  1  cup chicken broth
 ½  bay leaf
     Pinch of thyme
  3  tablespoons chopped fresh parsley
  1  teaspoon salt
 ¼  teaspoon freshly ground pepper
  4  or 5 carrots, peeled and sliced thick
  3  white turnips, peeled and quartered
```

Heat the oil in a nonstick skillet and brown the veal quickly. Blot with paper towels and arrange in an ovenproof casserole. Add the onions, wine, chicken broth, bay leaf, thyme, parsley flakes, salt, and pepper. Cover and bake at 325 degrees for 1 hour.

Add carrots and turnips and bake an additional 30 minutes or more until tender. *Six servings, 225 calories each.*

VEAL OSSO BUCO

Shinbone Italian Style

One of the delights of Italian cuisine is Osso Buco, a savory slow-simmered dish made from meaty veal shinbone. The word means "bone with a hole in it," which is what shinbone is. Also called shank or marrow bone, shinbone is cut from the leg: a hole surrounded by bone, surrounded by meat. And inside that hole is delicious marrow, too, that flavors the dish.

Although shinbone stew is supposed to be a hearty and economical dish, it's one Italians never apologize for. So delicious, it's frequently featured in the finest restaurants.

The veal shinbone dish is made with in Italy takes it out of the economy class on this side of the Atlantic—veal being expensive and sometimes hard to find. But sometimes you will find meaty veal bones in your supermarket meat section. Don't pass these up—they are not only meatier than you might suppose, but you will be amazed at the low price.

Here, then, is my slimmed-down version of Osso Buco.

2¾ **pounds lean veal shinbone sawed into pieces**
   16-ounce can whole or stewed tomatoes
 1 **large onion, chopped**
 2 **stalks celery, chopped**
 1 **carrot, grated (or ¼ cup baby-food carrots)**
¼ **cup dry white wine**
 1 **cup water**
 1 **bay leaf**
 1 **clove garlic, minced, or ¼ teaspoon instant garlic**
   Pinch of grated lemon rind
¼ **teaspoon basil (optional)**

Brown the meat under your broiler, turning to brown evenly. Pour off any fat. Arrange in a shallow layer in an ovenproof casserole. Break up tomatoes and combine with remaining ingredients. Pour over meat; cover and bake in a 350-degree oven until nearly tender—about 1 hour.

Tip the dish slightly to allow melted fat to accumulate on one side. Remove every bit of melted fat with a suction-type baster or spoon off with a tablespoon. Or, if you're making the dish ahead of time, cover and refrigerate. Fat will rise to the surface and harden. Lift it all off.

Return the dish to the oven, uncovered. Continue baking at 350 degrees until meat is tender and liquid is evaporated into a thick sauce (add water, if needed). *Serves four, 175 calories each.*

ITALIAN CROCKED VEAL

This is a "crockpot" special. If you don't have a crock cooker, you may still enjoy the pleasures of slow cookery—if your oven thermostat can be relied on to maintain a safe and steady 200-degree heat. Then any casserole or crock—even a cookie jar—can slow-cook in the oven.

Here's how to check your oven: beg, buy, or borrow two oven thermometers. Set the oven thermostat at "low" or 200, then check the thermometers hourly over a 4- or 5-hour period. If the thermostat and *both* thermometers agree, you've got it made! If both thermometers agree that the the temperature is somewhat lower than 200, experiment with resetting the oven thermostat higher, until you can determine the proper setting to assure a steady 200-degree heat. (Don't attempt to turn your oven lower than its lowest thermostat setting.)

What if the oven thermometers disagree with each other? Beg, buy, or borrow another and recheck them in the oven to find out which thermometer is mistaken.

1 **pound lean, fat-trimmed veal, cut in 1½-inch cubes**
1 **large onion, halved, then sliced**
1 **ripe tomato, peeled and cut in chunks**
1 **clove garlic, minced**
1 **red or green bell pepper, seeded and thinly sliced**
2 **tablespoons dry white wine or lemon juice**
2 **teaspoons oregano or Italian seasoning**
  Salt and freshly ground pepper to taste
3 **tablespoons all-purpose flour (optional)**
  Cold water (optional)

Combine all ingredients, in a crock cooker. Cover and cook 8 to 10 hours or longer on low heat, until meat is very tender. Sauce may be thickened, if desired, by making a paste of 3 tablespoons flour and a little cold water. Stir into crock and raise heat. Cover and cook until sauce is thick, stirring occasionally.

Without a crockpot, ingredients may be combined in a casserole or heavy covered crock or cookie jar. Place in the oven with thermostat set at 200 degrees. Slow-bake 8 to 10 hours. *Four servings, under 185 calories each; flour adds 20 calories per serving.*

Ground Veal "Cutlets"

Here is a way to beat the high cost of such ethnic delights as Italian veal parmigiana or German Wiener Schnitzel. Instead of the premium-priced cutlets—thin steaks cut from the leg—make your parmigiana or Schnitzel from chopped veal "hamburger" that comes from the less-expensive shoulder.

Then you can save calories as well. This parmigiana is baked in the oven instead of fried. And Schnitzel is stretched by mixing the meat with hamburger stretcher: TVP, the textured vegetable protein made from soy that's sold for turning one pound of hamburger into a pound and a half!

VEALBURGER PARMIGIANA

1½ pounds lean, fat-trimmed ground veal shoulder
 1 egg
 1 tablespoon olive oil
¼ cup Italian-seasoned breadcrumbs
 2 eight-ounce cans plain tomato sauce
 1 clove garlic, minced
   Salt and freshly ground pepper
 2 teaspoons oregano or Italian seasoning
 4 ounces part-skim mozzarella cheese, shredded

Divide ground veal into 6 equal oval patties and press flat into "cutlets."
Fork-blend egg and olive oil together. Dip each "cutlet" first into the egg
mixture, then into the seasoned breadcrumbs, coating lightly. Arrange in a
single layer in a nonstick baking dish. Bake in a preheated hot (450-degree)
oven until brown. Stir tomato sauce with seasonings and pour over "cutlets."
Continue to bake until sauce is simmering and thick. Sprinkle with shredded
cheese and return to oven only until cheese melts. *Six servings, 280 calories
each.*

GROUND VEAL "WIENER SCHNITZEL"

 1 pound lean, fat-trimmed ground veal shoulder
 1 envelope seasoned hamburger extender (textured vegetable protein)
   Water
¼ cup Toasted High-Fiber Breadcrumbs (page 302) or commercial unseasoned breadcrumbs
 2 tablespoons diet margarine
 1 beef bouillon cube
 2 tablespoons lemon juice
½ cup boiling water
 3 tablespoons chopped fresh parsley
   Coarsely ground pepper
   Additional fresh parsley (optional)
   Lemon wedges (optional)

Use packaged hamburger extender to turn 1 pound meat into 1½ pounds;
combine veal and extender with the amount of water called for on the package.
For extra flavor, choose the seasoned "Swedish Meatballs" mix. Shape into 6
oval steak-shaped patties and flatten into "cutlets." Press each "cutlet" into
the crumbs, coating lightly.

Heat 1 tablespoon diet margarine; cook the patties on one side. Add second tablespoon of margarine and brown on the other side. Don't overcook. Remove to a platter. Combine bouillon, lemon juice, and boiling water in the skillet. Cook quickly over a high flame, scraping the skillet well. Add the parsley at the last minute, then pour the hot pan juices over the "cutlets." Sprinkle with pepper. Garnish with additional fresh parsley and lemon wedges, if desired. *Six servings, 170 calories each.*

MOCK VEAL SCALOPPINE

1 **pound lean, fat-trimmed ground veal shoulder**
1 **egg or 2 egg whites**
1 **clove garlic, minced (optional)**
1 **tablespoon minced onion or 1 teaspoon dried onion flakes**
½ **cup Italian-seasoned breadcrumbs**
2 **tablespoons grated sharp Romano or shredded Provolone cheese**
 Lemon wedges (optional)
 Fresh parsley (optional)

Stir veal, egg, garlic, and onion together.

Combine breadcrumbs and cheese. Spread some of the crumb mixture on wax paper. Take a handful of the meat mixture and press it onto the crumbs. Sprinkle with additional crumbs and flatten the meat into a thin "cutlet," using a spatula or the palm of your hand. Lift, with a spatula, onto a shallow nonstick cookie sheet which has been liberally sprayed with cooking spray for no-fat frying. Continue shaping and bread-coating "cutlets." Discard excess crumbs.

Put the sheet in an oven which has been preheated to 450 degrees (oven *must* be preheated hot). Bake 8 to 10 minutes, turning once. Garnish with lemon wedges and fresh parsley if desired. *Four servings, about 250 calories each.*

VARIATION

Mock Veal Scaloppine Parmigiana: Follow preceding recipe. At the last minute top each cutlet with a thin ½-ounce slice of part-skim mozzarella cheese and return to oven just till cheese begins to melt. *Each ½-ounce slice of cheese adds about 40 calories.*

SWISS VEAL CUTLETS

1 pound lean, fat-trimmed ground veal, shaped into flat "cutlets"
  Salt or garlic salt and pepper
1 egg, beaten
4 ounces shredded Swiss-style low-fat cheese
7 tablespoons seasoned breadcrumbs
  Lemon slices (optional)

Season the cutlets lightly with salt and pepper. Dip into beaten egg, then into shredded cheese, then into breadcrumbs, until both sides are lightly coated. Arrange on a shallow nonstick cookie tin or baking tray. Bake in a preheated 450-degree oven, turning once, until brown and crisp, about 12 minutes. Garnish with lemon slices, if desired. *Four servings, 315 calories each.*

6
PORK
AND
HAM

From Roasts to Chops—Pork Is Permissible!

Once upon a time the porker deserved his pudgy, pound-provoking image, but today's pork is bred for leanness—figure conscious just like the rest of us! Of course, many pork products *are* too calorie laden for weight watchers: spareribs, sausage, bacon (but see page 89), lunch meats. But lean loin roasts or chops are definitely permissible. Ditto fresh ham roasts or lean pork steaks, cut from the leg. Fat-trimmed lean pork from the loin is 857 calories a pound; from the leg, only 667 calories!

ORIENTAL-SEASONED ROAST PORK

    Lean pork loin roast (about 4 pounds)
¼ **cup soy sauce**
½ **cup sherry**
  1 **teaspoon garlic powder**
  1 **teaspoon ground ginger**
  1 **teaspoon monosodium glutomate (optional)**

    Have the butcher saw across the backbone so it can be removed easily when you are carving the roast. Trim off and discard as much fat as possible, leaving just a thin covering for insulation. Place the roast fat side up on a rack in a roasting pan. Insert a meat thermometer in the thickest part. Be sure it does not touch bone. Combine remaining ingredients and spoon over roast. Place the pan in a slow (325-degree) oven and roast 2¼ to 3½ hours, or until the meat thermometer registers 170. (Allow about 35 to 40 minutes per pound.) Baste with pan juices frequently. *Each four-ounce serving, 220 calories.*

VARIATION

Boneless Polynesian Pork Roast: Choose a lean pork loin. Have it trimmed of fat and bone, then rolled and tied. Arrange the roast on a rack in a roasting pan. Follow preceding recipe, substituting pineapple juice for the sherry. Roast at 325 degrees, turning and basting frequently, 3 hours or longer. Insert a meat thermometer to check doneness. Roast is done when interior temperature reaches 170 degrees. *Each four-ounce serving, 220 calories.*

BONELESS PORK ROAST, ITALIAN STYLE

Pork loin, trimmed of fat and bone, rolled and tied (see note below)
Onion salt
Coarsely ground pepper
Garlic powder
Oregano, basil, or Italian seasoning
Tomato Velvet Sauce (page 308) (optional)

Arrange the rolled, tied roast on a rack in a roasting pan, or skewer in a rotisserie oven. Season liberally with onion salt, pepper, garlic, and herbs. Roast in a slow (325-degree) oven, turning frequently. Check with meat thermometer; roast is done when interior temperature measures 170 degrees. Serve with the Tomato Velvet Sauce, if desired. *Each four-ounce serving of pork, 215 calories; ¼ cup sauce adds 25 calories.*

Pork Broth

NOTE: Don't discard pork bones! Always ask for the bones and fat when ordering a boneless roast. (By obtaining the fat, you can see how many calories you've eliminated!) The bones can be used to make stock or broth. Cover the bones with salted water (1 teaspoon salt to 1 quart water). Simmer 2 to 3 hours. Skim off fat. Freeze in pint jars.

DEVILED PORK STEAK

Let's go to the devil. No, I don't mean a banana-split binge or doughnut orgy! Going to the devil diet-wise means a zesty, spicy food. Being devilish in the kitchen needn't be sinful if you're a Slim Gourmet cook!

Mustard and zingy spices are the ingredients usually found in deviled dishes. Mustard isn't fattening, considering the mighty wallop of flavor it packs. Most brands range between 4 and 8 calories a teaspoon. Fiery mustards are no more fattening than the chicken-yellow kidstuff squirted on hot dogs.

Try these dishes with your favorite type: the aforementioned kidstuff, the hearty brown variety, the hot Dijon-style mustard, or the pyromaniac Oriental mustard reserved for asbestos tongues!

1¼ **pound lean, fat-trimmed pork steak (fresh ham slice)**
¼ **cup chili sauce**
1 **tablespoon lemon juice**
2 **teaspoons prepared mustard**
2 **teaspoons Worcestershire sauce**
2 **teaspoons dried onion flakes**
½ **teaspoon garlic salt**
  Freshly ground pepper
¼ **teaspoon curry powder, or to taste**

Put pork steak in baking dish. Combine remaining ingredients and pour over pork steak. Bake uncovered in a slow (300-degree) oven until tender, about 1 hour and 20 minutes. Baste frequently. Add water, if needed. *Four servings, 190 calories each.*

DANISH PORK CHOPS AND POTATOES

6 **lean, fat-trimmed center-cut pork chops (about 2 pounds)**
2 **potatoes, peeled and halved**
1 **teaspoon salt**
  Pinch of freshly ground pepper
1 **teaspoon curry powder**
2 **chicken bouillon cubes**
2 **cups water**
1 **cup apples, peeled, cored, and cut up**

Brown the chops in a nonstick skillet (with no fat added). Drain off any accumulated fat. Add the potatoes, salt, pepper, curry powder, bouillon cubes, and water; cover and simmer 45 minutes.

Add the apples. Simmer 10 minutes more. *Six servings, 285 calories each.*

PORK CHOPS AND RED CABBAGE

8 lean, fat-trimmed pork chops (about 3 pounds) or 2 pork steaks (fresh
    ham slices, about 2½ pounds), cut into 8 serving pieces
½ cup apple juice or cider
3 tablespoons all-purpose flour
⅓ cup cider vinegar
    Large head of red cabbage, shredded (about 10 cups)
1 cup chopped onion
    1-ounce box raisins
1 teaspoon caraway seeds
1½ teaspoons garlic salt
1 teaspoon salt
    Pinch of freshly ground pepper

Spray a large nonstick skillet or electric frying pan with cooking spray for
no-fat frying. Add pork and 2 tablespoons apple juice. Cook until liquid
evaporates and pork begins to brown. Turn to brown evenly. Pour off fat, if
any. Add remaining apple juice. Cover tightly and simmer 1 hour. Skim off
fat, if any.

Blend flour into vinegar and add to the skillet. Stir until mixture simmers.
Remove meat, then mix remaining ingredients into sauce; place meat on top.
Cover tightly and simmer 40 minutes. Uncover. Cook, stirring occasionally,
until most of the liquid evaporates. *Eight servings, 385 calories each, if using
chops; 275 with steaks.*

Low-Cal Pork Cubes—to Skewer or Not

The Turks call them "kebabs," the French say "brochette," but food on
skewers is easy and low-calorie in any language. Because food on skewers is
generally broiled or barbecued, it's the least fattening way to cook. Following
are two calorie-wise kebab recipes, and then, just for good measure, some
recipes for now-skewered pork cubes—all guaranteed to make you a weight-
wary winner!

POLYNESIAN PORK AND PINEAPPLE

1¼ pounds lean, fat-trimmed pork steak (fresh ham slice)
1 tablespoon vinegar
1 tablespoon soy sauce
    16-ounce can juice-packed pineapple chunks, drained and juice reserved
    Skinny Rice (page 261) (optional)

Cut the meat into 1-inch cubes. Put into a plastic bag with the vinegar, soy sauce, and just enough juice from the pineapple to moisten thoroughly. Marinate at room temperature for 30 minutes, or for several hours in the refrigerator (the pineapple juice will help promote tenderness).

Thread the pork on skewers, alternating with pineapple chunks. Broil or barbecue, 3 inches from heat source, until pork is thoroughly cooked through, with no pinkness remaining, about 20 minutes.

Baste occasionally with reserved pineapple juice or a little soy sauce, if you wish. Serve with Skinny Rice (page 83) if desired. *Four servings, 265 calories each, without rice; 1/2 cup rice per serving adds 55 calories.*

OVEN-BARBECUED KOREAN KEBABS

A sprinkle of sesame seeds can do wonders for cooking. Even low-calorie cooking! Although sesame seeds are oil rich and, therefore, high calorie, their flavor is so pronounced that a spare scattering is all you need. One tablespoon's worth—about 42 calories—can turn on a main course for 4.

The nutty flavor of sesame is brought out by toasting or browning. You can toast sesame seeds by spreading them on a shallow cookie tin in a hot oven for a few minutes, or by shaking them in a nonstick skillet over high heat. When cool, store the seeds in a covered jar. Add a scant sprinkling to salads for a special dash. Or try this main-course pork recipe, decalorized from Korean cuisine.

1 **pound lean, fat-trimmed boneless pork shoulder, cut into 1-inch cubes**
1/2 **cup sherry**
1/4 **cup soy sauce**
1/4 **teaspoon garlic powder**
1/8 **teaspoon ground ginger**
1 **tablespoon toasted sesame seeds (see above)**

Thread the pork cubes on small wooden skewers and place in a shallow nonstick baking pan. Add sherry and soy sauce. Sprinkle with garlic powder and ginger. Cover with foil and bake in a 325-degree oven for 1 hour, or until tender. Uncover, raise heat to 450 degrees and sprinkle with sesame seeds. Bake uncovered until most of the liquid evaporates. Baste occasionally. *Four servings, 170 calories each.*

PORK WITH APPLEKRAUT

What could be better than fruits or vegetables? Fruits *and* vegetables, together with lean meat in a mini-caloried main course; and easy to do, too, if you're a Slim Gourmet cook.

We Americans tend to keep our fruits and vegetables separated—the former for desserts and snacks, the latter for salads and side dishes. But many foreign cuisines are much more imaginative, happily blending fruits and vegetables into savory main-course dishes.

Middle Europeans stuff poultry with onions and apples or prunes. Latins season stews or chopped-meat mixtures with raisins. Polynesians combine seafood with pineapple and scallions. Indians garnish meat and vegetable dishes with savory chopped fruits and nuts.

Here is a new low-cal version of a familiar favorite: pork with apples and sauerkraut. The fresh apple adds a touch of sweetness, plus color and crunch, to the slow-cooked meat-and-vegetable mixture.

Remember, fruits and vegetables are high-nutrition meat stretchers, low in fat and calories, high in fiber.

1   **pound lean, fat-trimmed pork steak (fresh ham slice)**
2   **cups sauerkraut, fresh or canned**
2   **large onions, minced**
     6-ounce can (¾ cup) apple juice or cider
1   **tablespoon caraway seeds**
2   **unpeeled red apples, cored and diced**

Cut the meat into 1½-inch cubes. Spray a large nonstick skillet or electric frying pan with cooking spray for no-fat frying. Brown the pork cubes quickly over high heat. Pour off melted fat, if any.

Rinse and drain the sauerkraut, then add to the skillet, along with the minced onion, apple juice, and caraway seeds.

Cover tightly and simmer over very low heat until pork cubes are tender, 1 hour or more (or cook in a crock cooker according to maker's directions). Uncover, stir in diced apple and heat through. *Four servings, 280 calories each.*

SZECHUAN PORK SKILLET

Give those diet-weary taste buds a lift . . . how about something hot and spicy? This zingy slimmer isn't Mexican, Spanish, or Indian in origin; it takes its inspiration from the Szechuan region of China. Szechuan cooks, like their counterparts in other hot regions, seem to favor foods that really zap the palate. Hot climates and hot foods seem to go hand in hand.

However, like many Chinese dishes, this main course is low in calories—even though it's made from pork. To make it, you'll want a pork steak cut from the leg, the very leanest pork there is.

This dish is simplified with canned tomato juice and crushed juice-packed pineapple, for natural sweetness. To turn on "the fire," use barely a pinch of cayenne pepper. If you don't have any cayenne pepper, use crushed Italian-style red pepper flakes or liquid red-pepper sauce. But with care—the management assumes no responsibility for scorched tongues!

If the folks at your place like scorchy stuff like chili, hot sausage, or horseradish, this will be their favorite Oriental dish; nobody will ever think of this as drab diet food!

1½ **pounds lean, fat-trimmed pork steak (fresh ham slice)**
1 **cup tomato juice**
½ **cup water**
1 **cup crushed juice-packed pineapple**
3 **tablespoons soy sauce**
4 **tablespoons minced green bell pepper (optional)**
½ **teaspoon ground ginger**
⅛ **teaspoon cayenne pepper**

Cut pork into 2-inch cubes. Place the cubes in a cold nonstick skillet and heat over a moderate flame. The pork will brown lightly in its own melting fat.

Add all remaining ingredients and cover. Simmer over very low flame for 45 minutes, checking occasionally, until very tender.

Add a little water, if necessary. Taste for seasoning, add more pepper, if you like. *Six servings, 210 calories each.*

CANTONESE PORK SKILLET

Here's another skillet-easy Chinese dish, ready in only a few minutes:

1 **pound pork steak (fresh ham slice)**
1 **tablespoon sherry or water**
2 **teaspoons salad oil**
3 **tablespoons chopped scallion or green onion**
½ **pound fresh mushrooms, sliced**
2 **tablespoons soy sauce**

Lay pork steak flat on a cutting board. Trim off and discard all fat. Using a sharp knife, slice the pork steak into very thin (¼-inch) diagonal slices.

Assemble all ingredients near your range. Add the sherry (or water) and oil to a nonstick skillet. Add the pork strips and stir-fry for 3 minutes, until pork loses its pinkness and all moisture evaporates. Add the scallions (or onions) and mushrooms. Stir-fry for 1 minute. Add the soy sauce; cook and stir for 2 more minutes. *Four servings, 220 calories each.*

INDIAN SPICED HOT 'N' SOUR PORK

Chili and vinegar combine delightfully in this toned-down and adapted Indian dish. Add more chili powder, if you wish. If you'd rather be cautious, simply serve with a bottle of Tabasco and let your tablemates add the "fire" to suit themselves.

 1 **pound lean, fat-trimmed pork, cut in 1½-inch cubes**
 1 **cup canned tomatoes, broken up**
 1 **large onion, chopped**
 2 **cloves garlic, minced, or ¼ teaspoon instant garlic**
¼ **teaspoon prepared mustard**
½ **teaspoon turmeric**
½ **teaspoon cumin seeds**
 1 **tablespoon mixed pickling spices**
¼ **teaspoon chili powder, or more to taste**
   Salt and freshly ground pepper to taste
 3 **tablespoons vinegar**
 2 **cups cooked rice (optional)**

Combine all ingredients in a heavy Dutch oven. Cover and simmer over very low heat—or place in a 200-degree oven—for 3 hours or more, until meat is tender. (May also be prepared in a crockery slow-cooker according to manufacturer's directions.) Serve with rice, if desired. *Four servings, about 240 calories each; cooked rice adds about 90 calories per 1/2-cup serving.*

HUNGARIAN PORK PAPRIKASH

1½ **pounds lean, fat-trimmed boneless pork, cut in 1½ inch cubes**
 1 **tablespoon water**
1½ **cups chopped onion**
 1 **clove garlic, minced**
 3 **tablespoons paprika**
 1 **chicken bouillon cube**
 1 **cup water**
 1 **teaspoon dill seed**
 1 **cup plain low-fat yogurt**
 1 **tablespoon all-purpose flour**
   Brown gravy coloring (optional)

Combine pork and 1 tablespoon water in a nonstick skillet over high heat. Cover and cook 1 minute. Uncover and continue to cook until liquid evaporates and pork cubes brown in their own melted inner fat. Drain off any fat. Add onion, garlic, paprika, bouillon cube, 1 cup water, and dill seed. Cover and simmer over low heat until meat is tender, about 1¼ hours. Uncover and continue to cook over moderate heat until nearly all the liquid evaporates.

Mix yogurt and flour; stir into the pan until well blended. Cook and stir over low heat until meat cubes are coated with a thick sauce. A little brown gravy coloring may be added, if desired. *Six servings, 255 calories each.*

Leftover Pork for Low-Calorie Meals

The only thing better than roast pork is leftover roast pork. There's so much a creative cook can do with it. If you're a low-calorie cook, so much the better, because roast pork has most of its fat calories already cooked out of it. There's no extra fat to ooze unwanted calories into a sauce or combination dish that's made with leftover pork.

ORIENTAL PORK WITH CASHEWS

1 cup thinly sliced celery
1 red or green bell pepper, thinly sliced
  10-ounce package frozen whole green beans, defrosted
½ cup water
2 teaspoons arrowroot or cornstarch
3 tablespoons soy sauce
¾ pound lean cooked pork, cubed
4 ounces canned water chestnuts, drained and sliced
2 tablespoons cashews

In a nonstick skillet combine celery, pepper, green beans, and water. Cover and simmer 4 minutes. Combine arrowroot with soy sauce and stir into skillet. Add pork cubes and water chestnuts. Cook and stir uncovered until sauce simmers and thickens and meat is heated through. Garnish with cashews and serve immediately. *Four servings, 290 calories each.*

SLIM GOURMET SWEET 'N' SOUR PORK

This recipe contains none of the sugar, starchy thickeners, or red food coloring often found in this dish. Don't be discouraged by the list of ingredients; this dish is easy.

8-ounce can crushed unsweetened pineapple, including juice
1 chopped dill pickle or ½ cup dill-pickle relish
2 tablespoons soy sauce
2 tablespoons sherry
4 cloves garlic, minced
2 teaspoons chopped fresh or dried ginger root (optional)
1 tablespoon molasses or 2 tablespoons plum preserves
2-ounce can sliced mushrooms (optional)
3 unpeeled purple plums or 8-ounce can juice-packed plums, pitted and diced; if canned, juice reserved
¼ cup water, more if necessary
3 large stalks celery, sliced
2 large onions, sliced
2 red or green bell peppers (or 1 of each), sliced
¾ pound lean roast pork, diced
2 cups cooked rice (optional)

In a nonstick skillet, stir together pineapple (with juice), pickle, soy sauce, sherry, garlic, ginger, molasses, and mushrooms (with canning liquid). Add the plums, plus juice if canned, and water. (Add about ⅓ cup water if you are using fresh plums.) Cover and simmer 10 minutes.

Uncover and stir in sliced celery, onion, and bell pepper. Simmer uncovered 5 minutes, stirring occasionally, until most of the liquid has evaporated and mixture is quite thick.

Meanwhile, trim all fat from roast pork and dice the lean cooked meat into ½-inch cubes. Stir in the meat at the last minute, gently heating through. Serve on rice, if desired. *Four servings, 295 calories each without rice; ½ cup cooked rice adds about 90 calories per serving.*

ROAST PORK KEBABS

¾ pound leftover lean roast pork, cut in 1-inch cubes
2 seedless oranges, in sections
8-ounce can unsweetened pineapple chunks, including juice
1 unpeeled red apple, in wedges
2 tablespoons lemon juice
2 tablespoons sugar
Pinch of dry mustard

Alternate cubes of meat with fruit on skewers.

Combine reserved pineapple juice with remaining ingredients. Stir well.

Broil kebabs over coals or under broiler, turning twice, until apple is tender but not soft. Baste with liquid. *Four servings, 340 calories each.*

Hold Those Bacon Calories!

Bacon, as every bulge battler knows, is a no-no. Even broiled and blotted, bacon is still more than 50 percent fat; much too devastating for the calorie conscious to consider, even as an accent. Yet there are weight-wary favorites in which the unique smoky flavor of bacon seems absolutely required.

That's when the premium-priced delicacy Canadian bacon can come to the rescue. Made from the lean loin instead of the fat belly, cured Canadian bacon packs all the flavor, for only 980 calories a pound instead of 3,000.

CANADIAN BACON, LIVER, AND ONIONS

¼ pound Canadian bacon
1 large Spanish onion
1 pound beef liver, sliced
3 tablespoons all-purpose flour
3 tablespoons water
4 level teaspoons soft butter or margarine
　 Salt and freshly ground pepper

Before cooking, dice the Canadian bacon into ½-inch cubes. Peel the onion and cut in half, then slice thin. Cut the liver into serving-size pieces and coat lightly with flour by pressing the liver into the flour on a shallow plate.

Brown the bacon cubes quickly in a nonstick skillet or electric frying pan, with no fat added. Remove and set aside.

Put the onion and water into the skillet. Cover and cook 3 minutes over moderate heat. Stir occasionally to separate. Remove the onions and set aside.

In the same skillet, melt 2 teaspoons butter or margarine, then add the liver in a single layer. Cook without turning about 2 to 3 minutes, until the under side is brown and blood appears on the flour-coated surface of the uncooked side. Then add remaining 2 teaspoons butter, turn the liver and cook 2 or 3 minutes more. (For maximum tenderness, liver should be medium rare.) At the last minute, stir in the onions and bacon cubes; cook and stir until crisp and heated through. Season to taste. *Four servings, 285 calories each.*

QUICKIE CANADIAN KEBABS

Good with sauerkraut.

Alternate chunks of unpeeled red apple with cubes of Canadian bacon on skewers. Sprinkle lightly with cider or white wine and caraway seeds. Broil briefly, only till apple is tender, but not soft; turn to cook evenly. (Canadian bacon is already cooked.) Allow 1 apple and ¼ pound Canadian bacon per serving. *About 270 calories each serving.*

For heat-and-eat convenience, nothing beats ham steak. For calorie saving, either, since ham steak, once it's trimmed of fringe fat, is less than 50 calories an ounce.

Unlike most beefsteaks, the inner part of a ham steak is mainly meat with little or no fatty marbling, yet it's always tender.

Most ham steaks available in supermarkets today are already cooked, needing little else than a creative warmup to make a meal.

You can heat a ham steak in a nonstick skillet with no fat added, then deglaze the skillet with some canned unsweetened crushed pineapple for an instant "sauce." Or toss a ham steak on the barbecue and baste with a little cider or unsweetened apple juice. Diced or shredded ham steak can add flavor to omelets, salads, or hot cooked vegetables.

Since ham steak is so versatile and has good keeping qualities under refrigeration, it's a good idea to have one always on hand.

Here are some of my favorite Slim Gourmet tricks with ham steak, from an adaptation of Broccoli Divan, made with ham and rice instead of noodles, to two barbecue versions, both featuring the verve of pineapple. All are low calorie.

HAM AND RICE DIVINE

1 **cup raw brown rice**
   Water
2 **onions, minced**
1 **tablespoon butter or margarine**
3 **cups skim milk**
3 **tablespoons all-purpose flour**
1 **teaspoon prepared mustard**
   Salt and freshly ground pepper
   Dash of Tabasco or cayenne pepper
2 **ten-ounce packages frozen broccoli spears, defrosted**
1 **thin, fat-trimmed ham steak, diced**
6 **ounces shredded part-skim mozzarella cheese**
6 **tablespoons fresh breadcrumbs, preferably from diet or high-fiber bread**
   Paprika

Cook the rice in 3 cups water until tender, about 45 minutes.

In a large nonstick skillet, combine the onion and butter with 1 tablespoon water. Cover and cook 2 minutes. Uncover and continue to cook until liquid has evaporated and onion is soft.

Stir milk and flour together, then add to the skillet. Cook and stir over moderate heat until sauce thickens and bubbles. Simmer 3 minutes. Season to taste with mustard, salt, pepper, and Tabasco.

Assemble all ingredients in layers in a shallow ovenproof casserole or baking dish: first rice, then broccoli, ham, and shredded cheese.

Top each layer with a little of the onion sauce. Top the casserole with remaining sauce, then sprinkle on breadcrumbs and paprika. Bake in a preheated 350-degree oven for 40 minutes. *Eight servings, 350 calories each.*

QUICK KEBABS POLYNESIAN

3/4 **pound fat-trimmed ham steak cut in 1½-inch cubes**
8 **ounces leftover cooked white meat of turkey or chicken, in cubes (1½ cups)**
   8-ounce can juice-packed pineapple chunks, including juice
1 **green bell pepper, seeded and cut into squares**
2 **onions, cut into chunks**
2 **tablespoons honey**
2 **tablespoons soy sauce**
2 **teaspoons salad oil**

On skewers, thread alternately the chunks of ham, turkey, pineapple, green pepper, and onion.

Mix ¼ cup reserved pineapple juice with the honey, soy sauce, and salad oil. Roll the skewers in this mixture, coating liberally.

Broil or barbecue about 5 minutes on each side, brushing the skewers with any remaining basting mixture. *Four servings, under 300 calories each.*

RAISIN-SPICED HAM STEAK

   Ready-to-eat, fat-trimmed ham steak (about 1¼ pounds)
½ **teaspoon pumpkin pie spice**
½ **cup unsweetened pineapple juice**
2 **tablespoons (1 ounce) raisins**

Spray a nonstick skillet well with cooking spray for no-fat frying. Put the ham steak into the cold skillet and turn on the heat. Cook uncovered until the under side is well browned, about 3 to 4 minutes, then turn. Continue cooking about 2 minutes, until heated through. Remove steak to a heated platter. Combine the remaining ingredients in the skillet over high heat. Cook and stir until the mixture is reduced to a few tablespoons. Pour over ham steak. Cut into serving-size pieces. *Four servings, 275 calories each.*

COOKOUT HAM STEAK WITH BROILED
PINEAPPLE RINGS

Ready-to-eat, fat-trimmed ham steak (about 1¼ pounds)
Canned unsweetened pineapple rings
Ground cloves or pumpkin-pie spice

Make shallow gashes around the border to prevent curling up. (Before broiling, ham steak may be marinated briefly in juice from canned pineapple to soak up extra flavor.) Before heating barbecue, spray the rack with cooking spray for no-fat frying to prevent meat from sticking.

When barbecue is hot, arrange ham steak and drained pineapple rings in a single layer on the rack, about 2 to 3 inches from the coals or heat source. Sprinkle surface of ham lightly with spice. When under side is brown, turn and cook briefly, only until heated through. *Each serving (¼ pound ham steak and 2 pineapple rings), about 240 calories.*

HAM, PINEAPPLE, ZUCCHINI KEBABS

1 pound fat-trimmed ham steak
1 medium zucchini
    8-ounce can unsweetened pineapple spears or chunks, drained; juice re-
    served
½ cup low-calorie Italian salad dressing

Cut ham steak into 1½-inch cubes. Quarter unpeeled zucchini lengthwise, then cut into 2-inch lengths.

Alternate ham, pineapple, and zucchini on small wooden skewers. Put the skewers in a shallow glass dish. Combine salad dressing with reserved juice from canned pineapple and pour over the skewers. Marinate 1 hour at room temperature or several hours in the refrigerator. Rotate occasionally.

. Spray grill rack with cooking spray to prevent sticking, then preheat. When grill is hot, arrange the skewers on the grill, about 3 inches from the heat source. Broil until heated through, turning to cook evenly. Don't overcook: zucchini should be well heated through but still crunchy. *Four servings, 240 calories each.*

7

HAMBURGERS, MEATBALLS, MEAT LOAVES, AND OTHER GROUND MEAT DISHES

For Nonfattening Flavor Try Mideast Hamburger

If you've got a hamburger budget but a traveler's tastes, try hamburger with a Middle Eastern accent!

There are almost as many Middle Eastern methods of preparing meatballs —and this includes Greece and Armenia—as there are American hamburger stands, so I'll focus on some of the nonfattening varieties.

Make your *kufta* (or *kafta, kofta, kuftah, keufta, konftah,* depending on the mood of the menu writer) with ground lean, fat-trimmed beef round, although you could just as readily use any lean ground meat. You might like to try it with chopped veal, or, for a more authentic touch, "lamburger," ground lean lamb.

QUICK KUFTA PIAZ

Chopped Steak with Onions and Parsley

1 pound lean, fat-trimmed ground beef round or leg of lamb
1 onion, finely chopped
¼ cup finely chopped fresh parsley
   Salt or garlic salt and coarse-ground pepper
   Lemon wedges

Cut the block of ground meat into quarters. Gently nudge into 4 oval "steaks." Put the chopped onion and parsley on a plate and gently press the "steaks" into the mixture, coating both sides well.

Spray a nonstick skillet with cooking spray for no-fat frying. Add the chopped "steaks." Cook on one side over moderate heat for 3 to 4 minutes, until under side is well browned. Turn, using a spatula, and brown the other side for an additional 1 or 2 minutes, depending on degree of doneness preferred. Season to taste after cooking, and squirt with lemon. *Four servings, 165 calories each.*

KUFTA IZMIR

Hamburgers with Cumin

2 slices stale or toasted high-fiber or protein diet bread
1 pound lean, fat-trimmed ground beef round
1 egg, beaten
1 cup finely chopped onion
1 teaspoon cumin seeds or ½ teaspoon cumin powder
1 teaspoon garlic salt
  Pinch of freshly ground pepper
  Chopped fresh parsley and lemon wedges (optional)

Soak the bread in water. Break up moistened bread and combine with remaining ingredients, except parsley and lemon wedges, tossing lightly. Shape into 6 hamburger patties. Broil, turning once, about 6 to 8 minutes. Garnish with chopped fresh parsley and serve with lemon wedges, if desired. *Six servings, under 145 calories each.*

ARMENIAN PARSLEYBURGERS

½ pound each lean, fat-trimmed ground beef round, lamb or veal, and pork,
  or 1½ pounds all lean ground beef
1 cup chopped fresh parsley, loosely packed
1 large onion, minced
1½ teaspoons salt or garlic salt
¼ teaspoon coarsely ground pepper
1 cup crushed ice (see note below)

Have meat trimmed of fat before grinding.

Toss ingredients (except lemon juice) together lightly and shape into 6 hamburgers. Broil or barbecue, turning once, to desired doneness. Baste with lemon juice, if desired. *Six servings, about 180 calories each.*

NOTE: To crush ice, wrap cubes in a clean dish towel and rap the towel on a hard surface. A powerful blender may also be used to crush ice.

HAMBURGERS À LA GRECQUE

2 slices bread, preferably high-fiber or diet protein bread
  water
1 small onion, peeled
1 clove garlic, peeled
1 carrot, peeled
1 pound lean, fat-trimmed ground beef round
2 tablespoons Chianti or any dry red wine
  Generous pinch of dried mint leaves
  Salt and freshly ground pepper to taste
1 ripe tomato, peeled and diced
  Lemon wedges (optional)

Moisten the bread in water, then squeeze out. Put in a mixing bowl.
Put the onion, garlic, and carrot through a shredder and add to the bowl.
Add remaining ingredients, except lemon wedges, and toss lightly. Shape into
6 hamburgers and broil or barbecue about 6 minutes on each side. Serve with
lemon wedges, if desired. *Four servings, about 205 calories each.*

VARIATION

Saucy Hamburgers à la Grecque: These hamburgers may also be browned on
both sides in a nonstick skillet, then simmered for 8 to 10 minutes in 1 cup
plain tomato sauce. *Adds about 75 calories to the total.*

MANDARIN MUSHROOM BURGERS

1 pound lean, fat-trimmed round
  2-ounce can mushroom pieces, drained and chopped
  Pinch of cayenne pepper
  Pinch of ground ginger
2 tablespoons soy sauce

Combine meat, chopped mushrooms, pepper, and ginger. Shape into 4
patties; broil, turning once. Baste liberally with soy sauce. *Four servings, 160
calories each.*

GREEK SPICEBURGERS

1 pound lean, fat-trimmed ground beef round
1 onion, finely chopped
1 teaspoon garlic salt
1 teaspoon ground cinnamon
1 teaspoon grated nutmeg
1 teaspoon oregano or Italian seasoning
1 cup plain tomato juice

   Combine meat with remaining ingredients, but just enough tomato juice to moisten. Shape into 4 patties. Broil, turning once. Baste with remaining tomato juice. *Four servings, 170 calories each.*

MEXICAN CHEESEBURGERS

1 pound lean, fat-trimmed ground beef round
1 teaspoon onion salt
1 teaspoon chili powder
¼ cup chopped green bell pepper
   6-ounce can plain tomato juice
2 slices (2 ounces) regular or diet American-style cheese

   Combine meat and other ingredients except tomato juice and cheese. Shape into 4 patties. Broil, turning once. Baste frequently with tomato juice. Slice cheese into 4 equal pieces. Top each burger with cheese at the last minute, so the burgers are served with the cheese just beginning to melt. *Four servings, 190 calories each with diet cheese, 215 calories with regular cheese.*

Lean, Lean "Lamburger" . . .

A whole leg of lamb can be cut into smaller roasts, or have part of it made into "lamburger."

ATHENIAN LAMB AND NOODLES

   If you like spaghetti and meatballs, you'll love this Greek inspiration.

1 pound lean, fat-trimmed ground leg of lamb
1 egg, beaten
2 tablespoons chopped fresh parsley
   Salt and freshly ground pepper
3 cups peeled, diced raw eggplant
   10½-ounce can fat-skimmed beef broth

1 cup water
   6-ounce can tomato paste
1 onion, chopped
1 clove garlic, minced
⅛ teaspoon grated nutmeg
½ teaspoon oregano or Italian seasoning
½ teaspoon basil
12 ounces dry wide noodles
6 teaspoons grated extra-sharp Romano cheese

Combine lamb, egg, parsley, salt, and pepper. Shape into 15 small meatballs. Brown under broiler, turning once.

In a large pot, combine eggplant, beef broth, water, tomato paste, onion, garlic, nutmeg, oregano, and basil. Stir well and add meatballs. Cover and simmer 30 to 40 minutes. Uncover and continue to simmer until sauce is thick. Meanwhile, cook noodles in boiling, salted water until tender (see page 245).

Serve sauce and meatballs over hot noodles, sprinkle lightly with cheese. *Six servings, about 380 calories each.*

LEMON LAMBURGERS

1 slice dry bread, preferably protein diet or high-fiber bread
1 pound lean, fat-trimmed ground leg of lamb
1 egg, lightly beaten
1 tablespoon catsup
½ teaspoon cumin seeds
½ teaspoon chili powder
1 clove garlic, minced, or ⅛ teaspoon instant garlic
1 teaspoon paprika
2 tablespoons chopped fresh parsley or mint
   Lemon juice
   Lemon wedges and additional parsley

Crush the bread into crumbs, and add to remaining ingredients, except lemon juice and lemon wedges. Toss lightly, then gently shape into four oblong hamburger steaks. Broil or barbecue as you would beefburgers. Baste with lemon juice. Serve medium rare, preferably, or at desired degree of doneness. Garnish with additional parsley and lemon wedges. *Four servings, 190 calories each.*

Make Low-Cal Meatballs, Enough for Two Dinners

Tonight why not make a dinner and a half? What's a dinner and a half? It's tonight's meal plus a head start on some other night's main course. It's easy if you like meatball dishes. All you need to do is make twice as many, then squirrel away extras in your freezer. Since the meatballs are low-calorie—browned under the broiler to eliminate fat—both night's meals will be figure-wise.

The first two recipes—favorites with the slim-thinking teenagers in some of the Slim Gourmet households I know—will give you the idea. Both are hearty dishes, just what big-appetite slimmers are looking for. The sweet 'n' sour cabbage dish is a savory plate filler, yet inexpensive (in cost and calories!). Both main courses are extra-easy one-dish meals. In the Italian noodle recipe, the noodles are cooked right along with the sauce. The international array of meatball dishes that follows can be handled in the same way.

OVEN-BROWNED MEATBALLS

  2 whole eggs or **4** egg whites
  2 pounds lean, fat-trimmed ground beef round
  ¼ cup water or **⅓** cup crushed ice
  ½ cup finely minced fresh parsley
  2 teaspoons salt
  2 teaspoons monosodium glutamate (optional)
  1 teaspoon freshly ground pepper
  1 clove garlic, finely minced (optional)
  3 tablespoons cracker crumbs, matzoh meal, or unseasoned breadcrumbs

Combine all ingredients, mixing well. Shape into 16 meatballs. Broil, turning once, until well browned on both sides. Allow to cool, then pack in 2 plastic bags and freeze. Each bag is enough for a 4-serving dinner. *Each meatball has 90 calories.*

ITALIAN MEATBALLS AND WINE NOODLES

  1 quart water
  2 beef bouillon cubes
      6-ounce can tomato paste
  1 cup dry red wine (optional)
      2-ounce can mushroom stems and pieces, including liquid
  1 clove garlic, minced
  1 onion, chopped
  1 green bell pepper, seeded and chopped
  1 teaspoon oregano or Italian seasoning
  ½ recipe Oven-Browned Meatballs (see above), defrosted if frozen
  4 ounces dry wide egg noodles
  ¼ cup grated Parmesan cheese (optional)

Heat water to boiling. Add bouillon and stir until dissolved. Stir in tomato paste until smooth. Stir in all remaining ingredients except noodles and cheese. Heat to boiling. Cover and simmer 4 minutes.

Uncover and stir in noodles gradually to retain simmering point. Simmer, stirring frequently, until noodles are very tender and sauce is thick, about 12 or 13 minutes. Spoon onto individual plates. Sprinkle each with 1 tablespoon cheese, if desired. *Four servings, 350 calories each without cheese; 380 each with cheese.*

SWEET 'N' SOUR CABBAGE AND MEATBALLS

2 cups water
2 beef bouillon cubes
1 tablespoon red wine vinegar
  6-ounce can tomato paste
1 onion, chopped
½ cup crushed unsweetened pineapple, including juice
½ recipe Oven-Browned Meatballs (see page 98), defrosted if frozen
1 medium head cabbage, quartered

Heat water to boiling in a large pot. Add bouillon and stir until dissolved. Stir in vinegar and tomato paste until smooth. Add onion and pineapple; cover and simmer 6 minutes, until onion is tender.

Add meatballs and quartered cabbage wedges. Cover and cook until cabbage is tender but still crisp and green, and sauce is thick. To serve, arrange cabbage and meatballs on individual plates and spoon on sauce. *Four servings, 280 calories each.*

KUFTA KARI

Baked Curried Meatballs

½ cup instant rice
½ cup boiling water
1 pound lean, fat-trimmed ground beef round
2 onions, chopped
2 eggs, lightly beaten
1 tablespoon curry powder, or to taste
¾ cup chopped fresh parsley
1 teaspoon dried dill weed
¼ cup defatted soy flour (see note below)
  Salt and freshly ground pepper to taste
  10-ounce can undiluted fat-skimmed chicken or beef broth
2 tablespoons lemon juice

Put rice into a mixing bowl. Add boiling water and stir. Cover and wait 10 minutes until water is absorbed. Add ground meat, half of the onion, eggs, curry powder, parsley, dill, and soy flour. Salt and pepper to taste. Toss lightly to mix well, then gently shape into 24 round meatballs.

Arrange meatballs and remaining onion in a shallow pan. Pour on broth and lemon juice. Bake at 350 degrees for 1 hour or more, basting frequently, until most of the liquid is gone. Add a little water, if necessary. *Eight servings, 150 calories each.*

NOTE: Soy flour is usually found in health-food stores. If not available, substitute ½ cup texturized vegetable protein meat extender, or ½ cup crushed high-protein cereal.

EASY HAMBOURGUIGNONNE

 1 pound lean fat-trimmed ground beef round
 Garlic salt and pepper
 4-ounce can sliced mushrooms, undrained
 8-ounce can whole boiled onions, drained
 16-ounce can small Belgian carrots, undrained
 1 cup Burgundy or any dry red wine
 1 teaspoon poultry seasoning
 1 tablespoon chopped fresh parsley
 1 tablespoon cornstarch
 ¼ cup cold water
 2 cups cooked instant rice (optional)

Assemble all ingredients. Shape ground meat into 16 small meatballs, or cut the block of meat into cubes. Spray a nonstick skillet with cooking spray for non-fat frying. Add the meat and brown quickly over high heat, with no fat added. Drain any fat from pan. Season liberally with garlic salt and pepper.

Add remaining ingredients, except cornstarch and cold water. Simmer uncovered 15 minutes, stirring frequently, to heat vegetables through and permit the liquid to reduce. Skim off fat, if any.

. Combine cornstarch and cold water, mixing well. Stir into simmering liquid, until thickened and bubbling. (Serve with prepared instant rice, if desired, ½ cup per serving.) *Four servings, under 225 calories each without rice; with rice, 330 calories.*

SWEET 'N' SOUR ARABIAN MEATBALLS

 1 large celery stalk with leaves
 ½ bunch fresh parsley
 1 pound lean, fat-trimmed ground beef round or leg of lamb

6　tablespoons lemon juice
⅛　teaspoon ground turmeric
　　Salt and freshly ground pepper
1　small onion, chopped
2　cups boiling water
2　tomatoes, peeled and chopped, or 1½ cups tomato juice
½　cup chopped fresh mint leaves
2　tablespoons honey

De-string celery if necessary and cut into 1-inch pieces. Chop celery leaves and parsley together and combine ½ cup of this mixture with the meat. Add 1 tablespoon lemon juice and a pinch of turmeric, salt, and pepper. Shape into 16 meatballs. Brown under broiler, turning once.

In a nonstick skillet combine browned meatballs with chopped onion, sliced celery, water, and tomatoes.

Add another pinch of turmeric. Cover and simmer 20 minutes, until celery is tender. Uncover, and stir in remaining celery-parsley mixture, remaining lemon juice, and mint.

Simmer uncovered until sauce is thick. Stir in the honey and salt and pepper to taste at the last minute. *Eight party servings, 105 calories each. Or four main-course servings, 210 calories each.*

POTTED MEATBALLS WITH PICKLED PINEAPPLE SAUCE

1½　pounds lean, fat-trimmed ground beef round
½　cup cooked rice or barley
1　egg, lightly beaten
2　or 3 sprigs fresh parsley, minced
1　onion, minced
1　teaspoon salt
¼　teaspoon freshly ground pepper
1　teaspoon monosodium glutamate (optional)
1　tablespoon prepared mustard
2　teaspoons Worcestershire sauce
　　Pickled Pineapple Sauce (page 305)

Combine the ground beef with the meatball ingredients, rice, egg, parsley, onion, and seasonings and toss lightly. Shape into meatballs and place in a shallow nonstick baking pan. Slip under the broiler, turning once, until browned.

Combine sauce ingredients in a large Dutch oven and heat to boiling. Add browned meatballs and simmer 20 minutes, covered. Serve sauce over meatballs. *Six servings, 260 calories each.*

VARIATION

Stuffed Cabbage with Pickled Pineapple Sauce: Separate a cabbage into leaves and drop the leaves into boiling water, only until limp. Drain and cool.

Combine ingredients for potted meatballs in preceding recipe and use as a filling for cabbage leaves. Put a little of the mixture onto each leaf and roll up tight. Arrange the rolls in a large Dutch oven. Add 1 cup water.

Combine ingredients for Pickled Pineapple Sauce (page 305) and add to the pot. Cover and simmer very gently 1½ hours. Add water if needed. *Six servings, about 280 calories each.*

FLEMISH MEATBALLS IN BEER SAUCE

Here's a beef-in-beer dish made with lean hamburger. Great as a main course or party dish.

3 **slices high-fiber or high-protein diet bread**
1 **pound lean, fat-trimmed ground beef round**
1 **egg**
½ **cup finely minced onion**
1 **clove garlic, finely minced**
¼ **cup chopped fresh parsley**
1 **teaspoon monosodium glutamate (optional)**
1 **teaspoon salt**
¼ **teaspoon coarsely ground pepper**
¼ **teaspoon thyme or poultry seasoning**
    12-ounce can low-calorie "light" beer
2 **teaspoons salad oil**
1 **tablespoon all-purpose flour**
    Few drops brown gravy coloring (optional)

Cut the bread into ½-inch cubes. Combine with meat, egg, onion, garlic, parsley, monosodium glutamate, salt, pepper, and thyme. Add enough beer (about ½ cup) to moisten, and lightly shape into 12 meatballs.

Spray a large nonstick skillet or electric frying pan with cooking spray for no-fat frying. Add oil and meatballs. Brown gently over a moderate flame, turning frequently; stir remaining beer and flour together and stir into skillet. Simmer, uncovered, until sauce is gravy thick. Season gravy with additional salt, pepper, monosodium glutamate, and thyme to taste. Add a few drops brown gravy coloring, if you wish.

May be served as a main course (with noodles or rice, if desired) or turned into a chafing dish for appetizers (recipe may be doubled or tripled). *Four main-course servings, about 300 calories each.*

SWEET 'N' SOUR PEKING PORKBALLS

This sauce is sweetened naturally . . . with fruit. The flavor is somewhat like Chinese duck sauce.

1½ **pounds lean, fat-trimmed ground pork**
1 **egg or 2 egg whites**
6 **tablespoons soy sauce**
   16-ounce can unsweetened apricot halves
2 **tablespoons vinegar**
½ **cup unsweetened white grape juice or apple juice**
½ **cup tomato juice**

Combine ground pork with egg and 3 tablespoons soy sauce. Shape into 12 meatballs. Spray a nonstick skillet with cooking spray for no-fat frying. Add the meatballs and 2 tablespoons liquid from the canned apricots. Cook over high heat until liquid evaporates and meatballs begin to brown in their own melted fat. Turn and brown on all sides. Drain off and discard any melted fat in the pan.

Meanwhile, combine all remaining ingredients in a blender, cover, and blend smooth, until apricots are pureed. Pour over meatballs. Cook uncovered, over moderate heat, until liquid has reduced to a thick flavorful sauce. *Six servings, about 235 calories each.*

POLYNESIAN SWEET 'N' SOUR MEATBALLS

1 **pound lean, fat-trimmed ground veal or beef round**
3 **tablespoons minced onion**
2 **tablespoons soy sauce**
½ **cup dry white wine**
2 **teaspoons arrowroot**
1 **green bell pepper, seeded and minced**
5 **tablespoons dill-pickle relish**
2 **tablespoons sugar**

Combine chopped meat, onion, and soy sauce. Shape into 1½-inch balls and arrange in a single layer in a shallow baking pan. Bake, uncovered, 15 minutes at 350 degrees. Drain off any fat. Combine all remaining ingredients and mix well. Stir into pan. Continue to bake, stirring occasionally, until sauce is hot and thick. *Four servings, 285 calories each.*

Meat-Loaf Recipes, Low-Cal and Cholesterol Wise

Meat loaf is a great idea for pennypinchers . . . but not always the prime choice for calorie counters or cholesterol watchers. Too often it is made with cheap hamburger meat—think of all that saturated fat—and held together with starchy fillers and eggs—all that cholesterol!

Here are savory meat loaves that are just what the doctor ordered—but so delicious nobody will know you've been tinkering with the calorie and cholesterol content.

Begin with the leanest meat—not ready-packaged hamburger, but lean meat you've had ground to order without the fat. These recipes contain no egg yolks, since it's the yolks, not the whites, that harbor the cholesterol.

ITALIAN MEAT LOAF

   16-ounce can Italian tomatoes
1 pound lean, fat-trimmed ground beef round
½ pound lean, fat-trimmed ground veal or pork
2 egg whites
2 onions, finely chopped
1 green bell pepper, seeded and chopped
1 cup minced fresh parsley
1 tablespoon oregano
1 teaspoon garlic salt
   Dash of cayenne pepper
   Green pepper rings (optional)

Break up tomatoes with a fork. Add all remaining ingredients except pepper rings and mix lightly. Shape into a loaf. If you wish, garnish the top with green pepper rings. Bake in a preheated 350-degree oven for 1 hour, or until a meat thermometer registers 170 degrees. *Six servings, 185 calories each.*

MEAT LOAF MEXICANA

   10¾-ounce can undiluted tomato soup
3 tablespoons water
2 teaspoons oregano or Italian Seasoning
2 teaspoons chili powder
1 teaspoon cumin (optional)
1½ pounds lean, fat-trimmed ground beef round
2 egg whites

1 **onion, finely chopped**
1 **teaspoon garlic salt**
1 **green bell pepper, finely chopped**

Combine soup, water, oregano, chili powder, and cumin. Measure out ½ cup.

Combine the ½ cup soup mixture with all remaining ingredients. Shape into a loaf in a shallow roasting pan. Pour on the remaining soup mixture. Bake in a preheated 350-degree oven for 1 hour, basting occasionally with the soup mixture in the pan. *Six servings, 200 calories each.*

Try Delicious Beef Ring, a Shapely New Meat Loaf

There's no law that meat loaf has to be meat loaf. Why not "meat ring"? Picture a savory circle of seasoned beef fresh from the oven, its center filled with glazed carrots or crisp Oriental vegetables. Same budget-sparing ingredients as mundane meat loaf, but so much more glamorous, thanks to its shape. And, speaking of glamorous shapes, keep yours by making beef ring low in calories.

How do you make a beef ring? Same as a meat loaf, except that the ingredients are shaped into a circle with the aid of a ring mold or center-hole angel-cake pan.

Yes, it's possible to bake your meat loaf right in the cake pan—many cookbooks suggest that you do—but I'm not in favor. I prefer to use this pan simply as a shaping device: first you fill it with meat, then invert it over a roasting pan. Lift off the ring mold and your raw meat mixture will retain its ring shape.

Then put it in the oven, uncovered, and bake it. The outside will be crispy brown. But, more important: the meat loaf will be less fattening because the melting fat will be able to escape. No trying to extract a cooked meat loaf from a cake pan, either!

BEEF RING WITH ORIENTAL VEGETABLES

MEAT LOAF:
2 **pounds lean, fat-trimmed ground beef round**
2 **eggs, beaten**
1 **cup skim milk**
2 **tablespoons soy sauce**
2 **teaspoons dry mustard**
1 **teaspoon monosodium glutamate (optional)**
   Salt and freshly ground pepper to taste
1 **cup finely chopped onion**
2 **cups high-protein cereal, crushed**

[continued]

VEGETABLE FILLING:
¼ cup dry white wine or water
2 tablespoons soy sauce
1 beef bouillon cube
 16-ounce can Oriental vegetables, drained
1 large onion, cut in half and then sliced
 2-ounce can mushrooms, including liquid
2 teaspoons arrowroot or cornstarch
1 cup cold water

Combine meat-loaf ingredients and pack into a ring mold. Invert on a shallow nonstick roasting pan and carefully lift the mold off, retaining the meat in a ring shape. Bake in a preheated 350-degree oven for 50 minutes or more.

About 10 minutes before serving time, prepare the vegetable filling. Combine in a nonstick skillet all ingredients except arrowroot and cold water. Cover and cook 4 to 5 minutes, only until onions are tender-crisp. Stir arrowroot and cold water together and stir into simmering vegetables until sauce thickens and clears. Season with additional soy sauce to taste.

At serving time, fill the meat ring with vegetables. *Eight servings, 225 calories each.*

FRENCH BEEF RING WITH CARROTS

MEAT LOAF:
2 pounds lean, fat-trimmed ground beef round
2 eggs
1 small onion, minced
2 teaspoons garlic salt
1 teaspoon freshly ground pepper
2 tablespoons prepared horseradish
2 teaspoons dry mustard
5 tablespoons catsup
1 cup chopped sweet pepper

FILLING:
2 ten-ounce packages sliced frozen carrots
1 tablespoon chopped fresh parsley
2 beef bouillon cubes
1 cup water

Combine meat-loaf ingredients and shape into a ring as in previous recipe. Bake at 350 degrees for 50 minutes.

About 20 minutes before serving time, combine filling ingredients in a covered saucepan and cook only until carrots are tender but still crisp. Serve meat ring with carrots in the center. *Eight servings, 220 calories each.*

Flavorful, Nonfattening Ground-Meat Skillet Dishes

HAMBURGER SKILLET OREGANATO

1 pound lean, fat-trimmed ground beef round
2 cups plain tomato juice
2 tablespoons Chianti or any dry red wine
1 large onion, sliced
2 medium zucchini, thinly sliced
1 teaspoon oregano or Italian seasoning
½ teaspoon fennel seeds
  Garlic salt and freshly ground pepper to taste
2 tablespoons grated sharp Romano cheese

Spray a large nonstick skillet or electric frying pan with cooking spray for no-fat frying. Flatten the ground meat in the skillet over high heat. When under side is brown, break up into chunks and turn over. Continue to cook until chunks are well browned. Drain off any fat carefully.

Add remaining ingredients except cheese. Cover and cook five minutes. Uncover and continue to cook until all liquid has evaporated, leaving a thick tomato sauce. Sprinkle on cheese and serve straight from the skillet. *Four servings, about 220 calories each.*

MACARONI AND BEEF À LA GRECQUE

2 pounds lean, fat-trimmed ground beef round
1 cup water
½ cup dry white wine
  6-ounce can tomato paste
1 large sweet onion, chopped
3 cloves garlic, minced
3 stalks celery, finely chopped
1 bay leaf
  Salt and freshly ground pepper
3 cups dry protein-enriched elbow macaroni

Spray a large nonstick skillet or electric frying pan with cooking spray for no-fat frying. Add the meat and cook slowly over low heat with no fat added. Turn frequently, breaking up, until the meat is browned. Pour on the water, reheat to boiling, and then drain off into a tall cup. When the fat has risen to the surface, skim with paper towel or a bulb-type baster.

Return the fat-skimmed liquid to the skillet. Add all the remaining ingredients, except macaroni.

Cover and simmer, stirring occasionally, until onion and celery are tender. Uncover and continue cooking until sauce is thick.

Meanwhile, cook macaroni in boiling salted water until tender (see page 245). To serve, top macaroni with meat and sauce, allowing ¾ cup macaroni per serving. *Eight servings, under 300 calories each.*

GREEK GREEN-BEAN-AND-BEEF BAKE

  2 cups sliced green beans—fresh, frozen, or canned
1½ pounds lean, fat-trimmed ground beef round
    8-ounce can plain tomato sauce
  ½ teaspoon garlic salt
    Pinch of ground cinnamon
  ½ teaspoon grated nutmeg
  2 eggs
1½ cups low-fat cottage cheese
  1 tablespoon minced fresh parsley (optional)
  2 tablespoons grated Parmesan cheese
  2 tablespoons seasoned breadcrumbs, homemade (see page 302) or commercial

If green beans are fresh, parboil 3 minutes and drain, reserving cooking water. If frozen, allow to defrost. If canned, reserve canning liquid. Arrange green beans in an ovenproof casserole.

Spread the chopped meat in a shallow nonstick skillet over a medium flame with no fat added. When under side is brown, break into chunks and continue browning until well rendered of any fat. Drain off and discard fat; then stir in tomato sauce, ¼ cup green-bean liquid or water, garlic salt, cinnamon, and nutmeg, and combine well. Layer meat-and-tomato mixture over the green beans.

Stir eggs, cottage cheese, and parsley together and layer on top of the meat. Sprinkle with Parmesan and crumbs. Bake in a preheated 350-degree oven for 30 minutes. *Six servings, about 260 calories each.*

GREEK EGGPLANT CHILI

1 pound lean, fat-trimmed ground beef round
1 medium eggplant, peeled and diced
1 large onion, minced
2 green bell peppers, seeded and sliced
  6-ounce can tomato paste
  10½-ounce can fat-skimmed beef broth or onion soup

1 clove garlic, minced
1 teaspoon oregano or Italian seasoning
½ teaspoon grated nutmeg
  Salt and freshly ground pepper to taste
  Chili powder to taste
½ cup shredded sharp Cheddar cheese

Brown ground meat in a large nonstick skillet with no fat added. Break into chunks as it browns. Pour off all fat. Stir in remaining ingredients except cheese. Cover tightly and simmer over very low heat 1½ hours (add a little water, if needed). Sprinkle with cheese before serving. *Six party servings, under 180 calories each.*

QUICK POLYNESIAN CURRY

1½ pounds lean, fat-trimmed ground beef round or leg of lamb
2 onions, halved and thinly sliced
2 stalks celery, thinly sliced
2 tablespoons soy sauce
½ teaspoon monosodium glutamate (optional)
1 clove garlic, minced
2 teaspoons curry powder, or to taste
  6-ounce can (¾ cup) plain tomato juice
  6-ounce can (¾ cup) unsweetened pineapple juice
¼ cup white raisins
1 unpeeled red apple, diced (optional)

Brown meat and break into chunks as directed in preceding recipe. Drain off and discard fat. Add all remaining ingredients except diced apple. Simmer, uncovered, stirring frequently, until nearly all liquid is absorbed. Stir in apples last and heat through. *Six servings, about 210 calories each without apple; apple adds under 15 calories per serving.*

DELHI SKILLET

1½ pounds lean, fat-trimmed ground beef round
1 onion, minced
2 medium potatoes, peeled and diced
2 medium tomatoes, diced
2 teaspoons curry powder
1½ teaspoons garlic salt
  Pinch of freshly ground pepper
  10-ounce package frozen cut green beans, thawed

Brown the meat along with the onion in a large nonstick skillet. Break up the meat as it cooks for about 5 minutes. Pour off any accumulated fat.

Add the potatoes, tomatoes, curry powder, garlic salt, and pepper. Stir lightly until well mixed.

Cover and cook over low heat for 20 minutes, stirring occasionally. Mix in the green beans. Cook 5 minutes more. *Six servings, 215 calories each.*

ARGENTINE BEEF SKILLET

1½ pounds lean, fat-trimmed ground beef round
    10½-ounce can fat-skimmed beef broth
½ cup sherry
 2 tomatoes, peeled, seeded, and chopped
 4 onions, halved and thinly sliced
¼ cup golden raisins
 6 dried apricot halves
 1 bay leaf
½ teaspoon thyme
 1 teaspoon salt
 2 unpeeled red apples, diced
 2 unpeeled pears, diced

Spread the chopped meat in a large nonstick frying pan or electric skillet over high heat, with no fat added. Permit the under side of the meat to brown. Then break up into bite-size chunks, turn, and brown the other side. Pour off all fat.

Add broth, sherry, tomatoes, onion, raisins, apricots, bay leaf, thyme, and approximately 1 teaspoon salt (or to taste). Simmer, uncovered, stirring frequently, until nearly all the liquid is absorbed. Stir in apples and pears. Continue to cook and stir until fresh fruit is tender but not soft. *Six servings, under 300 calories each.*

HAMBURGER PIZZA

The meat is the crust!

1 pound lean, fat-trimmed ground beef round
1 onion, finely minced
1 teaspoon garlic salt
1 cup tomatoes
⅓ cup shredded part-skim mozzarella cheese
2 tablespoons grated sharp Romano cheese
2 teaspoons oregano or Italian seasoning

Spray a nonstick 8-inch cake pan with cooking spray for no-fat frying. Combine the meat with half the onion. Season with garlic salt. Press the meat into the cake pan and up the sides to form a "crust." Bake in a preheated hot (450-degree) oven 12 minutes, until well browned.

Break up the tomatoes with a fork, and spoon into the meat crust. Top with cheeses and oregano. Return to the oven for 10 minutes. *Cut into four wedges, about 225 calories each.*

How to Stuff Peppers and Not Split Seams

How do *you* stuff a pepper? With 200 calories? Four hundred calories? A thousand calories? Depending on the recipe you follow, that lovable sweet bell pepper—only 14 or 15 calories by itself—can turn into a veritable calorific hand grenade, packed with hidden calories ready to explode into unwanted poundage!

The most popular stuffed-pepper dishes are usually seasoned combinations of ground meat and rice. Many unwary weight watchers think that simply eliminating or minimizing the rice is the right way to slim down a stuffed pepper. In fact, the real key to stuffed-pepper calories is the meat. If the ground meat is fatty, stuffed peppers will be fattening, because all the fat stays trapped in the pepper cases. If you brown other ingredients in added fat—the chopped onions, for example—that fat also remains trapped in the pepper cases.

Here I tell you how to make basic stuffed peppers with the least amount of fat possible. Vary the seasonings to suit your taste; the calories won't change!

SOUTH-OF-THE-BORDER BASIC STUFFED PEPPERS

4 well-shaped green bell peppers
½ pound lean, fat-trimmed ground beef round
2 tablespoons water or tomato juice
1 small onion, finely minced
1 small stalk celery, finely minced
¾ cup cooked rice
2 eggs or 4 egg whites
½ teaspoon salt or garlic salt
⅛ teaspoon freshly ground black pepper
  Pinch of cayenne pepper
  Chili powder to taste
  Generous dash of Worcestershire or steak sauce (optional)
  Pinch of oregano, basil, or Italian seasoning
4 teaspoons seasoned breadcrumbs, homemade (see page 302) or commercial
  6-ounce can (¾ cup) tomato juice or tomato cocktail

Slice off the tops of the peppers. Clean the pepper cases of seeds and membranes. Trim and discard the stem ends from the tops; mince any reserved pepper from the tops and set aside.

Put the chopped beef in a nonstick skillet with 2 tablespoons water or tomato juice over high heat. Cook undisturbed until under side is browned, then break up into chunks and continue to cook until meat is nicely browned. Drain off and discard any fat.

Stir together the browned meat, onion, celery, cooked rice, eggs, salt, pepper, red pepper, chili powder, Worcestershire, oregano, and minced green pepper reserved from the tops. Spoon the filling into the pepper cases and sprinkle with crumbs. Stand the stuffed peppers in a small ovenproof casserole or Dutch oven. Pour on ¾ cup tomato juice, cover, and bake in a preheated 350-degree oven 20 to 25 minutes, until tender. Uncover and continue to bake, basting frequently, until tops are browned. *Four servings, 190 calories each.*

VARIATIONS

Range-Top Stuffed Peppers: Stuffed peppers may also be cooked on top of the range in a covered Dutch oven over low heat about 20 to 25 minutes, or until tender.

Pressure-Cooked Stuffed Peppers: Stuffed peppers may also be cooked standing up in a pressure cooker in about 8 or 9 minutes. Add ½ cup water to the tomato juice. Follow manufacturer's directions carefully.

Microwave Stuffed Peppers: Stuffed peppers may also be cooked in a glass casserole in a microwave oven. Consult manufacturer's directions.

PARMESAN PEPPER HALVES

4 green bell peppers, cut lengthwise
   16-ounce can tomatoes
1 pound lean, fat-trimmed ground beef round
1 small onion, chopped
1 clove garlic, minced (optional)
1 egg
1 teaspoon salt
⅛ teaspoon freshly ground black pepper
⅛ teaspoon cayenne pepper
¼ cup grated Parmesan cheese
¼ cup seasoned breadcrumbs, homemade (see page 302) or commercial

Slice bell peppers in half lengthwise; remove the seeds and membranes. Drain the tomatoes and reserve the juice. Chop the tomatoes coarsely and mix with the ground meat, onion, garlic, egg, salt, pepper, and red pepper. Put the pepper halves in a shallow roasting pan and mound some of the meat filling in each. Pour the reserved tomato juice into the bottom of the roaster. Sprinkle the tops with Parmesan and breadcrumbs.

Cover the pan with foil and bake in a 350-degree oven 30 to 40 minutes. Uncover and bake an additional 10 minutes. *Four servings, 255 calories each.*

SLIM SKILLET HAVANA

"Meat-loaf mix" is ground beef, veal, and pork in equal proportions, widely sold in supermarkets across the United States. If you're weight wary, the one thing you should *not* do with meat-loaf mix is make it into meat loaf.

Why not? Because the ready-ground mixture contains another ingredient you don't want—fat. In meat loaf, the fat remains trapped in the mixture and eventually winds up on your waistline.

Okay then, what *do* you do with meat-loaf mix?

You could broil "comboburgers"—but only if you're willing to serve them very well done. The presence of pork in the mixture means that your combination burgers will have to be cooked all the way through.

A more interesting idea is this savory, spicy skillet main course, Cuban-inspired Skillet Havana. A mellow mélange of meat, tomatoes, celery, and onion, it is spiced with vinegar, raisins, oregano, and cumin seeds. Cumin, like oregano, is sold on supermarket spice shelves. The flavor of this dish is zesty but not hot. (A few generous shakes of Tabasco can add a torrid touch, if you like.)

SUBTRACT FAT: Note the special cooking technique that subtracts fat (and calories) instead of adding it. Brown the meat in its own melted fat, then add water, and drain the fat and water off into a cup. The liquid is then fat-skimmed before it is returned to the skillet.

After trying Skillet Havana try the same recipe with an Italian touch, as in Skillet Sorrento, or seasoned the Greek way, Skillet Athenia.

  1 **pound meat-loaf mix (ground beef, veal, and pork)**
  1 **cup water**
  1 **onion, chopped**
  4 **stalks celery, sliced**
    16-ounce can stewed tomatoes
1½ **tablespoons vinegar**
  1 **clove garlic, minced (optional)**
 ¼ **cup golden raisins**
 ½ **teaspoon oregano or Italian seasoning**
  1 **teaspoon cumin seeds**
  1 **teaspoon monosodium glutamate (optional)**
    Salt and freshly ground pepper

Spray a large nonstick skillet or electric frying pan with cooking spray for no-fat frying. Put the meat into a cold skillet. Heat slowly over a moderate flame without disturbing until the meat is browned on the under side in its own melted fat. Break the meat up into large chunks and continue to cook until all the chunks are well browned and rendered of fat. Add the water, reheat to boiling, then drain the liquid off into a cup. Set cup aside. Stir remaining ingredients into meat, cover, and simmer over low heat.

After the fat has risen to the surface of the drained liquid, skim it off with a bulb-type baster or spoon. Return the fat-skimmed broth to the skillet and continue to simmer, uncovered, until most of the liquid has evaporated and celery and onions are tender. Stir frequently. Serve with Tabasco on the side. *Four servings, about 225 calories each.*

VARIATIONS

Slim Skillet Sorrento: Follow the preceding recipe, omitting the raisins. Substitute red wine for the vinegar. Substitute fennel seeds for the cumin. (Add 1 teaspoon grated Parmesan cheese per serving, if desired.) *About 200 calories each serving without cheese; cheese adds 10 calories per serving.*

Greek Skillet Athenia: Follow first recipe, omitting raisins and cumin seeds. Substitute parsley flakes for the oregano (or 2 tablespoons fresh chopped parsley). Substitute white wine for the vinegar. Add ½ teaspoon ground cinnamon and ¼ teaspoon grated nutmeg. (Sprinkle with grated sharp Romano cheese, if desired.) *About 200 calories each serving without cheese, about 210 with.*

Save on Fat and Calories: BBQ Homemade Sausage

Instead of hot dogs or hamburgers on the grill, how about homemade sausage patties? It's easy—and nonfattening, if you're a Slim Gourmet backyard chef!

Most sausage products are 50 percent pork and 50 percent pork fat—with a whopping calorie and cholesterol count to match. You don't need all that fat to make sausage. In fact, you don't even need pork.

Here is a round-the-world collection of lean and luscious savory sausage patties that are perfect over the coals. Serve them on thin rounds of French bread. Add a big tossed salad and fresh fruit dessert for a super sundown supper.

FRENCH STEAK SAUSAGE

  2 pounds lean, fat-trimmed ground bottom round steak
  2 teaspoons salt
    Few drops liquid smoke seasoning or use smoke-flavored salt (optional)
 ½ teaspoon freshly ground black pepper
 ¼ teaspoon cayenne pepper (optional)
  2 teaspoons dried sage
  1 teaspoon dried savory
 ½ teaspoon grated nutmeg
 ½ cup crushed ice

Have the meat trimmed of fat and ground, or grind lean steak in a meat grinder or food processor. Combine with remaining ingredients and mix lightly. Gently shape into 16 patties. Wrap and freeze, if desired. Broil or barbecue for 2 minutes on each side (3 minutes, if frozen). *Each sausage, under 80 calories.*

ITALIAN VEAL SAUSAGE

2 pounds lean, fat-trimmed ground veal shoulder
2 teaspoons salt
2 cloves garlic, minced
2 teaspoons paprika
2 teaspoons thyme
2 bay leaves, crumbled
1 teaspoon anise or fennel seeds
¼ teaspoon black pepper
¼ teaspoon cayenne pepper or more, to taste
½ cup Chianti wine
Few drops liquid smoke seasoning (optional)

Follow directions in preceding recipe. *Sixteen patties, under 80 calories each.*

GERMAN VEAL SAUSAGE

2 pounds lean, fat-trimmed ground veal shoulder or leg, or lean, fat-trimmed fresh ham steak
2 teaspoons salt
1 teaspoon sugar (optional)
1½ teaspoons rosemary
½ teaspoon ground coriander or 1 teaspoon coriander seeds
1 teaspoon prepared mustard
½ teaspoon dried sage
Pinch of freshly ground black pepper
Pinch of cayenne pepper
¼ teaspoon grated nutmeg
½ cup crushed ice

Follow recipe directions on page 114. (Pork, if used, *must* be cooked through before serving.) *Sixteen patties, about 75 calories each for veal, 80 for ham.*

SPICY INDIAN LAMB SAUSAGES

2 pounds lean, fat-trimmed ground lamb, from leg or shoulder
2 teaspoons salt or smoke-seasoned salt
1 level tablespoon ground cumin
1 teaspoon curry powder, or to taste
1 onion, finely minced, or 2 tablespoons dried onion flakes plus ¼ cup water
2 tablespoons minced fresh parsley or 1 teaspoon flakes
2 eggs, lightly beaten

Follow recipe directions on page 114. *Sixteen patties, under 90 calories each.*

SPANISH TURKEY SAUSAGE

2 pounds ground raw turkey
2 teaspoons salt
1 clove garlic, finely minced
½ teaspoon red pepper flakes
1 teaspoon cumin seeds
2 teaspoons oregano or Italian seasoning
¼ cup dry red wine
   Few drops liquid-smoke seasoning (optional)

Follow recipe directions on page 114. *Sixteen patties, about 70 calories each.*

GREEK CUMIN SAUSAGE

1½ pounds lean, fat-trimmed ground leg of lamb or beef round
2 slices high-protein bread
½ cup water
2 cloves garlic, chopped
2 teaspoons salt or smoke-flavored salt
½ teaspoon freshly ground pepper
   Dash of Tabasco
1 teaspoon cumin seeds
1 egg or 2 egg whites

Have meat well trimmed of fat before grinding. Soak bread in water and squeeze out moisture. Combine meat and bread with remaining ingredients and toss lightly. Shape into 12 patties or sausage-shaped oblongs. To cook, barbecue over hot coals or broil about 3 or 4 inches from heat source until well browned. Or pan-fry, in a nonstick skillet, with no fat added. May be served with eggs, or topped with tomato sauce. *Six servings, 180 calories each.*

ITALIAN BEEFSTEAK SAUSAGE

2 **pounds fat-trimmed round steak, ground—twice, if possible**
1 **egg or 2 egg whites**
¼ **cup Chianti or any other dry red wine**
2 **teaspoons garlic salt**
1 **tablespoon instant onion**
1 **tablespoon fennel seeds**
1 **teaspoon crushed cayenne pepper; more, if desired**
1 **tablespoon oregano**
1 **teaspoon sage**
  Sausage casing (optional)

Combine meat, egg, wine, and seasonings. If you have a sausage-stuffing funnel and casing (sold in some supermarkets and butcher shops) stuff the mixture into the casing to form 2- or 3-inch links. Otherwise, shape the meat into uncased sausage-shaped oblongs, or into small, flat sausage cakes or patties.

Because this is uncured sausage, it should be cooked and served as soon as possible, or wrapped and frozen for later use. *Makes about forty small links or patties, about 35 calories each.*

VARIATION

Steak Sausage and Peppers: This dish uses half the above mixture for an Italian-style main course. Freeze the remainder. Or double this recipe to serve eight.

1 **pound Italian steak sausage (half the above recipe)**
  16-ounce can Italian plum tomatoes, broken up
  8-ounce can Spanish-style tomato sauce—no oil; check the label
1 **large Spanish onion, halved and then sliced**
2 **stalks celery, thinly sliced**
2 **green bell peppers, sliced**
1 **clove garlic, minced**
2 **teaspoons oregano or Italian seasoning**
  Crushed red pepper
  Salt and freshly ground pepper to taste

Combine all ingredients in a large nonstick frying pan or electric skillet. Cover and simmer 10 minutes. Uncover and continue to simmer until sauce is very thick. *Four servings, 235 calories each.*

Recycle Your BBQ Leftovers

What *do* you do with leftover hamburger?

If you're the backyard host or hostess with the mostest—leftovers—you're ready for our winning ways to recycle those weekend cookout gleanings into incredibly edible Monday-night dinners with a foreign flair. The makeovers that follow don't seem like leftovers. What's more, they're lean and low calorie!

RAGÙ ALLA BOLOGNESE (ITALIAN MEAT SAUCE) WITH LEFTOVER HAMBURGER

Remake your leftover hamburger into a sensational spaghetti dish with a savory Sauce Bolognese—Italian meat sauce. All the work of browning the meat is already done—so there's little fat left to clutter the sauce with unwanted calories. The smoky flavor is a bonus seasoning!

4 leftover broiled hamburgers (12 ounces, cooked), broken up
2 cloves garlic, minced, or ¼ teaspoon instant garlic
1 large onion, coarsely chopped
2 stalks celery, minced
1 carrot, coarsely shredded
  8-ounce can plain tomato sauce
  16-ounce can tomatoes, broken up
  10-ounce can fat-skimmed beef broth or onion soup
  Pinch of grated nutmeg (optional)
  Salt and freshly ground pepper to taste
  Oregano or Italian seasoning to taste
4 cups tender-cooked spaghetti (see page 245)

Combine all ingredients in a covered saucepan. Simmer 45 to 50 minutes. Uncover and continue to simmer until sauce is very thick. Serve over hot drained protein-enriched spaghetti. *Four servings, about 240 calories each with beef broth, about 265 calories with onion soup (plus 155 calories for each cup tender-cooked spaghetti.)*

"BARBECUED" CHILI CON CARNE

4 leftover barbecued burgers (from 1 pound lean ground round)
3 onions, chopped
1 green bell pepper, seeded and chopped

1 teaspoon garlic salt
1 teaspoon cumin
1 teaspoon chili powder
1 teaspoon oregano or Italian seasoning
1 cup canned stewed tomatoes
  8-ounce can plain tomato sauce
2 cups canned kidney beans, drained

Break up burgers into bite-size pieces. Combine with all remaining ingredients in an uncovered skillet. Simmer for 20 minutes or more, until onions are tender and chili is thick. Stir frequently. *Six servings, 225 calories each.*

8
CHICKEN
AND
GAME

Chicken is truly an international bird—a favorite main course in just about every country's cuisine. That's good news for both calorie counters and cholesterol watchers, because a chicken—especially the young, lean frying chicken —is one of the slimmest, most heart-smart choices you can make. The simple addition of spices and seasonings adds relatively little in the way of calories, yet provides a passport to a variety of new "ethnic" identities.

Hints For Low-Cal Chicken Cookery

• *Save calories!* Many of the recipes that follow use the Slim Gourmet technique for browning, sautéing, and frying chicken. You brown the chicken in its own melted fat with no oil added. Since the melted chicken fat is drained off and discarded, you actually cut calories instead of adding them. Although chicken is one of the least fattening main courses there is, you'll be surprised to see how much fat (and how many calories) you can drain off this way— sometimes ¼ cup or more. Each ¼ cup of chicken fat you remove represents a savings of about 400 calories.

• Save more calories with my "cake-pan cookery" method for baking chicken on a bed of vegetables. The important thing is to use a shallow pan just barely large enough to crowd the chicken pieces in a single layer. An ordinary 9-inch layer-cake pan is just about right for the average cut-up frying chicken.

The vegetables, seasonings, and wine simmer gently underneath, completely covered by the chicken pieces. Meanwhile, the chicken bakes to a golden crispness. At serving time, you simply spoon the vegetable mixture over the crisp chicken for a deliciously easy dish.

After trying the technique out in the recipes that occur throughout this chapter, use it to create your own favorite combinations of vegetables and seasonings.

BASIC BASTED CHICKEN

Here's the basic Slim Gourmet way to bake a cut-up chicken, and to add foreign flavor with easy variations. You could have chicken every night for two weeks and never have the same dish twice!

2 pounds cut-up frying chicken
Salt and freshly ground pepper to taste
1 onion, chopped
1 cup fat-skimmed chicken broth (homemade or canned)

Wash and dry chicken. Trim off fringe fat, if any. Arrange the chicken pieces skin side up in a shallow ovenproof nonstick pan. Bake in a preheated 450-degree oven 20 to 25 minutes, until the skin is crisp and well rendered of fat. Drain and discard fat.

Add remaining ingredients to pan. Lower heat to 350 degrees. Continue baking, basting occasionally, until chicken is tender (about 30 minutes). Spoon pan juice over chicken to serve. *Four servings, 205 calories each.*

VARIATIONS

African Chicken: Replace part of the chicken broth with 2 tablespoons lemon juice. Season the chicken with 1/8 teaspoon turmeric. Add a bay leaf and a minced clove of garlic to the pan. *About 205 calories per serving.*

Chinese Chicken: Replace part of the broth with 1/4 cup sherry and 2 tablespoons soy sauce. Season the chicken with garlic powder, monosodium glutamate (if desired), and 1/8 teaspoon ground ginger. *About 210 calories per serving.*

Cuban Chicken: Replace part of the liquid with 1/4 cup rum. Sprinkle the chicken with garlic salt and paprika. Add a bay leaf and a pinch of saffron. *About 210 calories per serving.*

Czechoslovakian Chicken: Replace part of the liquid with 1/2 cup tomato juice and 2 tablespoons dry white wine. Season chicken with garlic salt, paprika, a generous pinch of coriander seeds. *About 210 calories per serving.*

French Chicken: Replace part of the liquid with ¼ cup dry white wine. Season chicken with a pinch of grated nutmeg and a dash of poultry seasoning. After browning the chicken put 2 carrots and ½ cup sliced mushrooms under the chicken in the pan, if desired. *About 220 calories per serving with carrots and mushrooms.*

German Chicken: Replace part of the liquid with ½ cup "light" beer. Season chicken with garlic salt. Add a bay leaf and ½ teaspoon caraway seeds to the pot. *About 215 calories per serving.*

Greek Chicken: Replace the broth with ¾ cup tomato juice and 2 tablespoons lemon juice. Season with bay leaf, oregano, garlic salt, cinnamon, and nutmeg. *About 215 calories per serving.*

Hungarian Chicken: Reduce broth to ½ cup. Season chicken liberally with paprika, garlic salt, and dill weed. Just before serving, combine ½ cup plain low-fat yogurt with 1 tablespoon all-purpose flour. Add to pan juices and heat until bubbling. Serve over chicken. *About 225 calories per serving.*

Indian Chicken: Replace half of the liquid with ½ cup orange or pineapple juice. Sprinkle chicken lightly with curry powder, ground cinnamon, and garlic salt. Add 2 tablespoons raisins to the pan. *Under 235 calories per serving.*

Italian Chicken: Replace broth with 1 cup tomato juice, 2 tablespoons dry white wine. Add 1 diced seeded green pepper. Season with oregano, basil, garlic salt. Just before serving, sprinkle with 2 tablespoons shreddred extra-sharp Romano cheese. *About 230 calories per serving.*

Mexican Chicken: Follow preceding Italian chicken directions but add a pinch of chili powder and some cumin seeds. Use shredded Cheddar instead of Romano. *About 235 calories per serving.*

Spanish Chicken: Follow Italian Chicken directions but substitute ¼ cup orange juice for the wine. Add bay leaf instead of basil. Add 3 or 4 sliced stuffed green Spanish olives. Omit cheese. *Under 235 calories per serving.*

South Seas Chicken: Substitute ½ cup pineapple juice and 2 tablespoons soy sauce for part of the liquid. Season chicken with garlic salt and ginger. After browning the chicken, add 1 diced green pepper and ½ cup diced pineapple to the pan, under the chicken. *Under 240 calories per serving.*

The Ever-Versatile Frying Chicken

With rich ingredients and fattening cooking techniques, the calorie-foolish cook can multiply chicken's calorie count many times over.

Here you will make use of the special Slim Gourmet browning techniques to cook the following international variations on everyone's favorite frying chicken. In standard (fattening) recipes, the chicken would be browned in a skilletful of fat; here we subtract calories instead of adding them.

TÍA JUANA CHICKEN

3 pounds cut-up frying chicken
2 teaspoons garlic salt
½ teaspoon freshly ground pepper
½ teaspoon oregano
¼ teaspoon cumin
   Pinch or more of cayenne pepper
1 cup chopped onion
1 green bell pepper, seeded and chopped
2 chicken bouillon cubes
1 cup water
2 cups canned tomatoes
   8-ounce can sliced mushrooms, including liquid

Sprinkle chicken liberally with seasonings. Spread chicken pieces skin side up on a nonstick cookie sheet or shallow roasting pan. Bake in a preheated 450-degree oven for 15 minutes, until the skin is golden brown and inner fat is melted. Discard melted fat.

Combine browned chicken pieces with remaining ingredients in an oven-proof casserole dish. Lower oven heat to 350 degrees. Cover and bake until chicken is tender, about 30 to 40 minutes. Uncover and continue baking until most of the liquid has evaporated. *Six servings, 245 calories each.*

ARROZ CON POLLO

2½ pounds cut-up frying chicken
2 tablespoons water or olive-jar liquid
12 sliced pimiento-stuffed green Spanish olives
4 ounces lean cooked ham or Canadian bacon, cubed
2 teaspoons paprika
1 cup chopped onion
2 cloves garlic, minced
   16-ounce can peeled tomatoes, chopped
   10-ounce can fat-skimmed chicken broth
1 cup water
1 ½ cups raw rice
   Pinch of saffron
   10-ounce package frozen peas
2 tablespoons chopped fresh parsley
   Salt and freshly ground pepper to taste

Use a large nonstick skillet or chicken fryer. Place the chicken pieces skin side down. Add 2 tablespoons water or liquid from olive jar. Cover and heat slowly over moderate flame until the liquid evaporates and the chicken begins to brown in its own melted inner fat.

Uncover and continue to cook, turning once, until chicken is nicely browned on both sides. Remove chicken pieces to absorbent paper. Add the cubed ham and brown lightly with no fat added. Remove and set aside. Drain any fat from the pan.

Return the chicken to the pan skin side up. Sprinkle with paprika. Add the onion, garlic, tomatoes, chicken broth, water, rice, and saffron. Cover tightly and simmer 15 minutes. Add the peas. Cover and continue to cook until all the liquid is absorbed and rice is tender (another 10 or 15 minutes). Stir in parsley and browned ham cubes at the last minute. Season to taste. *Eight servings, 340 calories each.*

PEPPY POLYNESIAN CHICKEN

Salad making is only one way bottled diet dressings can help you to be creative in your Slim Gourmet kitchen. The low-calorie dressings can also add saucy tang to hot vegetables, barbecue bastes, casseroles, and all sorts of main courses. Here's an easy poultry dish made the low-calorie way, with bottled diet dressing as one of the ingredients.

2¼ **pounds cut-up frying chicken**
 ½ **cup juice-packed crushed pineapple**
 2 **tablespoons soy sauce**
 3 **tablespoons low-calorie Thousand Island salad dressing**

Brown chicken pieces skin side up in a 400-degree oven or under the broiler, to melt fat from skin. Arrange the browned chicken skin side up in a baking dish. Combine remaining ingredients and spoon over chicken.

Bake uncovered at 350 degrees until tender, about 25 minutes, basting occasionally with the sauce. *Six servings, 165 calories each.*

FRENCH PROVINCIAL CHICKEN

 ¼ **cup all-purpose flour**
1½ **teaspoons salt**
 ¼ **teaspoon freshly ground pepper**
 3 **pounds cut-up frying chicken**
 2 **cups water**
 1 **cup dry red wine**

½ teaspoon sage
2 bay leaves
Pinch of thyme
1 cup tomato juice

Combine flour, salt, and pepper in a large heavy paper grocery bag. Add all the chicken pieces, close, and shake up until chicken is lightly coated.

Place chicken pieces skin side down on a nonstick cookie sheet. Bake in a preheated 450-degree oven 15 minutes, turning once. Discard melted fat.

Put browned chicken skin side up in an ovenproof casserole and add remaining ingredients except tomato juice. Cover and bake at 350 degrees for 30 minutes. Uncover, add tomato juice, and continue baking until liquid evaporates to leave a thick sauce. *Six servings, 225 calories each.*

ATHENIAN CHICKEN AND ZUCCHINI

2 pounds cut-up frying chicken
¾ cup tomato juice (6-ounce can)
1½ tablespoons lemon juice
¾ cup water
½ teaspoon nutmeg
½ teaspoon cinnamon
2 cloves garlic, minced, or ¼ teaspoon instant garlic
1 teaspoon oregano or Italian seasoning
3 small onions, quartered
1 medium zucchini, sliced
½ cup low-fat yogurt
1 tablespoon all-purpose flour
¼ cup minced fresh parsley

Spray a large nonstick skillet or electric frying pan with cooking spray for no-fat frying. Add the chicken pieces skin side down. Cover and cook 3 minutes. Uncover and continue cooking until chicken skin is brown, crisp, and well rendered of fat. Drain and discard fat. Turn chicken skin side up. Pour on tomato juice, lemon juice, and water. Sprinkle chicken with spices, garlic, and oregano. Cover and simmer 30 minutes or more, until nearly tender.

Uncover skillet. Add onions and zucchini, putting them under the chicken. Continue to cook, uncovered, 6 to 8 minutes, allowing the liquid to reduce. Stir yogurt and flour together and stir into the simmering liquid. Gently heat and stir until gravy simmers and thickens. Sprinkle with parsley. *Four servings, under 270 calories each.*

SOUR-CREAMY CHICKEN STROGANOFF

2 pounds cut-up frying chicken
6-ounce can (¾ cup) tomato juice
⅓ cup dry sherry
2 teaspoons prepared mustard
Salt, or butter-flavored salt, and freshly ground pepper
1 medium onion, thinly sliced
¼ pound fresh mushrooms, sliced, or 4-ounce can mushrooms, drained
½ cup plain low-fat yogurt
2 tablespoons all-purpose flour
2 tablespoons minced fresh parsley (optional)

Brown chicken pieces skin side down in nonstick skillet as directed in preceding recipe. Turn chicken and add tomato juice, sherry, mustard, salt, and pepper. Cover and simmer till tender, about 30 minutes.

Add onions and mushrooms, placing under chicken. Simmer uncovered 6 to 8 minutes. Combine yogurt and flour; mix well and stir into the pot. Cook and stir until sauce simmers and thickens. Sprinkle with parsley and serve. *Four servings, 255 calories each.*

VARIATION

Hungarian Chicken and Mushrooms: Follow preceding recipe but omit sherry; substitute 1 tablespoon lemon juice and ¼ cup water for the sherry. Omit mustard. After browning chicken pieces, turn them skin side up and sprinkle with 1 tablespoon paprika. *Four servings, under 240 calories each.*

ITALIAN GARLIC CHICKEN

With long cooking, garlic loses a lot of its punch and pungency. It still adds plenty of flavor—similar to, yet different from, the sharp flavor of raw garlic in salad or salad dressing. Many hearty European dishes are heavy on garlic —until they're translated for American cooks.

1½ pounds cut-up young frying chicken
1 cup plus 1 tablespoon water
Salt and freshly ground pepper
6 cloves garlic
½ cup chopped fresh parsley

Put the chicken pieces skin side down in a nonstick skillet or electric frying pan. Add the 1 tablespoon water. Heat slowly, until water evaporates and chicken begins to brown in its own melted fat. When chicken is well browned, drain off fat and place the pieces skin side up. Season to taste with salt and pepper.

Chop or mince the garlic well and add to the skillet along with the 1 cup water and parsley. Cover closely and simmer over very low heat, basting occasionally with the liquid in the pan (add a little water if needed). Cook until tender, about 40 minutes or more. Uncover and continue cooking until the sauce is somewhat thickened. Skim off fat. Spoon over the chicken. *Four servings, about 160 calories each.*

SMOTHERED CHICKEN BASQUE STYLE

¼ **pound Canadian bacon, cubed**
 2 **pounds cut-up frying chicken**
 2 **tablespoons water**
 4 **onions, sliced**
 2 **green bell peppers, seeded and sliced**
 3 **cups canned tomatoes**
 4 **cloves garlic, minced**
 1 **bay leaf**
½ **teaspoon thyme or poultry seasoning**
    Salt or butter-flavored salt
    Freshly ground pepper

Spray the inside of a large covered chicken fryer with cooking spray for no-fat frying. Add the cubed Canadian bacon and cook over moderate heat, stirring frequently, until browned on all sides. Remove bacon from fryer and set aside.

Put the chicken pieces in the fryer skin side down. Add 2 tablespoons water. Cook over low heat until liquid evaporates and chicken browns in its own melted inner fat. Cook until well browned. Drain off all melted fat.

Turn chicken skin side up. Cover with onions, peppers, and tomatoes. Sprinkle with garlic and seasonings. Cover and cook over very low heat until tender, 40 minutes or more. Uncover and continue to cook until most of the liquid has evaporated. Adjust seasoning, remove bay leaf. Stir in browned bacon cubes at the last minute. *Four servings, 310 calories each.*

SKILLET CHICKEN TERIYAKI

 2 **pounds cut-up frying chicken**
 5 **tablespoons soy sauce**
½ **cup unsweetened pineapple, apple, or white grape juice**
 1 **clove garlic, minced, or ⅛ teaspoon instant garlic**
¼ **teaspoon ground ginger**

Spray a large nonstick skillet, electric frying pan or chicken fryer with cooking spray for no-fat frying. Put the chicken pieces in the skillet, skin side down. Sprinkle with 1 tablespoon soy sauce. Cover and cook over moderate heat for 1 minute. Uncover and continue to cook until liquid evaporates and chicken pieces begin to cook in their own drawn-out fat. Cook about 10 to 15 minutes, stirring to prevent sticking, until chicken is well browned. Drain off and discard all fat from the skillet. Turn chicken skin side up. Add remaining ingredients, cover, and simmer until tender, about 40 minutes. Uncover and continue to cook until pan juices simmer down to a thick tasty glaze. *Four servings, about 215 calories each.*

VARIATION

For delicious variations, substitute apple, white grape, orange, apricot, or any other natural unsweetened fruit juice.

ORANGE CURRIED CHICKEN

2 pounds cut-up frying chicken
1½ cups orange juice
2 tablespoons soy sauce
1 level teaspoon curry powder
1 clove garlic, minced, or ⅛ teaspoon instant garlic
1 teaspoon monosodium glutamate (optional)
2 large onions, cut in chunks
2 green bell peppers, seeded and cut in squares

Trim fringe fat, if any, from chicken. Brown chicken by placing pieces skin side up on a tray under the broiler until crisp and well rendered of fat. (Or spray a large nonstick skillet or chicken fryer with cooking spray and put the chicken skin side down over low heat. Gradually raise heat to high and continue cooking until skin is golden and well rendered of fat.) Drain off and discard fat.

Put the browned chicken pieces skin side up in a chicken fryer or large skillet. Combine juice, soy sauce, curry powder, garlic, and monosodium glutamate. Pour over chicken. Cover and simmer over low heat until nearly tender, about 30 to 40 minutes. Uncover and skim fat from liquid with bulb-type baster.

Add onion and green pepper. Cover and cook 2 minutes. Uncover and continue cooking until most of the liquid is evaporated and chicken is well coated with a thick sauce. Onion and pepper should be crisp. *Four servings, 265 calories each.*

ISRAELI ORANGE CHICKEN

Two of the main ingredients on Israeli menus.

3 pounds cut-up frying chicken
¼ cup lemon juice
½ cup orange juice
1 teaspoon grated lemon or orange peel
¼ teaspoon tarragon
¼ teaspoon thyme
   salt and freshly ground pepper to taste
1 teaspoon garlic powder
2 teaspoons paprika

Trim off fringe fat, if any, from chicken. Place chicken in a single layer skin side up in a shallow roasting pan. Bake in a very hot (450-degree) oven 20 to 25 minutes, until skin is crisp and well rendered of fat. Pour off and discard fat. Combine citrus juices, peel, tarragon, and thyme, and pour over chicken. Sprinkle with salt and pepper to taste, garlic powder, and paprika. Lower oven temperature to 325 degrees. Bake, basting occasionally, until chicken is tender, about 20 to 30 minutes more. Spoon sauce over chicken to serve. *Six servings, about 200 calories each.*

EASY POULET PROVENÇALE

1½ pounds cut-up frying chicken
1 carrot, very thinly sliced
1 cup sliced fresh mushrooms
1 onion, thinly sliced
2 tablespoons minced fresh parsley
   Small bay leaf
   Pinch of thyme
   Salt and freshly ground pepper
¼ cup sherry

Trim off chicken fat, if any. Arrange the chicken pieces skin side up in a round 9-inch nonstick layer-cake pan. Do not season. Bake uncovered in a hot (425-degree) oven for 20 to 25 minutes, until the skin is crisp and well rendered of fat. Meanwhile, prepare vegetables.

Remove the pan from the oven, pour the drippings into a cup, and set aside. Remove the chicken pieces with tongs. Arrange the vegetables and seasonings on the bottom of the cake pan. Cover them with the chicken pieces, skin side up.

Skim the chicken fat from the reserved drippings; discard fat. Combine the sherry and defatted drippings, and pour over the chicken. Lower the oven temperature to 350 and return the cake pan to the oven. Bake, uncovered, an additional 30 minutes, basting the chicken occasionally with the pan juices. Serve the chicken pieces smothered with vegetables. *Four servings, 165 calories each.*

"Cake-Pan" Chicken Cacciatore

1½ pounds cut-up frying chicken
  1 onion, thinly sliced
  1 stalk celery, very thinly sliced
  1 green bell pepper, seeded and chopped
  1 cup canned tomatoes, broken up
 ¼ cup dry white wine
 ½ teaspoon oregano or Italian seasoning
 ¼ teaspoon basil
   Salt and freshly ground pepper

The procedure for this recipe is essentially the same as for the preceding recipe; only the vegetables and seasonings are changed. *Four servings, 170 calories each.*

QUICKIE COQ AU VIN

1½ pounds cut-up frying chicken
  4 ounces Canadian bacon
 ⅓ cup dry red wine
 ⅓ cup tomato juice
 ⅓ cup water
   Small bay leaf
   Pinch of poultry seasoning
   Salt and freshly ground pepper
   Fresh parsley (optional)
   8-ounce can small onions, drained

Before cooking, trim fringe fat from chicken. Dice the Canadian bacon into ½-inch cubes.

Brown the bacon cubes quickly over high heat in a large nonstick skillet, chicken fryer, or electric frying pan that's equipped with a lid. Remove bacon and set aside.

Place the chicken pieces skin side down in the skillet, with no fat added. Cook slowly over moderate heat until the chicken has browned and crisped in its own melted inner fat. Drain and discard melted fat. Blot the chicken pieces dry.

Arrange the chicken skin side up in the same skillet along with all other ingredients except onions. Cover and simmer over low heat until chicken is tender, about 40 to 50 minutes.

Uncover and skim fat from liquid with a bulb-type baster (or pour the liquid into a tall glass and allow fat to rise to surface, then skim off fat; return the liquid to the skillet). Add the onions. Cook uncovered, until onions are heated through and the remaining liquid has evaporated to a thick sauce. *Four servings, 225 calories each.*

PARTY PAELLA

 2 **pounds cut-up frying chicken**
    Water
 3 **carrots, peeled and cut into 3-inch lengths**
 3 **onions, quartered**
 2 **stalks celery, in 3-inch lengths**
 1 **green bell pepper, seeded and sliced**
    10½-ounce can fat-skimmed chicken broth
⅔ **cup raw rice**
 2 **cloves garlic, minced, or ¼ teaspoon instant garlic**
 8 **green stuffed olives, sliced**
 1 **teaspoon oregano or Italian seasoning**
¼ **teaspoon saffron**
    10-ounce package frozen artichoke hearts, defrosted
¾ **pound raw shrimp, shelled and deveined**
 1 **dozen small clams in shells**

Spray a large nonstick skillet or electric frying pan with cooking spray for no-fat frying. Add chicken pieces, skin side down. Add water. Cook, uncovered, until liquid evaporates and chicken browns in its own fat. When skin is crisp and well rendered of fat, drain and discard fat. Stirring in the flour, add remaining ingredients except artichoke hearts, shrimp, and clams. Cover and simmer 30 to 40 minutes, until chicken is tender. Add artichoke hearts, shrimp, and clams. Cover and simmer 15 minutes more, or until clams open. *Ten servings, 225 calories each.*

CHICKEN TEQUILA SUNRISE

If you like the taste of Mexico, but not the temperature, you must try this Slim Gourmet chicken dish, spicy but not hot. This easy oven-baked dish has all the spices and seasonings we tender-tongued Yanquis love, without the palate-scorching peppers. Without the excess calories, too. This recipe is strictly low fat, but so flavorful that you'd never think to call it "diet." Incidentally, the alcohol in the tequila evaporates, along with the calories. Bravo!

2 **pounds cut-up frying chicken**
2 **onions, thinly sliced**
¾ **cup orange juice**
¼ **cup tequila**
1 **clove garlic, minced, or pinch of instant garlic**
2 **teaspoons dried oregano or Italian seasoning**
1 **teaspoon cumin seeds or ¼ teaspoon cumin powder**
  Salt and coarsely ground pepper

Spray a shallow nonstick baking pan with cooking spray for no-fat cooking. Put the chicken pieces skin side up, unseasoned, in it. Place pan in a preheated 425-degree (hot) oven for 25 minutes, to crisp the skin and melt the fat. Remove from oven and pour off all the fat.

Put the onion slices under the chicken. Combine remaining ingredients and pour over the chicken. Return to the oven for an additional 20 minutes or more, until chicken is tender and crisp and liquid is reduced to a thick glaze. Baste frequently with pan liquid, adding a tablespoon of water if the liquid evaporates too much. *Four servings, 235 calories each.*

Low-Cal Chicken Tricks with Your Crock Cooker

Crock cookery is very convenient but . . .

Differing from methods like baking or broiling, the crock doesn't allow melted fat (and calories) to escape. The fat remains trapped in the cooking liquid, which is eventually served as a sauce. Roast chicken or one that's broiled is naturally less fattening.

One more problem—particularly with chicken—is that the low heat doesn't permit the chicken to brown. The pale color is unappetizing to many people. Some slow-cooker recipes solve the browning problem by directing you to fry the chicken first in some fat. But this only adds calories.

If you're a calorie watcher and a crockery-cooker fan, you'll want to adapt those slow-cooker recipes by following these Slim Gourmet techniques.

1. Choose low-cal broilers or fryers rather than roasting or stewing chickens (less fat and calories); trim off as much fringe fat as possible.

2. Place the chicken pieces skin side up on a broiler tray or a sheet of heavy-duty aluminum foil. Brown under the broiler until the skin is golden crisp and well rendered of fat. Blot the chicken with paper toweling, and discard the melted fat.

3. Put the chicken into the pot and add remaining ingredients except the thickener. Cover and cook on the slow setting (190–200 degrees) for 8 hours or at 300 degrees for 4 hours.

4. Remove the chicken pieces to a heated platter and keep warm. With a bulb-type baster, skim fat from the surface of the liquid in the pot.

5. Turn heat to high. Combine thickening ingredients and stir into liquid. Cook until sauce is gravy thick. Serve over chicken.

POTTED CHICKEN CHAMPAGNE

2 **pounds cut-up frying chicken**
½ **cup water**
⅓ **cup champagne (can be flat)**
2 **chicken bouillon cubes**
1 **teaspoon freshly ground pepper**
1 **teaspoon basil**
1 **tablespoon minced fresh parsley**
4 **stalks celery, in 2-inch pieces**
8 **carrots, peeled and cut in 2-inch pieces**
¼ **cup cold water**
1 **tablespoon arrowroot**
1 **tablespoon all-purpose flour**

Follow directions given on page 132. *Four servings, 250 calories each.*

ALL-DAY COQ AU VIN

2 **pounds cut-up frying chicken**
1 **cup dry red wine**
3 **tablespoons brandy**
  10-ounce can fat-skimmed chicken broth
2 **tablespoons chopped fresh parsley**
  Pinch of ground cloves
1 **teaspoon thyme**
2 **cloves garlic, minced, or 1 teaspoon instant garlic**
1 **cup small white onions (fresh, defrosted, or canned)**
½ **pound mushrooms, sliced**
2 **tablespoons arrowroot or cornstarch**
¼ **cup cold water**

Follow directions given on page 132. *Four servings, 245 calories each.*

Try Chicken Drumsticks These New Low-Calorie Ways

Calorie-conscious chicken lovers are frequently told that dark meat is fattening. Fattening compared to what? The edible portion of chicken drumsticks contains only 115 calories (per 100 grams or 3½ ounces), compared with 250 to 400 calories for a similar quantity of hamburger or steak.

The same quantity of chicken breast is 110 calories! So, while white meat is less fattening, there's no reason for dark-meat lovers to avoid chicken drumsticks.

Here are some deliciously different ways to prepare them, all calorie wise.

"FRENCH-FRIED" CHICKEN LEGS WITH LEMON AND TARRAGON

An easy epicurean treat that's just as good served cold.

8 broiler-fryer drumsticks
1 cup lemon juice
1 cup unseasoned breadcrumbs, either Toasted High-Fiber Breadcrumbs (page 302) or commercial
4 teaspoons dried tarragon
1 teaspoon salt
1 teaspoon monosodium glutamate (optional)
¼ teaspoon freshly ground pepper

Roll the chicken legs in lemon juice, then roll lightly in breadcrumbs seasoned with tarragon, salt, monosodium glutamate, and pepper, making sure that not more than 1 tablespoon of the mixture adheres to each leg. (If you have time, allow the chicken legs to marinate 30 minutes in the lemon juice before coating them with the crumb mixture.)

Spray a shallow nonstick baking pan or cookie tin with spray for no-fat frying. Arrange the legs in a single layer. Bake in a preheated hot (450-degree) oven for 35–40 minutes, turning once, until legs are brown and crisp. *Four servings, 115 calories each.*

POLYNESIAN CHICKEN LEGS

A great entertainer, perfect for a buffet table. So flavorful nobody will guess it's low cal!

16 broiler-fryer drumsticks
6-ounce can frozen unsweetened pineapple juice, defrosted but undiluted
1 teaspoon Tabasco
2 tablespoons soy sauce
¼ cup grated white coconut

Arrange the drumsticks in a single layer in a shallow roasting pan. Bake in a very hot (450-degree) oven 15 minutes, turning once. Remove from the oven and drain off all melted fat. Combine undiluted pineapple juice, hot sauce, and soy sauce, and pour over the chicken.

Lower the oven heat to 325 degrees and bake 50 minutes, basting occasionally. Sprinkle with coconut and bake only until coconut is brown. *Eight servings, 170 calories each.*

TERIYAKI CHICKEN LEGS

12 broiler-fryer drumsticks
½ cup lemon juice
¼ cup dry white wine
¼ cup soy sauce
¼ teaspoon ground ginger
1 teaspoon garlic salt
1 teaspoon monosodium glutamate (optional)

Marinate drumsticks in a baste made of the remaining ingredients. Allow 1 hour at room temperature, or all day covered in the refrigerator.

Drain the drumsticks and reserve the marinade. Broil 3 to 4 inches from source of heat, over hot coals or under your broiler, basting frequently with the reserved marinade. Turn frequently. Chicken will be cooked in about 30 minutes. If you wish, simmer remaining marinade 1 minute and serve as a sauce. *Six servings, 115 calories each.*

ORIENTAL PLUM-GLAZED CHICKEN LEGS

Oriental in inspiration, this is a delicious way to serve chicken legs. The plums and other ingredients combine in a self-making sauce that glazes the chicken with delightful but nonfattening flavor. It's the kind of dish that will have your guests guessing; the ingredients are so subtly balanced that no one flavor predominates. Better yet, it's easy!

The plums should be quite ripe and soft—not hard and sour—and should be sliced thin but unpeeled. The peel adds flavor and a rich dark color to the glaze—but not a purple color; the peel "disappears" in cooking, melding into a thick sauce. Coriander seeds—available on supermarket spice shelves—add a pleasant bit of bite and texture.

[continued]

1½ pounds broiler-fryer drumsticks
3 large ripe purple plums
2 teaspoons vinegar
¼ cup dry sherry
¼ cup soy sauce
1 cup water
1 teaspoon coriander seeds
2 onions, finely chopped
1 small clove garlic, minced
2 teaspoons honey
Generous dash of Tabasco (optional)

Spray a large nonstick skillet or electric frying pan with cooking spray for no-fat frying. Put the drumsticks skin side down. Cover the skillet and raise the heat to high. Cook, covered, 7 to 10 minutes, until well rendered of fat. Remove the cover and drain off accumulated fat. Cook uncovered until skin is crisp and brown. Drain well. Turn the legs skin side up.

Meanwhile, slice the plums in half and remove the pits. Slice plums thin but do not peel. Put the plum slices in the skillet with all remaining ingredients. Lower the heat, cover, and simmer about 30 to 40 minutes.

Uncover and continue to simmer, stirring occasionally, until sauce is thick and chicken is well glazed. *Four servings, about 240 calories each.*

PHILIPPINE CHICKEN LEGS

2 pounds broiler-fryer drumsticks
5 tablespoons soy sauce
5 tablespoons wine vinegar
¼ teaspoon garlic powder

Broil drumsticks, turning as necessary, until crisp and fat is melted. Combine browned chicken legs with remaining ingredients in a shallow baking dish. Cover with foil and bake at 350 degrees for 40 minutes or until tender. Uncover and continue baking until sauce is somewhat reduced. *Six servings, 150 calories each.*

MANDARIN GLAZED CHICKEN LEGS

1½ pounds broiler-fryer drumsticks
1½ cups orange juice
¼ cup soy sauce
2 tablespoons minced fresh parsley
½ teaspoon liquid-smoke seasoning (optional)
½ teaspoon monosodium glutamate (optional)

Arrange drumsticks in a single layer in a nonstick baking dish. Bake uncovered in a hot (450-degree) oven 20 minutes or until crisp and brown. Pour off melted fat.

Combine remaining ingredients and pour over chicken. Bake uncovered at 350 degrees, basting occasionally, until sauce is thick and chicken is tender, about 25 minutes. *Four servings, 210 calories each.*

Chicken Thighs, Moist and Meaty

One of the most versatile choices of chicken parts is the moist and meaty chicken thigh. Its size makes it the perfect finger food. Moreover, the thigh has only one solid bone in the middle, so thighs are ideal for chicken dishes cooked in any type of sauce.

Here are some of my favorite ways to cook chicken thighs.

JAPANESE OVEN CHICKEN

Less fattening than fried.

```
2 pounds chicken thighs
1 egg
¼ cup Japanese-style soy sauce
6 tablespoons unseasoned breadcrumbs, either Toasted High-Fiber Bread-
    crumbs (page 302) or commercial
1 teaspoon monosodium glutamate (optional)
```

Stir egg and soy sauce in a small bowl. Shake bread crumbs and monosodium glutamate together in a brown paper bag.

Dip the chicken first in the soy mixture, put a few thighs at a time in the bag with the crumb mixture, and shake to coat thighs.

Arrange skin side up in a shallow nonstick baking pan. Bake without turning in a preheated 350-degree oven for 50 minutes or until brown and crisp. *Six servings, 185 calories each.*

SWEET 'N' SOUR PARTY CHICKEN

```
3 pounds chicken thighs
  Monosodium glutamate (optional)
  6-ounce can frozen apple-juice concentrate, defrosted
½ teaspoon ground ginger
¼ teaspoon freshly ground pepper
4 tablespoons lemon juice
5 tablespoons soy sauce
  Lemon slices (optional)
  Unpeeled apple wedges (optional)
```

Sprinkle the chicken thighs with MSG and bake in a preheated hot (425-degree) oven for 20 minutes, turning once, to brown the chicken and melt the fat from the skin.

Drain off and discard all melted fat. Combine remaining ingredients except lemons and apples, pour over chicken, and bake an additional 30 minutes, turning frequently, until well glazed. Add water, if needed. Garnish with lemon slices and unpeeled apple wedges, if desired. *Nine main-dish servings, 190 calories each.*

SORRENTO "FRIED" CHICKEN AND PEPPERS

2 pounds chicken thighs
2 cups tomato juice
2 cups sliced onion
2 cups sliced Italian frying peppers
1 clove garlic, minced (optional)
Salt and freshly ground pepper
Cayenne pepper (optional)
1 teaspoon oregano or Italian seasoning

Put the chicken thighs skin side down in a nonstick skillet over moderate heat. Heat slowly, until melted fat escapes and chicken begins to brown in its own fat. Turn frequently, until skin is crisp and brown and well rendered of fat. Remove chicken and blot carefully. Wipe melted fat from skillet.

Return the chicken to the skillet with the tomato juice. Cover and simmer 20 minutes. Uncover and add remaining ingredients. Cook uncovered, stirring frequently, until chicken is tender and sauce is reduced (about 25 minutes). *Six servings, 185 calories each.*

CHICKEN THIGHS ADOBO

4 chicken thighs
1 small green bell pepper, seeded and diced
1 medium onion, peeled and sliced
8-ounce can stewed tomatoes
¼ cup orange juice
2 teaspoons vinegar
½ teaspoon adobo seasoning (or a pinch each of garlic powder, oregano, and powdered cumin)

Spray a nonstick 8-inch cake pan with cooking spray for no-fat baking. Place chicken thighs in pan, skin side up. Bake in a preheated hot (450-degree) oven 20 minutes. Pour off fat.

Combine remaining ingredients and spoon over chicken. Bake an additional 20 minutes or more, basting frequently, until chicken is done and sauce is thick. *Two servings, about 280 calories.*

CHICKEN-NOODLE PAPRIKASH

```
 2  pounds chicken thighs
 1  cup plus 1 tablespoon water
 1  onion, sliced
 1  small bay leaf
 1  teaspoon caraway seeds
 2  teaspoons paprika
1½  teaspoons chopped fresh parsley
    10-ounce can fat-skimmed chicken consommé
1½  cups dry curly egg noodles
 ½  cup plain low-fat yogurt
 2  teaspoons arrowroot or cornstarch
    Additional paprika
```

Put the chicken thighs into a nonstick chicken fryer or heavy skillet in a single layer. Add the 1 tablespoon water and heat slowly over moderate flame until water evaporates and chicken pieces begin to brown in their own melted fat. Brown on all sides. Add the 1 cup water, heat to boiling, then drain off. When fat has risen to the surface, skim off fat with a bulb-type baster. Then return the liquid to the pot.

Add the onion, bay leaf, caraway seeds, paprika, parsley and consommé. Cover and simmer over very low heat 20 minutes. Add the noodles and continue to simmer until tender (see page 245). Combine yogurt and arrowroot. At last minute add to sauce. Cook and stir until thickened. Sprinkle with additional paprika. *Six servings, 235 calories each.*

SWEET 'N' SOUR CHICKEN WITH PINEAPPLE

Generally speaking, would-be skinnies should run the other way when they see the words "sweet and sour" on a recipe or menu. The "sour" won't hurt you, but the "sweet" is achieved with pure calories—lots of fattening, nutritionally-neutered sugar.

Here's a Slim Gourmet sweet and sour dish that leans to the lean side. Inspired by Polynesian cuisine, this easy dish is not only low-cal but nutritious and heart-smart as well. The sweet and sour accents are provided by vinegar and the natural sweetness of unsugared pineapple, plus a small amount of honey.

Take note of the special Slim Gourmet technique for "frying" the chicken in the oven with no fat added.

2 pounds chicken thighs or cut-up frying chicken
¼ cup cornstarch or arrowroot
1 teaspoon monosodium glutamate (optional)
   16-ounce can juice-packed pineapple chunks, including juice
1 tablespoon honey
¼ cup soy sauce
3 tablespoons vinegar
2 red or green bell peppers, or 1 of each
3 scallions or green onions, thinly sliced

Shake the chicken, cornstarch, and monosodium glutamate in a brown paper bag. Shake off the excess and put the chicken pieces skin side down in a shallow nonstick roasting pan which has been sprayed with cooking spray for no-fat frying. Put the pan into a preheated hot (450-degree) oven for 20 minutes.

After 10 minutes, turn the chicken pieces. When the chicken is crisp and golden and well rendered of fat, drain off and discard all the fat from the pan (there can be ½ cup or more—800 calories worth!). Blot the chicken pieces and return them to the pan, skin side up. Lower the heat to 325 degrees. Add the pineapple chunks. Combine the pineapple juice, honey, soy sauce, and vinegar, and add to the pan. Bake for 20 minutes, uncovered.

Seed the peppers and cut into 1-inch squares. Add to the pan. Bake another 8 to 10 minutes uncovered, stirring occasionally. Meanwhile, slice the scallions thin. Add to the pan at the last minute, and return to the oven only a minute or two until scallions are heated but not wilted.

Remove from the oven when most of the sauce has baked into a thick, rich glaze. *Four servings, 270 calories each.*

PERSIAN SPICED CHICKEN AND SQUASH

8 chicken thighs or 1½ pounds cut-up frying chicken
¾ cup water
¼ cup lemon juice
2 tablespoons soy sauce
¼ teaspoon ground cinnamon
¼ teaspoon grated nutmeg
   Salt and coarsely ground pepper
4 cups sliced summer squash, or 2 ten-ounce packages, defrosted
1 tablespoon snipped fresh parsley

Put the chicken pieces skin side down in a nonstick chicken fryer or electric skillet, with no fat added. Add 1 tablespoon water, cover, and cook over moderate heat 1 minute. Uncover and continue to cook; the chicken will begin to brown in its own melted inner fat. Cook slowly, uncovered, until chicken skin is golden brown and well rendered of fat.

Drain off and discard fat from the skillet. Add remaining ingredients except squash and parsley. Cover and simmer over low heat until chicken is tender; about 25 or 30 minutes for thighs, 40 to 50 minutes for larger pieces. Add water, if needed.

Tip the pan and skim the fat from the surface of the pan juices. Add the squash, cover and cook 2 minutes. Uncover and continue to cook until squash is tender-crunchy and the pan juices have reduced to a thick glaze. Stir in parsley at the last minute. *Four servings, about 200 calories each.*

SUMMER CHICKEN CACCIATORE WITH SQUASH

8 **chicken thighs or 1 cut-up frying chicken (1½ pounds)**
1 **clove garlic, minced**
1 **onion, chopped**
1 **tablespoon water**
1 **large tomato, peeled and diced, or 8-ounce can tomatoes**
1 **cup tomato juice**
¼ **cup dry white wine**
1 **green bell pepper, seeded and minced**
  Basil and oregano to taste
  8-inch green or yellow summer squash
  Salt and freshly ground pepper
4 **teaspoons grated Parmesan cheese**
  Snipped fresh parsley

Brown the chicken pieces skin side down in a nonstick chicken fryer or electric frying pan with no fat added, according to directions in preceding recipe.

Drain off and discard fat. Add garlic, onion, and 1 tablespoon water. Cook and stir 1 minute, until onion is limp. Add tomato, tomato juice, white wine, and minced pepper. Sprinkle with 2 tablespoons fresh basil or oregano, or 1 tablespoon of each. (If using dried herbs, use 2 teaspoons or 1 teaspoon of each.) Cover and simmer over low heat until chicken is tender, about 40 to 50 minutes. Stir occasionally, and add water, if needed.

Meanwhile, slice the squash into eighths, lengthwise, then slice the spears into 2-inch lengths.

Skim the fat carefully from the surface of the liquid in the skillet, then add the squash. Cover and cook 2 minutes. Uncover and continue to cook, stirring occasionally, until liquid is reduced to a thick sauce. Add salt and pepper to taste. Sprinkle with cheese and parsley before serving. *Four servings, about 200 calories each.*

Chicken Breast—Leanest Cut of All

The breast is the leanest and least fattening part of poultry. It's meaty and protein rich, too! A chicken breast half offers 25 grams of protein, half your daily need, for less than 150 calories.

TANDOORI "FRIED" CHICKEN BREASTS

3 whole chicken breasts, split (6 halves)
1 cup plain low-fat yogurt
¼ cup fresh lime juice
¼ cup water
3 cloves garlic, minced, or ½ teaspoon instant garlic
½ cup unseasoned breadcrumbs, either Toasted High-Fiber Breadcrumbs (page 302) or commercial
2 teaspoons ground coriander
1 teaspoon cumin
1 teaspoon fennel or anise seeds
1 teaspoon curry powder
Salt and freshly ground pepper to taste

Put chicken pieces into a heavy plastic bag or glass or ceramic bowl. Combine yogurt, lime juice, water, and garlic and add to chicken, mixing well. Close up bag or cover bowl and refrigerate 24 hours. Turn occasionally.

Put the breadcrumbs into a large heavy-duty brown paper bag. Add remaining seasonings.

Drain the chicken pieces and put them into the paper bag. Fold over the top and shake up well. Place the chicken pieces skin side up in a shallow nonstick baking pan and bake in a preheated 400-degree oven 50 to 60 minutes, until crisp and golden. *Six servings, under 160 calories each.*

CHICKEN BREASTS A LA SEVILLANA

Spanish food is so fattening that only flamenco dancers can afford the calories. And not always. On a recent trip, we saw one who looked more like a Wagnerian diva than a Spanish dancer. She was tall, as most flamenco dancers are, but her silhouette clearly betrayed too many *tapas.*

Though nearly 200 pounds, she was still the most talented of the troupe and performed with a passion and grace that her younger, slimmer counterparts couldn't match. But even under the ruffles and fringe her size was hard to hide, so it was only natural that the changing Spanish attitude toward food should become the table topic.

Our hostess, a handsome and slender woman in her late fifties, noted that it was typical for Spanish women to add weight along with years and children, owing mainly to *la cocina*—the cuisine. But more and more, at least among the affluent, retaining a youthful form is the fashion.

The Spanish aren't sweet freaks. The offending ingredient is oil—in enormous amounts—so much oil that the upsets tourists blame on water may very well be deranged digestion.

Hugh amounts of fat and oil aren't necessary to re-create the savor of Spanish dishes. I've taken a Sevillian chicken classic and translated it the Slim Gourmet way. The típico taste comes from olives, not olive oil. (A slimming tip for any dish that calls for olive oil: omit the oil and chop up a few olives instead.)

3   whole chicken breasts, split (6 halves)
3   tablespoons all-purpose flour
    10½-ounce can fat-skimmed chicken broth
3   tablespoons Spanish sherry
¼   teaspoon thyme
2   tomatoes, peeled and chopped, or 1 cup canned tomatoes
1   cup chopped onion
1   green bell pepper, seeded and cut in strips
18 stuffed green Spanish olives, sliced
½   pound fresh mushrooms, sliced

Shake the chicken breasts and flour in a large paper bag until lightly coated. Place chicken skin side up in an ovenproof baking dish. Bake in a preheated hot (450-degree) oven for 20 minutes, or until well browned and fat is melted. Drain off all fat.

Combine chicken broth, sherry, thyme, tomatoes, onion, and green pepper; pour over chicken. Cover with foil and bake at 350 degrees for 30 minutes. Uncover; stir in olives and mushrooms. Continue to bake, uncovered, until liquid is reduce to a thick sauce; baste occasionally. *Six servings, 210 calories each.*

CROCKED CHICKEN BREASTS

3   whole chicken breasts, split (6 halves)
2   ounces Canadian bacon or lean ham, diced
1   cup sliced scallion or green onion
8   small white onions, peeled
½   pound fresh whole small mushrooms
1   teaspoon garlic salt
¼   teaspoon freshly ground pepper
½   teaspoon poultry seasoning
1   cup fat-skimmed chicken broth
1   cup dry red wine

Brown chicken breasts, skin side up, and cubed Canadian bacon under broiler. Discard fat. Blot with paper towels. Combine all ingredients except wine in a slow-cooker. Cover and cook on low heat 8 to 10 hours. Add wine and cook on high heat 1 hour. *Six servings, 200 calories each.*

CHICKEN SANGRÍA BLANCO

White Sangría Chicken

2 whole chicken breasts, split (6 halves)
  Dash of ground cinnamon or grated nutmeg
  Salt and freshly ground pepper
1 cup white sangría
  8-ounce can juice-packed mandarin oranges
1 teaspoon grated orange peel (optional)
1 unpeeled red apple, diced
3 tablespoons golden raisins

Sprinkle the chicken with spice, salt, and pepper. Place skin side up in a small nonstick cake pan in a preheated very hot (450-degree) oven. Bake 20 to 25 minutes until skin is crisp and well rendered of fat. Drain off and discard melted fat. Pour on sangría and juice drained from oranges.

Lower heat to 350 degrees, and continue to bake until chicken is tender and liquid is reduced to a thick glaze. Stir in fruit at the last minute and continue to bake only until apples are heated through but still crisp. *Four servings, about 250 calories each.*

SPICED CHICKEN VALENCIANA WITH APRICOTS

When all the fresh fruits have fled (perhaps they go to Australia for the winter) that's the time to think dried apricots, one of my favorite fruits.

Their sunny color, cheerful disposition, and sweet-tart taste add adventure to lots of low-cal dishes. They're no slouch nutritionally, either. When you think apricots, think "A"—for the vitamin of the same name. It's nonsense to call dried apricots fattening, since a dried apricot half has the same calories as a wet one: 10

3 whole chicken breasts, split (6 halves)
  Garlic salt, pepper, and monosodium glutamate (optional)
½ cup orange juice
1 cup water
1 tablespoon instant minced onion
  ½-ounce package of raisins
¼ cup dried apricot halves

Place chicken skin side down in a nonstick skillet, and cover. Turn on heat and cook slowly until the chicken browns in its own melted inner fat. Drain off fat. Sprinkle with seasonings. Add all other ingredients. Cover and simmer over very low heat until chicken is nearly tender, about 35 minutes.

Uncover and skim off fat from liquid with a bulb-type baster. Continue to simmer uncovered until most of the liquid has evaporated and sauce is thick. *Six servings, 180 calories each.*

FRENCH CHICKEN WITH SHERRY-NUTMEG SAUCE

Like most spices, nutmeg has no calories to speak of. Unfortunately, too few cooks ever speak of it, except in fattening baked goods or unspeakably rich eggnog concoctions! If the only time you shake on the nutmeg is when you make apple pie, I'd like to shake up your thinking a bit. Nutmeg is a terrific turn-on for lean poultry.

Nutmeg is that certain *je ne sais quoi* flavor in some French chicken dishes topped with creamy wine sauce. Yet it's the cream—not the nutmeg or wine —that adds the calories. (In cooking, alcohol *calories* evaporate, not the *flavor.*) Here's my version, made with milk.

3 **whole chicken breasts, split (6 halves)**
1 **onion, minced**
1 **cup fat-skimmed chicken broth**
3 **tablespoons dry sherry**
½ **teaspoon grated nutmeg**
  Pinch of cayenne pepper
  Salt and freshly ground pepper
1 **tablespoon minced fresh parsley (optional)**
¾ **cup skim milk**
2 **tablespoons all-purpose flour**

Put the chicken skin side down in a nonstick or electric frying pan. Cook slowly over moderate heat with no fat added until the skin is well browned. Drain off melted fat. Put the chicken skin side up and add the onion, broth, and sherry. Sprinkle with seasonings. Cover and simmer over very low heat until nearly tender, 40 to 50 minutes. Uncover. Tip pan and skim fat from the liquid with a bulb-type baster.

Continue to simmer uncovered until the liquid is reduced by half. Whisk milk and flour together and stir into the pan. Cook and stir until sauce is bubbling and thick. *Four servings, about 215 calories each.*

DEVILED CHICKEN BREASTS

2 whole chicken breasts, split (4 halves)
Garlic powder
Soy sauce
2 or 3 tablespoons prepared mustard
¼ cup unseasoned breadcrumbs, either Toasted High-Fiber Breadcrumbs
   (page 302) or commercial

Sprinkle chicken breasts lightly with garlic powder. Broil skin side up for 8 to 10 minutes, until the skin is browned and the fat is melted. Remove from the broiler and coat both sides lightly with soy sauce and prepared mustard.

Sprinkle the breadcrumbs on a flat plate or sheet of wax paper and press the chicken pieces into the crumbs until lightly coated. Arrange skin side up on a baking sheet. Bake in a 325-degree oven until tender, about 35 minutes. *Four servings, 185 calories each.*

CHICKEN MUSCATEL WITH GRAPES

2 whole chicken breasts, split (4 halves)
1 cup muscatel or white port wine
Salt and freshly ground pepper
Grated nutmeg
1 tablespoon arrowroot or cornstarch
¼ cup cold water
1 cup green seedless grapes, halved

Place chicken breasts skin side up in a flameproof, ovenproof dish. Bake in a very hot (450-degree) oven 10 minutes. Drain off fat.

Add the wine. Sprinkle chicken with salt, pepper, and nutmeg. Bake at 350 degrees until tender, about 40 to 45 minutes. Remove the chicken pieces to a serving platter.

Combine arrowroot and cold water and stir into remaining juices in the dish. Heat over a low flame until sauce is smooth and thickened. Stir in grapes and heat through. Pour over chicken. *Four servings, 195 calories each.*

Dining (or Dieting) Alone? Here Are Ten Easy Recipes
for Chicken Breasts

Whether you live alone—or just eat alone—the chicken-breast half is a versatile choice for solo chefs. Especially if you also count your calories.

Here are 10 Slim Gourmet dishes single cooks can create from a chicken-breast half, all relatively easy, and most 200 to 300 calories a serving.

1. Oven-Fried Chicken Breast: Shake up the chicken in a closed paper bag with 2 tablespoons plain breadcrumbs. Place skin side up in a nonstick pie pan. Sprinkle with celery or onion salt, garlic powder, pepper, paprika, or other favorite seasonings. Bake in a preheated 350-degree oven 1 hour.

2. Solo Chicken Cacciatore: Bake chicken unseasoned and uncovered for 20 minutes at 400 degrees. Pour off fat. Add 1 small onion and 1 small bell pepper, chopped. Put under chicken. Pour on 1 cup plain tomato juice. Sprinkle with garlic powder and oregano. Bake uncovered 30 to 40 minutes at 325 degrees, basting frequently.

3. Chicken Tarragon: Place chicken skin side up in a nonstick cake pan. Sprinkle with the juice of 1 lemon, onion salt, pepper, and tarragon. Bake at 350 degrees for 1 hour.

4. Breast au Vin: Brown a chicken breast skin side down in a nonstick skillet with no fat added. Pour off fat. Add 3 tablespoons red table wine, 1 onion (quartered), 2-ounce can mushrooms, pinch of poultry seasoning. Cover and simmer till tender (about 40 minutes). Uncover and simmer until liquid evaporates. Add an 8-ounce can sliced carrots (drained) and heat through.

5. Chilled Chicken: Brown breast skin side down in a nonstick skillet; pour off fat. Turn chicken over. Add 1 cup tomato juice, 1 chopped onion, 1 chopped celery stalk, 1 small chopped green bell pepper, ¼ teaspoon chili powder, garlic salt to taste, a shake each of oregano and cumin. Cover and simmer until tender. Uncover and simmer till sauce is thick.

6. Spanish BBQ Chicken: Bake chicken uncovered and unseasoned 20 minutes at 425 degrees. Pour off fat. Combine 1 cup tomato juice (or Bloody Mary cocktail mix), 1 tablespoon dried onion flakes, 2 tablespoons vinegar, 1 tablespoon prepared mustard, 1 tablespoon Worcestershire sauce plus 1 teaspoon sugar or honey. Pour over chicken. Bake at 350 degrees for 40 minutes, basting frequently. Add a dash of liquid-smoke seasoning or seasoned salt, if desired.

7. Breast à l 'Orange: Bake uncovered an unseasoned chicken breast for 20 minutes; drain off fat. Combine 3 tablespoons low-calorie orange marmalade, ¼ cup dry white wine, 1 tablespoon soy sauce, and pour over chicken. Bake at 350 degrees for 40 minutes, basting occasionally. Garnish with fresh orange sections, if desired.

8. Singles Goulash: Brown chicken skin side down in a nonstick skillet; drain off fat. Turn chicken over. Add 1 cup canned chicken broth, 1 cup tomato juice, 1 chopped onion. Heat to boiling. Simmer 30 minutes. Stir in 1 ounce dry curly noodles. Cover and simmer until noodles and chicken are tender. Uncover, sprinkle with paprika. Simmer uncovered until sauce is thick.

9. Sauté Véronique: Brown chicken breast skin side down in a nonstick skillet; drain off fat. Turn breast over. Add ½ cup water and 2 tablespoons dry white wine. Sprinkle with nutmeg, celery or onion salt, a dash of poultry seasoning. Cover and simmer until liquid is reduced to a glaze. Stir in ¼ cup green seedless grapes and heat through.

10. Japanese Chicken: Brown chicken breast skin side down in a nonstick skillet; drain off fat. Turn breast over. Add 2 tablespoons soy sauce, 2 tablespoons sherry. Cover and simmer until tender. Uncover. Stir in 1 thinly sliced onion, 1 thinly sliced stalk celery, ½ cup sliced mushrooms. Cook and stir over high heat for 2 minutes, just until vegetables are crunchy.

Slimmest Chicken Cutlets for a Slimmest You

The dishes that follow use the leanest, least-fattening chicken there is—boneless, skinless white-meat cutlets cut from the breast. You can buy chicken cutlets already prepared, or save money and make them yourself from whole chicken breasts. (If you do, the leftover bones and skin can be simmered in water to make chicken broth.)

POLYNESIAN PEPPER CHICKEN

For an interesting flavor note here, add a pinch of fennel or anise seeds. Both are sweet spices with a vaguely licoricelike flavor that seems to boost the sweetness of the pineapple.

½ **pound chicken cutlets (skinless, boneless breast), cut to 1-inch cubes**
¾ **cup undiluted canned or homemade fat-skimmed chicken broth**
   6-ounce can (¾ cup) unsweetened pineapple juice
2 **tablespoons Japanese-style soy sauce**
2 **tablespoons sherry**
1 **large onion, sliced**
2 **green bell peppers, seeded and cut in 1-inch squares**
¼ **teaspoon fennel or anise seeds**
¼ **teaspoon monosodium glutamate (optional)**

Combine all ingredients in a nonstick skillet. Simmer 10 minutes, uncovered, stirring occasionally, until liquid evaporates into a thick glaze. Serve immediately. *Two servings, 215 calories each. Recipe may be doubled to serve four.*

VARIATION

With Leftovers: One cup cubed cooked chicken or turkey may be substituted. Follow preceding recipe, but stir in cooked poultry at the last minute. Cook and stir only until heated through.

CHINATOWN CHICKEN AND RICE

1 pound chicken cutlets (skinless, boneless breast)
2 tablespoons diet margarine
1½ cups sliced onion
1 cup diagonally sliced celery
1 can (5 ounces) bamboo shoots, drained
1 can (4 ounces) sliced mushrooms
¼ teaspoon freshly ground pepper
¾ cup chicken broth
3 tablespoons soy sauce
2½ cups cooked rice

Cut raw chicken in bite-size cubes. Heat diet margarine in a nonstick skillet. Add chicken and cook 5 minutes, stirring often. Add onion and celery and cook 5 minutes more. Add remaining ingredients and cook until liquid is absorbed. *Six servings, 245 calories each.*

ITALIAN "FRIED" CHICKEN FILLETS

1 pound chicken cutlets (skinless, boneless breast) or 2 whole chicken breasts, split (4 halves)
⅓ cup regular (not diet) Italian salad dressing
½ cup (4 slices) Toasted High-Fiber Breadcrumbs (see page 302)

To save time, buy chicken fillets already skinned and boned. To save money, buy two chicken breasts, split. Use a sharp knife to remove the skin. Then cut the meat away from the bone. (Save the bone and skin for soup or stock.)

Lightly pound the fillets with the edge of a heavy plate to flatten. Then marinate the fillets in the salad dressing for 15 to 30 minutes at room temperature, or all afternoon in the refrigerator. Turn frequently.

Preheat the oven to 450 degrees. Spray a nonstick cookie sheet or shallow baking pan with cooking spray for no-fat frying.

Sprinkle the crumbs on a shallow plate or sheet. Press each fillet into the crumbs, coating both sides lightly. Discard leftover marinade and crumbs. Arrange the fillets in a single layer on the baking sheet. Bake at 450 degrees for 5 to 6 minutes on each side. Turn carefully. *Four servings, about 275 calories each.*

ONE-PAN CHICKEN CACCIATORE WITH VERMICELLI

¾ pound chicken cutlets (skinless, boneless breast) or 2 small chicken
    breasts, skinned and boned
1 tablespoon diet margarine
2 cloves garlic, minced, or 1 teaspoon instant garlic
1 small green pepper, seeded and chopped
1 small onion, peeled and sliced
    2-ounce can sliced mushrooms, drained
    20-ounce can tomatoes, broken up
    6-ounce can tomato paste
    10-ounce can fat-skimmed chicken broth
2 tablespoons dry white wine
1½ teaspoons oregano or Italian seasoning
    Salt and freshly ground pepper to taste
1½ cups water
6 ounces very thin spaghetti (vermicelli)

Cut chicken in bite-size chunks. Heat margarine in nonstick skillet and brown chicken quickly over high heat. Stir in garlic, pepper, onion, and mushrooms. Cook and stir to brown lightly. Add tomatoes, tomato paste, broth, wine, seasonings, and water. Heat to boiling. Stir in broken-up spaghetti, a little at a time, to retain simmer.

Simmer uncovered, stirring occasionally, until spaghetti is tender and liquid is evaporated to a thick sauce. Add a little water if needed. *Four servings, 355 calories each.*

CHICKEN PARMIGIANA

1½ pounds chicken cutlets (skinless, boneless breasts)
1 egg
2 tablespoons olive oil
5 tablespoons Italian seasoned breadcrumbs
3 tablespoons grated Parmesan cheese
3 ounces part-skim mozzarella cheese, sliced thin or shredded
    Italian Tomato Velvet Sauce (page 308), made with chicken broth

Separate the cutlets into 6 pieces. Pound thin with the edge of a heavy plate. Fork-whip egg and oil in a shallow plate. Combine breadcrumbs and Parmesan cheese in another shallow plate.

Dip each cutlet first into the egg mixture, then into the crumb mixture, coating lightly. Arrange in a single layer on a shallow nonstick baking dish or cookie sheet (may be sprayed with cooking spray for no-fat frying). Bake in a preheated 450-degree oven for 10 minutes. Top with mozzarella and return to the oven only until cheese melts. Spoon on hot Italian Tomato Velvet Sauce and serve immediately. *Six servings, 275 calories each.*

VARIATION

Italian Chicken Rollettes: This recipe uses the same ingredients as the previous one, but the preparation is different. Separate the cutlets into 6 pieces, as above, and pound thin. Put ½ ounce sliced or shredded mozzarella cheese on top of each cutlet, then roll up tightly so the cheese is in the middle. (Secure with toothpicks, if necessary, but it usually isn't.) Then dip each rollette lightly in the egg-oil mixture, then in the breadcrumb-Parmesan mixture. Arrange in a single layer on a nonstick cookie sheet and bake in a preheated 375-degree oven 15 to 20 minutes until golden. Serve with Italian Tomato Velvet Sauce. *Six servings, 275 calories each.*

STUFFED CHICKEN BREASTS MILANO

 1 **pound chicken cutlets (skinless, boneless breast)**
½ **cup cooked rice, unbuttered**
 1 **cup finely minced celery**
 6 **tablespoons diet Italian salad dressing**
 1 **egg**
¼ **cup seasoned breadcrumbs, homemade (see page 302) or commercial**

Separate the cutlets into 4 pieces. Combine rice, celery, and 3 tablespoons salad dressing. Divide rice filling equally among the 4 pieces of chicken, then roll up. Stir 3 tablespoons salad dressing and the egg together.

Dip each roll first in the egg mixture, then in the breadcrumbs, coating lightly. Arrange on a nonstick baking dish and bake without turning in a 350-degree oven for 20 to 25 minutes, or until tender. *Four servings, 210 calories each.*

Cheap-Cheap Scallops from Boneless Chicken

You can put chicken breasts in company dress by cutting the meat into scallop-sized cubes and preparing them as if they were scallops. Luckily, many of the seasonings and cooking techniques that accent seafood go well with chicken, too.

FRENCH CHICKEN "SCALLOPS"

1 pound chicken cutlets (skinless, boneless breast) or 2 whole chicken breasts,
    boned and skinned
2 tablespoons sherry
2 tablespoons margarine
   Onion salt, pepper, paprika

Cut the meat into 1-inch cubes. Arrange in a single layer in a shallow flameproof dish. Add sherry. Dot with margarine. Sprinkle with seasonings. Slip under broiler about 6 minutes. Baste with pan juices several times while broiling. *Four servings, under 170 calories each.*

VARIATIONS

Lemon-Broiled Chicken "Scallops": Follow preceding recipe, substituting lemon juice for the sherry. Sprinkle with oregano or Italian seasoning, if desired.

Broiled Chicken "Scallops" and Mushrooms: Follow either preceding recipe. Add 1 cup fresh small mushroom caps to the pan, along with the cubes of chicken.

OVEN-FRIED CHICKEN "SCALLOPS" ITALIANO

1 pound chicken cutlets (skinless, boneless breast), cut in 1-inch squares
½ cup regular (not diet) Italian salad dressing
½ cup unseasoned breadcrumbs, either Toasted High-Fiber Breadcrumbs
    (see page 302) or commercial

Marinate chicken squares in salad dressing for 20 to 30 minutes, stirring frequently. Preheat oven to highest setting, 450 degrees or more. Sprinkle crumbs on a plate or sheet of wax paper. Spray a nonstick cookie sheet with cooking spray for no-fat frying. Roll each chicken "scallop" in the crumb mixture, then set on the cookie sheet, in a single layer. Bake in the oven, without turning, for 8 to 10 minutes. *Four servings, 330 calories each.*

VARIATION

"French-Fried" Chicken Scallops: Substitute regular French dressing for the Italian dressing. *295 calories per serving.*

MRS. BRODER'S STIR-FRY CHICKEN SKILLET

Mrs. Arthur M. Broder of Holmdel, New Jersey, sent me this delicious suggestion. "Extremely easy," she writes, "resembling chunks of lobster. Makes a lovely low-calorie hors d'oeuvre served on picks, or a company dinner dish served over fluffy rice."

> 3 tablespoons margarine or olive oil
> 1 pound chicken fillets (skinless, boneless breast), cut in 1½-inch cubes
> 3 cloves garlic, peeled and finely minced
> 1 teaspoon salt
> ¼ teaspoon thyme
>   Paprika and chopped fresh parsley

Heat margarine or oil in a nonstick skillet. Add chicken cubes and garlic. Sprinkle with salt and thyme. Cook and stir 5 minutes, just until chicken turns white (don't overcook). Sprinkle with paprika and parsley before serving. *Four servings, 195 calories each.*

Slim Cooking for Two is Easy with Chicken

Just the two of you. How intimate! How romantic! How difficult to cook for!

Today's "family" is often just one or two people—a fact overlooked by cookbooks and supermarkets. Recipes, meat, and produce are usually packaged as if everybody still sits down to an 8-foot dining table.

Here are a pair of recipes for making two "meals for two" out of one cut-up chicken. The vegetables served with the chicken on the first day help to season the sauce for our second-day Chicken Bolognese, a tomato-rich chicken-and-pasta dish.

Whether you're newlyweds or second honeymooners, keeping in trim is important, so I've made both dishes extra low in calories—but extra delicious. You won't mind chicken two nights in a row when the dishes are as different as these.

POTTED CHICKEN WITH CELERY AND CARROTS

> 2 pounds cut-up frying chicken
>   10-ounce package frozen carrots
> 3 stalks celery, sliced
> 1 onion, sliced
> 1 bay leaf
> ¼ teaspoon poultry seasoning
> ½ cup dry white wine
> 1½ cups water
> 2 teaspoons cornstarch or arrowroot dissolved in ¼ cup cold water
>   Salt and freshly ground pepper

Place the chicken pieces skin side up in a hot oven or under the broiler until skin is browned and fat is melted. Combine chicken pieces in a heavy pot or Dutch oven with all remaining ingredients except cornstarch and ¼ cup cold water (which will be used for thickening) and seasoning. Cover and simmer over low heat until tender, about 40 minutes. Uncover and continue cooking until liquid is reduced by half. Stir cornstarch and cold water into the simmering pot until liquid is slightly thickened. Season to taste. Serve half the chicken (see note below) and all of the vegetables, topped with some of the sauce. *Two servings, about 290 calories each.*

NOTE: Set aside remaining chicken and sauce until later. After dinner, when remaining chicken is cool enough to handle, remove the meat and discard the bones. Refrigerate the remaining chicken meat and sauce (can be done in the same pot) until the next day. Then make the following recipe:

VARIATION

Boneless Chicken and Spaghetti Bolognese: Yesterday's leftover boneless chicken, including sauce.

5-ounce can plain tomato sauce (no oil added)
½ **teaspoon oregano or Italian seasoning**
  Pinch of garlic powder
1½ **cups tender-cooked spaghetti (see page 245)**

Combine the chicken and its sauce, tomato sauce, and seasonings in a saucepan. Simmer about 5 minutes. Serve over the spaghetti. *Two servings, about 360 calories each.*

NOTE: Tossed salad with diet Italian dressing completes the meal.

Chicken on a Rotisserie—a Good Turn for Dieters

"Whirlybirds" are delicious waistline watchers any time of year, but especially during the outdoor season. What are "whirlybirds?" Whole chickens, roasted to a tender turn on a revolving spit.

Rotisserie devices are frequently found on electric or gas barbecues, but that's not the only place. Many ovens feature rotisseries. Countertop broilers do too, either the "open hearth" or enclosed glass-door varieties. Whatever way you set a chicken in motion, it's one of the most calorie-wise ways to cook.

For one thing, the type of chicken most suitable is also the leanest, least fattening, least expensive type; a whole broiler-fryer is only 385 calories per pound.

In the wonderful spin it's in, your chicken literally bastes itself to a golden crispness in its own melting fat. And, as the chicken turns, the fat drips off, out of harm's way.

In a rotisserie oven, the best temperature setting is around 350 degrees— the middle range—which will cook the average broiler-fryer in about 1 hour to 1 hour and 10 minutes. For more explicit guidance, however, you should check your operating instructions.

For best flavor, coat the chicken with a marinade of savory liquids and seasonings for about an hour before cooking—or at the last minute, if necessary. Baste chicken with any leftover marinade.

Once you get the hang of it, it's usually possible to secure a chicken to a spit without string; simply tuck the wing tips and drumsticks into the end clamps so they won't hang loose. If needed, small skewers can "nail" floppy appendages in place.

ORIENTAL LEMON CHICKEN BBQ

Great, hot or cold.

Broiler-fryers (1½ pounds each)
Lemon juice
Soy sauce
Freshly ground pepper
Paprika
Crushed dried tarragon

Clean and dry chickens; affix to rotisserie spit. Sprinkle liberally with seasonings. Cook at medium temperature, basting occasionally with additional lemon juice and soy sauce until done. *Each chicken serves four, fewer than 150 calories per serving.*

INDIAN CHICKEN TANDOORI BBQ*

1 **whole broiler-fryer (about 1½ pounds)**
   Few threads of saffron
1 **tablespoon boiling water**
½ **cup plain low-fat yogurt**
2 **tablespoons lime juice**
1 **clove garlic, crushed, or ⅛ teaspoon garlic powder**
1 **teaspoon salt**
½ **teaspoon ground ginger**
¼ **teaspoon cumin**
¼ **teaspoon turmeric**
   Dash of Tabasco or cayenne pepper
   Paprika (optional)
   Thin lime slices

*Adapted from *Best Ever Chicken* (New York: Family Circle Books). Reprinted courtesy *Family Circle* Magazine.

Wash, clean, and blot chicken. Soak saffron in the tablespoon boiling water for 5 minutes. Combine saffron water, yogurt, lime juice, garlic, salt, and seasonings in a shallow bowl. Turn the chicken in the mixture, coating well. Marinate 1 hour, turning occasionally.

Secure chicken on rotisserie spit and cook about 1 hour at medium temperature, until done. Sprinkle with paprika, if desired, and garnish with lime slices. *Four servings, 165 calories each.*

SOUTH SEAS SPITTED CHICKEN

1 whole broiler-fryer (1½ pounds)
2 tablespoons soy sauce
2 tablespoons lemon juice
½ of 6-ounce can defrosted apple-juice concentrate, undiluted
   Garlic or onion powder, monosodium glutamate, paprika (optional)

Wash, clean, and blot the chicken. Combine soy sauce, lemon juice, and apple-juice concentrate in a shallow bowl (for 2 chickens, double the quantities for marinade). Roll the chicken in the marinating mixture to coat evenly. Marinate 1 hour, turning frequently.

Secure the chicken on a rotisserie spit. If desired, sprinkle lightly with garlic or onion powder, monosodium glutamate, and paprika. Cook on a revolving spit at a medium temperature for 1 hour or more, until chicken legs move easily at the joint. *Four servings, 195 calories each.*

SPITTED LAUREL CHICKEN À LA GRECQUE

1 whole fryer (2 pounds)
3 or 4 bay leaves, broken up
1 lemon, sliced
1 onion, quartered
   Garlic salt and freshly ground pepper
   Lemon juice

Rinse and dry the chicken. Fill the cavity with the broken bay leaves, sliced lemon, and onion. Truss on a spit according to manufacturer's directions. Season with garlic salt, pepper, and lemon juice while cooking. Cook according to manufacturer's timetable, or until done (about 1 hour). *Four servings, 205 calories each.*

MOO GOO GAI PAN

This version is made with only 1 tablespoon oil, and fresh vegetables from American supermarkets instead of canned imports.

2 tablespoons sherry
1 tablespoon oil
½ pound small fresh whole mushrooms
1 cup fat-skimmed chicken or turkey broth (fresh or canned)
3 large onions, peeled and cut in chunks
3 stalks celery or celery cabbage
¾ pound roast white-meat chicken or turkey
1 tablespoon arrowroot or cornstarch
¼ cup cold water
  Salt and white pepper

In a nonstick skillet, combine the sherry, oil, and mushrooms. Cook and stir until wine evaporates and mushrooms brown lightly. Add the chicken broth and onions. Halve the celery lengthwise, then cut into 2- or 3-inch lengths. Add to the skillet. Gently simmer, uncovered, stirring occasionally. Cook only till celery is tender crisp. Break up the onions as you stir.

Meanwhile, cut the cooked poultry into bite-size cubes and set aside.

Combine arrowroot with cold water and gently stir into the skillet until the mixture simmers and thickens. Stir in cubed poultry at the last minute and heat gently, only till warmed through. Salt and pepper to taste. *Four servings, 260 calories each.*

BONELESS BBQ CHICKEN CACCIATORE

¼ cup dry red or white wine
2 teaspoons olive oil
¼ pound fresh mushrooms, sliced
4 pieces leftover broiled chicken
1 large onion, thinly sliced
  6-ounce can tomato paste
  10½-ounce can fat-skimmed chicken broth
¼ teaspoon poultry seasoning
  Oregano, basil, or Italian seasoning to taste (optional)
  Salt and freshly ground pepper to taste

In a large nonstick skillet or electric frying pan, combine 1 tablespoon wine, olive oil, and sliced mushrooms. Cook and stir over high heat until mushrooms are brown. Meanwhile, remove bones from chicken and cut meat into bite-size pieces. Combine all ingredients in the skillet. Simmer uncovered 20 to 25 minutes, until sauce is thick and onions are tender. *Four servings, 250 calories each.*

QUICK CACCIATORE

10-ounce can undiluted fat-skimmed chicken broth
1 cup Slim Gourmet Tomato Sauce Concentrate (page 306)
1 green pepper, finely chopped
1 teaspoon oregano or Italian seasoning
2 cups cubed cooked roast chicken or turkey

Combine chicken broth with Tomato Sauce Concentrate. Add 1 green pepper and oregano. Simmer uncovered until gravy thick. Stir in leftover roast chicken or turkey and heat through. *Four servings, about 195 calories each.*

CORNISH HEN VÉRONIQUE (IN RAISIN-WINE SAUCE)

Cornish hens are really miniature chickens, but they seem so festive that fancy dress is in order, as the recipes that follow prove. Cornish hens have the same low-calorie count as young frying chickens, only 382 per pound. In fact, the dishes can be made with cut-up chicken and will be equally delicious. A popular way to serve Cornish hens is "Véronique" or garnished with grapes. If you're fresh out of fresh grapes, you might like to try our any-season version, with golden raisins instead of grapes. Despite the fancy flavor, this dish is both fast to prepare *and* nonfattening!

2 Cornish hens, or 2 pounds cut-up frying chicken
2 tablespoons water
¾ cup fat-skimmed canned chicken broth or water
¼ cup dry white wine
  Salt and freshly ground pepper to taste
¼ teaspoon grated nutmeg
  Pinch of cayenne pepper
3 tablespoons golden raisins
1 cup skim milk (optional)
2 tablespoons all-purpose flour (optional)

Have Cornish hens split in half (or sawed, if frozen; defrost before cooking). Use a skillet, Dutch oven, or flameproof casserole with nonstick finish. Spray with cooking spray for no-fat frying. Put the poultry skin side down in skillet. Add 2 tablespoons water and raise heat. Cook slowly until water evaporates and poultry browns in its own melted fat. Move poultry frequently to prevent sticking. Continue cooking until skin is crisp and well rendered of fat. Drain and discard fat.

Turn poultry skin side up and add remaining ingredients, except milk and flour. Cover and simmer until tender, about 40 minutes. Uncover and continue to cook until most of the liquid evaporates. Spoon raisins over poultry to serve.

For a delicious "cream sauce," simply stir the milk and flour together, then stir into the simmering skillet over low heat until sauce thickens and bubbles. Thin with a little water, if needed. *Four servings, 220 calories each; or 255 calories with "cream sauce."*

CORNISH HENS IN CURRY "CREAM" SAUCE

Here's an Indian Cornish hen dish that's essentially prepared in a "cream sauce" like the preceding recipe but one with a totally different flavor. The sauce is flavored with onion, soy sauce, and curry powder instead of nutmeg, and diced apples are stirred in at the last minute.

2 **Cornish hens, split, or 2 pounds cut-up frying chicken**
3 **tablespoons raisins**
⅔ **cup fat-skimmed chicken broth**
2 **tablespoons soy sauce**
¼ **cup dry white wine**
   Salt and freshly ground pepper to taste
1 **teaspoon curry powder, or to taste**
1 **tablespoon minced onion or 1 teaspoon dried onion flakes**
2 **tablespoons all-purpose flour**
1 **cup skim milk**
3 **small unpeeled red apples, cored and diced**

Prepare poultry as in previous recipe, browning with no fat added in a nonstick skillet. (Or, if you prefer, poultry can be browned under the broiler, skin side up, until skin is crisp and well rendered of fat. Then transfer the poultry to a skillet or range-top Dutch oven, skin side up.) Add remaining ingredients except flour, milk, and diced apples. Cover and simmer until tender, about 40 minutes. Uncover, simmer until most of the liquid evaporates.

Combine flour and milk, and stir into the simmering pot until sauce thickens and bubbles. Thin with a little water, if needed. Stir in diced apples at the last minute and cook only until heated through. *Four servings, under 315 calories each.*

PLUM GOOD CORNISH HENS

Do you know how to season with "sour power"? Smart cooks have always known that a dash of vinegar or a squirt of lemon could turn on taste, adding just the right counterpoint to other seasonings. Sweet and sour is so much more sophisticated than just sweet!

Vinegar and lemon aren't the only sources of sour power. Other citrus juices, chopped pickles, even sweet 'n' sour fruits or vegetables can combine to create just the right tart and tangy overtones.

Here is a trim main course to show what we mean; fresh purple plums add the sweet and sour dash. Fresh plums are sour-skinned but sweet on the inside, so we slice the plums thin, leaving the skin on—which also adds a lovely winy color to the sauce.

2 Cornish hens, split, or 2 pounds cut-up frying chicken
4 unpeeled purple prune-type plums, pitted, thinly sliced
2 red onions, thinly sliced
5 tablespoons soy sauce
¼ cup red wine
  Pumpkin-pie spice
  Generous pinch of anise seeds (optional)

Put hen halves or chicken pieces skin side up in a shallow nonstick pan. Add no seasonings. Put the pan in a preheated hot (450-degree) oven. Bake 20 minutes, or until skin is crisp and well rendered of fat. Drain off and discard fat.

Put the plum and onion slices under the poultry. Sprinkle with remaining ingredients. Return to oven and continue to bake at 450 degrees, basting frequently, until poultry is tender and sauce is reduced, 30 to 40 minutes. (You can make a thicker sauce by stirring 1 teaspoon cornstarch or arrowroot into 3 tablespoons cold water; then add to the liquid in the pan, stirring well. Continue baking until sauce thickens.) *Four servings, under 270 calories each.*

Rabbit—the Uncommon Slimmer

After you've served every lean meat, poultry, and fish dish you can think of, there's always something else. How about rabbit, for a change?

Americans are inclined to think of rabbit as offbeat or exotic, but it's quite commonplace in other cuisines. Since rabbits reproduce like . . . well, rabbits . . . the dish is regarded a bit like hamburger, a delicious but familiar staple that could do with some dressing up. Hence the variety of interesting rabbit recipes.

Of course, rabbit is really more like chicken than like hamburger in the way it looks, cooks, and tastes. Even the calorie count is relatively low: rabbit is only 581 calories per pound. (A 2-pound rabbit serves 4.)

Young "frying" rabbits are found frozen—cut up and ready to cook—in 2-pound boxes in many American supermarkets. "Frying" rabbits and "frying" chickens have so much in common, culinarily speaking, that they are virtually interchangeable in most recipes. That means you can make this slim Hasenpfeffer with chicken—or make almost any favorite slim chicken dish with rabbit!

SLIM HASENPFEFFER

The slimmed-down version of this spicy German dish is "fried" in the oven. The marinade is sweetened with cider instead of sugar, and there's no fat added.

2 pounds cut-up young rabbit, defrosted
⅓ cup cider vinegar
1 cup unsweetened cider or apple juice
½ teaspoon whole cloves
1 onion, thinly sliced
3 or 4 bay leaves
2 teaspoons salt
¼ teaspoon freshly ground pepper
   Pinch of allspice
5 tablespoons all-purpose flour
   Worcestershire sauce (optional)

Combine rabbit pieces, vinegar, cider, cloves, onion, bay leaves, salt, pepper, and all spice in a plastic bag, set in a glass or ceramic bowl. Refrigerate 12 to 24 hours, turning occasionally.

To "fry" in the oven: Drain rabbit and reserve marinade. Shake up the rabbit pieces with the flour in a large paper bag; then arrange in a single layer in a shallow nonstick roasting pan which has been sprayed with cooking spray for no-fat frying. Put the pan in a preheated hot (450-degree) oven for 20 to 25 minutes, until crisp and crusty and rendered of fat.

Pour off any fat in the pan. Remove cloves and bay leaves from marinade and add marinade to the pan. Lower heat to 350 degrees. Bake until tender, about 35 to 45 minutes or more, basting occasionally. Add water if needed. Serve with pan juices and a dash of Worcestershire, if desired. *Serves four, 365 calories each.*

VARIATION

Chicken Hasenpfeffer: Substitute 2 pounds cut-up frying chicken for the rabbit. *265 calories per serving.*

FRENCH HARE À L'ORANGE

2 pounds cut-up young rabbit
Juice of 1 lemon
Salt and freshly ground pepper
1 cup orange juice
2 teaspoons grated orange rind
⅛ teaspoon grated nutmeg
½ teaspoon dried rosemary

Defrost rabbit; wash and pat dry. Rub with lemon; season with salt and pepper. Place pieces in a single layer in a shallow roasting pan or casserole.

Combine remaining ingredients and pour over rabbit. Bake in a preheated 350-degree oven, basting frequently, until tender, about 1 hour. Turn once during baking. *Four servings, 320 calories each.*

VARIATION

Chicken à l'Orange: Substitute 2 pounds cut-up frying chicken for the rabbit; *220 calories per serving.*

9
TURKEY

If you think turkey is only for midwinter holidays and family feasts, think again. Turkey, one of the trimmest, tastiest meats there is, is economical in cost as well as calories. And now that turkey-in-parts is widely sold in supermarkets, the calorie-cautious cook can enlarge his or her repertoire of slimming dishes by substituting turkey for more fattening meats.

Skinny Stews with Low-Cal Turkey Thighs

Dark-meat turkey in place of stew meat, for example. A large turkey thigh, found in your local supermarket's frozen meat case, contains about a pound of flavorful meat that can be used in place of beef chuck in any slow-simmered dish—at only 580 calories a pound instead of 1,166, cutting the calories in half!

With a small, sharp, pointed knife, simply slit through the defrosted turkey thigh and cut the meat away from the single bone in the middle. Then cut the meat into 1½-inch cubes. Add the bone to the pot for extra flavor, but discard it before making the sauce.

Try these delicious recipes, so rich-tasting nobody would ever suspect they're slimming.

TRIM TURKEY SUISSE

Tender tidbits of turkey in a rich-tasting wine-and-cheese sauce.

1 pound turkey meat, cut from defrosted turkey thigh, in 1½-inch cubes
½ cup dry white wine or champagne
     Celery salt and freshly ground pepper
¼ teaspoon thyme
1 small bay leaf
½ teaspoon onion powder
¼ teaspoon nutmeg
1 cup skim milk
2 tablespoons all-purpose flour
½ cup shredded Swiss cheese
1 tablespoon minced fresh parsley

Cut turkey meat from thigh bone, and cut meat in 1½-inch cubes, leaving skin on.

Spray a nonstick skillet, electric frying pan or heavy Dutch oven with cooking spray for no-fat frying. Add the turkey cubes, skin side down. Brown over high heat until skin is crisp, brown, and well rendered of fat. Pour off fat. Turn turkey cubes skin side up. Add wine. Sprinkle with seasonings. Cover tightly and simmer over low heat until tender, 1 hour or more. Uncover and raise heat. Cook until nearly all liquid evaporates. Remove bay leaf.

Stir milk and flour together, then stir into pan over moderate heat, until sauce is bubbling and thick. Sprinkle with cheese and parsley and serve immediately. *Four servings, 240 calories each.*

VARIATION

Turkey Tidbits Véronique: Follow preceding recipe, but omit Swiss cheese and parsley. Wash and halve ½ cup seedless green grapes (at room temperature, not chilled) and add to the skillet at the last minute. The heat of the sauce will warm the grapes. *Four servings, about 200 calories each.*

TURKEYAKI WITH VEGETABLES

1 pound turkey meat, cut from defrosted turkey thigh
3 tablespoons Japanese-style soy sauce
5 tablespoons sherry
1 small clove garlic, minced (optional)
4 small onions, quartered
3 stalks celery, split, sliced diagonally

1 red or green bell pepper, seeded and cut in 1-inch squares
 6-ounce can (¾ cup) tomato juice
1 teaspoon cornstarch or arrowroot

Brown turkey skin side down as directed in Trim Turkey Suisse, above. Turn over cubes, add soy sauce, sherry, and garlic. Cover and simmer till tender. Add vegetables. Cover and cook 5 minutes. Uncover. Stir tomato juice and cornstarch together and stir into pan over moderate heat until sauce simmers and thickens. *Four servings, about 210 calories each.*

VARIATION

With Frozen Vegetables: Substitute one 10-ounce package frozen sliced zucchini or green beans for the celery and bell pepper. *About 220 calories per serving.*

TURKEY CHILI

Differing from run-of-the-mill chili made with hamburger, this turkey chili has hardly any fat calories. It's a zesty tempter for both waistline watchers and cholesterol counters.

The dish, of course, is a Mexican-American inspiration. Which brings me to the deliberately noncommittal listing for "chili powder." Someone from the Southwest is likely to find my recommendation of "2 teaspoons" pretty tame. On the other hand, other folk, more tender-tongued, might think I was trying to poison them if I suggested the searing quantities some chili fans prefer.

So chili it up to suit your taste, but don't cut down on the cumin or oregano. Luckily for calorie watchers, the larger amounts of these seasonings don't raise the count one bit.

```
 2 turkey thighs, defrosted
 1 cup boiling water
   28-ounce can tomatoes, including liquid
 1 teaspoon monosodium glutamate (optional)
 2 large onions, chopped
 3 green bell peppers, seeded and chopped
 2 cloves garlic, minced
 2 or more teaspoons chili powder (to taste)
1½ teaspoons cumin
1½ teaspoons oregano or Italian seasoning
   Salt and freshly ground pepper to taste
 ¼ cup shredded extra-sharp Cheddar, jack, or American cheese (optional)
```

Put the turkey thighs on a cutting board and slice the meat away from the bones. Cut the meat in 1-inch cubes, discarding the skin. Spray a nonstick pot (or pressure cooker) with cooking spray for no-fat frying.

Add the cubed meat. Brown it over moderate heat in its own melted fat (no added oil is needed). Remove from flame and stir boiling water into juices in pot. Pour the water into a cup and set it aside until the fat rises to the surface. With a bulb-type baster, skim off and discard the surface fat.

Return the fat-skimmed liquid to the pot. (Add the bones to the pot for flavor; they can be removed before serving.)

Add all remaining ingredients except cheese. Cover and simmer over low heat until tender, about 1 hour in a conventional pot, or 20 minutes in a pressure cooker (follow manufacturer's instructions). Uncover and continue to simmer until most of the liquid is evaporated and chili is thick. Spoon into a serving dish. Top with shredded cheese (should be omitted for cholesterol dieters). *Four servings, 270 calories each with cheese, 240 calories without.*

MEXICAN RED TURKEY STEW

In Mexico, some Americans fear the food will be too hot. Others are wary of *turista*. But some are afraid of catching fat!

You'd better watch out for Mexican food, I was warned when I went there. It's so starchy. Look what it does to Mexicans!

But it's not the rice, beans, corn, and tortillas that make Mexican food fattening—it's the fat. Most native dishes are prepared with prodigious quantities of oil, lard, or butter—in amounts that double or triple the calories of all other ingredients combined.

But many of the ingredients that go into Mexican cuisine are nutritious and low calorie. Whole grains, beans, marvelous fresh fruits and vegetables, seafood, and poultry are all low-fat items. And the real flavor makers—spices, seasonings, herbs, tomatoes, garlic, onions, hot and sweet peppers—count for very few calories. So you *can* enjoy the taste of Mexico without putting on pounds if you're a Slim Gourmet cook.

Here is a zesty, quick and easy Mexican-style dish made with turkey thighs. Well seasoned but not hot, it is a streamlined adaptation of *Mancha Manteles;* the name means "tablecloth stainer," called so because of its savory red gravy. Fat (and other fattening ingredients) are kept to a minimum.

  1 turkey thigh, defrosted
  1 cup water
  8-ounce can plain tomato sauce
  1 teaspoon vinegar
  ¼ cup unsweetened crushed pineapple
  1 red bell pepper, seeded and diced
  2 onions, diced
  1 clove garlic, diced or ⅛ teaspoon instant garlic

1 teaspoon chili powder, to taste
¼ teaspoon ground cinnamon
  Salt and freshly ground pepper
1 small unpeeled red apple, diced (optional)
½ banana, peeled and diced (optional)

Trim the meat from the turkey thigh bone and cut in 2-inch cubes.

Put the meat skin side down in a large nonstick skillet which has been sprayed with cooking spray for no-fat frying. Cover and cook over a moderate flame until fat is rendered from turkey skin. Uncover and continue cooking until moisture evaporates and turkey is well browned in its own fat.

Add 1 cup water, mix well, then drain off. When fat has risen to the surface of the water, skim off and return water to the pot. Add the turkey bone and remaining ingredients, except apple and banana. Cover and simmer 1 hour or more, until tender.

Uncover and continue to simmer until liquid evaporates into a thick sauce. Remove turkey bone. Stir in banana and apple and gently heat only until warmed through. *Four servings, 225 calories each.*

OVEN-BAKED TURKEY YAKITORI

Soy sauce is the universal Oriental seasoning. Its proponents claim that this salty brew from fermented soybeans is what separates the world into fat and lean cuisines. The protein amino acids in naturally fermented soy sauce add a "roundness" to the basic salt-sweet-sour-bitter tastes of food—the same "roundness" that butter, fat, oil, and grease provide in the more fattening fare of the West. (Any dieter who has added a dash of soy sauce to boring broiled "diet" fare can attest to this belief.)

Poultry, of course, is among the leanest main-course meats. Here is a quick and easy basic Oriental recipe for calorie watchers. Crisp-cooked green vegetables and a side order of rice can complete the meal.

1 turkey thigh, defrosted
½ cup soy sauce
1 tablespoon honey
1 clove garlic, finely chopped, or ⅛ teaspoon instant garlic
½ teaspoon ground ginger

With a sharp knife, cut meat away from bone, then slice the raw turkey meat into 2-inch cubes. Thread the meat on small wooden or metal skewers and arrange in a nonstick cake pan. Add remaining ingredients and turn skewers so turkey is well coated with the sauce. Cover the pan with aluminum foil and bake in a preheated 350-degree oven 1 hour, or until meat is nearly tender. Uncover pan and continue to bake, turning the skewers frequently, until liquid is evaporated into a thick glaze. *Four servings, about 175 calories each.*

TURKEY BURGUNDY

2 turkey legs
2 cups dry red wine
1 clove garlic, minced, or ⅛ teaspoon instant garlic
2 large onions, cut in chunks
1 small bay leaf
¾ teaspoon poultry seasoning
1 pound carrots, sliced
1 teaspoon cornstarch or arrowroot
½ cup cold water
¼ cup chopped fresh parsley (optional)

In a Dutch oven, combine all ingredients except carrots, cornstarch, cold water, and parsley. Cover, put on low heat, and simmer until turkey is tender, about 2 hours. Remove turkey legs from broth and set aside to cool. Meanwhile, skim broth of fat with bulb-type baster. Add carrots and cook 20 minutes, until carrots are tender.

When turkey is cool enough to handle, cut meat from bones in bite-size pieces. Discard bones, skin, and sinews. Add turkey meat to pot and heat through.

Mix cornstarch and cold water, and stir into simmering liquid, until thickened. Garnish with minced fresh parsley, if desired, and serve over noodles. *Four servings, 295 calories each without noodles; 395 calories per serving with ½ cup cooked noodles.*

Ducky Idea! Fancy Fare in Low-Cal Turkey Thighs

Duck is a favorite among dark-meat-poultry lovers, but not among calorie counters. Duck, after all, is a whopping 92 calories per ounce. Closest in flavor to duck meat is turkey thigh, which has less than half the calories.

All you have to do to turn turkey into "duck" is have the dish dressed like a duck. Season and sauce the turkey meat as if it were duck and it will look and taste like duck.

Here are some ducky ideas for turkey thighs. The first is a French inspiration: *caneton* is the French word for duck, and *faux* means false.

CANETON FAUX MONTMORENCY
Mock Duck with Cherries

2 turkey thighs, defrosted
   Salt, pepper, and monosodium glutamate (optional)
¼ cup dry red wine

¼ cup unsweetened bottled red grape juice
1 small onion, minced
2 cups unsweetened pitted cherries, canned or frozen and defrosted
3 tablespoons all-purpose flour
½ cup cold water or juice from canned cherries
   Gravy coloring (optional)

With a sharp pointed knife, carefully trim the bone from the turkey thighs. Season the meat with salt and pepper and monosodium glutamate, if desired. Roll the thighs up, skin side out, and place in a shallow nonstick roasting pan, with the skin side up. Add the wine, grape juice, and onion. Bake in a 300-degree oven, basting occasionally, until the turkey meat is very tender, about 2 hours.

Drain the pan juices into a heat-resistant cup or glass; wait a few minutes until the fat rises to the surface, then remove the fat with a bulb-type baster.

Heat the pan juices and cherries in a saucepan. Thicken the sauce with a paste made of the flour and cold water or cherry juice. Stir in a few drops of gravy coloring, if desired. Season to taste with salt and pepper.

Slice the turkey thin on a hot platter, and garnish with the cherry sauce. *Each 4-ounce serving with ½ cup of sauce contains 245 calories.*

KOREAN MOCK DUCK ON SKEWERS

2 turkey thighs, defrosted
1 large lemon, very thinly sliced
3 tablespoons sherry
3 tablespoons soy sauce
1 teaspoon freshly grated ginger root
1 tablespoon minced onion
1 clove garlic, minced
2 teaspoons turmeric
¼ teaspoon chili powder

With a sharp knife, remove the bones from the turkey thighs; cut the meat into 1½-inch cubes. String the cubes on small wooden skewers, alternating with lemon slices. Arrange in a shallow roasting pan just large enough to fit. Stir remaining ingredients together and pour over skewers. Cover the pan with a lid or aluminum foil and bake at 300 degrees for 1 hour or more, until tender. Turn the skewers occasionally. Uncover during the last 20 minutes of baking. *Each 4-ounce serving contains about 215 calories.*

MOCK CHINESE DUCK WITH TANGERINES

 2 turkey thighs, defrosted
   Garlic salt and freshly ground pepper
   Monosodium glutamate (optional)
 2 tablespoons soy sauce
 1 cup water
 ¼ cup unsweetened tangerine or orange juice
 1 tablespoon vinegar
 ½ cup dried apricots
 1 teaspoon grated tangerine rind
 3 tangerines, sectioned and seeded

With a sharp knife, split open turkey thighs and remove the bone. Sprinkle inside of the meat with a little garlic salt, pepper, some monosodium glutamate, and soy sauce. Roll up and place in an ovenproof roasting pan. Add remaining ingredients—except tangerines.

Cover and bake at 350 degrees until turkey is tender, about 1 hour. Remove turkey and keep warm. Tip pan and drain off fat from sauce with bulb-type baster. Slice the turkey and pour on the sauce. Garnish with tangerine sections. *Six servings, 270 calories each.*

Slim Italian "White Steak" Is a Quick and Easy Dish

"White steak" is the cryptic but descriptive translation for a popular short-order dish in many northern Italian restaurants. Sautéed quickly in butter or oil, sometimes flavored with garlic or garnished with lemon or mushrooms, the "white steak" turns out to be turkey. Poor man's veal, but not a bit impoverished in flavor.

Luckily for waistline watchers, "white steak" is short on calories. In fact, this is one Slim Gourmet dish in which you'll find butter or oil on the ingredients list. Because with turkey steak you can afford a tablespoon or two—and that's all you need!

Turkey-breast steaks are now widely sold, fresh or frozen, in many supermarkets. Or you can make your own—and save money—by slicing ¼-inch-thin slices of raw turkey from a raw breast roast.

Although roast turkey takes hours to cook, thin turkey steaks take hardly any time at all. They're ready to serve the very minute they turn from pink to white.

WHITE STEAK SCALOPPINE

1¼ pounds raw turkey breast steaks, thinly sliced
¼ cup dry white wine
2 tablespoons butter
1 clove garlic, minced
¼ cup boiling water
   Salt and freshly ground pepper
   Parsley or lemon wedges (optional)

Use a skillet or electric frying pan with nonstick finish, or coat with cooking spray for frying with little or no fat. Combine steaks, wine, butter, and garlic in the skillet over high heat. Cook uncovered until all the wine evaporates. When the under side is nicely browned and the surface of the turkey is just beginning to turn from pink to white, turn and quickly brown the other side. Cook only a minute or so, just until pinkness disappears.

Remove steaks to a heated platter. Pour boiling water into skillet. Cook over high heat, scraping up residue, then pour the brown juices over the steaks. Season to taste and serve immediately, garnished with parsley and lemon wedges, if desired. *Four servings, 220 calories each.*

TURKEY SCALOPPINE WITH TOMATO-MUSHROOM SAUCE

1¼ pound raw turkey-breast steaks, thinly sliced
2 tablespoons olive oil
1 tablespoon dry white wine
   6-ounce can (¾ cup) tomato juice
   4-ounce can sliced mushrooms, including liquid
   Dash of oregano or Italian seasoning
   Onion salt and freshly ground pepper

Combine turkey, olive oil, wine, and canned mushrooms (including liquid) in a nonstick skillet or electric frying pan over high heat. Cook until liquid evaporates and under sides of turkey steaks begin to brown. Turn steaks and stir mushrooms to brown evenly, cooking only for a minute or so. Remove to a heated platter. Pour tomato juice into the skillet and shake on oregano, onion salt, and pepper. Cook and scrape over high heat until tomato juice is simmering and thick. Pour over steaks and serve immediately. *Four servings, 235 calories each.*

Trim Turkey Reruns—Even More Glamorous!

Hail the tireless turkey! Always ready for a glamorous comeback. There are so many quick and easy things to do with leftover turkey that it's worth cooking just for the reruns. Even if your family is small. Even if your family is only one! One swinging single senior I know roasts a whole turkey on the first of every month, then squirrels most of it away in the freezer, in single-serving portions.

Whether you're a swinger or a senior or not, the best thing about turkey is its low calorie count—only 50 or 60 calories an ounce.

TURKEY CHILI MAC

Here's a zesty main course that's a special favorite with teenagers and smallfry. No fuss, no muss! Make it all in a big skillet or electric frying pan. No fat added.

1¼ **cups fat-skimmed turkey broth, or 10½-ounce can fat-skimmed condensed chicken broth**
    6-ounce can tomato paste
1 **cup sliced celery**
1 **large sweet onion, chopped**
1 **clove garlic, minced (optional)**
1 **cup diced green or red bell pepper**
1 **or more teaspoons chili powder**
    Salt and freshly ground pepper
2 **teaspoons oregano or Italian seasoning**
1 **teaspoon cumin seeds**
3 **cups water**
1 **cup dry small elbow macaroni**
2 **cups cubed cooked white-meat turkey**
6 **tablespoons shredded extra-sharp Cheddar cheese**

In a large skillet or electric frying pan, stir turkey broth and tomato paste until blended. Add celery, onion, garlic, and sweet pepper. Season with chili powder, salt, pepper, oregano, and cumin. Add water and heat to boiling. Stir in macaroni a little at a time to prevent sticking. Cover and simmer until macaroni is nearly tender. Uncover and continue to simmer until sauce is thick. Stir in turkey; cook and stir until heated through. Sprinkle with Cheddar cheese and serve straight from the skillet. *Four servings, 340 calories each.*

SZECHUAN SKILLET TURKEY DINNER
WITH WALNUTS

Now let's travel in the opposite direction for another turkey rerun, Oriental style—also very low in calories.

½ cup tomato juice
2 tablespoons dry sherry
3 tablespoons soy sauce
4 cups sliced onion
2 cups thinly sliced celery
2 cups (9 ounces) cooked turkey meat, in bite-size cubes
1 teaspoon monosodium glutamate (optional)
1 teaspoon arrowroot
1 cup cold water
  Tabasco to taste
1 tablespoon chopped fresh ginger root (optional)
15 walnuts, halved

Combine first 7 ingredients in a covered skillet over moderate heat; cook till vegetables are tender-crunchy, about 6 minutes. Combine arrowroot and cold water; stir into skillet until sauce thickens and clears. Add several dashes of hot-pepper sauce to taste—dish should be hot and spicy. At the last minute, stir in ginger root and walnuts. *Four servings, 240 calories each.*

TRIM TURKEY SOUVLAKIA

Souvlakia is a tasty Greek dish that might ordinarily be made with lamb. You can make it in short order by substituting dark-meat roast turkey for lamb, thereby shortening the calorie count as well. It is made with the least-fattening ingredients.

¼ cup low-calorie Italian salad dressing
  Pinch of instant garlic
  Pinch of dried mint (optional)
1 pound cooked dark-meat turkey in 1½-inch cubes
4 green bell peppers, seeded and cut in squares
4 onions, quartered
8 cherry tomatoes
1 tablespoon salad oil

Mix the salad dressing with the garlic and mint. Marinate the cooked turkey cubes in the mixture for 30 minutes or more, or covered in the refrigerator several hours.

Thread the turkey cubes on skewers, alternating with the vegetables. Add 1 tablespoon oil to the remaining marinade, then use the combined mixture to brush the skewers. Broil or barbecue 2 inches from the heat source for about 5 minutes on each side, just until seared and heated through. Vegetables should be hot but crunchy. *Four servings, about 325 calories each.*

TRIM TEN-MINUTE TURKEY

4 stalks celery
1 cup fat-skimmed condensed chicken broth
1 cup unsweetened pineapple juice
1 large Spanish onion
1 green pepper
3 cups trimmed diced white-meat roast turkey (or any lean leftover roast)
  Soy sauce (optional)

Slice the celery diagonally and put in a large nonstick skillet or electric frying pan, along with the chicken broth and pineapple juice. Simmer uncovered. Meanwhile, peel the onion and cut in half. Slice thin and add to the skillet.

Stir to separate and allow to simmer. While it cooks, remove the top, seeds, and membrane from the pepper and cut into squares. Add to the skillet.

When the juice and broth have thickened into a nice sauce, stir in the turkey. Cook and stir until turkey is heated through and well coated.

Serve with soy sauce, if desired. *Four servings, about 260 calories each.*

TURKEY À LA QUEEN

4 ounces dry ziti (or large macaroni)
½ pound fresh mushrooms, sliced
1 tablespoon butter
½ cup dry sherry
¼ cup minced onion
¼ teaspoon grated nutmeg
2 cups cubed cooked turkey or chicken
2 cups skim milk
¼ cup all-purpose flour
6 tablespoons grated Parmesan cheese

Salt and freshly ground pepper to taste
¼ **cup chopped fresh parsley**
   Paprika

Cook ziti until tender (see page 245) in boiling salted water.

Quarter mushrooms, or slice them (not too thin). Combine them in a non-stick skillet with 1 tablespoon butter and 3 tablespoons sherry. Cook and stir over moderate heat until wine evaporates and mushrooms brown. Add remaining sherry, onion, nutmeg, and turkey. Simmer 1 minute.

Combine milk and flour. Stir into skillet over low heat until sauce thickens and bubbles. Stir in 3 tablespoons Parmesan until melted. Salt and pepper to taste. Stir in parsley.

Spoon over hot drained ziti. Sprinkle with remaining Parmesan and paprika. Serve immediately. *Four servings, about 335 calories each.*

10
SEAFOOD

Fillet Your Fish for Easy Dishes the Slim Gourmet Way

Want to be slimmer? Make friends with fish!

Fish is so *un*fattening it's the ideal main course for waistline watchers. A whole pound of flounder fillets has fewer calories than many a hamburger— or single serving of steak.

Of course, when we say "fish," we don't mean the kind that comes smothered in a heavy overcoat of grease-soaked starch: "fish sticks" or "frozen fried fillets." We mean plain fillets, that leave the culinary creativity to you. (Not only less fattening, but a lot less expensive as well. Why pay seafood prices for breadcrumbs and grease?)

For an example of how low calorie fish really are, consider these calorie counts per pound for some of the most popular species of boneless fillets (meat only): flounder, 360; sole, 360; haddock, 360; perch, 535; turbot, 660; fish sticks, 800.

FISH FILLETS IN MUSHROOM-CHEESE SAUCE

2 twelve-ounce packages frozen fish fillets, defrosted, or 1½ pounds fresh
10¾-ounce can undiluted cream of mushroom soup
4-ounce can chopped mushrooms, including liquid
2 tablespoons grated Parmesan or Romano cheese

2 tablespoons chopped fresh parsley
2 tablespoons dry white wine

Arrange fillets in a single layer in a shallow ovenproof baking dish. Stir remaining ingredients together until cooking sauce is smooth. Pour over the fish. Bake in a preheated 375-degree oven 20 minutes or more, until fish flakes easily. *Six servings, 155 calories each.*

EASY CHEESY FISH FILLETS

1 pound fish fillets (sole, flounder, or halibut), fresh or defrosted
1 onion, thinly sliced
¼ cup low-calorie mayonnaise
2 tablespoons chopped fresh parsley
¼ cup grated Parmesan or Romano cheese

Place the fillets in a single layer in an ovenproof dish. Top with thinly sliced onion. Spread with mayonnaise. Sprinkle with parsley and cheese. Cover and bake in a preheated hot (450-degree) oven for 10 minutes. Uncover and bake 4 to 6 minutes more, until browned. *Four servings, 150 calories each.*

SKILLET SOLE À LA BONNE FEMME

Here's how to take the excess calories—and the complexity—out of a French classic. The French phrase *à la bonne femme* means "good wife" or the way a "good wife" cooks it. I'll be more liberated and translate it to mean the way a "good cook" cooks it. And my definition of a "good cook" (or "good wife," "good husband," or "good friend") is one who is considerate of calories and cholesterol!

Most recipes for this dish involve lots of added fat—and a sinkful of dirty dishes. This one-pan technique is so much simpler.

2 teaspoons butter or margarine
½ cup dry sherry or dry white wine
4 ounces sliced mushrooms, fresh or canned
3 tablespoons minced onion or 1 tablespoon dried onion flakes
1 pound fillets of sole or flounder, fresh or defrosted
   Salt, or butter-flavored salt, and freshly ground pepper
   Tarragon to taste
½ teaspoon monosodium glutamate (optional)
1 cup skim milk
2 tablespoons all-purpose flour
   Paprika
2 tablespoons minced fresh parsley

Combine the butter with 1 tablespoon wine in a nonstick skillet or frying pan. Add the mushrooms (drain, if canned). Cook and stir over high heat until liquid evaporates and mushrooms begin to brown in the remaining fat (2 teaspoons is all you need!). Remove mushrooms and set aside.

Put onion and remaining wine in the skillet. Add the fish fillets in a single layer. Sprinkle lightly with salt, pepper, a pinch of tarragon, and monosodium glutamate. Simmer, uncovered, over low heat about 5 to 8 minutes, depending on thickness of fillets, until fish is opaque and most of the wine has evaporated (add a little more wine or water if it threatens to evaporate completely). Spoon wine over fish occasionally while it simmers.

Stir milk and flour together, then stir into the simmering skillet and cook until sauce simmers again and thickens. Sprinkle browned mushrooms on top of fillets; top with paprika and parsley. Heat through. Serve from the skillet. *Four servings, about 160 calories each.*

FLOUNDER TETRAZZINI

Here's a decalorized seafood version of a famous chicken dish, with flounder or sole. The preparation technique is similar to that in the previous recipe.

- **4 ounces sliced mushrooms, fresh or canned**
- **2 teaspoons butter or margarine**
- **½ cup dry white wine**
- **1 pound fillets of flounder or sole, fresh or defrosted**
  Salt, or butter-flavored salt, and freshly ground pepper
  Dash of grated nutmeg
- **2 tablespoons all-purpose flour**
- **1 cup skim milk**
- **2 tablespoons grated Parmesan cheese**
- **1 ounce Swiss cheese, chopped or shredded**
- **2 tablespoons chopped fresh parsley**
- **2 tablespoons seasoned breadcrumbs, homemade (see page 302) or commercial (optional)**
- **2 cups tender-cooked spaghetti (see page 245)**

Brown mushrooms in a nonstick skillet in butter and 1 tablespoon wine, according to directions in the previous recipe. Meanwhile, cut fillets into 2-inch squares. Remove mushrooms and set aside. Combine fish and remaining wine in the skillet. Sprinkle with salt, pepper, and nutmeg. Simmer, uncovered, until fish is opaque and most of the wine has evaporated. Spoon wine over fish occasionally while cooking.

Mix flour and milk together, blend well, then add to the simmering skillet. Stir gently until sauce simmers again and thickens. Add more seasonings to taste, if needed. Sprinkle with cheeses, mushrooms, and parsley. Heat through. Or, if skillet has a burnproof metal handle, you may add a light topping of breadcrumbs and slip the skillet under the broiler briefly until topping is brown. Serve from skillet. *Four servings, 200 calories each; breadcrumbs add about 5 calories per serving. Serve combined with tender-cooked spaghetti, if desired, at 80 calories per ½ cup.*

WINE-POACHED FISH FILLETS WITH MUSHROOMS AND CHEESE

This reader recipe is from Charles Silversmith of Jupiter, Florida, who went from 205 pounds to 145 pounds by becoming a Slim Gourmet cook.

Mr. Silversmith won with his own adaptation of Julia Child's Filets de Poisson Bercy aux Champignons, wine-poached fish with mushrooms and cheese, from *Mastering the Art of French Cooking.* *

Mr. Silversmith cut calories by eliminating all the butter and cream called for in the original recipe, and using diet margarine and evaporated skim milk instead.

¼ **pound fresh mushrooms, sliced**
4 **teaspoons diet margarine**
2 **tablespoons minced scallion or green onion**
1 **pound flounder or sole fillets, fresh or defrosted**
¾ **cup dry white wine**
¾ **cup water**
  Salt and white pepper
2 **tablespoons all-purpose flour**
¾ **cup evaporated skim milk**
¼ **cup grated Swiss cheese**
  Lemon juice

Spray a nonstick skillet with cooking spray for no-fat frying. Add mushrooms and 2 teaspoons diet margarine. Toss lightly over moderate heat, but do not brown.

Spray a shallow flameproof baking dish with cooking spray. Arrange half the onions in the bottom. Add the fish fillets in a single layer, slightly overlapping. Top with remaining onions, mushrooms, wine, and water. Sprinkle on salt and white pepper. Dot with 2 teaspoons diet margarine. Cover with foil or a lid. Put in a preheated 350-degree oven and bake 15 minutes. The fish will simmer (poach) in the liquid.

Remove from the oven and drain the liquid into a saucepan. Preheat the broiler.

Boil down the poaching liquid until it is reduced to 1 cup.

In a small cup, combine the flour and ½ cup evaporated skim milk, then

*New York: Alfred A. Knopf, 1961.

stir into the simmering poaching liquid. Cook and stir until thick, then thin with additional evaporated skim milk. Season to taste with a little lemon juice and additional salt and white pepper.

Spoon this sauce over the fish and sprinkle with grated cheese. Put the dish 6 or 7 inches from the broiler flame and broil 2 or 3 minutes to reheat the fish and brown the sauce lightly.

Four servings, 225 calories each.

HIGH-FIBER FLOUNDER AU GRATIN

2 slices dry high-fiber toast
1 pound flounder or other fish fillets, fresh or defrosted
   Garlic salt and freshly ground pepper
   Paprika
3 tablespoons melted butter or margarine
2 tablespoons fresh lemon juice
   Lemon wedges

Process the high-fiber toast into crumbs. Spray a shallow square nonstick baking pan or other flameproof dish with cooking spray for no-fat frying. Cut the fish into 4 equal pieces; arrange in a single layer in the dish. Sprinkle evenly with crumbs and seasonings. Combine melted butter with lemon juice and sprinkle over the crumbs to moisten evenly.

Slip under a preheated broiler about 5 inches from the heat source and broil for about 8 to 12 minutes. Do not turn. (Exact time depends on thickness of fillets. Fish is done when it flakes easily. Don't overcook or it will dry out.) Garnish with lemon wedges. *Four servings, about 190 calories each.*

POLYNESIAN FLOUNDER

Here's a decalorized recipe adapted from a dish served a group of food editors on Coconut Island, the marine life preserve where the University of Hawaii is conducting fish-farming experiments. The original dish was made with giant prawns (supersize shrimp) but the recipe has been adapted to go with any fish fillets available in your supermarket freezer case.

1 onion, thinly sliced
1 green bell pepper, seeded and chopped
1 stalk celery, finely minced
   8-ounce can small carrots, drained
   Garlic salt
2 pounds flounder or sole or other frozen fish fillets, defrosted
2 cups plain tomato sauce
1 cup unsweetened crushed pineapple, well drained

Spread the bottom of an ovenproof baking dish with onion, green pepper, celery, and carrots. Sprinkle with garlic salt.

Cover vegetables with fish fillets, white side up. Combine tomato sauce with pineapple and pour over fish fillets.

Bake in a preheated hot (450-degree) oven for 20 minutes, basting frequently with pan liquid. Dish is ready when fish flakes easily and most of the liquid has evaporated into a thick sauce. *Eight servings, 140 calories each.*

ISRAELI SPICED FISH FILLETS

Lemons and oranges. Lots of garlic, olives, and tomatoes. Savory spices and herbs. Does that sound like Jewish food? It does if you live in Israel!

Israeli cuisine is a spicy blend that's more Middle Eastern than Middle European. Light and spicy rather than rich and heavy. Less fattening, too.

So why not add a taste of Israel to your Slim Gourmet recipe repertoire? Here is a simple idea to try, adapted for calorie watchers from recipes developed by Ruth Sirkis, cookbook author and wife of an Israeli diplomat.

1 **pound flounder or other thin fillets, fresh or defrosted**
2 **tablespoons lemon juice**
1 **tablespoon olive oil**
½ **teaspoon cumin**
¼ **teaspoon Tabasco, or to taste**
   Salt and freshly ground pepper
   Paprika

Arrange fillets in a single layer in a shallow broiling pan. Combine lemon juice, oil, cumin, and pepper sauce, and spread over fish. Sprinkle with salt and pepper to taste, and with paprika. Broil 5 to 6 minutes, or more, without turning, until fish flakes easily. (Don't overcook!) *Four servings, under 125 calories each.*

FISH FILLETS IN CHILI SAUCE

1 **pound flounder fillets, defrosted**
1 **cup Slim Gourmet Tomato Sauce Concentrate (page 306)**
1 **cup water**
1 **cup minced green bell pepper**
2 **teaspoons chili powder**
1 **teaspoon cumin**
2 **tablespoons lemon juice**
1 **teaspoon salt**

Arrange flounder fillets in an ovenproof dish. Combine Tomato Sauce Concentrate with water, minced green pepper, chili powder, cumin, lemon juice, and salt. Stir together and pour over fish. Bake uncovered in a 350-degree oven, until fish flakes easily with a fork, about 20 minutes. *Four servings, 130 calories each.*

CUBAN BAKED FISH FILLETS WITH ALMONDS

2 bay leaves, broken up
1 small onion, thinly sliced
1 pound fish fillets, fresh or defrosted
2 tablespoons lime juice
2 tablespoons water
2 tablespoons olive oil
1 tablespoon freshly chopped parsley
⅛ teaspoon instant garlic
½ teaspoon thyme
  Salt and freshly ground pepper
2 tablespoons sliced almonds

Put the bay leaves and onion slices in the bottom of a shallow nonstick baking dish. Arrange the fish fillets in a single layer over the onion and bay leaves. Combine the lime juice, water, olive oil, chopped parsley, garlic, and thyme, and pour over fish.

Bake in a preheated very hot (450-degree) oven for 8 to 10 minutes, basting frequently with the pan juices. Sprinkle with salt, pepper, and almond slices during the last 2 or 3 minutes of baking. Fish is done when it flakes easily. *Four servings, 185 calories each.*

FILLET OF SOLE VÉRONIQUE

Ever since some super-spoiled despot commanded, "Peel me a grape," the sweet and succulent fruit has enjoyed an indulgent image. At 66 calories a cup, they're not the least fattening of fruit, but still slim enough to be enjoyed by the calorie-wise.

Here is a trimmer treat for friends of the grape—a streamlined version of the classic Sole Véronique. "Véronique," by the way, means trimmed with grapes in Menuese.

Enjoy yourself, no peeling needed! This recipe is designed to help you peel off pounds without stripping away the enjoyment of good eating!

1½ pounds fillet of sole, fresh or defrosted
1 cup white wine
1½ cups skim milk
3 tablespoons all-purpose flour
Juice of ½ lemon
Dash of white pepper
Dash of mace
¼ teaspoon salt or butter-flavored salt
1 cup green seedless grapes

Put fillets and wine in a shallow glass baking dish. Cover dish with aluminum foil and bake in a hot oven 12 to 15 minutes, until fish is opaque.

Stir milk and flour in saucepan over low heat until thickened. Drain wine from baking dish into sauce. Add lemon juice and seasonings. Cook until well blended. Arrange grapes over fish and pour on sauce. Return to oven at 350 degrees for 6 to 8 minutes, until sauce is bubbly. *Six servings, 150 calories each.*

FILLETS OF SOLE IN TOMATO-CURRY SAUCE

1-pound can tomatoes
1 onion, chopped
½ teaspoon curry powder
Salt and freshly ground pepper
1½ pounds sole fillets, fresh or defrosted
1 tablespoon diet margarine
1 tablespoon all-purpose flour
¼ cup low-fat lemon yogurt

Combine tomatoes, onion, curry powder, salt, and pepper in a saucepan. Cook uncovered, until some of the liquid has evaporated and the mixture has thickened, about 20 minutes.

Lightly sauté the fish in the margarine.

Stir the flour into the yogurt. Add to the tomato mixture. Cook and stir until thickened. Pour over fish; heat through. Serve immediately. *Six servings, under 135 calories each.*

FISHERMAN'S RICE CASSEROLE

½ cup sliced fresh mushrooms
⅔ cup chopped onion
2 tablespoons diet margarine
2½ cups cooked rice
2 tablespoons chopped fresh parsley
1 jar (2 ounces) diced pimiento
½ teaspoon poultry seasoning
1 teaspoon salt
Dash of pepper
1½ pounds flounder or other fillets, fresh or defrosted
1 tablespoon lemon juice
6 tablespoons grated extra-sharp Cheddar cheese
6 slices firm fresh tomatoes

In a nonstick skillet cook mushrooms and onion in diet margarine until onions are tender. Stir in rice, parsley, pimiento, and seasonings. Mix well. Turn into a greased shallow, 2-quart casserole. Brush fillets with lemon juice and arrange on top of rice. Season with salt and pepper.

Bake at 350 degrees 20 minutes. Spoon 1 tablespoon cheese onto each tomato slice, place over fish, and continue baking 5 minutes. *Six servings, 215 calories each.*

Slim Mexican Fish Dishes Well Seasoned . . . Not Hot

Two delicious fishes found on nearly every Mexican menu are *robalo* and *huachinango.* A surreptitious under-the-table check of your pocket dictionary reveals that these are none other than haddock and red snapper—both frequently available here at home! Seafood stores near major cities often feature red snapper flown in fresh from Florida waters. And haddock is commonly available in many supermarket frozen-food sections at (relative) bargain prices.

Here are two decalorized recipes for fixing these fishes (or any fish fillets) in the Mexican manner, popular with both natives and visitors. Neither dish is "hot."

Fillet of haddock and red snapper are both exceedingly low in calories, only 360 and 420 calories per pound, respectively. Low in cholesterol and fat, these dishes are smart for your heart as well as for your waistline.

MEXICAN GARLIC-BROILED FISH

Since garlic is a primary ingredient in this dish, be sure to use fresh garlic, not instant. However, cholesterol watchers may substitute soft margarine for butter.

1 **pound fresh haddock or red-snapper fillets (or other fresh fish)**
4 **(or more) cloves garlic, coarsely chopped**
3 **tablespoons butter or margarine**
2 **tablespoons water**
3 **tablespoons lime or lemon juice**
  Salt and freshly ground pepper

Spray a shallow nonstick roasting pan with cooking spray for no-fat baking. Arrange the fillets in a single layer.

In a small saucepan, cook and stir the garlic, butter, juice, and water until butter is melted, then pour over fish. Season the fish with salt and pepper. Slip under the broiler, about 4 or 5 inches from the heat source, and broil until fish flakes easily. Spoon the liquid in the pan over the fish occasionally while it broils. *Four servings, about 180 calories each with haddock, 195 with red snapper.*

PESCADA A LA VERACRUZANA

Fish Vera Cruz Style

In deference to gringo tastes, this dish is generally served mild in tourist haunts—too tame in fact for some Southwesterners and other "chiliheads." You can add considerably more chili powder. But a safer option is to have a bottle of hot sauce on the table. Adding "fire" doesn't increase the calorie count!

1 **pound haddock or red-snapper fillets (or other fish), fresh or defrosted**
2 **tablespoons lemon or lime juice**
  Salt and freshly ground pepper
2 **onions, peeled and chopped**
1 **clove garlic, minced or ⅛ teaspoon instant garlic**
1 **tablespoon olive oil**
½ **cup water**
  8-ounce can plain tomato sauce
  8-ounce can stewed tomatoes, well broken up, or 1 large ripe tomato, peeled and chopped
¼ **cup coarsely chopped stuffed Spanish olives (green olives)**
¼ **cup olive liquid (from jar)**
1 **large bell pepper, seeded and thinly sliced**
1 **small bay leaf, broken up**
¼ **teaspoon chili powder, or to taste**
  Tabasco (optional)
  Lemon wedges (optional)

Cut the fish into serving-size pieces. Sprinkle with juice. Season with salt and pepper and set aside.

Combine onions, garlic, and oil in a large nonstick skillet or electric frying pan, over medium heat. Cook and stir only until onions are golden. Stir in remaining ingredients and heat to boiling. Add the fish to the skillet and spoon on the sauce. Cook gently, uncovered, until fillets are cooked through and sauce is thick.

Or: Arrange the fillets in a single layer in a baking dish and spoon the hot sauce mixture over them. Bake in a preheated hot (425-degree) oven, uncovered, for 10 to 15 minutes, until fish fillets are opaque and break easily. Serve with Tabasco and lemon wedges, if desired. *Four servings, about 185 calories each with haddock, 200 with red snapper.*

Sea Steaks, Done to a Turn—Much Trimmer than Beef

Steak is the busy cook's choice because it's so fast. Unfortunately, steak is also fattening. Unless it's a fish steak! Steaks from the sea can be every bit as delicious as beefsteak, but with only a fraction of the calories and cholesterol. Consider this: cod steak is only 360 calories a pound while beef rib is 1,800!

Fish steaks can be baked or broiled, but baking is simpler. Since fish is always tender and flakes when it's done, sea steaks can break up if broiled too long on one side before turning. Baking—without turning—is easier.

TURKISH BAKED FISH STEAKS

> **6 or 7 bay leaves, broken up**
> **2 or 3 cloves garlic, finely chopped, or ½ teaspoon instant garlic**
> **1½ pounds swordfish or other fish steaks, at least 1 inch thick**
> **3 or 4 tablespoons lemon juice**
> **Salt and freshly ground pepper**
> **Paprika**
> **1 lemon, thinly sliced**
> **Finely minced fresh parsley**

Put bay leaves and chopped garlic into a shallow baking dish; arrange the fish steaks in a single layer on top of them. Sprinkle with lemon juice, salt, pepper, and paprika. Bake in a hot (425-degree) oven 12 to 20 minutes, basting frequently with pan juices, until fish flakes easily. Top with lemon slices and chopped parsley to serve. *Six servings, under 145 calories each.*

GREEK BAKED FISH STEAKS

> **2 pounds cod, swordfish, halibut, or other fish steaks, cut at least 1½ inches thick**
> **2 onions, chopped**
> **2 green bell peppers, seeded and thinly sliced**

1½ cups canned tomatoes, well broken up
½ cup water
2 tablespoons lemon juice
2 cloves garlic, finely minced
1 lemon, thinly sliced

Arrange fish steaks in a single layer in a shallow baking pan. Combine other ingredients, except lemon slices, and pour over fish. Bake 50 to 60 minutes at 325 degrees, or until fish flakes easily. Garnish with lemon slices. *Eight servings, about 115 calories each with cod, 160 with swordfish, 140 with halibut.*

BROILED SEA STEAKS WITH ORANGE CURRY SAUCE

   Halibut (or salmon or swordfish) in 6 serving pieces (about 5 or 6 ounces each)
¼ cup orange juice
1 tablespoon salad oil
   Salt and freshly ground pepper to taste
½ cup low-fat mayonnaise
¼ cup plain low-fat yogurt
3 tablespoons catsup
2 teaspoons grated orange peel
½ teaspoon curry powder
   Fresh parsley
1 eating orange, peeled, halved, and thinly sliced

Arrange fish steaks on a broiler platter.
Combine 2 tablespoons orange juice with oil and brush steaks lightly with this combination. Sprinkle with salt and pepper. Broil or barbecue close to the heat source about 4 or 5 minutes on each side, until fish loses its translucency and flakes easily.
Meanwhile, combine remaining 2 tablespoons orange juice with low-fat mayonnaise, yogurt, catsup, orange peel, and curry powder.
Garnish fish steaks with parsley and orange slices before serving, and serve with the sauce. *Six servings, about 180 calories each.*

IRISH CIDER-BAKED FISH STEAKS

1½ pounds fish steaks, 1½ inches thick
1 cup cider
   Salt, freshly ground pepper, and paprika
1 tablespoon all-purpose flour
2 tablespoons finely chopped fresh parsley

Arrange fish steaks in a single layer in a shallow, ovenproof, nonstick dish. Pour on ¾ cup cider. Sprinkle with salt, pepper, and paprika. Bake in a preheated 375-degree oven about 20 minutes, basting frequently with pan liquid, until fish flakes easily.

Stir flour and remaining ¼ cup cider together in a small saucepan. Carefully drain hot cider from baking dish into the saucepan. Cook and stir over low heat until sauce thickens. Spoon over fish. Slip under broiler, until sauce is bubbling. Sprinkle with chopped parsley and serve immediately. *Six servings, about 140 calories each.*

OVEN-BARBECUED SEA STEAKS MEXICANA

2 **fresh cod or other fish steaks, about 6 ounces each**
  6-ounce can (¾ cup) Bloody Mary mix
1 **teaspoon vinegar**
⅛ **teaspoon cumin (optional)**
  Dash of oregano or Italian seasoning
1 **tablespoon dried onion flakes**

Arrange fish steaks in a small shallow nonstick baking pan. Combine remaining ingredients and pour over fish. Bake in a preheated 350-degree oven 10 minutes or more, basting frequently with the sauce. Fish is done when it flakes easily and the liquid has evaporated into a thick sauce. *Two servings, 145 calories each.*

Bake Slim Salmon Steak for Calorie-Wise Treat

Salmon is considered a fatty fish, but that's only in comparison to other seafoods that are exceedingly low in fat. Compared with most meats, salmon is still a dieter's delight.

Most varieties average about 750 calories per pound, less than half the calories in most steaks, chops, or hamburger. Moreover, the small amount of fat found in salmon is highly unsaturated.

If your salmon savvy is limited to salads and sandwich spreads made with the canned variety, you might like to try some easy main courses made with fresh or frozen salmon steaks. I've also provided a leftover cooked salmon dish, just in case your salmon steaks aren't wolfed down at the first sitting.

JAPANESE SESAME SALMON STEAKS

6 **salmon steaks (2¼ pounds)**
3 **tablespoons dry sherry**
3 **tablespoons Japanese soy sauce**
1 **teaspoon liquid-smoke seasoning (optional)**
6 **teaspoons sesame seeds**

Defrost fish if frozen. Arrange in a shallow ovenproof dish, just large enough to hold the steaks in a single layer. Combine sherry, soy sauce, MSG, and smoke seasoning, and pour over steaks. Sprinkle with sesame seeds.

Bake in a preheated hot (450-degree) oven for 7 to 10 minutes, until fish flakes easily. *Six servings, under 300 calories each.*

SALMON STEAKS SAUTERNE

2 bay leaves
2 tablespoons finely chopped onion
6 salmon steaks (2¼ pounds)
½ cup sauterne
1 tablespoon lemon juice
1 teaspoon salt or butter-flavored salt
  Paprika
  Freshly ground pepper

Break up the bay leaves into the bottom of a shallow ovenproof dish; add the onion. Arrange the steaks on top in a single layer. Pour on the wine. Sprinkle with lemon juice, salt, and paprika.

Bake in a preheated 450-degree oven for 7 or 8 minutes, basting occasionally with the pan liquid, until the fish flakes easily. Sprinkle with freshly ground pepper just before serving. *Six servings, 285 calories each.*

SPANISH SALMON AND RICE

An all-seafood paella. Use leftover cooked salmon or canned salmon for this budget-wise Spanish seafood dish.

    16-ounce can peas
    16-ounce can tomatoes, broken up
    16-ounce can artichokes
    10½-ounce can fat-skimmed chicken broth
    Water
1½ cups brown rice
  1 onion, chopped
  1 clove garlic, minced
  3 stalks celery, chopped
  1 red or green bell pepper, seeded and sliced
  1 teaspoon salt
  ⅛ teaspoon freshly ground pepper
    Pinch of cayenne pepper or dash of Tabasco
  1 pound salmon, cooked or canned, in chunks
  1 lemon, cut in wedges

Drain the canned peas, tomatoes, and artichokes, reserving the liquid from each can. Measure the liquid. Add fat-skimmed chicken broth and water to make 3 cups liquid. Pour into a large nonstick skillet or paella pan.

Add the rice, tomatoes, onion, garlic, celery, and bell pepper. Season with salt, pepper, and cayenne. Cover and simmer until rice is nearly tender, about 40 minutes. Add peas, artichokes, and salmon chunks. Cover and cook until heated through, about 5 minutes. Garnish with lemon wedges. *Eight servings, 300 calories each.*

Hearty Dinners That Start with Low-Cal Tuna

At only 210 calories per 7-ounce canful, tuna is so trim it shouldn't be left to languish in the pantry. Here are some main courses the Slim Gourmet cook can whip up with tuna. (Take note, however, that the weight-wary calorie count applies only to water-packed tuna. The oil-packed variety is more than twice as fattening.)

Remember: oil adds no flavor, just calories.

SLIM SCALLOPED TUNA

2 **cups skim milk**
7 **tablespoons all-purpose flour**
1 **teaspoon salt or butter-flavored salt**
1 **teaspoon freshly ground pepper**
3 **eggs, lightly beaten**
2 **seven-ounce cans water-packed tuna, drained and flaked**
1 **onion, minced**
1 **cup chopped fresh parsley**
1 **tablespoon lemon juice**
2 **teaspoons Worcestershire sauce**
3 **tablespoons unseasoned breadcrumbs, either Toasted High-Fiber Bread-**
    crumbs (page 302) or commercial

Stir milk and flour in a nonstick saucepan over low heat until mixture thickens and bubbles. Season with salt, or butter-flavored salt, and pepper. Remove from the heat and gradually beat into the eggs. Stir in the tuna, onion, and parsley. Season with lemon juice and Worcestershire. Spoon into an ovenproof casserole and sprinkle lightly with breadcrumbs. Bake in a preheated 375-degree oven until set, about 30 minutes. *Four servings, 280 calories each.*

LEAN LASAGNE WITH TUNA FISH

1 onion, minced
2 stalks celery, minced
1 clove garlic, minced
  29-ounce can Italian plum tomatoes, broken up
2 teaspoons oregano
  Pinch of cayenne pepper (optional)
6 dry curly-edged lasagne noodles
1 egg
1½ cups low-fat cottage cheese
1 cup chopped fresh parsley
2 seven-ounce cans water-packed tuna, flaked
8 ounces shredded part-skim mozzarella cheese
2 tablespoons grated extra-sharp Romano cheese

In a saucepan, cook the onion, celery, garlic, and tomatoes gently for 30 minutes. Season with oregano and hot pepper. Meanwhile, cook the lasagne in boiling salted water until very tender (about 18 minutes).

Stir the egg, cottage cheese, and parsley together.

Now combine all ingredients in a shallow nonstick baking pan in layers: noodles, some flaked tuna, some tomato sauce, cottage cheese mixture, then more noodles, tuna, sauce, and cottage cheese.

Top with tomato sauce, shredded mozzarella, and grated Romano cheese. Bake in a preheated 350-degree oven for 40 minutes. *Eight servings, 270 calories each.*

TUNA CACCIATORE AND SPAGHETTI

2 cups canned Italian tomatoes
1 cup chopped onion
1 green bell pepper, seeded and diced
1 teaspoon garlic salt
½ teaspoon oregano or Italian seasoning
¼ cup dry white wine
1 cup sliced mushrooms
2 seven-ounce cans water-packed tuna
½ teaspoon arrowroot or cornstarch
¼ cup cold water
2 tablespoons minced fresh parsley
4 cups tender-cooked protein-enriched spaghetti (see page 245)

Break up tomatoes with a fork in a heavy saucepan. Add onions, green pepper, garlic salt, oregano, and wine. Cover and simmer over very low heat 45 minutes.

Uncover and add mushroom slices and flaked tuna. Cook uncovered until most of the liquid has evaporated. Combine arrowroot and cold water and stir into simmering sauce until thick (this keeps sauce from separating). Stir in parsley and serve over the hot cooked spaghetti. *Four servings, 310 calories each.*

TUNA LASAGNE MARINARA

½ cup chopped onion
½ cup chopped celery
2 six-ounce cans tomato paste
3 cups water
2 teaspoons garlic salt
1 teaspoon oregano or Italian seasoning
1 pound lasagne noodles
2 seven-ounce cans water-packed tuna
1 cup low-fat cottage cheese
4 ounces shredded part-skim mozzarella cheese

Combine onion, celery, tomato paste, water, garlic salt, and oregano. Simmer 30 minutes, covered, until celery is tender. Meanwhile, cook lasagne according to package directions.

In a 13-by-9-inch baking dish, arrange layers of lasagne, tomato sauce, flaked tuna, and cottage cheese. Top with a layer of sauce and shredded mozzarella.

Bake in a 375-degree oven for 30 minutes or more, until cheese is well melted. Let stand 10 minutes before cutting. *Eight servings, 360 calories each.*

TUNA RISOTTO PIZZA

1½ cups cooked rice
1 egg, lightly beaten
1 cup shredded part-skim mozzarella cheese
7-ounce can water-packed tuna, drained and flaked
2 teaspoons dried onion flakes
8-ounce can plain tomato sauce
1 teaspoon oregano or Italian seasoning

Combine rice, egg, and ½ cup of the shredded cheese. Spray a nonstick cake pan with cooking spray for no-fat baking, then press the rice mixture firmly into the pan, spreading evenly. Bake in a preheated 450-degree oven 20 minutes.

Top with flaked tuna, onion, tomato sauce, oregano, and remaining cheese.
Bake 10 minutes more. *Cut into four wedges, about 230 calories each.*

Easy Cooking on the Go with Low-Calorie Tuna

On vacation? Here are "can-do" ideas for getaway cooks—who are not only
on the go but are calorie wise as well.

This trio of easy main courses is based on canned tuna, which can be ever
ready in anybody's pantry, galley, cabin, or trailer . . . no refrigeration needed!
To make these recipes extra easy for getaway cooks, most of the ingredients
need no refrigeration, and can be cooked in one dish on top of the stove.

TUNA THERMIDOR WITH RICE

 1 **cup instant rice**
 1 **cup boiling water**
   10½-ounce can cream of mushroom soup
¼ **cup dry white wine**
 1 **cup skim milk (fresh, canned, or reconstituted)**
½ **teaspoon prepared mustard (optional)**
 1 **tablespoon bottled lemon juice (optional)**
   4-ounce can sliced mushrooms, undrained
 3 **seven-ounce cans water-packed tuna, drained and broken up**
   Grated Parmesan cheese (optional)

Combine rice and boiling water in a dish, cover and set aside.

Meanwhile, stir soup, wine, milk, mustard, and lemon juice together in a
saucepan over moderate heat until smooth. Add mushrooms and simmer until
bubbling. Stir in tuna and simmer until heated through.

Serve over rice. Top each serving with 1 tablespoon grated cheese, if desired.
Six servings, 245 calories each without cheese; 275 calories with cheese.

TUNA MARINARA WITH SPAGHETTI

 8 **ounces dry very thin spaghetti (vermicelli)**
 3 **eight-ounce cans plain tomato sauce (no oil added)**
1½ **teaspoons oregano or Italian seasoning**
 3 **seven-ounce cans water-packed tuna, drained and broken up**
   Grated Parmesan cheese (optional)

Cook vermicelli in boiling water as package directs. Drain without rinsing.
Place in a bowl, cover, and set aside.

Use the pot in which the vermicelli was cooked to heat tomato sauce and oregano to boiling. Add broken-up tuna and simmer gently until heated through.

Serve cooked vermicelli with sauce. Top each serving with 1 tablespoon grated Parmesan cheese, if desired. *Six servings, 275 calories each without cheese; 305 calories with cheese.*

TUNA CHOP SUEY

    1 cup instant rice
    1 cup boiling water
       8-ounce can beef gravy
    ¼ cup soy sauce
       16-ounce can Oriental vegetables, drained
    1 cup sliced onion or 3 tablespoons dried onion flakes
    2 seven-ounce cans water-packed tuna, drained and broken up

Combine rice with boiling water in a bowl. Cover and set aside for 5 minutes.

Combine beef gravy and soy sauce in a saucepan. Cook and stir over moderate heat until smooth. Stir in drained vegetables and onion. Cook and stir until bubbling. Stir in tuna and simmer until heated through. Serve over rice. *Four servings, 280 calories each.*

Live Alone and Love It with Easy Low-Cal Tuna

What do single swingers and senior citizens have in common? Fattening convenience foods and frozen dinners!

Usually they're live-aloners, in tiny quarters without a well-stocked pantry or freezer. One single we know refers to his closet galley as an "eat-out kitchen." But eat-out isn't the answer for most singles or seniors, who usually have minuscule budgets to match.

They often have another common goal: the avoidance of overweight. Newly seated in a nine-to-five job, yesterday's football hero or cheerleader finds that an athletic appetite is a disadvantage. And grandma or grandpa finds that the new "efficiency" doesn't take the upkeep—or calorie outgo—that the old place did. Yet swinger and senior both need just as much protein as ever to keep the vitality needed to enjoy their new freedom.

One convenience food that's ideal for solo cooks is canned tuna. The smallest single-serving can—3½ ounces—packs a meal-size powerhouse of protein: 25 grams, about half your day's requirements. Packed in water instead of oil, tuna is a calorie bargain, only 105 calories or so per can. (Packed in oil it's 265 calories.) And those tiny cans are always handy: they take little space and need no refrigeration.

It doesn't take much time or trouble to turn a can of tuna into a "something special" main course for one. Toss together a generous salad and you've got a complete meal that's nourishing but nonfattening. Here are some ideas to try:

SINGLE-SERVING TUNA ROMANOFF WITH NOODLES

2 ounces dry noodles
¼ cup plain low-fat yogurt
   3½-ounce can water-packed tuna, drained and flaked
   Salt, or butter-flavored salt, and freshly ground pepper
   Chopped fresh parsley
2 teaspoons grated Parmesan cheese

  Boil noodles according to package directions. Drain and return the hot noodles to the same saucepan. Stir in yogurt and tuna over very low heat, only until heated through. Season to taste with salt (or butter-flavored salt) and a grind of fresh pepper. Sprinkle with parsley and cheese and serve immediately, with salad. *One serving, 375 calories.*

SOLO TUNA CACCIATORE WITH SPAGHETTI

  2 ounces dry protein-enriched very thin spaghetti (vermicelli)
    Boiling water
1½ cups tomato juice
  2 tablespoons chopped onion
 ½ green bell pepper, sliced
    3½-ounce can water-packed tuna, drained and flaked
    Garlic salt and pepper
    Oregano or Italian seasoning

  Cook vermicelli in boiling unsalted water. Meanwhile, in another saucepan. combine tomato juice, onion, and green pepper. Boil uncovered, while spaghetti cooks, until reduced to a sauce.
  Stir in tuna and seasoning to taste; reheat. (Check before adding salt.) *One serving, about 395 calories each.*

ORIENTAL STIR-FRY TUNA FOR ONE

⅓ cup instant rice
⅓ cup boiling water
2 stalks celery, diagonally sliced
½ sweet onion, sliced
1 tablespoon soy sauce
½ cup tomato juice
  3½-ounce can water-packed tuna, drained and flaked
  Tabasco or dry-roasted nuts (optional)

Combine rice and boiling water in a small bowl; cover and set aside. In a skillet, combine sliced celery, onion, soy sauce, and tomato juice. Cook and stir, uncovered, only until celery is crunchy-tender and juice is reduced to a thick sauce.

Stir in tuna and heat through. Add a dash of Tabasco for a spicy Szechuan-style dish if you like, or scatter with a tablespoon of dry-roasted peanuts for crunch. Spoon over hot rice and serve. *One serving, 285 calories each without peanuts; about 325 calories with peanuts.*

Slim Scallop Dishes Choice Among Seafoods

Scallops are to seafood what steak is to beef. Definitely prime! Luckily for Slim Gourmets, scallops are also calorie wise, only 386 calories per pound. And because scallops are all meat—no bones, no waste, no fat—a pound of scallops easily serves 4.

Scallops usually are sold frozen, unless you're lucky enough to live in areas where they're available fresh. Defrost scallops slowly in the refrigerator—never under hot running water! Cook quickly for the best flavor and texture.

Restaurant or heat-and-serve scallops may contain more bread and fat calories than "meat," so do your figure a favor with these:

"OVEN-FRIED" SCALLOPS

2 **pounds scallops**
1 **egg**
2 **tablespoons salad oil**
5 **tablespoons unseasoned breadcrumbs, either Toasted High-Fiber Bread-crumbs (see page 302) or commercial**
   Paprika
   Lemon juice
   Low-Cal Tartar Sauce (page 305) (optional)

Fork-blend egg and oil together. Cholesterol-free liquid egg substitute or 2 egg whites may be used in place of the whole egg. Roll scallops in egg mixture, then roll lightly in crumbs. Spray a nonstick cookie sheet with cooking spray for no-fat frying; arrange scallops in a single layer. Sprinkle with paprika and lemon juice. Bake in a preheated hot (450-degree) oven for 12 minutes without turning. Serve immediately, with Lo-Cal Tartar Sauce, if desired. *Four servings, 205 calories each without sauce; add 20 calories per tablespoon of sauce used per serving.*

SCALLOPS ON SKEWERS

1 pound scallops
¼ pound small fresh mushrooms
1 green pepper, cut in squares
½ cup low-calorie French dressing

Alternate scallops with vegetables on skewers; coat lightly with dressing. Grill over charcoal or under broiler approximately 10 minutes, turning and basting frequently. *Four servings, about 150 calories each.*

SCALLOP SCAMPI

1 pound scallops
1 or 2 cloves garlic, minced
1 tablespoon olive oil
3 tablespoons white wine
½ teaspoon oregano or Italian seasoning
   Paprika
4 slices protein-bread toast

Arrange scallops in a single layer in a shallow ovenproof dish. Combine garlic, olive oil, wine, and oregano and pour over scallops. Sprinkle with paprika. Broil without turning about 10 to 12 minutes. Serve on triangles of toasted protein bread. *Four servings, 175 calories each.*

SCALLOPS MARINARA

3 onions, chopped
2 cloves garlic, minced
   20-ounce can Italian tomatoes, broken up
3 cups tomato juice
1 teaspoon oregano or Italian seasoning
1 pound scallops
6 cups tender-cooked protein-enriched spaghetti (see page 245)
6 tablespoons grated extra-sharp Romano cheese

Combine first 5 ingredients in a saucepan. Cover and simmer 45 minutes. Uncover and simmer, stirring frequently, until sauce is reduced and quite thick. Add scallops and simmer 10 minutes longer. Serve over drained hot spaghetti and sprinkle with cheese. *Six servings, 325 calories each.*

THIN MAN'S COQUILLES ST. JACQUES

These cash- and calorie-saving versions of the French scallop dish Coquilles St. Jacques were suggested by two Slim Gourmet readers. Mrs. Frederick Wilson of Wakefield, Rhode Island, submitted her Thin Man's Coquilles St. Jacques, and Lee Nelke of West Acton, Massachusetts, offers Lee's "Pauvre Coquilles."

Mrs. Wilson adapted her recipe from one learned years ago in a gourmet cooking class in New York City. Only 5 feet 2, Mrs. Wilson writes that three years ago she weighed 140 pounds and wore a size 16. Then she began to cut way down on fattening ingredients. Today she weighs 107 pounds and wears a size 8 or 10.

The original French recipe calls for butter, heavy cream, and mushrooms sautéed in lots more butter.

1 **pound small scallops, fresh or defrosted**
2 **cups dry white wine**
1 **tablespoon dried onion flakes**
2 **tablespoons diet margarine**
3 **tablespoons all-purpose flour**
1 **jumbo or 2 small egg yolks**
½ **cup skim milk**
   3-ounce can drained mushroom pieces
   Salt, white pepper, grated nutmeg
½ **cup (2 ounces) grated Gruyère cheese**

Combine scallops, wine, and onion in a heavy nonstick skillet over medium heat. Poach gently in the wine 5 minutes. Remove scallops with a slotted spoon and place in 4 baking shells or a shallow ovenproof dish. Boil wine in the skillet until reduced to about 1 cup. Pour into a saucepan and set aside over very low heat.

Melt the margarine in the same skillet over low heat. Gradually blend in the flour. Add the warm wine slowly. Cook and stir until thickened.

In a small bowl beat egg yolks with milk. Gradually beat in some of the hot wine sauce. Return the hot wine-and-egg sauce to the skillet over very, very low heat. Add the mushrooms. Cook and stir over very low heat until thickened, but do not boil. Season to taste with salt, pepper, nutmeg.

Spoon the sauce over the scallops and top with grated cheese. Bake in a preheated 450-degree oven 10 to 12 minutes, until top is lightly browned and bubbly. *Four servings, 205 calories each.*

VARIATION

Lee's "Pauvre Coquilles": "Have you tried to buy scallops lately?" writes Lee Nelke. She teaches gourmet cooking classes at the Acton-Boxborough Adult School. "I use firm white fish. This way you can prepare Coquilles St. Jacques for a fraction of the cost."

To make mock scallops, substitute 1 pound fresh firm white fish fillets, preferably cusk, cod, haddock, or turbot. Rinse under cold water. Then gently cut the fish into 1-inch scallop-size cubes.

Use in the foregoing recipe.

Start with a Bloody Mary for Slim 'n' Spicy Seafood

A Bloody Mary mix can be the start of a great evening for two, even if you're out of vodka. Even if you don't like a Bloody Mary!

Because there's a lot more you can make with Bloody Mary mix than a Bloody Mary . . . especially if you're a Slim Gourmet cook. How about a spicy Crab Creole or an Oriental-inspired Szechuan shrimp dish? These quick-and-easy dinners for two start with Bloody Mary mix.

By "Bloody Mary mix" I mean a canned or bottled blend of tomato juice, salt, and a hot green chili pepper—not a chemicalized combination of synthetics. Several brands are available; just read the print on the labels.

Luckily for calorie counters, the pepper-spiked tomato-juice blend isn't much more fattening than plain tomato juice, only 40 or 50 calories or so for a 6-ounce (¾ cup) serving. If you don't like the spicy bite of chili peppers, simply use plain tomato juice instead—as I do for the easy leftover shrimp-for-two dish that follows the Bloody Mary mix recipes.

SPICY CRAB CREOLE

      7½-ounce can crabmeat
      6-ounce can (¾ cup) Bloody Mary mix or plain tomato juice
      Dash of garlic powder
  1 stalk celery, minced
  1 onion, minced
½ small green bell pepper, minced

Rinse and drain crabmeat, picking over carefully, and set aside. Combine remaining ingredients in a nonstick skillet. Cover and simmer 3 minutes. Uncover and simmer 3 more minutes, until celery and onion are tender-crunchy and tomato juice is thickened into a sauce. Stir in crabmeat at the last minute and heat through. *Two servings, 150 calories each. Serve on hot cooked rice, if desired, 110 calories per ⅔-cup serving.*

SZECHUAN SHRIMP

2 onions, quartered
1 stalk celery, thinly sliced on the diagonal
1 cup cut frozen green beans, defrosted
3 tablespoons soy sauce
2 tablespoons dry sherry
  Dash of ground ginger
  6-ounce can (¾ cup) Bloody Mary mix
½ pound cleaned raw shrimp, fresh or defrosted

Combine all ingredients except shrimp in a large nonstick skillet or electric frying pan. Heat to boiling. Stir in shrimp and reheat to a simmer. Simmer 3 to 5 minutes over low heat, stirring occasionally. *Two servings, 190 calories each.*

EASY SHRIMP FOR TWO

If there's ever any shrimp left over from a party, here's how to make it a meal.

½ pound shrimp cleaned cooked
¾ cup (6-ounce can) unsweetened pineapple juice
¾ cup (6-ounce can) tomato juice
1 tablespoon soy sauce
1 green bell pepper, seeded and diced
1 onion, cut in chunks

Simmer all ingredients except shrimp about 7 or 8 minutes, until vegetables are tender-crisp and juice is simmered into a thick sauce. Stir in cooked shrimp at the last minute. Cook only until heated through. Serve with rice if desired. *Each serving, about 195 calories without rice; add about 90 calories for ½ cup rice per serving.*

11
OMELETS, QUICHES, CRÊPES, AND OTHER EGG DISHES

What can you serve for dinner when you're fresh out of meat, money, and time? When you need something in a hurry that won't leave a sinkful of dishes? And, while I'm at it, be delicious, nutritious, and diet-wise as well?

Nothing meets this tall order like eggs. Not breakfast-style eggs, but a hearty main-course dish that goes with salad and wine. Eggs, after all, are a complete protein—just like meat, only cheaper and less fattening.

In this chapter I serve up a full range of low-calorie egg main-coursers, from the simplest of "scrambles" and easy omelets through frittatas, quiches (with and without crusts), crêpes, and timbales—about which more later.

GERMAN SCRAMBLE

2 leftover broiled frankfurters or 1 large knockwurst
6 eggs
2 tablespoons water
  Salt and freshly ground pepper to taste
  Chopped fresh parsley

Slice franks into thin disks, set aside. Beat eggs, water, salt, pepper, and parsley. Spray a large nonstick skillet with cooking spray for no-fat frying. Put the skillet over medium heat. When hot, add the eggs all at once. Stir in the sliced franks. Scramble lightly. *Three servings, 225 calories each.*

Omelets—Quick 'n' Easy (Especially on the Calories)

An unbeatable suggestion for hurry-up calorie watchers is the versatile omelet. Same eggs, but much more special than a scramble, especially when you add a saucy topping or filling.

ONE-PAN "SPANISH OMELET"

An omelet for 2 can be quickly made in a nonstick skillet with no fat added; just follow directions. Then you can use the same skillet to simmer up a 2-minute tomato sauce that switches its nationality just by switching the seasonings.

4 **eggs**
3 **tablespoons water**
  Salt and freshly ground pepper
  8-ounce can plain tomato sauce
3 **tablespoons finely minced onion**
¼ **cup chopped red and green bell pepper**
1 **small clove garlic, minced**
  Chili powder to taste

Put 2 plates in a 200-degree oven to keep warm. Spray a nonstick omelet pan or skillet with cooking spray for no-fat frying. Heat skillet over high flame until hot—until a drop of water bounces and sizzles. Beat eggs and water together, then add all at once to the skillet. Season with salt and pepper. The edges will begin to set immediately.

Gently lift edges with a spatula, permitting the uncooked portion to run underneath.

Continue cooking and lifting until eggs are set but surface is still moist and creamy (don't overcook or eggs will be rubbery). With spatula, gently fold omelet over on itself, then roll out of the skillet onto a heated plate. Cut in half and put half on the other plate. Return plates to oven to keep warm.

Put remaining ingredients in the same skillet, uncovered, over high heat. Check label on tomato sauce and choose a brand with no fat or oil.

Simmer 2 minutes, until sauce is bubbling and thick. Pour over omelet halves and serve immediately. *Two servings, 205 calories each.*

VARIATIONS

Mexican Cheese Omelet: Just before omelet is ready to turn out of the pan, sprinkle the surface with ¼ cup shredded extra-sharp Cheddar, American, or Monterey jack cheese. Season the sauce with a pinch of cumin and oregano, if desired. *230 calories per serving.*

Italian Omelet: Follow directions for Spanish Omelet, but omit chili powder. Season the sauce with a dash of cayenne pepper and oregano or Italian seasoning.

Italian Pizza Omelet: Follow Italian Omelet directions, but just before eggs are ready to turn out of the pan, sprinkle with 4 tablespoons shredded mozzarella cheese.

Low-Cholesterol "Omelets": Cholesterol watchers can prepare these using cholesterol-free liquid egg substitute (Eggbeaters or Second Nature). Use 1 cup liquid (as directed) in place of 4 eggs. Omit water. Cholesterol watchers should eliminate or minimize high-fat cheeses like Cheddar, American, or Monterey jack. In some areas, supermarkets stock low-fat "imitation" diet cheese, which can be shredded and used instead.

FRENCH QUARTER OMELET

¼ cup chopped green bell pepper
¼ cup chopped celery
2 tablespoons chopped onion
2 ripe tomatoes, peeled and chopped
¼ cup water
¼ teaspoon oregano or Italian seasoning
    Salt and freshly ground pepper
4 eggs, lightly beaten

Combine pepper, celery, onion, tomatoes, water, and oregano in a saucepan and simmer uncovered 20 minutes, stirring occasionally. Add water if needed. Season to taste.

Meanwhile, prepare a 2-serving omelet; spray a nonstick skillet with cooking spray for no-fat frying. Heat over a high flame. When skillet is hot, add the eggs. When eggs begin to set, lift the edges gently to permit unset portion to run underneath. Roll out onto a heated plate and top with sauce. Cut in half to serve. *Two servings, 200 calories each.*

MAXIM'S ROQUEFORT OMELET, DECALORIZED

"Maigrir!" ("Slim down!") demands an ad for a French bouillon producer. "You don't have the right to get fat!" chides the headline in a newspaper ad for a mineral-water bottler. There's even a Paris franchise of Weight Watchers. And Printemps, the big Paris department store, has a low-calorie restaurant featuring such dishes as broiled rabbit.

Even Maxim's, the Paris restaurant, grants recognition to calorie counters in its public cooking school by providing the calorie counts for its recipes.

This omelet makes a light luncheon or supper, served with chilled dry white wine or champagne. A tossed salad with ripe tomato wedges is a good addition.

2½ **ounces Roquefort, grated (see note below)**
12 **eggs**
 1 **tablespoon milk**
    Salt and freshly ground pepper
 2 **tablespoons butter**
    Fresh parsley (optional)

Beat together the eggs, milk, salt, and pepper. Spread the butter on the sides and bottom of a large nonstick skillet. Heat over high flame. When skillet begins to sizzle, add the eggs. Shake the pan lightly, or use a rubber spatula to lift up the omelet and allow the uncooked portion to run to the bottom of the pan. Sprinkle the cheese evenly over the omelet and stir into the surface.

When cheese is melted and egg is cooked, tip the skillet and loosen the edge of the omelet. It will roll over onto itself. Have a heated platter ready. Garnish with fresh parsley, if desired. *Six servings, 230 calories each.*

NOTE: To grate Roquefort cheese, put it in the freezer. When frozen, it is easy to grate with a hand grater. You will need about ⅔ cup for this recipe.

GREEK SPINACH OMELET IN A HINGED SKILLET

One of the greatest gadgets for a "stuffed" omelet is the hinged folding omelet pan or divided skillet. You've probably seen these inexpensive utensils in the housewares section. Making a filled omelet is simply a matter of pouring eggs in each side, partially cooking, adding the filling, and closing the pan. When you open it, there's a perfectly-shaped, neatly-filled omelet.

You can use any combination of low-calorie ingredients (even low-choles-terol egg substitute), but one of my favorites is this Greek Spinach Omelet.

 3 **medium (or 2 jumbo) eggs, lightly beaten, or ½ cup cholesterol-free egg**
    substitute
    Salt and pepper
¼ **cup drained, chopped canned or cooked spinach**
 1 **tablespoon minced onion (optional)**
    Grated nutmeg
½ **ounce cubed Provolone or feta cheese**

To make a filled low-calorie omelet in a hinged skillet, first spray both inner surfaces well with cooking spray. Open the pan flat over a moderate flame to heat both sides. When hot, pour an equal amount of beaten eggs into each side. When the edges of the eggs begin to set, gently but quickly lift the eggs on each side to permit uncooked portion to run underneath. When surface is nearly set but still moist, divide remaining ingredients between the sides. Then close the hinged skillet and turn off the heat. Wait 2 minutes before opening; remove the omelet onto a plate. (The heat of the eggs will warm the filling.) *One serving, about 275 calories.*

MICROWAVE BACON-CHEDDAR OMELET

Here's a low-calorie version of an omelet technique developed by Sharp's test kitchen for their carousel microwave oven with revolving turntable.

4 eggs
¼ cup skim milk
  Salt and freshly ground pepper
2 ounces shredded extra-sharp Cheddar cheese
1 tablespoon bacon-flavored bits

Spray a heatproof glass pie plate with cooking spray for no-fat frying, until the surface is wet and slick. Beat eggs and milk together and pour into pie plate. Sprinkle with salt and pepper. Cover tightly with plastic wrap or a nonmetal lid or a plate and put in the microwave oven. Cook on full power about 2 to 2 ½ minutes (rotate every 30 seconds). Uncover. Using a fork or rubber spatula, lift up cooked portion to let uncooked portion run underneath. Cover and cook again until eggs are nearly (but not quite) set, about 2 minutes. Sprinkle with cheese and cover. Wait a minute or 2 until cheese is melted, then uncover and sprinkle with bacon bits. Use a spatula to fold the omelet over on itself. Cut in half and serve. *Two servings, about 290 calories each.*

International Omelets That Begin with Leftovers

What do you do with leftover meat when what's left over is barely enough to make a meal? Make an omelet! A stuffed omelet is so much more special than a sandwich. More filling and nourishing, too.

HOW TO MAKE A NO-FAT-ADDED "STUFFED" OMELET. You'll need a small nonstick skillet, or an omelet or crêpe pan, and some cooking spray for no-fat frying. Spray the pan well, then heat over a moderate flame. Beat the eggs (no liquid added), then pour all at once into the hot pan. Shake the pan lightly, then lift up the edges of the egg to let the unset portion run underneath. When the surface is nearly set, add your filling. Then roll the omelet out onto a heated plate. Cover with wax paper or an upended pie tin and keep warm in the oven while you prepare the sauce. Or, if you are lucky enough to have a microwave oven, reheat briefly to warm the filling through. (It helps if all the filling ingredients are at room temperature rather than refrigerated.)

Low-cholesterol egg substitutes can also be used. If cholesterol watching, choose combinations that don't involve cheese or shellfish.

ITALIAN PARMIGIANA OMELET

2 eggs, beaten
1 ounce thinly sliced lean leftover roast veal
  Pinch of oregano or Italian seasoning
  Garlic salt, freshly ground pepper, red pepper flakes
  2 tablespoons shredded part-skim mozzarella cheese
  6-ounce can (¾ cup) tomato juice
1 teaspoon dried onion flakes

Cook omelet according to directions on page 205 and fill with veal. Sprinkle the veal lightly with seasonings and 1 tablespoon mozzarella before rolling out onto a plate. Cover and keep warm.

In the same skillet, put the tomato juice, onion flakes, and additional seasonings. Cook uncovered over high heat until the mixture reduces to a thick sauce. Pour the hot sauce over the omelet and sprinkle with remaining shredded cheese. Serve immediately, with a tossed salad as a side dish. *One serving, about 305 calories.*

VARIATION

Mexican Enchilada Omelet: Follow the preceding recipe, but substitute cooked white-meat chicken or turkey for the veal, extra-sharp Cheddar for the mozzarella. Add a dash of Tabasco to the tomato juice (or use canned Bloody Mary mix); add a dash of chili powder and cumin with the oregano, and substitute minced green pepper (or dried bell-pepper flakes) for the onion. *One serving, about 310 calories.*

PORK FOO YUNG FOR FOUR

8 eggs, beaten
4 ounces lean leftover roast pork, diced
1 cup well-drained canned Chinese chop suey vegetables
2 tablespoons finely chopped onion or 2 teaspoons dried onion flakes
3 tablespoons soy sauce
1 cup fat-skimmed beef or chicken broth
2 teaspoons arrowroot or cornstarch

Make 4 individual omelets in a small skillet or omelet pan, following directions on page 205, filling each with some of the diced pork, Chinese vegetables, and chopped onion. Set aside. To make sauce, combine soy sauce, broth, and arrowroot. Heat until mixture simmers and thickens. Pour over omelets. Serve with additional soy sauce and hot mustard. *Four servings, about 260 calories each.*

FRENCH HAM, CHEESE, AND SPINACH OMELETS FOR TWO

    8-ounce can chopped spinach, well drained
1   tablespoon dried onion flakes
    Pinch of grated nutmeg
    Salt and freshly ground pepper
4   eggs, beaten
¼   cup shredded or chopped Swiss cheese
2   ounces thinly sliced leftover lean baked ham

(You may prepare one large omelet in a large skillet and cut in half, or make two smaller omelets separately, dividing the ingredients between them.)

Drain and chop the spinach and combine with onion flakes and a dash of nutmeg. Season lightly with salt and pepper.

Prepare omelet (or 2 small omelets), following instructions on page 205. When set, fill with spinach, cheese, and ham. Roll out onto a plate and heat briefly in a warm oven or microwave oven to warm through and melt cheese. Serve with hot mustard. *Two servings, about 295 calories each.*

FETA-CHEESE OMELET

Now that all things Greek are very "in," it's only natural that feta is the big cheese. Feta looks like cream cheese, crumbles like Roquefort, cooks like ricotta and tastes like—well, it tastes like itself. Unique. Tangy yet mild, sort of salty, crumbly, but creamy. So rich tasting, in fact, that every week I get letters asking the calorie count. "It must be fattening," people write. Others take a more hopeful view: "It looks a little bit like cottage cheese." Some letter writers aren't sure of the name, calling it "Greek salad cheese," a reference to their first encounter with it. One reader called it "Greek fat cheese," expecting the worst, and another called it "Greek fetid cheese," a definite disservice in view of its delicious flavor.

None of the calorie guides widely available lists feta. However, the federal government, as part of its nutrient information update, recently released a new book on dairy and egg products, *Agriculture Handbook 8–1*, which does provide data on feta. According to the U.S. Department of Agriculture, feta cheese is 75 calories an ounce—more fattening than cottage cheese (24 per ounce), but a lot less than Cheddar (114 per ounce). Feta cheese is 20 percent fat, mostly saturated, and offers 4 grams of protein per ounce. What this means is that if you can have cheese, feta is better than most.

Sliced ripe tomatoes or diced cucumbers topped with yogurt would make a nice salad for this omelet.

2 eggs, lightly beaten
2 tablespoons skim milk
1 ounce feta cheese, cubed or crumbled
  Salt and freshly ground pepper to taste
  Chopped fresh parsley (optional)
  Pinch of onion or garlic powder (optional)

Lightly beat eggs and milk. Spray a small nonstick omelet pan with cooking spray for no-fat frying, or wipe lightly with salad oil on a paper towel. Heat pan over moderate flame. Add beaten-egg mixture. Shake pan lightly, and gently lift the eggs with a rubber spatula to allow uncooked portion to run underneath. When egg is set, top with cheese and seasonings.

Fold over. Turn off the heat. Leave the folded omelet in the skillet 1 minute, covered with a plate. (This will heat the serving plate and warm the cheese.) *One serving, about 260 calories.*

NOTE: Low-cholesterol egg substitute may be used in place of the eggs. *One serving would be under 300 calories.*

Save Calories, Save Time with the Fabulous Frittata

Here are some versions of the most fuss-free omelet of all, the flat, oven-baked Italian "pancake" called *frittata*. I've also used this incredibly easy method for an adaptation of the fabulous (but fat-laden) Spanish omelet that recreates the authentic dish but cuts the calories way, way down.

OVEN-BAKED FRITTATA

9 eggs, lightly beaten
½ pound diced cooked lean poultry or leftover roast pork, ham, or veal
3 ripe tomatoes, peeled and diced
2 red or green bell peppers (or one of each), seeded and chopped
1 large onion, finely chopped
1 clove garlic, minced, or ⅛ teaspoon instant garlic
2 tablespoons minced fresh parsley (optional)
2 teaspoons oregano or Italian seasoning
2 tablespoons grated sharp Romano cheese

Spray a nonstick piepan or layer-cake pan with cooking spray for no-fat frying. Combine all ingredients except grated cheese and pour into the pan. Bake uncovered in a preheated 350-degree oven until set, about 25 minutes. Sprinkle with cheese and cut into wedges to serve. *Six servings, about 230 calories each.*

LOW-CALORIE VEAL FRITTATA

A delightful dish, so delectable you'll plan leftover veal just to make it. Good with cooked chicken or turkey, too.

1 tablespoon diet margarine
½ cup finely minced onion
1 green bell pepper, seeded and finely chopped
½ cup finely chopped celery
2 cups diced leftover lean roast veal
Dash of Tabasco or Worcestershire sauce (or both)
1 teaspoon tarragon
2 tablespoons minced fresh parsley or 2 teaspoons parsley flakes
6 eggs, slightly beaten
6 tablespoons grated Romano or Parmesan cheese

Heat the margarine in a large skillet and cook onion, pepper, and celery until just tender. Add veal, Tabasco, and tarragon, and toss. Combine eggs, cheese, and parsley, and pour over veal mixture; cook over low heat until eggs begin to set. Put the skillet under a preheated broiler for a few minutes until browned on top; then serve. *Six servings, 205 calories each.*

PIZZA FRITTATA

This Italian-style "flat omelet" is goof-proof—and a great way to stretch leftover meat.

6 eggs, beaten
1 teaspoon dried onion flakes
Garlic powder to taste
1 cup diced cooked lean pork roast or other leftover meat
8-ounce can plain tomato sauce
¼ cup shredded part-skim mozzarella cheese
1 teaspoon oregano or Italian seasoning

Use an all-metal skillet or omelet pan that can go under the broiler (no plastic handles!). Spray the skillet well with cooking spray for fat-free frying. Heat over high flame. Add eggs. As they cook, lift edges to permit uncooked portion to run underneath.

Sprinkle surface with onion flakes, garlic powder, and cooked pork. Pour on tomato sauce. Sprinkle with shredded cheese and oregano. Slip under Heat over high flame. Add eggs. As they cook, lift edges to permit uncooked portion to run underneath.

Sprinkle surface with onion flakes, garlic powder, and cooked pork. Pour on tomato sauce. Sprinkle with shredded cheese and oregano. Slip under broiler for 4 or 5 minutes until tomato sauce is bubbling and cheese is brown and melted. To serve, cut in four wedges. *Four servings, 245 calories each.*

MEXICAN TURKEY FRITTATA

10 eggs
2 cups diced cooked turkey (see note below)
2 bell peppers, seeded and chopped
2 cups diced peeled ripe tomatoes
1 onion, chopped
2 tablespoons minced fresh parsley or 2 teaspoons dried parsley flakes
1 teaspoon salt or garlic salt
1 teaspoon chili powder
½ teaspoon oregano or Italian seasoning
1 teaspoon cumin seeds (optional)

Beat eggs lightly, then stir in remaining ingredients until well blended. Spray a nonstick cake pan with cooking spray for no-fat baking. Pour in egg mixture. Bake in a preheated 350-degree oven for 30 minutes, until set. Cut in wedges to serve. May be served hot or cold. *Eight meal-size servings, about 185 calories each; or sixteen appetizer servings at 95 calories each.*

NOTE: For interesting variations, use cooked smoked turkey or diced "turkey ham" or julienne strips of "turkey salami" or "turkey pastrami," now available at many cold-cuts counters.

FOO YUNG FRITTATA

2 cups diced cooked turkey, chicken, or lean roast pork
3 tablespoons soy sauce
10 eggs
16-ounce can mixed Chinese vegetables, rinsed and drained
1 Spanish onion, minced
1 small red or green bell pepper, diced

Marinate leftover roast poultry or meat in soy sauce 30 minutes or more.

Beat eggs lightly, then stir in all other ingredients. Turn into a nonstick 9-inch pie plate that has been sprayed with cooking spray for no-fat baking. Bake in a preheated 350-degree oven 30 minutes or more, until set. Cut into wedges to serve. *Eight servings, 185 calories each with turkey, 155 with chicken, 210 with pork.*

OVEN-BAKED SPANISH POTATO OMELET

The native Spanish omelet has nothing whatsoever to do with the ubiquitous Spanish omelet of roadside-diner fame—as any American who orders one for breakfast soon finds out! The diner version is really a French omelet with Spanish sauce—rolled-over eggs topped with tomato, onion, and pepper.

To further confound would-be food linguists, the Spanish call their omelet a "tortilla," but a traveling Texan who expects a crisp cornmeal Mexican-style tortilla is in for a surprise also.

What, then, is a Spanish omelet? Basically, it's an egg-onion-potato mixture fried in oil and served in pie-shaped wedges. It's so thick and dense it could never be folded or rolled up, as a French or American omelet is. In texture and appearance it's more like a thick pancake (or fallen soufflé) than our omelet . . . but delicious.

To the basic mixture the inventive Spanish cook is likely to add chopped pepper, olives, green peas, seasonings, or bits of cooked meat. The true Spanish omelet is not only a work of art and expression of individuality, it's a great way to use up leftovers.

Unfortunately, the true Spanish omelet also requires lots of oil—too much oil—an indifference to calories, and a strong wrist. The mixture is usually cooked in a skilletful of oil, then flipped over to brown the other side. It takes practice. So I've come up with an oven-baked version that's easier on the cook, easier on the calories—no fat, no frying, no flipping. And it's nonfattening. As do Spanish cooks, you can vary this dish according to what's in your refrigerator. The cooked ham can be replaced with leftover roast, poultry, seafood, or water-packed tuna.

 5 eggs
 2 cups peeled cooked cubed potatoes
 1 onion, finely chopped
 1 green bell pepper, minced
12 stuffed green Spanish olives, sliced
 1 teaspoon salt
 4 ounces lean cooked ham, cubed

Beat eggs until fluffy. Fold in remaining ingredients. Spray a round nonstick cake pan with cooking spray for no-fat frying. Spoon in omelet mixture. Bake in a preheated 350-degree oven 25 to 30 minutes, until eggs are set. Cut into wedges to serve. *Four servings, 230 calories each.*

Make a Meal of Crêpes, Easy, Elegant, and Slim

Crêpes are skinny pancakes, but they can be very, very fattening. What goes in them and on them makes the difference.

Since crêpes are also easy, elegant, and very versatile they can be lunch, dinner, or dessert (see the yummy recipes for which on pages 212–14). Every calorie watcher should know how to make "skinny pancakes" even slimmer.

These crêpes are nutrition rich, filling but nonfattening. Begin with some batters (take your choice!) that are more dairy protein than starch. "Fry" the crêpes in a nonstick skillet with no fat. Then, to top it off, fill and sauce the crêpes with low-fat nutrition-rich ingredients.

BASIC EGG CRÊPES

One plus two and three equals four. That's my easy-to remember recipe for the protein-rich, low-calorie crêpes. One egg plus 2 tablespoons flour and 3 tablespoons milk equals 4 crêpes. Need more? Simply multiply—as you see, this recipe is for 8 crêpes.

For a dozen crêpes triple the recipe. Use 3 eggs, 6 tablespoons flour, and 9 tablespoons skim milk (a little more than ½ cup).

What makes my crêpe formula different from most recipes is the higher proportion of protein-rich ingredients—milk and eggs—and the lesser amount of flour. My egg-rich mixture is really a cross between an omelet and a skinny pancake. It makes delicious crêpes in a nonstick omelet pan, or in one of the new crêpe gadgets now rushing to the market.

6 **tablespoons skim milk**
2 **large eggs**
⅛ **teaspoon salt**
¼ **cup all-purpose flour**

Fork-whip ingredients until blended. Spray a small nonstick skillet or omelet pan with coating for no-fat frying. Preheat over a moderate flame, until a drop of water will bounce off the pan. Add about 2 tablespoons batter and rotate skillet to spread. When the surface of the crêpe is dry and bubbled, flip out onto a plate. Continue making crêpes one at a time. *Makes about eight, 45 calories each.*

VARIATIONS

Low-Cholesterol Crêpes: Replace the 2 eggs with 4 egg whites. Or, use ½ cup liquid low-cholesterol egg substitute.

Soy-Enriched Crêpes: Substitute soy pancake mix for the flour, and omit salt.

Mexican Crêpes: Replace the flour with white or yellow cornmeal. (Use Mexican crêpes in place of fried tortillas in enchilada-type combinations.)

LOW-CAL CHEESE CRÊPES

The cheese you need for these crêpes is low-fat, dry-curd "pot-style" cottage cheese. Look for a brand that's 99 percent fat free.

3 eggs
⅓ cup low-fat, dry "pot-style" cottage cheese
2 tablespoons all-purpose flour
¼ teaspoon salt

Combine all the ingredients in your blender, cover, and blend. Scrape down with a rubber spatula. Cover and blend again, until batter is completely smooth.

Use a skillet, omelet pan, or small crêpe pan. Spray the inside well with cooking spray for no-fat frying. Heat over a moderate flame. When hot, add 3 tablespoons batter. Swirl the pan to spread the batter. When surface of crêpe is dry, turn the pan over and drop the crêpe onto a sheet of wax paper (no need to cook the other side). Continue making 1 crêpe at a time until all the batter is used. Stack crêpes with wax paper in between, then fill with filling of your choice. *Makes about six, 60 calories each.*

NOTE: If you have a dip-type crêpe maker, keep in mind that some of the batter is wasted, so you'll need extra. Follow the manufacturer's directions to make crêpes.

FRENCH SEAFOOD CRÊPES

Basic Egg Crêpes (see page 212)
1½ cups skim milk
1 tablespoon all-purpose flour
2 teaspoons cornstarch
½ cup shredded Swiss cheese
Salt and nutmeg to taste
Pinch of cayenne pepper
1½ cups drained canned crabmeat, lobster, or shrimp
Chopped fresh parsley or minced onion (optional)

Prepare Basic Egg Crêpes. Then, in a small saucepan over low heat, stir together skim milk, flour, and cornstarch until thick. Stir in Swiss cheese until melted. Season with salt, nutmeg, and a pinch of cayenne pepper. Then combine ½ cup of the hot sauce with crabmeat, lobster, or shrimp. Stir in some chopped fresh parsley or minced onion, if you like.

Spoon seafood mixture into the middle of each crêpe. Roll up, then warm in a 325-degree oven. At serving time, pour the remaining hot sauce over the crêpes. *Makes eight, 110 calories each.*

CHICKEN ENCHILADA CRÊPES

Mexican Crêpes (see page 212)
10-ounce can fat-skimmed condensed chicken broth
6-ounce can tomato paste
Chili powder, cumen, or oregano to taste
1½ cups minced cooked turkey

Prepare Mexican Crêpes. Then, in a small saucepan over moderate heat, stir together chicken broth and tomato paste. Season to taste with chili powder cumin, or oregano. Simmer until thick and smooth. Combine ½ cup of the hot sauce with chicken or turkey. Spoon chicken filling onto crêpes and roll up. Warm in a 325-degree oven. Top with the remaining hot sauce. *Makes eight, 120 calories each.*

MINI-CALORIE MANICOTTI

Recycle lean leftover roast beef or other meat into a luscious Italian dish that's made in minutes.

6 Low-Cal Cheese Crêpes (page 213)
½ pound lean roast beef or crumbled leftover cooked hamburgers
2 teaspoons instant onion
¼ cup low-fat, dry-curd "pot-style" cottage cheese
4 cups shredded part-skim mozzarella cheese
Oregano or Italian seasoning
Garlic salt
Freshly ground pepper
8-ounce can plain tomato sauce

Cook crêpes and set aside.

Combine finely minced cooked meat, onion, cottage cheese, and 2 table-spoons mozzarella. Season lightly with oregano, garlic salt, and pepper. Spoon a little of the meat mixture onto each crepe and roll up. Arrange in a nonstick cake pan that has been sprayed with cooking spray for no-fat frying. Cover the pan with foil and put in a preheated 250-degree oven to warm through (or heat through in a microwave oven).

Meanwhile, heat sauce in a small saucepan. Season lightly with oregano. Pour over crêpes and sprinkle with shredded mozzarella. *Each crêpe, 175 calories.*

If you like ham and cheese . . . and eggs . . . and pie, you'll love the nifty French dish known as Quiche Lorraine. If you hate frumpy calories, you'll especially love this version.

In case you don't *comprenez* culinary French, *quiche* is pie—but not as in apple, mince, or pumpkin. A French quiche is a protein-rich main course usually made with eggs, cream, cheese, and such savory extras as bacon, ham, or onions. Today, quiche is considered a very chic partygoer, but the thrifty French farmers' wives, who developed the dish, did it as a budget stretcher, eggs, cream, and cheese being cheaper than meat.

One thing they did not economize on was calories; farm families needed all the energy they could get. Since that is just the reverse of our problem, Slim Gourmet quiche puts the emphasis on protein and minimizes fat.

Quiche is handy at holiday time—a quick and easy supper, needing little else than a salad and some dry white wine. Or make a quiche and serve it in slender appetizer portions at your next party.

SLIM QUICHE LORRAINE

Ham and Cheese Pie

      Frozen ready-to-bake pie crust, defrosted
4 ounces cubed cooked lean ham or Canadian bacon
1 small onion, finely minced
½ cup (2 ounces) shredded Iceland Swiss or other part-skim white cheese
3 eggs
1 cup skim milk
¾ cup low-fat cottage cheese
1 teaspoon salt
1 teaspoon prepared mustard
      Pinch of pepper
3 tablespoons minced fresh parsley

Have the pie crust at room temperature. Remove it from its pie pan and put it in a straight-sided 9-inch nonstick round cake pan. Press the pastry thin to fit the pan. Trim away and discard the excess pastry that overlaps the edges.

Sprinkle the ham, onion and Iceland Swiss cheese in the bottom of the pan. Combine remaining ingredients in a bowl or blender and beat smooth. Pour into pan. Bake in a preheated 325-degree oven for 40 to 50 minutes or until set. Serve warm. *Six meal-size servings, 230 calories each; sixteen appetizer servings, 85 calories each.*

CHOLESTEROL WATCHERS' QUICHE

POLYUNSATURATED OIL PASTRY:

¾ cup all-purpose flour
½ teaspoon salt
¼ teaspoon baking soda
3 tablespoons safflower oil
4 to 6 teaspoons ice water

FILLING:
2 cups low-fat cottage cheese
1 tablespoon arrowroot or cornstarch
1 tablespoon lemon juice
3 egg whites
1 teaspoon salt
3 ounces lean cooked ham, cubed
2 onions, finely chopped
1 or 2 drops yellow food coloring (optional)
2 tablespoons grated Parmesan cheese

Prepare the pastry first. Stir dry ingredients together. Cut in oil with a fork; add only as much ice water as needed, until pastry will leave the sides of the bowl. Flatten, wrap, and chill. Roll out on a floured board with a floured roller. Line a round 9-inch nonstick cake pan, discarding the excess.

Beat the cottage cheese, arrowroot, and lemon juice smooth. In another bowl, beat the egg whites and salt until soft peaks form. Gently fold together the cottage-cheese mixture, the egg-white mixture, the ham, and onions. Stir in yellow food coloring, if desired. Spoon the mixture into the pie crust and sprinkle with Parmesan cheese. Bake in a preheated 350-degree oven for 1 hour, or until set. *Six meal-size servings, 225 calories each; sixteen appetizer servings, 85 calories each.*

LOW-CAL BACON-MUSHROOM QUICHE

Single frozen piecrust
1 small onion, thinly sliced
½ cup shredded Swiss cheese
1 tablespoon minced fresh parsley or 1 teaspoon parsley flakes
½ cup sliced fresh mushrooms or 4-ounce can, drained
¾ cup skim milk
2 whole eggs
3 tablespoons dry white wine
½ cup low-fat cottage cheese

1 teaspoon prepared mustard
½ teaspoon salt or butter-flavored salt
⅛ teaspoon freshly ground pepper
3 tablespoons bacon-flavored bits

Defrost piecrust. Carefully fold in quarters and remove to a nonstick deep-dish 8- or 9-inch pie pan or cake pan. Stretch to fit with fingertips.

Put onion, cheese, parsley, and mushrooms on the bottom of the pie shell. Combine remaining ingredients except bacon bits. Beat or blend well. Pour into pie shell. Sprinkle with bacon bits. Bake in a preheated 375-degree oven for 30 to 40 minutes, until filling is set. Cut into wedges to serve. *Six meal-size servings, 230 calories each; sixteen appetizer servings, 85 calories each.*

TUNA-CHEDDAR-YOGURT QUICHE

Single frozen piecrust
6½-ounce can water-packed tuna, drained and flaked
1 small onion, thinly sliced
½ cup extra-sharp Cheddar cheese, shredded
2 whole eggs
8-ounce container plain low-fat yogurt
¼ cup low-fat cottage cheese
1 tablespoon lemon juice
2 teaspoons Worcestershire sauce
Dash of Tabasco
½ teaspoon garlic salt

Prepare piecrust according to preceding recipe. Place tuna, onion, and Cheddar cheese in the bottom of the pie shell. Beat remaining ingredients well and pour into pie shell. Bake in a preheated 375-degree oven 30 to 40 minutes, until set. *Six meal-size servings, 250 calories each; sixteen appetizer servings, under 95 calories each.*

EASY TURKEY-MUSHROOM "BREADCRUST" QUICHE

4 slices bread, preferably diet, whole wheat, protein, or high-fiber
½ cup thinly sliced fresh mushrooms
1 tablespoon dried onion flakes
¾ pound sliced cooked turkey
2 cups skim milk
2 eggs

2 one-serving envelopes instant mushroom soup
3 tablespoons dry sherry
2 tablespoons breadcrumbs
¼ cup grated Parmesan cheese

Toast bread lightly. Cut each slice in quarters. Arrange in the bottom of an 8-inch square nonstick cake pan. Top with mushrooms, onion flakes, turkey.

Combine milk, eggs, soup mix, and sherry in blender or mixer bowl and beat until well mixed. Pour over turkey. Sprinkle with crumbs and Parmesan. Bake in a preheated 375-degree oven 30 to 40 minutes, until set. *Eight servings, 215 calories each.*

GREEK SPINACH PIE

The Greeks' favorite spinach dish is Spanakopitta—spinach pie. Conventionally made, it's plenty fattening, with lots of layers of oiled phyllo pastry. The pastry itself isn't that fattening, only about 38 calories a sheet. This version uses just one layer. Phyllo pastry is available frozen in some supermarkets. If you can't get it, try this alternative suggestion, an upside-down deep-dish spinach pie topped with a single layer of ready-to-bake piecrust. Either way, my Greek Spinach Pie is a lot less fattening.

2 eggs, lightly beaten
1 onion, finely chopped
2 tablespoons chopped fresh parsley
   10-ounce package frozen chopped spinach, defrosted and drained well
1½ cups skim milk
3 tablespoons instant-blending flour
   Salt
¼ teaspoon grated nutmeg
8 ounces low-fat cottage cheese
½ cup cubed feta cheese
1 6-by-16-inch sheet of phyllo pastry (strudel leaf)
1 tablespoon salad oil

Beat the eggs in a large mixing bowl and set aside.

Cook onion, parsley, and spinach together in a small amount of water; drain very well and set aside.

Combine milk, flour, a pinch of salt, and nutmeg in a small saucepan. Cook and stir over moderate heat until sauce simmers. Simmer 1 minute. Very slowly stir ½ cup of the white sauce into the beaten eggs. Mix in the spinach mixture, then the remaining white sauce. Stir in the cottage and feta cheeses. Turn into an 8- or 9-inch square nonstick cake pan.

Brush phyllo pastry lightly with oil and fold in half. Brush again with oil and fold in half again to form an 8-by-8-inch square. Place on top of spinach mixture.

Bake at 325 degrees 30 to 40 minutes, until top is golden and crusty. Cut in squares to serve. *Four meal-size servings, about 355 calories each; eight side dish or appetizer servings, about 175 calories each.*

VARIATION

Greek Upside-Down Spinach Quiche: If you can't find phyllo pastry, try this. Substitute a defrosted ready-to-use single pie shell. Turn filling mixture into a round 9-inch pie pan or cake pan. Arrange piecrust on top. Make slits with the point of a sharp knife. Bake at 350 degrees for 20 minutes, until crusty. Serve in wedges, topped with crust. *Adds about 150 calories to a meal-size serving, about 75 to an appetizer serving.*

HAM AND CHEESE ON RYE PIE

Leftover baked ham or roast turkey makes a great sandwich, or you can dress it up as a savory slimmer's "quiche." This calorie-saving translation, made into a square "pie," uses crisp rye crackers as a base.

      About 9 seasoned rye crackers (Ry-Krisp or similar)
    4 ounces lean cooked ham, diced
    4 ounces Swiss cheese, diced
 1½ cups low-fat cottage cheese
   ½ cup skim milk
   ¼ cup dry white wine
    3 eggs
    1 small onion, minced, or 1 tablespoon dried onion flakes
    1 teaspoon prepared mustard
    3 or 4 sprigs fresh parsley, chopped
      Dash of Tabasco

Spray a 9-inch nonstick square cake pan with cooking spray for no-fat baking. Arrange crackers to cover the bottom, breaking to fit. Spread diced ham and Swiss cheese over the crackers, evenly.

Combine remaining ingredients in blender or food processor. Cover and blend smooth. Pour over ham and cheese.

Bake in a preheated 350-degree oven for 45 minutes, or until set. Serve warm. *Six servings, under 210 calories each.*

Glamorous Leftovers with Egg-Rich "Timbales"

Question: What's a crustless "quiche," an unscary "soufflé," or a custard you have for dinner instead of dessert? Answer: A timbale.

A timbale, in case the word has escaped your culinary lexicon, is a creamy egg-and-meat mixture cooked in custard cups, then unmolded and served hot and steaming. Or egg and seafood, egg and poultry, egg and cheese, egg and vegetable, egg and whatever.

Like a quiche, it's a great way to glamorize leftovers—but the timbale has no fattening pastry crust. A timbale is more like a single-serving soufflé. Except it won't deflate at the crucial moment the way a soufflé might.

And—like quiche, soufflé, or custard—the timbale can be calorie laden if made according to standard recipes; it can also be delightfully decalorized. The timbale really has a lot going for it if you have to count both calories and pennies.

Ordinary ovenproof custard cups can hold your timbale fillings. Coat the cups lightly with spray for no-fat frying and the mixture will unmold easily. The custard cups should be filled about two-thirds full, then set in a shallow pan. Pour about 2 inches of boiling water into the pan around the custard cups, then put the pan in a preheated 350-degree oven and bake about 20 to 30 minutes until set (a table knife inserted in the middle will come out clean).

Seasoning variations won't change the calorie counts too much, so experiment with combinations according to your whim and what's on hand.

VEAL OR BEEF TIMBALES

2 cups cooked, finely chopped lean veal or beef
1 cup fat-skimmed beef or veal broth
2 tablespoons all-purpose flour
1 tablespoon minced onion
½ teaspoon basil or oregano
    Juice of ½ lemon
½ teaspoon grated lemon rind
    Salt and freshly ground pepper
2 eggs, beaten
6 teaspoons grated Parmesan cheese

Trim off and discard any fat from the meat before chopping. In a saucepan, cook and stir the broth and flour together until mixture simmers and thickens. Season with onion, basil, lemon juice and rind, salt and pepper if needed. Stir in meat and eggs; spoon into 6 custard cups. Set the cups in a shallow pan filled with 2 inches of water.

Bake in a preheated 350-degree oven until set, about 20 minutes. Upend and unmold on dinner plates; sprinkle each with 1 teaspoon grated cheese. *Six servings, 180 calories each.*

CHICKEN MUSHROOM TIMBALES

2 **cups minced cooked white meat of chicken or turkey**
  4-ounce can mushroom pieces, drained and chopped
3 **eggs, separated**
2 **tablespoons dry white wine**
½ **cup evaporated skim milk**
  Salt and freshly ground pepper
  Dash of Tabasco
  Pinch of grated nutmeg
  Paprika
  Fresh chopped parsley

Stir the chopped poultry, mushrooms, egg yolks, wine, and milk together. Season to taste with salt, pepper, Tabasco, and nutmeg. In another bowl, add a dash of salt to the egg whites and beat until stiff. Fold into the poultry mixture. Spoon into 6 custard cups.

Put the cups in a shallow pan with 2 inches of water. Bake in a preheated 350-degree oven until set, 20 to 30 minutes. Invert and sprinkle with paprika or chopped fresh parsley. *Makes six timbales, 120 calories each.*

VARIATION

Seafood Timbales: Follow the preceding recipe, substituting drained, flaked water-packed tuna for the poultry; or any leftover cooked or canned fish or shellfish can be used.

What to serve with timbales? Try a big tossed salad, some broiled tomato halves, a green vegetable, and fresh fruit dessert.

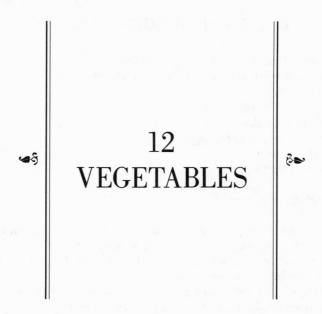

12
VEGETABLES

CRUNCHY "STEAMED" ASPARAGUS

We think it's a mortal sin to murder vegetables with overcooking, but never is the sin more grievous than when the vegetable is asparagus. Expensive even at its peak, it's the royalty of vegetables, entitled to coddling.

Asparagus is one indulgence even calorie counters can afford. A whole pound is only 66 calories—about 3 per spear—and chock-full of appetite-appeasing fat-fighting fiber.

Fresh is always better than frozen or canned, but in no vegetable is the taste and texture difference more marked than with asparagus. To overcook fresh asparagus is to take a premium-priced delicacy and reduce its flavor to what's available processed the rest of the year.

Our own preference is to cook fresh asparagus even less than the generally accepted norm. We like it just heated through, still crunchy and bright green. We enjoy eating steaming spears of asparagus as finger food, dipping them in little bowls of lemon juice, Worcestershire or soy sauce, or in low-calorie salad dressing. Try it our way and you might join us. If not, you can always cook asparagus a little longer, but never limp and olive drab.

Asparagus should be cleaned in running water. The tough woody ends should be snapped off, not cut. Then asparagus should be steamed to the desired crunchiness or tenderness. The exact time really depends on the thickness of the stalks and your own preference.

But one way asparagus should never be cooked is boiled. The cook who drops asparagus into a bubbling cauldron of water, like so much spaghetti, should have her hot pad retired!

How do you "steam" asparagus? In a vegetable steamer, if you have one. If not, try this:

IN A COVERED SKILLET: Set a small wire cake rack in the skillet. Lay the spears on top of the rack and pour water underneath, so the water is not touching the asparagus. Cover and steam to desired tenderness.

ON FOIL: No cake rack? Crumple foil in the bottom of a skillet. Punch some holes in the foil to let the steam through. Then add water. Lay the spears on its bed of foil. Cover the skillet and steam.

IN A COFFEEPOT: Stand the spears head up in a tall percolator. Put 2 inches of water in the bottom. Put on the top and steam.

IN A MICROWAVE OVEN: If you have one, and really like your asparagus crunchy, just lay the spears on a paper plate in a single layer. Close the door and cook for 30-second periods. Open the door, check the temperature and texture with your fingers, then rotate the plate. Continue to cook for 30-second periods until thoroughly hot (time depends not only on the thickness of the stalks but on how many you're cooking at once.)

LOW-CAL SAUCES

If you prefer your asparagus cooked tender and topped with a sauce, here are some low-calorie toppings to try:

Mock Hollandaise: Gently warm some low-fat mayonnaise, thinned with a little water and some lemon juice. *About 20 calories per tablespoon.*

Bottled Italian Salad Dressing: The low-fat, low-calorie version, of course!

Greek Garlic Tomato Sauce: Chop 3 cloves garlic and sauté in 1 tablespoon olive oil. Stir in 1 tablespoon lemon juice and 1 cup plain tomato sauce. Simmer 1 minute, then season to taste with salt, fresh pepper, and chopped parsley. *About 12 calories per tablespoon.*

The Simplest Way Yet to Grow Bean Sprouts

Try your hand at some indoor gardening under the sink. Or in the pantry. Or in that second oven you rarely use.

The "crop" we're referring to is bean sprouts—only 16 calories a half-cup serving, and a nutritional bargain.

Sprouting couldn't be simpler; the beans do most of the work. They need no dirt, only darkness, moisture, and room temperature. They take up hardly any space at all. They're just what the impatient "farmer" ordered: start your garden Monday morning and you'll be enjoying a Chinese dinner before the weekend. It only takes 3 or 4 days to harvest time.

Many beans can be sprouted, but the beginner will probably reap the most enjoyment from sprouting mung beans, the basic bean sprout found in chow mein, chop suey, and other super-popular Chinese meals.

They're really worth the minimal effort required; the difference between home-grown sprouts and the canned variety is like the difference between fresh tomatoes and canned. If your "homemade" chow mein from a can doesn't taste like takeout, try it with fresh sprouts.

Here's how:

First buy some mung beans from health-food store or a Chinese grocery. Then remove ½ cup from the package. Don't be overambitious: remember Jack and his beanstalk? . . . Beans sprout to 4 or 5 times their original volume.

Cover the beans with tepid water to soak overnight. Next day, pour the beans into a colander to drain. Then set the colander in a larger bowl to catch the drippings. Now put the colander-bowl assembly in some dark place. At least 3 or 4 times a day, submerge the colander full of beans in a bowlful of tepid water to rinse and rewet. Then lift the colander out of the water and set it back in the bowl, in the aforementioned dark place. As soon as they're 2 inches long, they're bean sprouts.

By that time most of the green hulls will be loose and will wash off, but those that don't are edible, so don't worry. And that's all there is to it. There are kits sold for sprouting beans and directions that involve layering the beans in wet paper, but I never saw the need for complicating the matter.

Sprouting is simply a matter of getting the bean wet and keeping it moist until it does its thing. If you've ignored the suggestion about the quantity to sprout and now find yourself knee deep in a bumper crop of bean sprouts, be advised that they keep quite well in the refrigerator, bagged in plastic.

After a while they lose their crispness, but can be recrisped with a chilly rinse of ice water. The same bagged bean sprouts can also be frozen. They're not as crisp as fresh, but are still better than canned.

BASIC CHOP SUEY

With fresh sprouts available, chop suey is the one basic recipe every calorie counter and nutrition watcher will want to know. Of course it's not Chinese at all, but who cares? Kids love it; so do vegetable haters! It's so economical and versatile. And luckily for the figure conscious, it's low in fat and calories.

That great American dish, ideal for calorie counters.

  1 cup fat-skimmed chicken or beef broth
¾ pound chicken cutlets, cut in bite-size pieces
  3 cups fresh bean sprouts
  1 large Spanish onion, cut in half, then thinly sliced
  4 large stalks celery, diagonally sliced
½ pound fresh mushrooms, sliced

½ teaspoon monosodium glutamate (optional)
   Soy sauce
2 tablespoons arrowroot or cornstarch
2 cups cooked rice

In a large skillet combine ½ cup broth with all remaining ingredients except soy sauce, arrowroot, and rice. Heat to simmering and stir well. Cover and cook 7 to 10 minutes, only until celery is tender crunchy.

Stir 3 tablespoons soy sauce, arrowroot, and remaining ½ cup cold broth together in a small bowl. Stir into simmering skillet, stirring constantly until sauce thickens and clears. Serve with the cooked rice and additional soy sauce. *Four servings, 170 calories each without rice. Each ½ cup of rice adds about 90 calories per serving.*

VARIATIONS

With Leftover Poultry: Dice cooked white-meat chicken or turkey into bite-size chunks. Follow above recipe, but add the cooked poultry at the last minute. Simmer and stir only until heated through.

Shrimp Chop Suey: Use ¾ pound shelled, deveined small shrimp instead of chicken. If shrimp is canned or already cooked, add it at the end and simmer-stir until heated through. *165 calories per serving.*

Beef, Pork, or Veal Chop Suey: Use 2 cups cooked meat, cut into cubes; trim off and discard any fat. Use beef broth as the simmering liquid. Add cubed cooked meat at the end and heat through. *Less than 200 calories per serving.*

Tuna, Lobster, or Crab Chop Suey: Use two 6½- or 7-ounce cans seafood—if tuna, the water-packed, not the oil-packed kind. Rinse, drain, and pick over canned lobster or crab carefully. Add canned seafood at the last minute and heat through. *About 175 calories each.*

Hamburger or Steak Chop Suey: Use ¾ pound lean beef round, trimmed of fat, ground into hamburger or diced into bite-size cubes. Fry the meat quickly in a nonstick skillet with no fat added, only until brown. Stir in 1 cup cold water. Drain the water into a cup or bowl. Wait till the fat rises to the surface, then skim off with a bulb-type baster. Use this fat-skimmed liquid in place of the broth in the recipe. Add salt or additional soy sauce to suit. *Less than 200 calories per serving.*

"HAWAIIAN" HARVARD BEETS

Submitted by Joseph Blumenfeld of East Rutherford, New Jersey, this recipe wins the prize for simplicity! Mr. Blumenfeld just combines canned beets and canned pineapple and thickens their juices to make a sweet-sour sauce with no sugar. What could be easier!

16-ounce can diced or sliced beets
8-ounce can unsweetened pineapple chunks
¼ cup lemon juice
2 tablespoons cornstarch
Salt and freshly ground pepper

Heat beets in their own juice in a saucepan. Add pineapple chunks and heat to simmering. Stir juice from canned pineapple, lemon juice, and cornstarch together and stir into simmering beets. Cook and stir until thickened. *Six servings, about 55 calories each.*

CHOPPED BROCCOLI À LA GRECQUE

10-ounce box frozen chopped broccoli or spinach, defrosted
1 chicken bouillon cube
¼ cup water
1 tablespoon low-fat mayonnaise
2 teaspoons dried onion flakes

Combine all the ingredients in a saucepan, then cover and cook 2 minutes. Uncover. Break up vegetables with a fork. Simmer uncovered until nearly all the liquid has evaporated and vegetables can be served without draining. *Three servings, under 45 calories each.*

SWEET 'N' SOUR RED CABBAGE

Florence Absheer of St. Louis, Missouri, had a favorite recipe for sweet 'n' sour cabbage, but it called for bacon grease and brown sugar. Now she substitutes a dash of butter flavoring and liquid-smoke seasoning in this calorie-saving winner:

¼ cup water or unsweetened apple juice
1 capful liquid butter flavoring or butter-flavored salt
Few drops liquid-smoke seasoning
2 tablespoons vinegar
Dash of Tabasco
1¼ teaspoons salt
½ teaspoon caraway seeds
4 cups shredded red cabbage
3 tablespoons sugar, white or brown

Combine all ingredients. Cook, tightly covered, over very low heat for 15 minutes or more, until as tender as desired. Stir occasionally. *Four servings, about 65 calories each.*

Fruit Accents Sauerkraut: It's German, but Low-Cal

Unfortunately for calorie counters, practically everything German is fattening. With one delicious exception: sauerkraut. And even that tends to be calorie laden when prepared according to many traditional Germanic recipes.

Here are three German-inspired sauerkraut dishes that aren't fattening. All three profit from the marriage of sauerkraut with fruit.

GERMAN PINEAPPLE KRAUT

16-ounce can German sauerkraut
2 cups unsweetened pineapple juice
½ fresh pineapple or 2 cups canned chunks in juice

Combine sauerkraut and pineapple juice in a saucepan. Cover and simmer 1½ to 2 hours, stirring occasionally, until most of the liquid is absorbed.

If using fresh pineapple, hollow it out to use as a serving shell. Chop the fruit into small cubes. Discard woody core. Combine fresh fruit with cooked sauerkraut and reheat to boiling. Mound kraut in pineapple shell to serve.

If using canned pineapple, drain off the juice and use it as part of the cooking liquid. Stir in reserved canned fruit at the last minute. Reheat and serve. *Six servings, 90 calories each.*

OKTOBERFEST KRAUT WITH WINE AND GRAPES

16-ounce can sauerkraut
1 cup Rhine wine
¼ pound green seedless grapes

Simmer sauerkraut and wine in a covered saucepan until most of the liquid is absorbed (1½ to 2 hours). Stir in grapes at the last minute, and reheat. *Four servings, 40 calories each.*

APPLE-CARAWAY KRAUT

This is an ideal vegetable to bake in the oven while lean roast pork or fresh ham is roasting.

16-ounce can sauerkraut
2 teaspoons caraway seeds
1 onion, chopped
1 cup unsweetened applesauce
1 cup boiling water
Fat-skimmed pork drippings

Combine sauerkraut, caraway, onion, and applesauce in a baking dish, cover, and put in the oven while pork cooks. About ½ hour before pork is finished cooking, add 1 cup boiling water to the roasting pan the pork is cooking in. Drain off the water into a cup. Wait until the fat rises and then skim off the fat, using a bulb-type baster. Stir the pork liquid into the sauerkraut. Continue cooking until most of the liquid is absorbed. *Four servings, 55 calories each.*

FRENCH CARROT MEDLEY

10-ounce package frozen sliced carrots
1 onion, sliced
2-ounce can sliced mushrooms, including liquid
2 stalks celery, thinly sliced
Chopped fresh parsley or dried parsley flakes to taste (optional)
1 cup fat-skimmed chicken broth
Salt and freshly ground pepper to taste

Combine ingredients in a saucepan; cover and cook 10 minutes. Uncover and continue cooking 5 to 7 minutes, until vegetables are tender and well glazed. *Six servings, 30 calories each.*

CONTINENTAL CONFETTI CARROTS

If you're nutrition conscious and calorie careful, one of the greatest kitchen gadgets to own is a vegetable shredder, electric or hand operated. Powered by "elbow grease," the latter is relatively inexpensive and the only energy it takes is yours (which, when used, also helps burn up some calories, by the way). But, if you're lazy or in a hurry (and who isn't?) the former is well worth owning.

There are several types available, some free-standing and others that attach to electric mixer systems. They all make short work of shredding vegetables for salads and slaws. Or for making one of my favorite hot vegetable dishes— shredded carrots.

Shredded carrots are quick and easy to make. They need no scraping or peeling and they're cooked in only a fraction of the time it takes to cook whole or sliced carrots. Quick-cooked and tender-crunchy, shredded carrots keep their bright color and have plenty of eye appeal; they look like lots of orange confetti.

1 **carrot, coarsely shredded**
1 **teaspoon butter**
2 **tablespoons dry sherry**
2 **tablespoons water**
  Generous dash of ground cinnamon
  Salt and freshly ground pepper

Use the largest plate on your vegetable shredder. Put the washed, unpeeled carrot through the shredder. (The processed carrot should resemble noodles or pieces of thin spaghetti.)

Combine all ingredients in a small nonstick saucepan or skillet, cover, and simmer 3 minutes. Then uncover and continue to simmer until shredded carrot is tender-crunchy and most of the liquid has evaporated. *One serving, about 65 calories.*

VARIATION

Some Other Ideas: Add finely chopped onion to the carrots; or crushed juice-packed pineapple and a sprinkle of raisins and pumpkin-pie spice.

CARROTS WITH PINEAPPLE SAUCE

4 **cups sliced carrots**
  6-ounce can (¾ cup) unsweetened pineapple juice
1 **tablespoon cornstarch**
¼ **teaspoon salt**
¼ **cup water**

Cook carrots in pineapple juice until tender.

Mix cornstarch, salt, and water together. Add to carrots and cook, stirring constantly, until clear and thickened. *Eight servings, under 25 calories each.*

Slim Cauliflower Dishes

Since cheese is one of the world's most fattening foods, one of the best places to put it is on cauliflower, one of the least fattening. Even after trimming, a whole pound of cauliflower is only 122 calories. But a pound of cheese is about 1,800 calories . . . how depressing!

In addition to being nonfattening, cauliflower is filling because it's one of the most fiber-rich foods in the world. Its calorie-fiber ratio is even better than that of bran cereal.

Here are some cheesy-flavored cauliflower dishes (and a Hungarian "sour-cream" cauliflower slimmer) that are chintzy only about calories. Choose the sharpest cheese you can find, for the most flavor and the fewest fat calories.

CAULIFLOWER WITH WHITE CHEESE SAUCE

  1 large head cauliflower (2¼-2½ pounds) or 3 boxes frozen
     Salted water
1½ cups skim milk
  3 tablespoons all-purpose flour
  2 teaspoons prepared mustard
     Salt and white pepper
     Pinch of cayenne or dash of Tabasco
  1 cup (4 ounces) coarsely shredded, lightly-packed extra-sharp white Cheddar, American, or Italian Fontina cheese
  2 tablespoons grated Romano or Parmesan cheese

Wash fresh cauliflower and trim. Break into florets. Cook in salted water, uncovered, only till tender-crisp, about 6 minutes.

Meanwhile, combine remaining ingredients except cheeses in a small saucepan. Blend well, then cook and stir over very low heat until sauce thickens. Remove from heat and stir in cheeses until melted. Correct seasonings to taste. Spoon over hot, drained cauliflower. *Eight servings, 105 calories each.*

QUICK CAULIFLOWER AU GRATIN

  2 ten-ounce boxes frozen cauliflower
     Water
½ cup plain low-fat yogurt
¾ cup (3 ounces) coarsely shredded lightly packed sharp American cheese
     Salt and freshly ground pepper
  3 tablespoons unseasoned breadcrumbs, either toasted High-Fiber Breadcrumbs (page 302) or commercial
     Paprika

Cook cauliflower in water according to package directions only till tender-crisp. Drain, then stir with yogurt, cheese, salt, and pepper. Spoon into a shallow ovenproof casserole and sprinkle with breadcrumbs and paprika. Bake in a 350-degree oven about 15 minutes, until crumbs are brown and sauce is bubbly. *Six servings, 100 calories each.*

QUICK CHEESY CAULIFLOWER

    10-ounce package frozen cauliflower
¼ **cup water**
    Salt or butter-flavored salt
 1 **tablespoon all-purpose flour**
½ **cup skim milk**
⅛ **teaspoon grated nutmeg**
½ **teaspoon prepared mustard**
    Pinch of cayenne or dash of Tabasco
 2 **tablespoons shredded extra-sharp Cheddar cheese**

Cook frozen cauliflower in salted water according to package directions. Don't overcook, and don't drain.

In a covered jar shake flour, milk, mustard, nutmeg, and cayenne together, then stir into the cauliflower over low heat, until sauce thickens and bubbles. Stir in grated cheese at the last minute; the heat of the sauce will melt the cheese. *Three servings, 65 calories each.*

HUNGARIAN CAULIFLOWER IN "SOUR-CREAM SAUCE"

    10-ounce package frozen cauliflower
¼ **cup water**
    Salt or butter-flavored salt
½ **cup plain low-fat yogurt**
 2 **teaspoons cornstarch**
    Imported paprika

Cook frozen cauliflower in salted water according to package directions, just till tender, don't drain.

Stir yogurt and cornstarch together until smooth. Stir yogurt mixture into the cauliflower over very low heat, just until the sauce bubbles and thickens. Spoon into a serving dish and sprinkle liberally with paprika. *Three servings, 50 calories each.*

CONFETTI CORN CREOLE

10-ounce package frozen whole-kernel corn
1 stalk celery, minced
1 green bell pepper, seeded and diced
1 chicken bouillon cube
5 tablespoons water
1 teaspoon dried onion flakes
 Salt, or garlic salt, and freshly ground pepper to taste
1 fresh ripe meaty tomato

Combine all ingredients except tomato in a saucepan. Cover and cook, stirring occasionally, about 6 minutes. Peel and dice the tomato. Stir in at the last minute and cook only until heated through. *Six servings, 50 calories each.*

MEXICAN CORN

½ cup chopped onion
½ cup chopped celery
1 small green bell pepper, seeded and chopped
2 cups canned tomatoes, broken up
2 cups fresh or frozen whole-kernel corn
 Salt and cayenne pepper to taste

Simmer onion, celery, green pepper, and tomatoes 20 minutes. Stir in corn and seasoning, and cook 5 minutes more. *Six servings, 75 calories each.*

ITALIAN EGGPLANT CAESAR

Eggplant is a calorie sneak. At only 92 calories a pound, it's deceptively slim, but it has a spongelike ability to sop up calories from other ingredients with which it comes in contact. Cooking oil, for example. Most eggplant dishes begin with frying. Except these.

I love the golden-crisp texture of breaded and fried eggplant, but just can't afford all those calories! So I've devised a better way—not only slimmer but easier too.

I "fry" eggplant in the oven. But first I spread the slices with a thin coating of low-fat mayonnaise—the kind that's labeled "imitation" because it doesn't meet federal standards for fat content. Less fat—and fewer calories—is what we want. The egg-and-lemon content makes this mixture the perfect base.

Then press the slices lightly in grated Parmesan or Romano cheese and seasoned breadcrumbs. The small amount of fat in the low-fat mayonnaise and grated cheese is all that is needed to make a crisp coating. The slices are then baked in a very hot oven on a nonstick surface. The high heat gives the coating a crusty finish that tastes and looks like fried.

1 **pound raw eggplant, in thick slices**
6 **tablespoons low-fat "imitation" mayonnaise**
6 **tablespoons grated Romano cheese**
¼ **cup Italian-seasoned breadcrumbs**
   Salt and freshly ground pepper

Soak eggplant slices in cold water 15 or 20 minutes. Drain and blot dry. Spread lightly on both sides with low-fat mayonnaise, then press lightly into the grated cheese, then into the seasoned crumbs, lightly coating both sides. Spray a shallow nonstick baking pan with cooking spray for no-fat frying. Arrange the eggplant in a single layer. Bake in a preheated hot (475-degree) oven 5 minutes. Turn and bake an additional 3 or 4 minutes, until eggplant is golden and crisp on the outside, tender inside. *Six servings, 110 calories each.*

LOW-CAL EGGPLANT PARMIGIANA

1 **recipe Eggplant Caesar (see above)**
   16-ounce can plain tomato sauce
¼ **cup water**
⅛ **teaspoon instant garlic**
2 **teaspoons oregano or Italian seasoning**
4 **ounces shredded part-skim mozzarella cheese**

Follow the preceding recipe, using Parmesan cheese in the coating rather than Romano. When the eggplant is golden-brown, remove from the oven and lower the heat to 375 degrees. Stir together the tomato sauce, water, instant garlic, and oregano, and pour over the eggplant. Bake uncovered 10 minutes. Sprinkle with mozzarella and return to oven until mozzarella is melted. *Six servings, 185 calories each.*

EGGPLANT LASAGNE

Here's another eggplant main course, this one submitted by Mrs. S. J. Couch of Florissant, Missouri, who writes that she and her husband have always loved lasagne, but noodles are a "no-no" on their diet. So she invented a dish that's a cross between Lasagne and Eggplant Parmigiana, but very low-cal.

2 medium eggplants
¼ cup water
1 cup low-fat cottage cheese
1 whole egg
   8-ounce can plain or onion tomato sauce
   Salt, or garlic salt, freshly ground pepper, and Italian seasoning to taste
4 ounces diced or shredded part-skim mozzarella cheese
2 tablespoons grated Parmesan or sharp Romano cheese

Peel eggplants and slice ¼ inch thick. Simmer in a small amount of water just until soft, then drain. Mix cottage cheese and egg together.

Spray a baking dish with cooking spray for no-fat frying. Combine all ingredients in 2 layers. First use half the eggplant. Then top it with half the cottage-cheese mixture, half the tomato sauce sprinkled with seasonings, and half the diced and grated cheese. Repeat to make a second layer.

Bake in a preheated 350-degree oven about 30 minutes, until bubbly and melted. *Four servings, about 220 calories each.*

GREEN BEANS CANADIENNE

2 ounces Canadian bacon, diced
½ small onion, thinly sliced
1 pound fresh green beans, trimmed and sliced diagonally
¼ cup water
½ teaspoon salt
   Pinch of freshly ground pepper

Spray a nonstick saucepan lightly with cooking spray for no-fat frying. Heat the bacon over a moderate flame, stirring until lightly browned. Remove from the saucepan and set aside.

Combine onion, beans, and water in the saucepan. Cover and cook until the beans are tender-crisp, about 12 minutes. Drain and season. Add brown bacon cubes and stir through lightly. *Six servings, 40 calories each.*

GREEN BEANS AMANDINE

1½ tablespoons blanched slivered almonds
   10-ounce package frozen green beans
¼ cup water
   Butter-flavored salt and freshly ground pepper to taste

Put the almonds in a nonstick saucepan over moderate heat with no fat. Stir with a wooden spoon until lightly toasted. Remove from pan and set aside.

Put the beans and water into the saucepan and cover. Cook according to package directions. Drain. Season to taste and sprinkle with toasted almonds. *Three servings, 55 calories each.*

QUICK GREEN BEANS WITH MUSHROOMS

Good for camp or boat cookery.

   2-ounce can sliced mushrooms
1 tablespoon diet margarine
   15-ounce can cut green beans
1 chicken bouillon cube

Drain the mushrooms well. Heat the diet margarine in a nonstick saucepan or small skillet. Add the mushrooms and brown lightly, stirring occasionally with a wooden spoon. Add the undrained green beans and bouillon cube. Heat to boiling, stirring constantly, until bouillon is dissolved. Continue to cook, uncovered, until most of the liquid has evaporated. *Four servings, 40 calories each.*

GREEK GREEN BEANS IN TOMATO SAUCE

Butter is not only the most boring thing to put on green beans, it's also the most fattening. At 100 calories a tablespoon, the topping is triple the calories of the vegetable: a whole cupful of cooked green beans is only 33 calories.

One of the sauciest ways to jazz up green beans (or "string beans") is to serve them Greek style, simmered in a savory tomato sauce spiked with herbs. Here's how:

4 ripe tomatoes, peeled, or 16-ounce can tomatoes
2 onions, finely chopped
3 tablespoons chopped fresh parsley
1 clove garlic, minced
½ cup water
1 tablespoon chopped fresh mint or 1 teaspoon dried mint
2 teaspoons oregano or Italian seasoning
   Salt and freshly ground pepper to taste
1½ pounds green beans, cut up, or 2 ten-ounce packages frozen green beans, defrosted

Peel and dice the tomatoes. If using canned tomatoes, break up with a fork. Combine tomatoes (including juice) with remaining ingredients, except green beans. Cover and simmer 10 minutes, stirring frequently. Meanwhile, wash, tip, and cut up fresh beans. (If using frozen, allow to defrost.)

Add green beans to the pot and simmer uncovered, stirring frequently, until beans are tender and sauce is thick. *Eight servings, about 50 calories each.*

QUICK GREEK GREEN BEANS

10-ounce package frozen French-style green beans, defrosted
8-ounce can plain tomato sauce
1 tablespoon dried onion flakes
Garlic salt and freshly ground pepper to taste
1 teaspoon Italian seasoning
½ teaspoon dried mint

Combine all ingredients in a pan and cover. Cook 3 minutes. Uncover and stir well; continue cooking until beans are tender. *Three servings, 50 calories each.*

SKINNY GREEN-BEAN-AND-BACON SKILLET

1 pound fresh green beans
1 slice raw lean bacon
Salt and freshly ground pepper to taste

Wash and trim beans but leave whole. Arrange in a single layer in a nonstick skillet. Add just enough water to come to the top of the beans. Mince the bacon into tiny bits and add to the water. Cook, uncovered, about 8 to 10 minutes, stirring occasionally, until beans are cooked crisp and all water has evaporated. Cook and stir until bacon is crisp and beans are slightly sautéed. *Four servings, under 65 calories each.*

CHOLESTEROL WATCHER'S GREEN BEANS WITH "BUTTER"

1 pound fresh green beans
Butter-flavored salt and freshly ground pepper to taste
Water
1 tablespoon polyunsaturated margarine or safflower oil

Wash and trim beans; leave whole. Arrange in a single layer in a nonstick skillet. Sprinkle with butter-flavored salt and pepper. Add water just to top of beans. Add margarine or oil. Cook, uncovered, until tender-crisp and most of the liquid has evaporated, stirring occasionally. Stir well to coat evenly and add additional salt and pepper to taste, if needed. *Four servings, about 60 calories each.*

VARIATIONS

More calorie-conscious ways with a box of frozen beans:

Green Beans and Pimiento Italiano: Combine one 10-ounce package frozen green beans with ⅓ cup low-calorie Italian dressing, 1 tablespoon minced onion, 3 tablespoons diced fresh or canned red pepper. Cook and stir, uncovered, 4 minutes. (Frozen Italian green beans may be substituted.) *Three servings, 40 calories each.*

Microwave Green Beans: One 10-ounce box frozen beans—put the box in the microwave oven 7 to 9 minutes. Open the door and turn the package once or twice during cooking.

Two 10-ounce boxes—increase microwave cooking time to 11 to 13 minutes.

Pressure-Cooked Green Beans: Peel box from a 10-ounce package frozen green beans. Put the frozen beans in a pressure cooker, with ½ cup cold water. Put on the cover and pressure regulator weight. Time cooking when rocking of the pressure regulator begins. Pressure cook 2 to 3 minutes. Reduce pressure according to manufacturer's directions.

Slim Stir-Fried Oriental Green Beans: Defrost green beans at room temperature. Put in a nonstick skillet or wok, along with 2 teaspoons oil and 2 tablespoons water or liquid (can be chicken broth or soy sauce). Cook and stir over high heat until all the liquid evaporates, about 2 to 4 minutes.

Cooked Green Beans, French Style: Defrost beans at room temperature. Drop the beans into a quart of rapidly boiling salted water and cook, uncovered, only until tender-crisp, about 3 minutes. (This method, while disapproved by nutritionists because the large amount of water leeches out some nutrients, does result in bright green beans.)

Steamed Green Beans: This method is nutritionally superior. Put a 10-ounce block of green beans, frozen or defrosted, on a rack or in a steaming basket in a saucepan. Add 1 inch or 2 of water, not touching the beans. Cover and steam 6 to 8 minutes if frozen; 3 to 4 minutes if defrosted.

PEAS PARMESAN

    10-ounce package frozen peas
1 **medium onion, chopped**
½ **fresh red bell pepper, diced**
1 **chicken bouillon cube**
5 **tablespoons water**
1 **cup skim milk**
1 **tablespoon all-purpose flour**
4 **teaspoons grated Parmesan cheese**
    Paprika

Combine first 5 ingredients in a saucepan, cover tightly, and cook over low heat 5 minutes. Blend milk and flour and stir into saucepan. Cook and stir until sauce is thick. Sprinkle with Parmesan and paprika. *Four servings, 105 calories each.*

GREEK PEPPERS

8 green bell peppers, seeded and sliced
4 cups canned tomatoes, broken up
   Salt and freshly ground pepper to taste
¼ teaspoon dill weed
¼ teaspoon oregano
¼ teaspoon savory
¼ teaspoon thyme

Combine all ingredients in a covered pan and simmer slowly over low heat until peppers are tender. Uncover and continue to simmer until most of the liquid evaporates. *Eight servings, under 40 calories each.*

SPINACH-CHEESE CUSTARD À LA GRECQUE

Kojak star Telly Savalas has done wonders for the image of bald men . . . and Greek food. Unfortunately, Greek food can be very fattening, which isn't good for *your* image. Maybe the many Greeks with svelte physiques stay that way because they dance a lot.

Even if you don't dance a lot, you can still enjoy Greek-inspired dishes if you're a Slim Gourmet cook. (I promise it won't make you bald.)

One popular—and fattening—dish is Greek Spinach Pie, a troublesome but ecstatically delicious dish of phyllo pastry filled with a subtly seasoned spinach-egg-cheese mixture. Without the pastry (or as prepared in my own slimming version on page 218), it's no longer troublesome—or fattening. But then it's no longer Greek Spinach Pie, either. It *is,* however, a protein-rich side dish that can really dress up a simple, low-cal main course like lemon-basted chicken or fish. A big tossed salad or some vine-ripe tomatoes would be nice, too.

1 pound raw spinach or 1 cup chopped cooked spinach
2 eggs
1 cup skim milk
¼ teaspoon salt or butter-flavored salt
⅛ teaspoon grated nutmeg
   Dash of cayenne pepper
⅔ cup grated Parmesan cheese

Wash spinach and cook quickly in a covered saucepan, using only the water adhering to the leaves. Chop coarse. Or use 1 cup well-drained canned or defrosted chopped spinach.

Beat eggs, milk, and seasonings together in a mixing bowl. Stir in cheese and spinach. Spoon into an 8-inch nonstick pie pan or four small soufflé dishes wiped lightly with oil. Bake in a preheated 350-degree oven for 25 or 30 minutes or until set. *Four servings, 170 calories each.*

ITALIAN SPINACH

The idea of seasoning spinach with nutmeg is Italian in origin. Here's how: Simply wash and tear spinach and put it into a tightly covered pot with no added water, just the moisture on the freshly washed leaves. Add a dash of nutmeg and cover tightly. Cook only until wilted. *Each ½-cup serving, under 20 calories.*

SAUCEPAN SQUASH SICILIAN

Zinnias and marigolds are nice, but for my money one of the most colorful sights in the garden is summer squash. Bright yellow or patterned with speckled stripes of green, fresh squash is not only delicious to look at but delightful to eat as well. One of its best aspects is its low calorie count. Most varieties of winter squash are at least 50 calories a cupful, but fresh yellow summer squash has only about 16 calories per ½ cup.

Yes, there's nothing better than fresh vegetables. On the other hand, there's nothing more convenient than canned or frozen. For the best of both, why not mix the best of both? Garden-fresh goodies can add just-picked flavor to convenient (and often cheaper) frozen or canned vegetables. The seasonal and out of season can be combined creatively to produce imaginative dishes—low in calories yet high in nutrition! Here is a favorite mix.

2 **cups sliced fresh yellow squash or 10-ounce package frozen sliced yellow squash**
1 **green bell pepper, seeded and diced**
⅛ **teaspoon instant garlic**
    6-ounce can (¾ cup) tomato juice
¼ **teaspoon oregano or Italian seasoning**
    Salt and freshly ground pepper to taste
4 **teaspoons grated sharp cheese (optional)**

Combine all ingredients except cheese in an uncovered saucepan. Break up vegetable, if frozen, as it cooks in simmering tomato juice. Cook, stirring frequently, until tomato juice evaporates into a thick sauce (about 5 minutes). Sprinkle each serving with 1 teaspoon sharp grated cheese, if desired. *Four servings, 25 calories each, without cheese; with cheese, 35 calories each.*

A-Z: Zucchini May Be Last, but It's Not Least in Flavor

Not too many years ago, zucchini occupied the same place in the vegetable popularity poll that it does in the alphabet. Most people thought of it, if they thought of it at all, as an ethnic oddity or garden curiosity—something Aunt Emma put in behind the cabbage patch or Mrs. Monteleone brought back from the Italian market.

Now both gardening and ethnic food are "in," and so is zucchini. And you don't have to grow your own to enjoy it. Zucchini pops up on produce stands and in frozen food cases just as eagerly as it does in the garden.

Sometimes called "Italian squash" or "green summer squash," zucchini has become widely popular. Its availability is no longer limited to summer nor does its versatility confine it to Italian cuisine. And, most important, zucchini is one of the least fattening vegetables there is—fewer than 15 calories per ½-cup serving.

Here are some ways to enjoy it (you can short-cut the calories, too!).

"BUTTERED" ZUCCHINI

1 **medium zucchini, sliced, or 10-ounce package frozen zucchini**
  Butter-flavored salt and freshly ground pepper
2 **level teaspoons soft butter or margarine**
2 **tablespoons water**
2 **teaspoons minced fresh parsley**

If using frozen zucchini, defrost first at room temperature. Put the sliced zucchini in a single layer in a small nonstick skillet or saucepan. Sprinkle with butter-flavored salt. Add a liberal grating of pepper. Add the butter and water. Cover and simmer until just tender (about 6 minutes), shaking the pan occasionally.

Uncover and continue to cook, stirring occasionally, until the liquid evaporates and the zucchini is evenly coated. Stir in the parsley at the last minute. *Three servings, 40 calories each.*

PRONTO ZUCCHINI PARMESAN

1 **cup tomato juice**
½ **teaspoon garlic salt**
⅛ **teaspoon freshly ground pepper**
  10-ounce package frozen zucchini
1 **tablespoon grated Parmesan cheese**
2 **teaspoons cracker crumbs**
½ **teaspoon oregano or Italian seasoning**

Combine tomato juice, garlic salt, pepper, and frozen zucchini in an uncovered saucepan. Simmer 10 minutes uncovered, stirring occasionally, until squash is tender and juice has reduced into a sauce. Turn into a small shallow flameproof casserole. Sprinkle with cheese, cracker crumbs, and oregano. Slip under the broiler for 2 to 3 minutes, until topping is browned. *Three servings, 50 calories each.*

BAKED CAESAR ZUCCHINI

1 **medium zucchini, diced or thinly sliced**
4 **medium tomatoes, peeled and diced**
3 **tablespoons minced onion**
1 **teaspoon oregano or Italian seasoning**
1 **teaspoon basil**
  Pinch of red pepper flakes
¼ **cup shredded sharp Provolone cheese**
½ **cup Caesar-seasoned salad croutons**

Combine vegetables in an ovenproof baking dish. Sprinkle with seasonings, cheese, and croutons. Bake uncovered at 400 degrees 35 minutes or more, until top is well browned. *Eight servings, 40 calories each.*

RISOTTO-STUFFED ZUCCHINI

4 **medium zucchini (about 1 pound)**
1 **clove garlic, minced**
1 **medium onion, chopped**
1 **teaspoon olive oil**
2 **tablespoons zucchini cooking water**
1 **cup chopped tomatoes, fresh or canned**
¾ **cup cooked rice**
½ **teaspoon oregano or Italian seasoning**
  Garlic salt and cayenne pepper to taste
¼ **cup grated extra-sharp Romano cheese**

Trim stems from zucchini. Cut zucchini in half lengthwise. Arrange cut side up in a frying pan. Add water. Cover and simmer until barely tender, 3 or 4 minutes. Allow to cool, then scoop out seeds with a spoon and discard. Set zucchini aside.

Put the garlic, onion, and olive oil in the same skillet with 2 tablespoons zucchini cooking water. Cook, uncovered, over high heat until water evaporates and onion sautés lightly in remaining oil. Add tomatoes, rice, oregano, garlic salt, and hot pepper. Stir well. Spoon this mixture into the zucchini cases and top with cheese.

Arrange in a single layer in a baking dish. Bake at 450 degrees 15 to 20 minutes. *Eight servings, 75 calories each.*

"Butter" Vegetables Mediterranean Style

If you can't afford butter calories, serve your vegetables Mediterranean-style . . . "buttered" with tomato sauce! Even people who don't like vegetables are willing to try them this way and the calorie savings aren't to be sneered at.

Consider this: it takes only 1 level teaspoon butter (or margarine) to double the calorie count of a cupful of green beans or cauliflower. At 33 calories a scant teaspoon, butter and margarine are among the most fattening foods there are.

The idea of simmering vegetables with tomato sauce abounds in the sunny climes around the Mediterranean, where there are a lot more tomatoes than cows. Most food fans are familiar with Italian zucchini or eggplant with tomatoes, or the Southern French dish ratatouille, summer vegetables simmered in tomatoes. We offer versions of those, as well a Romanian recipe and, last but not least, Pisto Machego, a Spanish version.

Note that for calorie-wary cooks in a hurry, a small can of tomato juice serves as the cooking liquid and self-making sauce when added to a box of frozen vegetables.

See also the vegetable suggestions included with the recipe for Greek Tomato Sauce for Vegetables (page 307).

EASY ITALIAN VEGETABLE CASSEROLE

1 **large eggplant, peeled and diced**
9-ounce package frozen Italian green beans, defrosted
16-ounce can undrained Italian plum tomatoes, well broken up
Salt or garlic salt to taste
Freshly ground pepper or cayenne pepper to taste
1 **teaspoon oregano or Italian seasoning**
3 **tablespoons grated extra-sharp Romano cheese**
3 **tablespoons Italian-seasoned breadcrumbs**

Combine vegetables in an ovenproof casserole. Stir in seasonings; mix well. Sprinkle with cheese and crumbs. Bake at 375 degrees 30 to 40 minutes. *Six servings, under 75 calories each.*

SKILLET RATATOUILLE

1 medium or ½ large eggplant, peeled and diced
1 unpeeled medium zucchini, thinly sliced
2 green bell peppers, seeded and diced
1 large onion, thinly sliced
2 tomatoes, peeled and diced
1 or 2 cloves garlic, minced
   Pinch of thyme or poultry seasoning
4 pitted large black olives, sliced
2 tablespoons olive liquid (from can)
   6-ounce can (¾ cup) tomato juice
   Salt and freshly ground pepper to taste

Combine all ingredients in a large nonstick skillet or electric frying pan. Cover and simmer 25 minutes. Uncover and continue to simmer until most of the liquid evaporates. Season to taste. Serve hot or cold. *Eight servings, 45 calories each.*

GHIVETCH

Romanian Vegetables

4 tomatoes, peeled and diced
1 unpeeled green or yellow squash, diced or sliced
1 small or ½ medium eggplant, peeled and diced
1 cup sliced fresh or drained canned green beans
2 stalks celery, thinly sliced
3 sprigs parsley, minced
1 clove garlic, minced, or ⅛ teaspoon instant garlic
1 potato, peeled and diced
   10-ounce can fat-skimmed beef broth
   Salt and freshly ground pepper to taste
1 teaspoon dried dill or tarragon, or to taste
   Dash of cayenne pepper (optional)

Combine all ingredients in a large nonstick skillet, electric frying pan, or heavy Dutch oven. Cover and simmer 30 minutes, uncover, and continue to simmer another 30 minutes or more, until all vegetables are very tender and liquid is reduced. *Eight servings, 55 calories each.*

SPANISH PISTO MACHEGO

A decalorized Spanish-style ratatouille.*

1 tablespoon olive oil
¼ cup olive juice (from jar)
3 cups chopped onion
2 unpeeled green or yellow summer squash, diced
2 green bell peppers, seeded and diced
4 ripe tomatoes, peeled and chopped, or 16-ounce can tomatoes
½ cup water
   Salt and freshly ground pepper
1 hard-cooked egg, chopped
4 Spanish olives (green olives), sliced

Spray a nonstick skillet or electric frying pan with cooking spray for no-fat frying. Add olive oil, 2 tablespoons olive juice, and chopped onion. Cook and stir over moderate heat until liquid evaporates and onion begins to brown lightly.

Add the squash, peppers, tomatoes, water, and remaining 2 tablespoons olive juice. Cover and simmer over very low heat 30 minutes. Uncover and continue to simmer until vegetables are very tender and sauce is thick. Season to taste. Garnish the top of the mixture with coarsely chopped egg and sliced olives. Serve directly from the skillet. *Eight servings, 75 calories each.*

VARIATION

Mediterranean Hurry-up Vegetables: 6-ounce can (¾ cup) tomato juice or tomato cocktail and a 10-ounce package plain frozen vegetables in a covered saucepan over low heat and simmer until defrosted and tender-crisp. Uncover and continue to simmer until tomato juice evaporates into a thick sauce. Season to taste, and add instant garlic or onion, parsley flakes, and dried herbs, if desired. *Three servings, about 35 calories each (with green beans).*

*Adapted from Peter S. Feibleman, *The Cooking of Spain and Portugal* (New York: Time-Life Books, 1969).

13
PASTA, POTATOES, AND RICE

❧   ⧉

As calories go, pasta, potatoes, and rice are fairly light. That's because they have no fat to speak of. The meat that they replace, on the other hand, is much more fattening. So there's no need to say no to noodles, pass up potatoes, or refuse rice.

BASIC TENDER-COOKED PASTA

Traditionally, Italian spaghetti, linguine, and other pastas are cooked only till firm (*al dente,* resistant to the teeth). But, if you cook it longer—about 18 minutes, until tender—it will be fuller and less fattening. The longer-cooked pasta absorbs more water, swells up plumper, and therefore less makes more! It takes only 6 ounces dry pasta to make 3 cups tender-cooked pasta at about 155 calories a cupful (that's also 8 ounces of dry pasta for 4 cups of cooked, or a basic rule of 2 ounces dry for 1 cup cooked).

By comparison, a cupful of *al dente* pasta adds up to more than 200 calories.

Simply bring a pot of salted water to a rapid boil. Drop in the pasta, a few strands at a time to maintain the boil, and cook, stirring occasionally for 18 minutes or until tender. Drain in a collander and proceed with whatever your recipe calls for.

Easy, Cheesy Spaghetti with Dairy-Rich Sauces

What can you put on spaghetti besides tomato sauce? Here we answer that question the protein-rich low-calorie way.

These saucy "white" spaghetti dishes are rich in lean dairy ingredients like cottage cheese, skim milk, and eggs. They're easy, too. In fact, they're ideal for using up leftover spaghetti. To recycle yesterday's spaghetti, simply boil a potful of water. When the water reaches a rolling boil, drop in the cold cooked spaghetti. Stir until heated through. Then drain and proceed as if you were using freshly cooked spaghetti.

DIETER'S NOODLES ROMANOFF

8 ounces dry noodles
1 cup low-fat cottage cheese
1 cup plain low-fat yogurt
1 tablespoon grated Parmesan cheese
   Onion salt and freshly ground pepper
   Few drops Worcestershire sauce
¼ cup chopped fresh parsley

Have cottage cheese and yogurt at room temperature. Cook noodles in boiling salted water according to package directions. Drain and toss lightly with remaining ingredients. *Eight servings, 160 calories each.*

NOODLES ALFIE

. . . which is short for Alfredo. This is a calorie-abbreviated adaptation of the Italian classic Fettucini Alfredo.

8 ounces dry noodles
2 tablespoons diet margarine
1 teaspoon butter-flavored salt
   Freshly ground pepper
¼ cup grated Parmesan cheese
2 tablespoons skim milk
¼ cup chopped fresh parsley ¼ cup

Cook noodles, without salt, in boiling water for 18 minutes, or until tender (see page 245). Drain and toss with remaining ingredients until noodles are well coated with cheese. *Eight servings, 140 calories each.*

EASY SPAGHETTI ANGELICA

6 ounces dry protein-enriched spaghetti or linguine
1 cup low-fat cottage cheese
½ cup shredded or grated Swiss cheese
2 tablespoons minced fresh parsley
  Salt and freshly ground pepper to taste
¼ teaspoon grated nutmeg

Cook spaghetti in boiling salted water for 18 minutes, or until tender (see page 245). Drain. Return to the same pot it was cooked in. Stir in remaining ingredients over very low heat until Swiss cheese is melted. Serve immediately. *Six servings, under 140 calories each.*

BAKED SPAGHETTI ROMANOFF

6 ounces dry protein-enriched spaghetti
1 cup low-fat cottage cheese
1 cup low-fat "imitation" sour cream-type dressing
1 clove garlic, minced, or ⅛ teaspoon instant garlic
2 tablespoons chopped onion or 2 teaspoons onion flakes
1 tablespoon minced fresh parsley or 1 teaspoon parsley flakes
1 teaspoon Worcestershire sauce
½ teaspoon salt
  Dash of Tabasco
3 tablespoons shredded or grated extra-sharp Romano cheese
2 tablespoons seasoned breadcrumbs

Cook spaghetti in boiling salted water until tender. Drain. Combine hot spaghetti in a casserole with remaining ingredients except breadcrumbs. Sprinkle top with breadcrumbs. Bake in a 350-degree oven 30 to 40 minutes. *Six servings, 195 calories each.*

SPAGHETTI ALLA CARBONARA

With eggs, Canadian bacon, cheese, and milk, this dish contains enough protein to serve as a main course for supper, lunch, or dinner. A tossed salad with diet dressing and a glass of dry wine are all you need to complete the meal. Some fresh fruit would serve as dessert.

6 ounces dry protein-enriched spaghetti
4 ounces Canadian bacon or cooked lean smoked ham
2 eggs
3 tablespoons skim milk
4 tablespoons grated extra-sharp Romano cheese
2 tablespoons minced fresh parsley
1 teaspoon oregano or Italian seasoning
  Salt, or butter-flavored salt, and coarsely ground pepper

Cook spaghetti in boiling salted water for 18 minutes, or until tender (see page 245).

Meanwhile, dice Canadian bacon and brown in a nonstick skillet, with no fat added.

When the spaghetti is cooked, drain it. Beat the eggs and milk together, and stir into the hot spaghetti. Stir in the bacon cubes, grated cheese, and seasonings. Serve immediately. *Three servings, 310 calories each.*

SWISS SPAGHETTI

A calorie counter shouldn't be lulled into a false sense of security by the phrase "part skim." Often the lower-fat cheeses are not that much lower in calories, perhaps only 20 or so per ounce. But a calorie saved is a calorie that won't fatten! And the displaced fat is made up with extra protein, so the part-skim cheese is generally more nutritious.

Part-skim cheeses can be used creatively in low-cal cookery. Here is a Slim Gourmet idea to try.

4 ounces dry spaghetti
  Boiling salted water
1 whole egg
  Pinch of grated nutmeg
½ cup plain low-fat yogurt
2 tablespoons chopped fresh parsley
3 ounces shredded part-skim Iceland cheese or Swiss cheese
  Salt and freshly ground pepper

Cook spaghetti in boiling salted water for 18 minutes, or until tender (see page 245). Drain and return to the pot. Stir egg, nutmeg, and yogurt together and stir into hot spaghetti over a very low flame. Quickly stir in parsley, cheese, and seasonings, until spaghetti is well coated. Serve immediately. *Four servings, 195 calories each.*

Ziti: Last but Not Least for Diet-wise Pasta Fans

If you like macaroni, you'll love ziti, the biggest macaroni of all! Last, but hardly least, in the alphabet of pasta, these giant-size tubes are nearly half an inch in diameter. They're not really any lower in calories than other forms of pasta. It's just that they take up so much plate room that less seems like more. And fooling the eye is the first step in fooling the appetite! Using ziti in place of macaroni—or even in place of spaghetti or noodles—is a trick any waistline watcher can use.

ZITI AL FORNO

For a delicious side dish with very little fat, how about this Italian version of baked macaroni and cheese, made with ziti and tomatoes? The Italians use sharp Provolone for the cheese; you can use Romano.

8 ounces dry ziti
   8-ounce can undrained stewed tomatoes, well broken up
   8-ounce can plain tomato sauce
1 onion, finely chopped
1 clove garlic, minced
½ teaspoon dried basil
   Salt and freshly ground pepper to taste
1 ounce aged sharp Provolone, diced, or ¼ cup grated Romano cheese
2 tablespoons Italian-seasoned breadcrumbs

Cook ziti in salted water until tender-firm; then drain. Combine with all ingredients except breadcrumbs. Turn into a casserole and sprinkle with crumbs. Bake at 400 degrees 20 minutes. *Six servings, about 110 calories each.*

SLIMMED-DOWN ZITI PIEDMONTESE

A northern-style side dish; very easy!

8 ounces dry ziti
2 tablespoons plain low-fat yogurt
2 eggs, lightly beaten
5 tablespoons grated Parmesan cheese
2 tablespoons chopped fresh parsley
   Salt and freshly ground pepper to taste
   Pinch of grated nutmeg (optional)

Cook ziti in boiling salted water for 18 minutes, or until quite tender (see page 245). Drain well, then return the drained ziti to the pot it was cooked in. Quickly stir in the yogurt, then the eggs, then the cheese, until well coated. Stir in parsley; add salt and pepper to taste (and nutmeg, if desired). *Six servings, under 100 calories each.*

Super, Slimming Main-Course Pasta Dishes

SPEEDY SKILLET SPAGHETTI MILANESE

Skillet suppers are super-swift; no wonder we liberated cooks love 'em! Too bad they're usually so fattening; the one thing we work-all-day types can't afford is unneeded calories.

Here's a no-fuss, no-mess skillet spaghetti dish that's been liberated from extra calories. Pasta really isn't pudgy-making. What makes most spaghetti dishes high-caloried is the greasy ingredients that go into the sauce—oil, fatty chopped meat, and the like. This skillet spaghetti dish is designed to eliminate as much fat as possible—especially important in one-dish main courses in which all ingredients are cooked together. Note that in this recipe there's no need to boil the spaghetti separately. Add it right to the skillet and let it cook in its own self-making sauce. The kind of spaghetti you want for this is the super-thin, quick-cooking type known as "vermicelli."

¾ **pound ground fat-trimmed lean beef round**
1 **cup boiling water**
2 **cloves garlic, minced, or ¼ teaspoon instant garlic**
   20-ounce can tomatoes, broken up
1 **onion, chopped**
   6-ounce can tomato paste
   4-ounce can sliced mushrooms, including liquid
1½ **teaspoons oregano or Italian seasoning**
¼ **teaspoon freshly ground pepper**
½ **teaspoon salt**
3 **cups cold water**
6 **ounces dry very thin spaghetti (vermicelli)**

Brown the chopped meat in a nonstick skillet with no fat added, breaking up the meat as it browns. Add the boiling water, then drain off. Set aside to allow the fat to rise to the surface.

To the skillet add the garlic, tomatoes, onion, tomato paste, canned mushrooms, including liquid, and seasonings. Add 3 cups cold water and heat to boiling. With a bulb-type baster, skim the surface fat off the drained liquid and add that liquid to the skillet. When the skillet is simmering, break up the vermicelli and add it a little at a time.

Simmer uncovered, stirring frequently, until the vermicelli is tender and the liquid has evaporated to a thick sauce. *Four servings, 350 calories each.*

ITALIAN SPAGHETTI WITH MEAT SAUCE

1 pound ground fat-trimmed lean beef round
2 cups water
2 cups Slim Gourmet Tomato Sauce Concentrate (page 306)
2 teaspoons oregano or Italian seasoning
   2-ounce can sliced mushrooms, juice included
   Salt, freshly ground black pepper, and cayenne pepper to taste
12 ounces dry protein-enriched spaghetti

Brown 1 pound ground fat-trimmed beef in a nonstick skillet with no fat added. Break the meat up with a fork as it cooks. Add 2 cups water to the skillet, then pour off the water into a jar or container. Allow the melted fat to rise to the surface, then skim off with a spoon or bulb-type baster. Return the remaining liquid to the skillet.

Add tomato sauce concentrate, oregano or Italian seasoning, and sliced mushrooms. Simmer uncovered until gravy thick. Season to taste with salt, pepper, and cayenne.

Meanwhile, cook spaghetti in boiling salted water about 18 minutes, or until tender (see page 245). Serve the sauce over the hot drained spaghetti. *Six servings, 360 calories each.*

LAZY LASAGNE

You can enjoy homemade lasagne, even if you're calorie shy. Even if you're lazy! This low-cal lasagne is extra easy as well as nonfattening.

Conventional lasagne is a real mess maker, filling your sink with dirty dishes. First you have to boil the lasagne. Then brown the ground meat. Then make a sauce. And finally combine them all in yet another dish and bake it all in the oven.

I've trimmed the trouble as well as the calories.

In this lazy lasagne you brown the meat and make the sauce in the same nonstick skillet with no fat added. Then you combine everything—including the uncooked lasagne noodles—in a baking dish. The lasagne cooks itself—in the oven.

This lazy lasagne is also low-cal because it uses fewer lasagne noodles, more high-protein ingredients like meat, eggs, and cheese. The meat is the leanest you can buy, ground fat-trimmed round. You will also use low-fat pot-style cottage cheese, instead of whole-milk ricotta, and part-skim mozzarella cheese. The entire dish is made with no oil or other fats added.

Here's a step-by-step guide:

¾ pound ground fat-trimmed lean beef round
16-ounce can tomatoes, broken up
8-ounce can plain tomato sauce
2 tablespoons dried onion flakes
1 teaspoon instant garlic, or to taste (optional)
1 teaspoon monosodium glutamate (optional)
1 teaspoon oregano or Italian seasoning
¼ cup chopped fresh parsley, preferably Italian
4 ounces dry high-protein lasagne noodles (about 6)
1½ cups boiling water
1 cup low-fat cottage cheese
½ cup shredded part-skim mozzarella cheese
2 tablespoons seasoned breadcrumbs

Spray a nonstick skillet with cooking spray for no-fat frying. Spread the meat in the skillet and cook over moderate heat until under side is cooked. Break up and turn. Continue cooking until chunks are well browned. Drain off and discard fat, if any (there should be none).

Stir in tomatoes, tomato sauce, instant onion and garlic, monosodium glutamate, oregano and parsley. Heat to boiling.

Break the uncooked lasagne noodles in half or into thirds.

TO ASSEMBLE: Spoon some of the meat mixture into the bottom of an 8-inch square cake pan or ovenproof casserole. Arrange a layer of the dry noodles to fit. Pour on a little of the boiling water, then spoon on the cottage cheese. Spoon on some more of the meat mixture, pour on a little more water, and arrange a second noodle layer on top, using up the remaining noodles. Spoon on some more meat mixture and pour on remaining water. Sprinkle evenly with mozzarella, then breadcrumbs. Cover the pan with a double layer of aluminum foil.

TO BAKE: Put the covered cake pan or caserole on top of a cookie tin in a preheated 350-degree oven and bake 1 hour. Uncover and bake 10 minutes more, until top is brown.

Or: Store in the freezer. Bake frozen, on top of a cookie tin, for 2 hours at 300 degrees. Uncover and bake 15 minutes more.

Or: Store all day or overnight in the refrigerator. Then bake only 45 minutes at 375 degrees. Uncover and bake about 5 minutes or so, until brown. *Six servings, 265 calories each.*

WHITE LASAGNE FLORENTINE

Italians and Greeks don't need Popeye to promote spinach! It's a favorite vegetable in both cuisines. Italians frequently use spinach as a stuffing for pasta, or chopped up in flavorful meatballs. But one of our favorite ways to use spinach Italian style is in a meatless "white" lasagne. Protein-powered, this dish has a rich, creamy flavor that belies its low calorie count.

  2 ten-ounce packages frozen chopped spinach, cooked and well drained
  8 tender-cooked protein-enriched lasagne noodles (see page 245)
2½ cups skim milk
  3 tablespoons instant-blending flour
1½ teaspoons salt, or butter-flavored salt, and pepper
  ¼ teaspoon grated nutmeg
    Pinch of cayenne pepper or dash of Tabasco
  1 cup low-fat cottage cheese
  2 hard-cooked eggs, thinly sliced
  3 tablespoons grated Parmesan cheese
  2 tablespoons Italian-seasoned breadcrumbs

Cook spinach according to package directions and drain well. Cook lasagne according to package directions, rinse, and drain.

Combine milk and flour in a saucepan. Cook and stir over low heat until sauce is thick. Season with salt, pepper, nutmeg, and cayenne pepper. Pour half of the sauce into the cooked spinach and set aside.

To assemble casserole: Pour a little of the remaining white sauce into a shallow baking dish. Add 3 or 4 cooked noodles. Top with half of the spinach mixture. Add half of the cottage cheese and a layer of egg slices. Add layers of lasagna, spinach, cottage cheese, and egg. Pour on remaining white sauce. Sprinkle with Parmesan and breadcrumbs. Bake at 375 degrees 30 to 40 minutes. *Six servings, under 200 calories each.*

VARIATION

Tuna or Turkey White Lasagne Florentine: Add a layer of drained water-packed white-meat tuna flakes (6½-ounce can) or 1 cup diced cooked turkey, for an interesting variation. *Eight servings, about 175 calories each with tuna, about 185 with turkey.*

ONE-PAN GREEK PASTITSIO

Now that ethnic food is "in" Greek is chic! One dish that's perennially popular is pastitsio—"Greek lasagne" was the way one Greek waiter described it to a questioning customer.

Like lasagne, pastitsio is a richly-seasoned casserole of ground meat, pasta, tomatoes, and cheese. And, like lasagne, it's also fattening, and a lot of trouble to make.

We make it the Slim Gourmet way—low calorie, quick, and easy, all in one pan. (Our trim version includes shredded zucchini or cucumber for extra flavor and fiber.)

MACARONI AND MEAT MIXTURE:
- ¾ pound ground lean round steak
- 16-ounce can tomatoes, broken up
- 2 cups plain tomato sauce (no oil added, check ingredients)
- 1 cup water
- 1 onion, finely minced
- 1 small zucchini or cucumber, shredded
- 1 clove garlic, minced, or ⅛ teaspoon instant garlic
- ½ teaspoon salt
- ⅛ teaspoon freshly ground pepper
- 4 ounces (1 cup) dry protein-enriched elbow macaroni

TOPPING:
- 1 cup plain low-fat yogurt
- 2 eggs
- 1 tablespoon minced fresh parsley or 1 teaspoon parsley flakes
- 2 tablespoons grated sharp Romano cheese

Spread the meat in the bottom of an 8- or 9-inch square metal cake pan (preferably one with a nonstick finish). Slip under a preheated hot broiler for about 5 minutes, or until the meat is browned and well rendered of any fat. Pour off any melted fat. Break the meat up with a fork into bite-size chunks. Stir in remaining ingredients, except topping ingredients.

Stir topping ingredients together and spoon onto the surface of the mixture, spreading evenly. (The meat and macaroni mixture will be very liquid and the topping will almost float on the surface.)

Cover the pan tightly with heavy-duty foil or a double sheet of regular foil, shiny side in. Place the pan on top of a cookie tin or baking sheet, and place in a preheated 400-degree oven. Bake 1 hour. Remove the foil carefully and continue to bake uncovered for an additional 30 to 45 minutes, until most of the liquid has evaporated. *Four servings, 360 calories each.*

TURKEY PASTITSIO

MACARONI AND TURKEY MIXTURE:
- 6 ounces (1½ cups) dry protein-enriched large macaroni
- 1 egg, lightly beaten
- ¼ cup plain low-fat yogurt
- ¼ cup grated Parmesan cheese
- 2 cups diced cooked white-meat turkey
- 8-ounce can plain tomato sauce
- ¼ cup finely minced onion or 2 tablespoons onion flakes
- 3 tablespoons chopped fresh parsley
- 1 teaspoon oregano or Italian seasoning

½ teaspoon ground cinnamon
Pinch of ground mace or grated nutmeg

SAUCE:

1½ cups skim milk
3 tablespoons instant-blending flour
Salt, or butter-flavored salt, and freshly ground pepper to taste
1 egg, lightly beaten

TOPPING:

3 tablespoons grated Parmesan cheese
Grated nutmeg

Cook macaroni in boiling salted water until tender, about 18 minutes (see page 245). Drain but don't rinse. Stir beaten egg into hot macaroni. Stir in yogurt and Parmesan.

Combine turkey, tomato sauce, onion, parsley, oregano, cinnamon, and mace. Set aside.

In a saucepan combine milk, flour, salt and pepper. Cook and stir over moderate heat until simmering. Slowly stir ¼ cup white sauce into beaten egg. Wait 1 minute, then stir in remaining hot white sauce.

To assemble casserole: Layer half of the macaroni mixture in a nonstick 8-inch square cake pan. Top with turkey mixture. Add remaining macaroni mixture. Top with white sauce. Sprinkle with cheese and nutmeg. Bake at 350 degrees for 40 to 50 minutes, until set. Cut in squares to serve. *Six servings, under 245 calories each.*

GREEK MACARONI AND MEAT

An easy one-pot recipe traditionally made with lamb, but any lean meat can be substituted

1½ pounds fat-trimmed lamb, cut from leg, or beef, veal, or lean pork
1 large onion, peeled and sliced
2 cloves garlic, peeled and chopped, or ¼ teaspoon instant garlic
2 cups plain tomato sauce
2 cups water
10½-ounce can fat-skimmed beef or chicken broth
Salt and freshly ground pepper to taste
1 teaspoon dried mint
2 tablespoons chopped fresh parsley
¼ teaspoon ground cinnamon
¼ teaspoon grated nutmeg
6 ounces (1½ cups) dry protein-enriched large macaroni

Spray a nonstick skillet or Dutch oven with cooking spray for no-fat frying. Add meat cubes and brown over moderate heat, turning frequently to prevent sticking. Add remaining ingredients, except macaroni. Cover and simmer over low heat until meat is very tender, 2 hours or more. Skim all fat from surface (or chill until fat hardens, then lift off). Reheat to boiling.

Stir macaroni into simmering liquid. Cover and cook, stirring frequently, until macaroni is tender, about 15 minutes. Uncover and cook until liquid is absorbed. *Six servings, about 320 calories each with lamb; 325 calories each with beef; 330 calories each with veal; 390 calories each with pork.*

CHICKEN-NOODLES ITALIANO

Chicken meat and stock from 2 pounds chicken necks (see page 23)
6-ounce can tomato paste
4 ounces (1 cup) dry protein-enriched elbow macaroni
4 small onions, peeled and chopped
4 stalks celery, finely minced
1 bell pepper, seeded and chopped
¼ cup chopped fresh parsley (optional)
1 clove garlic, minced,
⅛ teaspoon instant garlic (optional)
2 teaspoons or more oregano or Italian seasoning
Salt and freshly ground pepper to taste
8 teaspoons grated Parmesan or Romano cheese

In a large pot or nonstick electric skillet, combine fat-skimmed chicken broth and tomato paste. Stir smooth and heat to boiling. Add macaroni a little at a time. Stir in remaining ingredients except reserved chicken meat and Parmesan cheese. Simmer uncovered about 15 minutes, stirring frequently, until noodles are tender and liquid is reduced to a thick tomato sauce. Stir in meat and heat through. Sprinkle with cheese. *Four servings, about 325 calories each.*

TURKEY TETRAZZINI

2 teaspoons margarine
1 tablespoon sherry
½ pound fresh mushrooms, sliced
2 cups tender-cooked noodles (see page 245)
2 cups cubed roast white-meat turkey
2 tablespoons minced fresh parsley or 2 teaspoons parsley flakes
⅓ cup low-calorie blue-cheese salad dressing
2 tablespoons seasoned breadcrumbs

Heat margarine in a nonstick skillet; add sherry and sliced mushrooms. Sauté quickly over high heat, until wine evaporates and mushrooms are lightly browned. Combine well with other ingredients except breadcrumbs in a casserole; sprinkle with breadcrumbs last. Bake 20 minutes at 350 degrees. *Four servings, about 285 calories each.*

Mash, Bake, Fry, Stuff! Potatoes Can Be Low-Cal

Mashed, baked, fried, stuffed . . . who doesn't love 'em? Potatoes, of course, the undeserved "heavy" in so many fad diets.

At 80 or 90 calories each, potatoes aren't at all the villain they're made out to be. It's the go-withs that give them their bulge-inducing reputation: butter, margarine, sour cream, rich sauces, and gravies. Even "fried" potatoes can be nonfattening, if you're a Slim Gourmet cook.

Here's how to enjoy potatoes without unneeded calories. And don't forget them in salads (pages 284–87).

SLIM GOURMET OVEN "FRENCH FRIES"

2 **baking potatoes**
1 **tablespoon salad oil**
Salt, freshly ground pepper, and paprika

Peel potatoes and cut into thick strips. Soak in a bowl of ice cubes and water 20 minutes. Meanwhile, preheat oven to 450 degrees.

Drain potatoes and blot dry. Toss lightly with salad oil to coat evenly. Spread in a single layer in a shallow nonstick baking pan (which can be sprayed with cooking spray to prevent sticking).

Bake 30 minutes or longer, until tender, turning frequently. Sprinkle with salt, pepper, and paprika. *Four servings, about 100 calories each.*

SLIM GOURMET "BUTTERY" MASHED POTATOES

Cut potatoes in quarters and boil in a tightly-covered pot until tender, 20 to 30 minutes. Remove skins. With an electric mixer or potato masher, whip potatoes smooth, gradually adding skim milk till they are the right consistency. Whip in a little butter-flavored salt or butter flavoring. Add additional seasonings to taste (salt, pepper, chopped parsley). Scoop out individual servings; at the last minute top each serving with a teaspoon of diet margarine, or, if you are serving the potatoes with a roast, with Defatted Pan Gravy (see page 303–4) *Each ½-cup serving, 70 calories.*

VARIATION

With Instant Potatoes: Follow package directions, but omit butter or fat. Use skim milk in place of whole milk. Season with butter flavoring or butter salt. *Each ½-cup serving, 70 calories.*

BAKED POTATOES

Pierce baking potatoes with a fork and put them unwrapped on an oven rack. They can be baked at any temperature, ranging from 325 to 450 degrees (depending on what else is being cooked at the same time). At 400 degrees, a medium potato will bake tender in 45 minutes. *Each medium potato, 90 calories.*

Slim Baked-Potato Toppings: Instead of butter or margarine at 100 calories per tablespoon, top your baked potato with a tablespoon of plain yogurt (8 calories), grated cheese (25), low-fat "imitation" sour-cream-type dressing (25), or low-fat cottage cheese blender-whipped with milk or buttermilk (15). Season your dressing with chopped chives, minced parsley, onion flakes, herbs, or bacon-flavored soy bits.

VARIATION

Stuffed Baked Potatoes: Bake 4 potatoes; cut in half lengthwise. Scoop out potato; leave skins intact for restuffing. Whip potato with 1 cup low-fat cottage cheese and ½ cup skim milk, buttermilk, or plain yogurt. Season with salt or butter-flavored salt. Stuff filling into potato shells and sprinkle with paprika and parsley flakes. Bake potatoes an additional 10 minutes, until golden. *Eight servings, 75 calories each.*

POTATO-CARROT SOUFFLÉ

  1 cup mashed potatoes
    1 (7½-ounce) jar baby-food carrots
  2 eggs, separated, plus 1 egg white
⅛ teaspoon grated nutmeg
⅛ teaspoon ground cinnamon

Mix the mashed potatoes, carrots, egg yolks, nutmeg, and cinnamon. Beat the 3 egg whites stiff. Fold the carrot mixture gently into the egg whites. Pour into a nonstick 1½-quart baking dish. Place baking dish in a pan of hot water. Bake at 350 degrees for 40 minutes. *Six servings, 60 calories each.*

EASY POTATO MOUSSAKA

1 **pound ground fat-trimmed lean round**
1 **medium onion, chopped**
2 **medium potatoes, peeled and sliced**
  8-ounce can tomato sauce
1 **teaspoon garlic salt**
1 **teaspoon oregano or Italian seasoning**
  Dash of freshly ground pepper
2 **eggs**
1 **cup plain low-fat yogurt**
½ **teaspoon ground cinnamon**
¼ **teaspoon grated nutmeg**

In a large, heavy nonstick skillet with ovenproof handle, brown meat and onion. Drain off any accumulated fat.

Add potatoes, tomato sauce, garlic salt, oregano, and pepper. Cook, stirring, 5 minutes. Spread evenly in bottom of skillet.

In a medium bowl, with a fork, lightly beat eggs; blend in yogurt. Spread over meat mixture. Sprinkle with cinnamon and nutmeg. Bake at 350 degrees for 1 hour or until topping is set. *Four servings, about 310 calories each.*

POTATO CURRY

A quick main course.

2 **cups thinly sliced potatoes**
2 **hard-cooked eggs, sliced**
2 **cups cubed cooked chicken, turkey, or roast lamb**
  10¾-ounce can condensed cream of potato soup
1 **tablespoon curry powder**
½ **cup water**

In a nonstick 9-inch-square baking pan, arrange in layers as follows: 1 cup potatoes, eggs, chicken, remaining 1 cup potatoes.

In a small bowl blend soup, curry powder, and ½ cup water; pour over casserole.

Bake uncovered at 375 degrees for 1 hour or until potatoes are tender. *Five servings, about 360 calories each.*

HAM AND POTATOES AU GRATIN

1½ cups skim milk
   3 tablespoons all-purpose flour
   1 cup shredded sharp Cheddar cheese
   1 cup diced cooked ham
   2 cups sliced cooked potatoes
   1 tablespoon chopped fresh parsley

Combine milk and flour in a large saucepan over medium heat, stirring constantly, until mixture thickens and bubbles. Add cheese and cook, stirring, until cheese melts. Gently stir in ham and 1 cup potatoes. Pour into a casserole. Arrange remaining potato slices on top. Sprinkle with parsley.

Bake at 400 degrees about 20 minutes or until casserole is hot and bubbly. *Four servings, about 295 calories each.*

JEWISH POTATO PUDDING PUFFS

   3 medium potatoes, cut up
   ½ cup water
   1 egg
   1 small onion, diced
   ½ teaspoon salt
   ¼ teaspoon baking powder
     Dash of freshly ground pepper

In an electric blender on grate setting, blend potatoes with ½ cup water for a few seconds.

Pour into a fine strainer, pressing potatoes against the sides with the back of a spoon to drain off all liquid possible. Return potatoes to blender; add remaining ingredients. Blend at low speed a few seconds.

Spoon into 9 small nonstick muffin-pan cups, filling each two-thirds full. Bake at 350 degrees for 45 minutes. Serve immediately. *Nine puffs, about 40 calories each.*

GERMAN POTATO DUMPLINGS FOR STEW

   2 cups mashed potatoes, made with skim milk (see page 257)
   1 egg
   ¼ cup all-purpose flour
   1 tablespoon minced onion
   1 tablespoon chopped fresh parsley
   ½ teaspoon salt

In a small bowl combine all ingredients, mixing well.

Drop by rounded spoonfuls on top of hot stew. Cover and simmer 20 minutes. *Twelve dumplings, about 40 calories each.*

No Need to Reject Rice! Try These Low-Cal Dishes

Rice is often needlessly shunned by waistline watchers. Like other foods that grow, it's mainly "carbohydrate," a word that sends certain fad followers into a tizzy of illogic. If you're still limping along under the carbohydrate-diet delusion, be advised that it's excess calories—not carbohydrates—that pile on weight.

You don't see many fat Orientals or vegetarians, and they love rice! It's not until the Chinese begin adopting our fat-heavy diet that they begin to develop Buddhalike bulges. Of course rice can be fattening, if other ingredients are high in fat. Rice is very absorbent, and will suck up fat and calories like thousands of little sponges.

SKINNY RICE

2 cups finely minced celery
1 cup water
1 cup instant rice
   Salt, pepper, and soy sauce (optional)

Combine celery with water. Cover and simmer 5 minutes.

Add the instant rice. Cover and let stand until serving time. Season with salt, pepper, and soy sauce, if desired. *Four servings, 110 calories each.*

LESS-STARCH BROWN RICE

If you're calorie wary, cook rice "spaghetti style" in lots of boiling salted water, then rinse in more hot water. No, it's not as nutritious as rice cooked in a minimum of water, but some of the nutrition you're rinsing away is the starch and calories. (If you don't *have* to be calorie careful, follow the directions on the box.) Brown rice is higher in fiber content than white rice, and more nutritious to begin with.

½ cup raw brown rice
6 cups boiling water
1 teaspoon salt

Add rice slowly to boiling salted water (omit salt if rice will be served with soy sauce). Cook uncovered, stirring occasionally, for 45 minutes. Pour into a strainer and rinse twice with more boiling water. Rice grains will be tender and separate, not sticky or starchy. *Four servings, 95 calories each.*

CHINESE-FLAVORED QUICK RICE

2 chicken bouillon cubes
2 teaspoons soy sauce
1 cup water
2 teaspoons dried onion flakes
1 cup instant rice

In a small saucepan combine chicken-bouillon cubes, soy sauce, water, and onion flakes. Heat to boiling. Add instant rice and stir well. Remove from heat and cover. Wait 10 minutes, then stir and serve. *Six 1/3-cup servings, under 40 calories each.*

LOW-CAL VIETNAMESE FRIED RICE

Eat-out, take-home, canned, or frozen, fried rice is fattening—upward of 300 calories a cupful. If you're a fried-rice fan, you'll love the Vietnamese version, less fattening and more protein-rich than the Chinese kind, because Vietnamese cuisine uses far less oil.

The Slim Gourmet version of Vietnamese Fried Rice is adapted for American kitchens. It's full of flavorful protein adders like eggs, shrimp, Canadian bacon, and crabmeat. Make it in a nonstick skillet using hardly any oil at all. This Vietnamese fried rice would make a great side dish for a simple main course like broiled fish or chicken.

2 cups boiling water
1 cup raw long-grain rice
1 cup finely chopped celery (3 stalks)
2 eggs, beaten
2 ounces Canadian bacon, cubed
1 tablespoon salad oil
1 tablespoon water
1 onion, chopped
  4-ounce can mushroom pieces
  6-ounce can small shrimp
  8-ounce package crabmeat, defrosted
3 scallions, sliced
  Soy sauce (optional)

Heat the water to boiling and add the rice and celery (the celery should be chopped almost as fine as cooked rice grains). Reheat to boiling. Lower heat, cover, and simmer about 20 to 25 minutes, stirring occasionally, until water is absorbed.

Spray a large nonstick skillet with cooking spray for no-fat frying. Add the beaten eggs and heat gently, until partly set. "Frizzle" with a fork until eggs are broken up. Remove from frying pan and set aside. Wash out skillet.

Cook the cubed bacon in the clean nonstick skillet with no fat added, until lightly browned. Remove bacon and set aside.

Put 1 tablespoon oil and 1 tablespoon water into the skillet. Add the onion and cook, stirring occasionally, until water evaporates and onion is golden.

To the onion in the skillet add the cooked rice-and-celery mixture, the canned mushrooms (including liquid), the shrimp (including liquid), the crab-meat, the "frizzled" eggs, and browned Canadian bacon cubes. Cook and stir gently over medium heat until most of the liquid has evaporated and everything is heated through. Stir in the scallions at the last minute and serve with soy sauce, if desired. *Eight servings, 190 calories each.*

QUICK CHINESE "FRIED" RICE
(DECALORIZED)

1½ **cups instant rice**
1½ **cups boiling water**
 2 **eggs, lightly beaten**
 1 **onion, chopped**
   16-ounce can mixed Chinese vegetables
 2 **tablespoons dry sherry**
 3 **tablespoons soy sauce**

Prepare instant rice by combining it with the boiling water. Cover and set aside 10 minutes.

Spray a nonstick skillet with cooking spray for no-fat frying. Heat over a moderate flame. Add beaten eggs and heat undisturbed until partly set. Then frizzle with a fork until broken up.

Add onion, drained Chinese vegetables, rice, sherry, and soy sauce. Cook, stirring constantly, until dry and heated through. *Eight servings, 115 calories each.*

SPANISH VEGETABLES WITH RICE

A special side dish to serve with a simple fish or poultry main course.

2 cups raw rice
10½-ounce can fat-skimmed chicken broth
2 cups water
1 tablespoon lemon juice
16-ounce can peeled tomatoes, chopped
8 ounce can artichokes, including liquid
2-ounce can sliced mushrooms, including liquid
1 onion, chopped
1 stalk celery, minced
10-ounce package frozen French-cut green beans
10-ounce package frozen peas
¼ teaspoon saffron threads
1 bay leaf

Combine all ingredients in a top-of-range casserole, and cover. Simmer gently until rice is tender and liquid is absorbed. Stir frequently. *Twelve servings, 170 calories each.*

Great Leftovers: For an easy one-dish dinner, combine leftover Vegetables with Rice with bite-size pieces of cooked meat, seafood, or poultry. Bake in a covered casserole until just heated through.

RICE 'N' NOODLES

½ cup fine dry egg noodles
⅔ cup finely minced celery
½ cup raw rice
10-ounce can fat-skimmed condensed chicken broth
3 tablespoons water
1 tablespoon minced fresh parsley (optional)
Salt and pepper

Crush the noodles in a plastic bag. Mince the celery as fine as rice. Combine all ingredients in a nonstick saucepan and heat to boiling. Cover and simmer until liquid is absorbed, about 20 minutes. *Six servings, 100 calories each.*

GREEK RICE DRESSING FOR POULTRY

3 onions, chopped
1 cup raw rice
2½ cups fat-skimmed chicken or turkey broth
2 tablespoons pine nuts
3 tablespoons golden raisins
2 teaspoons ground cinnamon
  Salt and pepper to taste

Simmer onion and rice in broth until rice is tender and liquid is absorbed. Add remaining ingredients. Use as poultry stuffing, or bake in a covered dish for 20 to 30 minutes at 350 degrees. *Serves twelve, about 90 calories each.*

VARIATION

Greek Dressing with Meat: Sauté 1 pound lean ground fat-trimmed lamb, beef, or pork in a nonstick skillet, breaking meat up as it browns. Drain and discard all fat. Add the meat to the ingredients in the preceding recipe. *Twelve servings, about 140 calories each with lamb or beef, about 165 calories each with pork.*

ALMOND PILAF

½ cup sliced scallions
2 teaspoons margarine
1 cup raw rice
2 cups fat-skimmed chicken broth
  Salt and pepper to taste
3 tablespoons toasted sliced almonds

Sauté scallions in margarine until tender-crisp. Add rice. Stir in broth, and salt and pepper to taste. Heat to boiling. Cover, reduce heat, and simmer 15 minutes, or until rice is tender and liquid absorbed. Add almonds before serving. *Six servings, 175 calories each.*

14
SALADS
AND
SALAD
DRESSINGS

"Salad Days" Are Every Day

Once upon a time, "salad days" meant the good ol' summertime. Now salad ingredients are available year round and Americans can enjoy them whatever the weather, whatever the occasion.

ISRAELI SHREDDED SALAD

The ingredients aren't any different from your common garden-variety American salad; what makes this different is that everything is finely chopped or shredded . . . sort of a salad slaw. Vary the ingredients to suit yourself.

1 large cucumber
1 red or green bell pepper
2 carrots
¼ head of lettuce
3 tomatoes
4 or 5 radishes
1 or 2 tablespoons chopped fresh parsley
1 tablespoon olive oil
1 tablespoon lemon juice
   Salt and coarsely ground pepper to taste

Peel cucumber and quarter lengthwise; cut away the seeds. Dice or finely chop the cucumber into a bowl. Discard the top and seeds of the bell pepper; finely dice the rest. Peel and dice the tomatoes, shred the carrots and lettuce, trim and chop the radishes. Mix all ingredients together, and serve immediately. *Eight servings, about 40 calories each.*

MANDARIN BEAN-SPROUT SALAD

 2 cups fresh or canned bean sprouts (if canned, wash in cold water and drain thoroughly)
    8-ounce can juice-packed mandarin oranges, drained but juice reserved
 1 cup green seedless grapes
 2 tablespoons fresh lemon juice
 3 tablespoons honey
¼ teaspoon ground ginger
 1 teaspoon finely chopped lemon peel
    Salad greens
    Soy sauce

Combine bean sprouts, mandarin oranges, and grapes in a serving bowl. Chill. In a blender, whirl 2 tablespoons reserved orange juice from can and lemon juice, honey, and ginger. Add lemon peel and toss salad lightly with dressing; serve on crisp salad greens. Add soy sauce to taste. *Four servings, about 120 calories each.*

MARINATED COLD GREEN-BEAN SALAD

    10-ounce box green beans, defrosted
½ small onion, chopped
½ red bell pepper, diced
 4 black or green olives, sliced
 2 tablespoons olive liquid (from jar)
 1 tablespoon olive oil
1½ tablespoons vinegar
    Garlic salt, black pepper, cayenne pepper, and oregano or Italian seasoning to taste

Cook green beans only until tender-crisp and combine in a glass bowl with chopped onion, diced red bell pepper, olives, olive liquid (from jar), olive oil, and vinegar. Season to taste with garlic salt, pepper, cayene pepper, and oregano. Cover and chill several hours in the refrigerator before serving. *Four servings, 55 calories each.*

GREEN-BEAN SALAD ARRIVEDERCI

Pack tonight's leftover cooked green beans in a glass bowl or plastic refrigerator bowl, with a little chopped onion, diced canned pimiento, a shake of instant garlic, and bottled low-calorie Italian salad dressing. Serve tomorrow as a chilled green-bean salad. *Less than 50 calories a serving.*

CHILLED MARINATED CAULIFLOWER

   10-ounce package frozen cauliflower
¼ cup water
 2 tablespoons diced red or green bell pepper
 2 tablespoons sliced scallions or green onions
 5 tablespoons low-calorie Italian salad dressing

Cook cauliflower in water according to package directions, only till tender crisp. Stir remaining ingredients into the undrained cauliflower and chill several hours until serving time. *Three servings, 35 calories each.*

GREEK HILLBILLY SALAD

1 small cucumber
1 small onion, minced
2 tomatoes, peeled and cubed
1 tablespoon olive oil
1 tablespoon lemon juice
4 black olives, pitted and sliced
2 tablespoons olive liquid (from jar)
  Salt, or garlic salt, and coarsely ground black pepper
1 ounce cubed feta cheese or Provolone

Peel and quarter the cucumber lengthwise, then strip away and discard the seeds. (This step may be omitted; the seeds are high in fiber—good for calorie counters.) Then slice the cucumber into bite-size chunks. Add remaining ingredients. *Four servings, 90 calories each.*

GREEK FETA–COTTAGE-CHEESE PLATE

Here's how to jazz up a diet cottage-cheese plate.

1 ounce feta cheese
½ cup large-curd low-fat cottage cheese
1 tablespoon chopped scallion or green onion

1 tablespoon chopped fresh parsley
Salt, or garlic salt, and freshly ground pepper to taste
Raw vegetables for garnish

Dice the feta cheese into pieces about the same size as the cottage cheese. Combine all ingredients, then mound on lettuce. Garnish with ripe tomato slices, green pepper rings, or other raw vegetables for a delicious lunch. *One serving, under 160 calories.*

GREEK FETA FRUIT SALAD

1 cup green seedless grapes
1 cup red grapes, halved and seeded
1 large Bermuda onion, sliced
2 large eating oranges, peeled, seeded, and sliced or diced
4 ounces (1 cup) feta cheese, broken into chunks
1 cup watercress leaves
Few sprigs fresh mint (optional)
1 tablespoon olive oil
2 tablespoons lemon juice
Salt and freshly ground pepper to taste

Toss all ingredients in a large bowl. *Four servings, about 230 calories each.*

ROMANOFF FRUIT SALAD

If you like Waldorf salad, you'll love my Romanoff fruit salad, a slim and nutritious mélange of colorful fruits in a tangy low-fat dressing. Simply delicious!

1 cup sliced fresh strawberries
1 eating orange, peeled, seeded, and diced
1 unpeeled yellow apple or ripe pear, diced
2 cups diced celery
¼ cup plain low-fat yogurt
3 tablespoons low-fat mayonnaise
2 tablespoons defrosted orange-juice concentrate

Combine fruit and celery in a bowl. Stir remaining ingredients together and stir into salad mixture. Chill. *Six servings, about 65 calories each.*

GREEN APPLE SALAD

1½ cups unpeeled diced green apples
2 cups diced celery
½ cup halved green seedless grapes
2 tablespoons mayonnaise or low-calorie mayonnaise
5 tablespoons vanilla yogurt

Combine and chill. Serve on lettuce. *Six servings, 70 calories each with regular mayonnaise; only 45 calories with diet mayonnaise.*

QUICK PEAR SALAD

1 unpeeled fresh pear, cored and diced
1 cup diced celery
6 tablespoons low-cal blue-cheese dressing

Combine and serve on lettuce. *Four servings, 55 calories each.*

Four Foreign Favorites for Slim Coleslaw Fans

Here is a Slim Gourmet's grand tour of coleslaw, featuring foreign favorites sans unneeded calories. I've adapted some of the most-loved cabbage salads of other lands, omitting the extra pound makers—like a lot of sugar or mayonnaise, or huge quantities of oil. The salads lose nothing in the translation.

Bagged shredded cabbage or coleslaw mix from the produce counter can make short work of coleslaw making.

DUTCH COLESLAW

3 cups shredded cabbage
½ red bell pepper, chopped
1 stalk celery, chopped
½ onion, chopped
   Sprig of parsley, chopped
2 tablespoons plain low-fat yogurt
2 tablespoons diet (imitation) mayonnaise-type salad dressing
2 tablespoons lemon juice
2 tablespoons bacon-flavored bits

Combine everything except bacon bits. Chill. Add bacon bits at serving time. *Six servings, 35 calories each.*

POLYNESIAN PINEAPPLE SLAW

3 cups shredded cabbage
¼ cup chopped red or green bell pepper
¾ cup unsweetened crushed pineapple, including juice
1 teaspoon salt
1 tablespoon sugar
3 tablespoons vinegar
2 carrots, shredded
   Dash of Tabasco or pinch of cayenne pepper

Combine all ingredients and chill. *Six servings, 35 calories each.*

GERMAN RED CABBAGE COLESLAW

3 cups shredded red cabbage
3 red apples, cubed—don't peel
2 carrots, shredded or chopped
3 tablespoons brown or white sugar
3 tablespoons vinegar
1 tablespoon salad oil
   Salt and freshly ground pepper to taste

Combine all ingredients and chill. *Eight servings, about 75 calories each.*

ITALIAN COLESLAW

2 cups shredded cabbage
1 green bell pepper, chopped
1 red bell pepper, chopped
1 clove garlic, chopped
2 tablespoons catsup
2 tablespoons low-calorie Italian salad dressing
   Salt and freshly ground pepper to taste

Combine all ingredients and chill. *Six servings, 25 calories each.*

For Nutrition's Sake, Don't Peel That Cucumber!

Three good reasons to enjoy cucumbers: they're low in calories, high in appetite-appeasing fiber, and rich with flavor.

Cucumbers that don't need to be peeled (that aren't waxed) are high in vitamin A and have twice as much fiber.

Here's how they compare:

Large Cucumber	Peeled	Unpeeled
Calories	39	45
Vitamin A (units)	0	750
Fiber (grams)	0.9	1.8

JAPANESE CUCUMBER SALAD

1 cucumber, thinly sliced
1 tablespoon white vinegar or white-wine vinegar
1 tablespoon sake wine or sweet sherry
2 teaspoons Japanese-style soy sauce

Combine all ingredients in a nonmetallic bowl, cover, and chill 1 hour or more before serving. *Two servings, about 35 calories each.*

VARIATION

Cold Seafood Salad: Drain and add one 6½- or 7-ounce can flaked water-packed white-meat tuna. (Canned or cooked crab or lobster meat may also be used.) For a colorful accent, peel and section a fresh tangerine and add it to the mixture. *Two servings, under 145 calories each without tangerine sections, under 165 calories with tangerine sections.*

GREEK YOGURT AND CUCUMBER SALAD

Ja Juck

1 small cucumber
1 cup plain low-fat yogurt
2 cloves garlic, minced
½ teaspoon salt
   Pinch of freshly ground pepper
¼ cup chopped fresh mint leaves, loosely packed, or 1 tablespoon dried mint
   Chopped fresh parsley (optional)

Slice cucumber thin. Arrange on 4 small plates. Combine yogurt, garlic, salt, pepper, and mint in blender, or stir well by hand, and spoon over cucumber slices, covering completely. Sprinkle with parsley, if desired. *Four servings, about 40 calories each.*

ITALIAN MARINATED CUCUMBERS

1 large cucumber
1 ripe tomato
2 teaspoons dried onion flakes
⅛ teaspoon instant garlic
¼ teaspoon oregano or Italian seasoning
2 teaspoons olive oil
2 tablespoons chopped fresh parsley or 2 teaspoons parsley flakes
2 tablespoons red-wine vinegar
   Salt and freshly ground pepper

Quarter cucumber lengthwise, then slice into ½-inch chunks. Peel tomato if skin is tough, then dice. Combine all ingredients, salt and pepper to taste, and chill 30 minutes. *Six servings, 30 calories each.*

MARINATED CUCUMBERS

1 medium cucumber, thinly sliced
1 onion, peeled and thinly sliced
   Water and cider vinegar
   Salt and freshly ground pepper
1 teaspoon sugar (optional)

Put cucumber and onion in a nonmetallic bowl. Cover with equal parts water and vinegar. Salt and pepper to taste, and add sugar, if desired. Cover and chill. *Four servings, 20 calories each.*

CUCUMBER COTTAGE CHEESE

A light lunch.

1 small cucumber, unpeeled (if not waxed)
2 cups low-fat cottage cheese
1 teaspoon dried onion flakes
1 tablespoon chopped fresh parsley
½ teaspoon dill seed
   Lemon juice and Tabasco (optional)
   Salt and freshly ground pepper

Cut cucumber in half lengthwise. Scoop out seeds. Shred coarsely, using hand grater or shredder attachment on electric grinder, food processor, or mixer. Press out moisture. Combine with remaining ingredients, mixing well. Season to taste. Chill, then mound individual servings on lettuce. *Four servings, about 90 calories each.*

UNCLE JOHN'S HUNGARIAN CUCUMBER SALAD

1 **medium cucumber**
1 **large stalk celery**
½ **small onion (optional)**
1 **clove garlic**
1 **sprig parsley**
5 **tablespoons sour cream or sour half-and-half or plain low-fat yogurt**
1 **tablespoon cider vinegar**
¼ **teaspoon sweet Hungarian paprika**
   Salt and freshly ground pepper

Peel the cucumber and slice with a vegetable slicer at the thinnest setting. Set aside for about 20 minutes, then drain and discard the moisture. Cut the celery in half lengthwise, then slice into ½-inch pieces. Peel the onion and slice razor thin; break into rings. Mince the garlic and parsley. Combine all ingredients; add salt and pepper to taste. Marinate in the refrigerator several hours before serving. *Four servings, 45 calories each with sour cream; 40 calories each with half-and-half; 25 calories each with yogurt.*

De-Oiled Marinades for Mini-Calorie Mushrooms

Although lots of lovable vegetables all but disappear in winter, one reliable treat is fresh mushrooms. At only 125 calories for a whole pound, mushrooms are an indulgence even calorie counters can afford. They're terrific added to soups and stews, sautéed with seafood or steak, stuffed with ground meat or tuna mixtures, threaded on skewers with other vegetables, tossed in salads, or served raw as snacks.

One more thing to do with fresh mushrooms is to marinate them. Most mushrooms marinades call for ridiculous amounts of oil—at 1,900 calories a cupful! I don't know why. Most salad oils, except for olive oil, have absolutely no flavor whatsoever, just calories!

Here are my de-oiled marinades for mini-caloried mushrooms.

MARINATED MUSHROOMS

Olives and olive juice add to the olive-oil flavor.

2 tablespoons olive oil
3 black olives, pitted and chopped
¼ cup olive juice (from jar)
¾ cup boiling water
¼ cup lemon juice
2 or more cloves garlic, chopped, or ¼ teaspoon instant garlic
½ teaspoon salt
1 tablespoon mixed pickling spices
1 pound fresh small white mushrooms

Heat all ingredients except mushrooms. Simmer 10 minutes. Add mushrooms, and simmer 4 or 5 minutes. Pour into a strainer. When cool pick out mushrooms and add to strained marinade. Cover and chill. *Eight servings, 45 calories each.*

SHORTCUT MARINATED MUSHROOMS

½ cup low-calorie Italian dressing
½ cup water
½ pound fresh small white mushrooms

Combine dressing and water and heat to boiling. Add mushrooms and simmer uncovered 4 to 5 minutes. When cool, pour into a covered container and chill in refrigerator. *Four servings, 35 calories each.*

MAKE-DO MARINATED MUSHROOMS

8-ounce can button mushrooms, including liquid
¼ cup vinegar
1 cup water
1 tablespoon salad or olive oil
1 envelope Italian (or garlic Italian) dressing mix
¼ teaspoon instant garlic (optional)

Cook and stir ingredients in a saucepan 2 minutes. Cool, then chill all day or overnight. *Four servings, 55 calories each.*

MARINATED RAW MUSHROOMS

1 pound fresh small white mushrooms
1 red onion, sliced into rings
⅔ cup white vinegar
¼ cup water
2 tablespoons olive or other salad oil
1 clove garlic, minced, or ⅛ teaspoon instant garlic
1½ teaspoons salt or garlic salt
¼ teaspoon coarsely ground pepper
  Pinch of cayenne pepper (optional)

Combine all ingredients in a covered bowl and refrigerate 2 days before serving. *Eight servings, about 55 calories each.*

Hail the Salad-Bowl Lunch

While salads are usually first courses or side dishes, main-course salads are especially welcome whenever the weather turns warm. Particularly for lunch. And especially by calorie counters.

A salad-bowl lunch can be every bit as easy to make as a sandwich. The turkey, ham, or cheese that might normally go on bread can be tossed with crisp greenery and low-cal dressing for a quick and easy chef's salad. Leftover chicken or turkey combines with fruit and celery for an easy, tangy chilled curry. Lean leftover steak or rare roast beef is great with romaine and cherry tomatoes. Etc., etc.

CLASSIC CHEF'S SALAD (DECALORIZED)

2 cups torn lettuce or other salad greens
2 tablespoons minced onion
2 slices (2 ounces) cooked white-meat turkey
1 slice (1 ounce) cooked lean "boiled" ham
1 slice (1 ounce) Swiss cheese
3 tablespoons low-calorie commercial salad dressing, any flavor

Combine lettuce and onion in a large salad or soup bowl. Shred or dice the turkey, ham, and cheese, and add. Pour on the dressing and serve. Mix well. *One serving, 325 calories.*

MEAL-SIZE GREEK CHEF'S SALAD

2 cups shredded lettuce
4 or 5 small black olives, pitted and sliced
1 small ripe tomato, quartered
2 hard-cooked eggs, quartered
1 ounce feta cheese, diced
1 tablespoon chopped fresh parsley
2 tablespoons olive juice (from can)
1 teaspoon olive oil
2 tablespoons chopped red or yellow onion
2 tablespoons lemon juice or wine vinegar
½ teaspoon oregano
  Garlic salt and freshly ground pepper

Cut or tear lettuce into bite-size pieces in a large soup bowl. Arrange olives, tomato, eggs, and feta dice on top. Sprinkle with parsley. Stir remaining ingredients together and pour over salad. Serve immediately. *One serving, about 360 calories.*

CURRIED CHICKEN SALAD BOWL

1 eating orange
1 unpeeled red apple
5 stalks celery
2 teaspoons minced onion
2 tablespoons raisins
2 tablespoons low-fat mayonnaise
4 tablespoons plain low-fat yogurt
1¼ cup (7 ounces) cubed cooked white-meat chicken
2 tablespoons soy sauce
½ teaspoon curry powder
  Salt and freshly ground pepper

Peel the orange and slice in half; remove seeds with the tip of a knife. Cut the orange in bite-size chunks, catching and reserving any juice. Core and dice the apple. Cut the celery in thin diagonal slices. Stir the orange, apple, celery, onion, and raisins together with the low-fat mayonnaise and yogurt. Spoon into 2 large soup bowls or onto 2 beds of lettuce. Stir the cubed chicken with the soy sauce and arrange on top of the salad. Sprinkle with curry powder, salt, and pepper, and serve. Mix well. *Two servings, 295 calories each.*

RUSSIAN BEEFEATERS' BOWL

½ cup (3½ ounces) thinly sliced rare leftover lean roast beef or broiled beef round
¼ small red onion, thinly sliced
2 cups torn romaine lettuce
5 ripe cherry tomatoes, halved
   Salt, or garlic salt, and freshly ground pepper
2 tablespoons low-calorie Russian dressing

Slice the beef very thin, then into bite-size strips; break the onion into rings. Combine all ingredients in a large soup bowl or salad bowl and serve. *One serving, 295 calories.*

CURRIED APPLE CHICKEN MOLD

1 envelope plain gelatin
¼ cup cold water
1 cup boiling water
2 chicken bouillon cubes
1 tablespoon lemon juice
1 teaspoon prepared mustard
1 teaspoon curry powder
   Dash of onion powder
1 cup plain low-fat yogurt
1 cup diced cooked white-meat chicken or turkey
1 cup diced celery
1 cup unpeeled diced apple

Sprinkle gelatin on cold water in blender. Wait 1 minute, then add boiling water. Cover and blend on high speed, scraping often, until gelatin granules are dissolved. Add bouillon cubes, lemon juice, mustard, curry powder, and onion powder.

Cover and blend. Add yogurt, cover, and blend smooth. Pour into a bowl. Chill in refrigerator until mixture just begins to set. Stir in chicken, celery, and apple. Chill in a large bowl or individual molds until firm. *Four servings, 115 calories each.*

CHICKEN SALAD VÉRONIQUE

½ cup diced cooked white-meat chicken or turkey
1 cup thinly sliced celery
½ cup green seedless grapes
1 tablespoon low-calorie mayonnaise
2 tablespoons plain low-fat yogurt
1 tablespoon minced onion
  Salt and freshly ground pepper

Combine all ingredients and chill. Serve on lettuce leaves. *One serving, 245 calories.*

TURKEY AMBROSIA FALL FRUIT SALAD

If you're a salad fan, cold cooked turkey is ready to make an almost instant meal—a complete lunch or supper in a bowl, high in protein and fiber—with the addition of fresh fruits and sliced celery. A generous dash of curry powder adds exotic flavor. Spice it up with Tabasco to taste.

½ cup cubed cooked white-meat turkey
1 tablespoon soy sauce
1 cup diagonally sliced celery
1 purple plum, pitted and diced
1 small yellow unpeeled apple, diced
1 tablespoon raisins
1 tablespoon low-fat mayonnaise
1 tablespoon plain low-fat yogurt
1 tablespoon dry-roasted peanuts
  Curry powder to taste
  Tabasco (optional)

Sprinkle turkey with soy sauce and stir well. Add celery, plum, apple, and raisins. Stir in mayonnaise and yogurt. Pile on a crisp bed of lettuce or mound in an individual salad bowl. Sprinkle with peanuts and curry powder. Serve with additional soy sauce and Tabasco, if desired. *One serving, 350 calories.*

DUTCH MACARONI SALAD

An electric shredder (or shredder attachment to your mixer) makes short work of preparing produce for salads like this. It is well worth having if you've got to watch your calories.

8 ounces dry protein-enriched elbow macaroni
5 stalks celery
½ onion, peeled
1 large carrot
1 small green bell pepper, seeded
2 tablespoons low-calorie mayonnaise
2 tablespoons plain low-fat yogurt
½ teaspoon prepared mustard
Pinch cayenne pepper, or to taste
¼ cup minced fresh parsley
Salt and freshly ground pepper
Additional minced parsley and paprika (optional)

Cook macaroni in salted water until tender (See page 245). Drain and rinse in cold water. Cut vegetables into large chunks and put through a shredder. Combine all ingredients except paprika, adding salt and pepper to taste. Chill well. Garnish with additional parsley and a sprinkle of paprika, if desired. *About sixteen ¹/₂-cup servings, 60 calories each.*

VARIATIONS

Quick Tuna Macaroni Lunch: Remove 1 cup prepared Dutch Macaroni Salad (see above) from the refrigerator. Drain a chilled 3 ½-ounce can water-packed tuna and break into flakes. Toss with Macaroni Salad and arrange on lettuce. *One serving, 225 calories.*

Quick Macaroni-and-Egg Salad Lunch: Garnish 1 cup prepared mini-caloried Dutch Macaroni Salad (see above) with 2 chilled hard-cooked eggs, cut in wedges. Arrange on lettuce, with a few slices of vine-ripe tomatoes. *One serving, 280 calories.*

POLYNESIAN SHRIMP-STUFFED PAPAYA RINGS

1 large Hawaiian papaya
½ pound fresh shrimp, cooked and shelled
¼ teaspoon oregano or Italian seasoning
2 tablespoons finely chopped scallions or green onion
Low-calorie salad dressing to taste
2 tablespoons dairy low-fat sour dressing
Squeeze of lemon juice
Lettuce leaves

Cut end off papaya and carefully scoop out seeds and discard. Chop shrimp very fine and blend well with rest of ingredients except lettuce. Pack firmly into papaya shell. Chill. Slice into rings. Serve on lettuce leaves. *Two servings, 200 calories each.*

These Slim Meal-Size Salads Start with Spinach

If you eat a salad lunch every day through the summer, variety is the key to avoiding monotony.

After you've tried every conceivable combination of meat, poultry, cheese, eggs, and seafood, topped by every variety of low-fat salad dressing, it's time to rethink the base. There's no law that every salad begins with a bed of lettuce. How about spinach for a change?

Any combination of lean low-cal ingredients that tastes appealing with lettuce takes on a new dimension when you exchange the lettuce for a crisp bed of torn raw spinach. But spinach has a personality of its own and, therefore, its own preferred companions—eggs, cheese, tuna, rare cooked beef, bacon-flavored bits, and Italian- or French-style salad dressings. Here are some meal-size single-serving combinations that make quick and easy slimming lunches for one.

FRENCH SPINACH, STEAK, AND MUSHROOM SALAD

A tasty way to use up cold steak, left over from your weekend BBQ.

3 ounces chilled broiled lean beef round or flank steak
2 cups coarsely chopped raw spinach
2 tablespoons minced onion
½ cup sliced raw mushrooms
¼ cup low-calorie French or blue-cheese dressing
   Garlic salt and coarsely ground pepper

Steak should be rare. Trim away any fat, then slice thin against the grain in julienne strips. Toss all ingredients together in a large soup bowl. *One meal-size serving, 260 calories.*

TUNA SALAD FLORENTINE

2 cups coarsely chopped raw spinach
1 stalk celery, thinly sliced
½ small red onion, sliced into rings
¼ cup low-calorie Italian salad dressing
1 tablespoon lemon juice
   Salt, or garlic salt, and coarsely ground pepper
   3½-ounce can water-packed white-meat tuna
   Cherry tomatoes for garnish (optional)

Toss and serve garnished with cherry tomatoes, if desired. *One serving, 200 calories.*

Spinach Shrimp Louis: Substitute chilled shrimp for the tuna, low-cal Thousand Island dressing for Italian.

FRENCH SPINACH AND EGG SALAD

  2 **cups coarsely chopped raw spinach**
  2 **tablespoons minced onion**
¼ **cup low-cal French dressing**
  2 **hard-cooked eggs, sliced or shredded**
  1 **tablespoon bacon bits**
  1 **tablespoon chopped fresh parsley**
     Salt and freshly ground pepper

Toss spinach, onion, and salad dressing together in a large salad or soup bowl. Garnish with eggs and sprinkle with bacon bits, parsley, and seasoning. *One meal-size serving, 275 calories.*

CHEF'S CAESAR SPINACH SALAD

  2 **cups torn raw spinach, washed**
¼ **small red onion, sliced in thin rings**
  3 **or 4 radishes, sliced**
  1 **tomato, in wedges**
  1 **(1-ounce) slice each cooked lean ("boiled") ham and cooked turkey**
½ **ounce part-skim mozzarella cheese, diced**
  1 **raw egg or ¼ cup liquid egg substitute**
  3 **tablespoons low-calorie Italian dressing**
     Salt, or garlic salt, and coarsely ground pepper

In a large soup bowl, combine spinach, onion, and radishes. Add tomato wedges. Cut ham and turkey in julienne strips and arrange on top. Add cheese. Beat egg and salad dressing together and pour on. Season to taste. *One meal-size serving, 310 calories.* (Toasted diet bread croutons may be added.)

Slim Salad Lunches for Crabmeat Fans

In Maryland, crab is king. Luckily, even inland dwellers can enjoy crabmeat any time of the year, thanks to the can opener and deep freeze. Canned or frozen crabmeat can be a handy inspiration for a quick salad lunch that's low in calories. Crabmeat is only 25 or 30 calories per ounce. (Unfortunately, crab should be avoided by cholesterol watchers.)

Here we feature some superquick meal-size salads with canned or frozen crabmeat. Be sure to pick over crabmeat for bits of shell. Have it well drained of liquid.

CRAB IMPERIAL SALAD

½ **pound cooked or defrosted lump crabmeat (or 7-ounce can)**
 1 **cup finely chopped celery**
½ **green bell pepper, minced**
 1 **tablespoon minced onion**
 2 **tablespoons diet (imitation) mayonnaise**
 6 **cherry tomatoes, halved**
   Lettuce

Combine crab, celery, pepper, onion, and mayonnaise; toss lightly. Chill. Line 2 salad plates with lettuce and heap on crabmeat mixture. Garnish with tomatoes. *Two servings, about 215 calories each.*

CRAB-APPLE SALAD

A sort of crabby Waldorf!

½ **pound cooked or defrosted lump crabmeat (or 7-ounce can)**
 1 **cup diced celery**
 2 **unpeeled red apples, diced**
 1 **tablespoon regular or diet mayonnaise**
 2 **tablespoons plain low-fat yogurt**
   Salt and freshly ground pepper
   Pinch of curry powder (optional)

Combine all ingredients and chill. Serve on lettuce. *Two servings, 260 calories each.*

CRAB LOUIS SALAD PLATE

   Lettuce
½ **cup cooked, defrosted, or canned crabmeat**
1½ **tablespoons diet mayonnaise**
1½ **tablespoons plain low-fat yogurt**
 1 **teaspoon chili sauce**
   Dash of dried onion flakes
   Lemon wedge
 1 **hard-cooked egg, quartered**

Arrange drained crabmeat on lettuce. Combine mayonnaise, yogurt, chili sauce, and onion and spoon over crabmeat. Garnish with a lemon wedge and egg quarters. *One serving, about 250 calories.*

SOUTH PACIFIC CRAB-STUFFED PAPAYAS

- 4 fresh ripe papayas or cantaloupes
- 3 cups cooked brown rice
- 3 tablespoons low-fat mayonnaise
- 3 tablespoons plain low-fat yogurt
- 1½ teaspoons curry powder (or to taste)
- 1 teaspoon salt
- 2 teaspoons cider vinegar
- 3 tablespoons raisins
- 2 tablespoons chopped cashews
- ¼ cup chopped fresh parsley
- ½ pound cooked crabmeat, cleaned and flaked (or (7-ounce can) crabmeat, drained

Cut papayas or melons in half; scoop out seeds. In a bowl, combine cooked rice with diet mayonnaise and yogurt, stirring lightly with a fork; add curry powder. Add remaining ingredients, mixing lightly; chill. Just before serving, fill hollows with salad mixture. *Eight servings, about 185 calories each with papaya, 160 with cantaloupes.*

Turn Leftover Potatoes into Meal-Size Lunch

Cold potatoes aren't very appealing. But tonight's tired leftovers can be the start of something sensational for tomorrow's lunch. Those cold potatoes, for example, can encore as a very Continental Salade Niçoise, the famous meal-size salad from the French Riviera. Got some leftover steak or roast beef? Why not a steak-and-potato salad seasoned with wine? And why not stretch your leftover potatoes into a meal-size salad with ham and apples? Try the German or Scandanavian versions with some thinly sliced lean cooked meat. These salads are as easy to make as a sandwich, but so much more special. You'll feel as if you're lunching at the Ritz.

But what about calories?

These makeovers are calorie wise, much more filling and a lot less fattening than the usual hurry-up lunch fare. Moreover, our salad-bowl lunches are a delicious way to enjoy vegetables at midday.

NIÇOISE SALAD-BOWL LUNCH

French Tuna and Potato Salad

- 1 cup sliced cooked potatoes
- 1 cup cooked green beans (leftover or canned)
- ⅛ teaspoon instant garlic

  3 ripe olives, pitted and sliced
  3 tablespoons olive liquid (from can)
  1 tablespoon olive oil
 ½ teaspoon Worcestershire sauce
  2 tablespoons wine vinegar
     7-ounce can water-packed white tuna
 ¼ red onion, thinly sliced
  1 tomato, sliced
 ¼ red or green bell pepper, sliced (optional)
     Salt and freshly ground pepper
     Romaine lettuce (optional)

After dinner, slice the leftover potatoes into a nonmetallic bowl. Add the green beans, garlic, and olives. Combine the olive liquid, olive oil, Worcestershire, and vinegar, and pour over the mixture. Cover and refrigerate.

Next day, just before lunchtime, add the flaked white tuna (including liquid), the onion, tomato, and sliced pepper. Stir to combine and season to taste. Serve on romaine lettuce, if desired. *Two servings, 270 calories each.*

POTATO–STEAK STROGANOFF SALAD BOWL

  1 cup thinly sliced leftover broiled flank steak or rare roast beef round
  1 cup sliced cooked potatoes
     2-ounce can sliced mushrooms
1½ tablespoons wine vinegar
1½ tablespoons dry red or white wine
  1 teaspoon catsup
     Dash of dry mustard
1½ teaspoons minced fresh parsley or ½ teaspoon dried parsley flakes
  3 tablespoons plain low-fat yogurt
     Salt and freshly ground pepper
     Lettuce leaves

After dinner, combine all ingredients except yogurt, salt, and pepper in a nonmetallic bowl. Cover and refrigerate.

The next day, just before lunch, add yogurt and mix well. Season to taste and serve on lettuce leaves. *Two servings, 215 calories each.*

DANISH MEAL-SIZE POTATO SALAD
WITH HAM AND APPLES

2 medium potatoes, cooked, peeled, and diced
1 tablespoon salad oil
3 tablespoons lemon juice
2 tablespoons apple juice
1 tablespoon Dijon-style mustard
½ teaspoon salt
  Pinch of freshly ground pepper
4 ounces cooked lean ("boiled") ham, diced
2 unpeeled red apples, cored and diced or sliced
4 hard-cooked eggs, peeled and sliced
2 stalks celery, thinly sliced
  Lettuce
  Chopped fresh parsley
  Paprika

Combine hot diced potatoes with oil, fruit juices, mustard, salt, and pepper. Cover and refrigerate several hours. Toss lightly with ham, apples, eggs, and celery just before serving. Mound on lettuce and sprinkle with chopped parsley and paprika. *Four lunch-size servings, about 245 calories each.*

QUICK GERMAN POTATO SALAD (HOT)

  10¾-ounce can condensed cream of celery soup
2 tablespoons lemon juice
¼ cup water
4 medium potatoes, cooked, peeled, and cubed
½ cup sliced celery
¼ cup chopped fresh parsley
2 teaspoons salt
½ teaspoon sugar (optional)
  Dash of freshly ground pepper
1 tablespoon bacon-flavored bits

In a large saucepan, combine soup, lemon juice, and water. Heat, stirring occasionally.

Stir in remaining ingredients, except bacon bits. Cook just until heated through, stirring constantly and gently. Serve immediately, topped with bacon bits. *Eight servings, about 75 calories each.*

SCANDINAVIAN POTATO SALAD

½ cup plain low-fat yogurt
2 tablespoons lemon juice
2 teaspoons salt
Pinch of freshly ground pepper
1 tablespoon dill
6 potatoes, cooked, peeled, and cubed
1 onion, sliced
1 cup chopped cooked beets
2 tablespoons capers (optional)

Mix the yogurt with the lemon juice, salt, pepper, and dill. Toss with the potatoes, onion, beets, and capers. Chill. *Twelve servings, 55 calories each.*

"Creamy" Low-Cal Salad Dressings—with Yogurt

God made salads and the devil made salad dressings. Or so it seems to us waistline watchers. Most toppings account for 10 times the calories of the greens they cover. A whole pound of lettuce is only 56 calories, about the same as 1 level tablespoon of most commercial dressings. A tablespoon of mayonnaise is 100!

The "fat maker" in salad dressing—whether commercial or homemade—is oil, the most fattening food there is.

Luckily for homemade-dressing fans, there's another base that's both low-cal and protein rich: plain, low-fat yogurt—only 8 calories a tablespoon instead of 115 or so for salad oil. In addition to good dairy nutrition, yogurt also provides a creamy tang that combines beautifully with the crisp texture of fresh vegetables and fruits. Here are some easy homemade, calorie-wise blends to try:

YOGURT GREEN GODDESS

1 cup plain low-fat yogurt
1 hard-cooked egg, peeled
1 teaspoon Worcestershire sauce
1 tablespoon lemon juice
1 teaspoon celery salt
1 teaspoon prepared hot mustard
1 bunch parsley, chopped
¼ cup chopped chives

Combine all ingredients in a blender, cover, and blend smooth. *About 12 calories per tablespoon.*

YOGURT CAESAR DRESSING

½ cup plain low-fat yogurt
1 raw egg
1 tablespoon lemon juice
2 tablespoons grated Parmesan cheese
½ teaspoon Worcestershire sauce
½ teaspoon garlic salt
   Freshly cracked pepper
   Minced fresh parsley (optional)

Stir together with a fork until well blended. Spoon onto Romaine lettuce. Garnish with chopped onion and toasted protein-bread croutons, if desired. *About 17 calories per tablespoon.*

YOGURT MAYONNAISE

1 cup plain low-fat yogurt
1 hard-cooked egg, peeled
2 tablespoons lemon juice
1 teaspoon prepared mustard
1½ teaspoons celery salt

Combine in blender, cover, and beat smooth. Refrigerate. *About 11 calories per tablespoon.*

MORE YOGURT IDEAS

Fluffy Fruit Salad Dressing: Spray some aerosol whipped cream into a measuring cup: add an equal amount of plain low-fat yogurt. Gently fold together; season with grated citrus peel, if desired. *About 10 calories per tablespoon.*

Real Yogurt Roquefort: Stir plain low-fat yogurt with an equal amount of grated Roquefort (or any blue cheese). Season to taste with salt, mashed garlic, minced onion, chopped chives, or parsley. (Roquefort can be grated, if frozen.) *About 30 calories per tablespoon.*

Yogurt Russian: Blend smooth in blender 1 cup plain low-fat yogurt, 1 peeled hard-cooked egg, 5 tablespoons catsup. Stir in 2 tablespoons chopped green bell pepper, salt and pepper to taste. *About 12 calories per tablespoon.*

Yogurt "French": Mix equal parts plain low-fat yogurt and catsup. Add a few drops of vinegar or lemon juice, salt and pepper to taste. *About 10 calories per tablespoon.*

Yogurt Thousand Island: Stir 1 cup plain low-fat yogurt with 3 tablespoons chili sauce, a pinch of dry mustard, 2 tablespoons dill-pickle relish. Season with celery, salt, and pepper. *About 12 calories per tablespoon.*

15

SANDWICHES
AND
BREAD
IDEAS

ᥱᢓ   ᢓᥱ

What's an all-American meal with ethnic roots? The sandwich.

Sandwich meals seem uniquely American, but of course they're not. Nor are they British. The Earl of Sandwich merely lent his name, but he wasn't the first person to order up a fast-food meal. Even the Greeks and Romans stuffed bits of meat into loaves of bread . . . and are still doing it! Some say the Jews invented sandwiches; they still mark Passover with bitter herbs between matzohs, but it wouldn't sell at the Stage Door Deli! The hamburger—without sesame-seed bun and special sauce—was invented by the Germans, along with frankfurters, bologna, and other wurst stuff.

Submarine sandwiches—also known as hoagies, or heroes, depending on where you hail from—are really variations on the French poor-boy sandwich, an entire meal on French bread. Or is it Italian bread? If you stuff your lunch into a tortilla, what you've got is a Mexican taco. Put it in a pita pocket and it's Middle Eastern. Wrap it up, and it's an egg roll from column A! So there's nothing new under the neon at the lunch counter, except the idea that bread is fattening and should, therefore, be avoided. Which led to the development of the "diet plate special" which *is* uniquely American and a low point in American culinary history. On top of being so boring it makes your teeth hurt, such so-called diet plates are bad nutrition—and not even nonfattening! A recent study disclosed that the typical diet plate can be upward of 700 calories and far too high in protein, fat, and cholesterol. Most sandwiches would not only be better, but less.

Of course, a sandwich can be fattening, but usually not because of the bread.

Some of the best breads are also the lowest in calories: true French or Italian bread and Middle Eastern flat breads are really just flour, salt, water, and leavening—no fats or oils, sugars or syrups. Bagels are extra satisfying because they're protein rich, made with high-protein (high-gluten) flour. And there are special high-protein and high-fiber breads available for diet-conscious sandwich lovers that add extra appetite satisfaction because of the types of flour with which they're made. The only bread a dieter needs to avoid is one made with extra shortening or sugars (check the label).

What really makes a sandwich fattening is the fat in the filling: mayonnaise or salad dressing, butter or margarine, fatty meats or high-fat cold cuts. Some of the most interesting "ethnic" variations manage to avoid all that. Many add extra appetite satisfaction and nutrition to sandwich meals with leafy vegetable garnishes.

Here are some tips from our Slim Gourmet sandwich board:

BREAD. The most calorie-wise choices are high-fiber, high-protein, or slim-slice diet breads made without unneeded shortening or sugar. Read the label to be sure, and check for the calorie count per slice (if the baker won't say, don't buy!). The new high-fiber diet breads average 50 calories a slice. Other low-cal, low-starch, and high-protein breads range between 35 and 50 calories, compared to 65 or more for ordinary white bread. Rye, pumpernickel, whole-wheat, cracked-wheat, and no-fat French or Italian breads are generally lower in calories by weight, but the slices are often larger. Rolls are about 150 calories each, but can be "decalorized": slice in half, then pull out and discard the doughy center, leaving only the deliciously crusty shell.

MEAT. The most healthful and least fattening filling is lean fat-trimmed slices of leftover roast chicken, turkey, or lean cuts of beef, lamb, veal, ham, or pork. Home-cooked cold meats invariably have less fat than "cold cuts." Luncheon meats are often a third fat or more. Three ounces (a generous filling) of really lean beef, ham, or lamb is 160 calories or less, while salami or bologna is 230 calories or more. Turkey or chicken is 150 calories or less. Calorie bargains from the deli counter include "boiled" ham, 120 calories; turkey or chicken loaf, about 140 calories. All estimates are for 3-ounce portions.

SALAD FILLINGS. Tuna, crabmeat, egg salad, and other fillings will be fattening if made with mayonnaise (100 calories a tablespoon) or low-cal if made with low-fat ("imitation") mayonnaise (about 24 calories per tablespoon for the low-fat "dairy" varieties). Bottled low-cal salad dressings or plain yogurt can also be used for blending sandwich fillings. In choosing tuna, be sure to get the packed-in-water type (105 calories per 3 ½-ounce can) instead of packed in oil (267 calories).

CHEESE. Virtually all cheeses, even the part-skim varieties and processed cheese foods, are relatively high in fat, 100 calories or more for each 1-ounce slice. Look for low-fat or "diet" cheeses, only half the calories and much richer in protein.

SPREADS. Butter and margarine are *pure fat,* and 100 calories per tablespoon. If you simply must spread your bread, switch to diet margarine (only half the calories). Or low-fat "imitation" cream cheese or Neufchâtel cheese, one-third lower in calories than ordinary cream cheese. (Don't be put off by the word "imitation"; it is required on the label of products that don't meet federal standards for fat content. The low-fat "imitations" are usually higher in valuable protein!)

OTHER TOPPINGS. Catsup, 18 calories per tablespoon; dietetic sugar-free catsup, 7 calories; mustard, 21; horseradish, 9; regular Russian or Thousand Island dressing, 75; low-calorie dressing, 24; sweet-pickle relish, 21; dill pickle relish (no sugar), 3.

AND DON'T OMIT lettuce, tomatoes, green pepper, dill pickles, raw onion, and other crunchy stuff which make a sandwich seem like more for very few calories!

ZINGY OPEN-FACED HAM SALAD SANDWICHES

1 cup chopped lean ham
1 teaspoon dry mustard
2 tablespoons dill-pickle relish
3 tablespoons crushed unsweetened pineapple
3 tablespoons low-calorie mayonnaise or French dressing

Stir together. Serve on thin rye or pumpernickel. *Three servings, 110 calories each (salad only).*

Put Hamburger in Pita Pockets for Slim "Ethnic" Variety

Here's how to glamorize hamburger and cut calories as well: enclose them in pita bread pockets instead of those fluffy, puffy kidstuff hamburger buns.

Pita bread is Middle Eastern flat bread, now available in stores and supermarkets all over the country, both fresh and frozen. It looks like a big, flat, 5-inch pancake, but when you cut the "pancake" in half (into 2 half moons) it opens to form 2 "pockets." Into the "pocket" go your lean broiled burger, onions, catsup, tomatoes, pickle slices, or any glamorous garnish you can think of.

Why pita bread instead of common hamburger rolls? Because pita bread is simply flour, salt, water, and yeast—no sugar, shortening, or other calorie adders. (Read the label; if it contains anything else, it's not true pita bread.) A pita pocket is only 80 calories instead of the 120 calories common hamburger buns cost. You can use pita bread as the envelope for a number of "ethnic" variations on the ordinary all-American hamburger. Here are some slim variations to try, all based—of course—on lean, fat-trimmed hamburger (such as ground round steak) cooked with no fat added.

And since it goes without saying that pita bread can be used as a "shell" for all kinds of sandwich fillings, I'm including a ham 'n' cheese "hero" on pita bread, just to give you the idea.

P.S. If you can't find pita bread in your area, look for Italian or French rolls —the kind made without sugar or fat, and used to make hero or hoagie sandwiches. Split each roll lengthwise and pull out the doughy (and fattening) center, leaving only the flavorful crust. Prepare the filling and spoon it into the cavity. The flavor will be authentic even if the container isn't.

GREEK HAMBURGER HERO SANDWICHES

¾ **pound lean fat-trimmed ground beef round or lamb**
   Monosodium glutamate (optional)
¼ **teaspoon ground cinnamon**
¼ **teaspoon grated nutmeg**
 2 **teaspoons oregano or Italian seasoning**
 1 **tablespoon lemon juice**
 1 **small onion, finely chopped**
½ **cucumber, peeled and diced**
 2 **tablespoons minced fresh parsley**
 1 **small tomato, diced**
   Garlic salt and freshly ground pepper
 2 **pitas, cut in half, or 4 Italian hero or hoagie rolls, split in half, doughy centers removed**
   Tabasco (optional)
   Plain low-fat yogurt (optional)

Shape the chopped meat into one big flat hamburger and put it in a nonstick skillet over moderate heat, no fat added. After the underside is well browned, break up the meat into chunks. Add the monosodium glutamate, cinnamon, nutmeg, and oregano. Cook and stir until the chunks are browned. Drain off fat. Stir in the lemon juice and chopped vegetables, and heat through. Season to taste with garlic salt and pepper.

Fill the bread with the hot meat mixture and serve immediately. For an authentic flavor, dash on a few drops of Tabasco and spoon on some yogurt. *Four servings, 200 calories each.*

VARIATION

Italian Hamburger Heroes: For an Italian version, follow the previous recipe, using beef or lean ground veal. Substitute finely diced green pepper or zucchini for the cucumber. Omit cinnamon, nutmeg, lemon juice, and yogurt. At serving time, split and remove dough from center of Italian rolls, then spread with the hot meat mixture and sprinkle each serving with 1 teaspoon sharp Romano cheese instead of yogurt. *Four servings, about 200 calories each.*

PIZZABURGER

3 ounces lean, fat-trimmed ground beef round
¼ cup plain tomato sauce
1 tablespoon chopped onion
    Garlic salt and freshly ground pepper
    Oregano or Italian seasoning
½ of 5-inch pita
1 tablespoon shredded part-skim mozzarella cheese

Brown hamburger quickly in a nonstick skillet. Drain fat from pan. Add tomato sauce, onion, and seasonings, and heat to boiling. Insert burger in pita pocket. Spoon in hot tomato sauce and cheese. *One serving, 250 calories.*

VARIATION

Tacoburger: Follow directions in preceding recipe, but add a dash of chili powder or hot sauce and a pinch of cumin to the tomato sauce. Fill the pita bread with some shredded lettuce and 1 tablespoon finely minced green bell pepper. Substitute shredded sharp Cheddar or Monterey Jack cheese for the mozzarella. *One serving, 280 calories.*

BOEUFBURGER AUX CHAMPIGNONS

3 ounces lean, fat-trimmed ground beef round
    Pinch of poultry seasoning
    Salt and freshly ground pepper
½ of 5-inch pita
2 tablespoons chopped onion
¼ cup sliced fresh mushrooms
2 tablespoons dry white wine

Brown hamburger quickly in a small nonstick skillet over high heat, no fat added. Season with poultry seasoning, and salt and pepper as it browns. Drain fat from pan. Insert burger in pita pocket. Combine remaining ingredients in skillet over high heat. Cook and stir 1 minute; spoon over hamburger. *One serving, 215 calories.*

CHINABURGER

3 ounces lean, fat-trimmed ground beef round
1 tablespoon soy sauce
  Monosodium glutamate (optional)
  Garlic salt and freshly ground pepper
½ of 5-inch pita
  1 tablespoon chopped raw onion
  3 tablespoons chopped fresh bean sprouts
  1 tablespoon catsup
  Additional soy sauce (optional)

Season the hamburger with soy sauce, monosodium glutamate, garlic salt, and pepper as it broils. Stuff into pita pocket and fill with onion and sprouts. Top with catsup and additional soy sauce, if desired. *One serving, 235 calories.*

GREEKBURGERS

3 ounces lean, fat-trimmed ground beef round or lamb
  Garlic salt and freshly ground pepper
  Ground cinnamon and grated nutmeg
½ of 5-inch pita
  1 tablespoon chopped onion
  1 tablespoon chopped or thinly sliced cucumber
  2 tablespoons plain low-fat yogurt

Season the meat with the garlic salt and pepper, cinnamon, and nutmeg as it broils. Place in pita pocket. Combine onion, cucumber, and yogurt. Spoon over meat. *One serving, 220 calories.*

FETA CHEESEBURGERS

3 ounces lean, fat-trimmed ground beef round
  Garlic salt and freshly ground pepper
½ of 5-inch pita
  1-ounce slice feta cheese
  1 tablespoon chopped fresh parsley or mint
  Thin slice onion (optional)

Shape meat into a flat patty and cook quickly under a broiler or over coals, turning once. Season with garlic salt and pepper. Put the cooked hamburger, cheese, parsley, and onion into the pita pocket and serve immediately. *One serving about 275 calories.*

BLUE CHEESEBURGERS

1 pound lean, fat-trimmed ground beef round
1 onion, minced
1 cup low-calorie blue-cheese dressing
2 five-inch pitas, each cut in half

Combine beef, onion, and dressing; shape into 4 burgers. Broil, turning once, then put each into a pita pocket. *Four servings, 270 calories each.*

CUBAN HERO SANDWICH

½ of 5-inch pita or small crisp French or Italian roll, cut in half lengthwise
    and doughy center removed
1 teaspoon hot mustard
1 teaspoon low-fat mayonnaise
2 ounces (4 thin slices) lean cooked ham
1 ounce (2 thin slices) Swiss, Gruyère, or low-fat white diet cheese
½ green bell pepper, sliced
½ dill pickle, thinly sliced
    Garlic salt and coarsely ground pepper
1 tablespoon chili sauce

Slit the roll in half lengthwise and pull out the bready filling, leaving a crisp shell. Spread one side lightly with mustard, the other with low-fat mayonnaise. Fill with ham, cheese, sliced pepper, and pickle. Season with garlic salt and pepper; top with chili sauce. *One serving, about 375 calories.*

Slim Sausage and Pepper Hero Sandwiches

Prepare the recipe for Steak Sausage and Peppers (page 117). Crisp 6 Italian hero rolls in a hot oven. Remove, halve, pull out doughy centers. Discard dough, leaving only crisp shells. Fill rolls' cavities with sausage and sauce, dividing evenly. Serve immediately. *Six servings, about 250 calories each.*

For a Diet-Wise Lunch, Try a French-Toast Sandwich

Who says "French toast" is limited to breakfast? Here we've got a trio of toasted goodies that are definitely welcome for lunch, brunch, or supper.

Welcome also if you happen to be calorie counting, because these tasty treats are really nutrition-rich diet dishes. Differing from breakfast French toast, these recipes don't need any sugary syrups. Basically, they're grilled-cheese sandwiches all done up in fancy dress.

What makes them calorie-wise is attention to detail in choosing ingredients and grilling techniques. Everything in them is low- or no-fat. We grill them without fat by using a nonstick skillet coated with cooking spray. You can try these treats even if eggs are off limits. We've double-tested the recipes with cholesterol-free egg substitute, and they work just as well. Who says dieting is drab!

CROQUE MONSIEUR

French-Toasted Ham and Cheese Sandwich

2 slices (1 ounce) Swiss cheese or low-fat white diet cheese
2 thin slices diet or high-protein bread
2 ounces sliced lean cooked ("boiled") ham
  Mustard
1 egg or ¼ cup egg substitute

Put 1 slice cheese on each slice of bread. Add ham. Spread lightly with mustard; close the sandwich. Beat the egg with a few drops of water in a shallow dish or pour in the egg substitute. Put the assembled sandwich into the dish; turn frequently until all the egg is absorbed and both sides are well coated. Spray a nonstick skillet liberally with cooking spray for no-fat frying. Heat over moderate flame. Add the sandwich and grill, turning once, until both sides are browned and cheese is melted. *Each sandwich about 305 calories.*

FRENCH-TOASTED REUBEN SANDWICH

2 thin slices rye bread
2 thin slices (1 ounce) part-skim Iceland or white diet cheese
2 ounces thinly sliced lean corned-beef round—*not* brisket!
  Mustard
2 tablespoons well-drained finely chopped canned sauerkraut
1 egg or ¼ cup egg substitute

Assemble the sandwiches as in the previous recipe, with the cheese closest to the bread and the sauerkraut in the middle. Coat with egg or substitute. Cook in a well-sprayed nonstick skillet according to previous directions. *Each sandwich 375 calories.*

FRENCH-TOASTED ITALIAN SANDWICHES

2 thin slices loaf-style Italian bread (made without fat)
2 thin slices (1 ounce) thinly sliced part-skim mozzarella cheese
2 ounces sliced lean cooked ("boiled") ham
  Thinly sliced ripe tomato

Oregano or Italian seasoning
Salt and freshly ground pepper
1 **egg or ¼ cup egg substitute**

Assemble sandwiches as in previous recipes, with the tomato in the middle. Season filling. Dip in egg or substitute and grill in nonstick skillet according to previous directions. Serve with a tossed green salad. *Each sandwich 365 calories.*

FRENCH-TOASTED MOZZARELLA SANDWICH

6 **slices high-fiber white bread**
3 **slices (about 3 ounces) part-skim mozzarella cheese**
2 **tablespoons sliced pimiento-stuffed olives**
2 **eggs, lightly beaten**
2 **tablespoons skim milk**
1 **tablespoon butter or margarine**
  Parsley sprigs

Trim crusts from bread. Place cheese on 3 slices bread; top with olives and remaining slices bread. In a bowl combine eggs and milk. Dip both sides of bread into the egg mixture. In a skillet brown the sandwiches in butter. Garnish with parsley. *Three sandwiches, 285 calories each.*

"FRENCH DIP" SANDWICHES

What to do with the leftovers? Here's the Slim Gourmet version of a really special meal-size sandwich that's popular in New York area "beef restaurants." Hot, sliced rare beef is served on crusty fingers of French bread, along with a cup of broth for dipping . . . hence the name "French Dip." (See also the turkey version on page 298.) Serve with crisp celery, dill-pickle spears, or coleslaw made with diet dressing.

2 **French or Italian rolls (2½ ounces each)**
  10½-ounce can fat-skimmed beef broth or bouillon
6 **ounces thinly sliced, fat-trimmed rare roast beef round**

Toast rolls in oven or in toaster-oven until crisp and heated through. Heat undiluted broth in a saucepan until boiling. Add meat to heat through.

Cut rolls in half lengthwise. Open and pull out doughy centers. Fill the cavities with sliced hot meat. Cut each sandwich in quarters and serve on a plate. Pour the heated broth into 2 cups and put a cup on each plate. Dip the sandwich quarters in the hot broth and eat. *Two servings, 325 calories each.*

Slimming Sandwiches Made with Turkey

What follows Thanksgiving—almost as surely as Christmas and New Year—
is turkey sandwiches.

But the type of turkey sandwich needn't be that predictable . . . nor that
predictably fattening. Instead of the usual mayonnaise-slathered fare, here are
some trim turkey makeovers for post-holiday lunching. Add eye appeal, if you
wish, with pickles, tomato wedges, and celery sticks.

TURKEY "FRENCH DIP"

A turkey version of what restaurants do with roast beef (see page 297).

1 decalorized French roll (see below)
3 ounces sliced cooked turkey
1 cup fat-skimmed well-seasoned turkey broth (canned or from turkey bones)
  Minced fresh parsley

To decalorize a French roll, heat briefly in the oven or in an oven-toaster
until crisp. Slice lengthwise, then pull out and discard the doughy center,
leaving a crusty hollow for the turkey.

Gently heat the turkey in the broth. Put the hot turkey in the hollow, then
slice the sandwich in quarters. Pour the hot broth into a cup and sprinkle with
a little minced parsley. Put the cup in the center of a plate and surround with
sandwich sections.

To eat, dip the sandwich in the hot broth and eat with your fingers. *One
serving, about 275 calories.*

TURKEY SWISS TOAST

French-Toasted Turkey-Cheese Sandwich

4 slices protein-enriched or high-fiber diet bread
4 teaspoons low-fat mayonnaise
2 ounces (4 thin slices) Swiss cheese
4 ounces sliced cooked white-meat turkey
  Salt, or celery salt, and freshly ground pepper
  Dash of grated nutmeg
1 egg
6 tablespoons skim milk

Spread the bread lightly with diet mayonnaise. Cover bottom slice with
cheese, turkey, then cheese. Season, then cover with top slice of bread.

Beat the egg and milk together in a shallow bowl, then add the sandwiches.

Turn after a minute or two, so that both sides of the sandwiches soak up the egg-milk mixture.

Spray a nonstick skillet or electric sandwich grill with cooking spray for no-fat frying, then grill the sandwiches on both sides, until bread is golden and cheese is melted. *Two servings, 385 calories each.*

TURKEY MINI-PIZZAS

1 English muffin, halved and toasted
2 ounces (2 slices) cooked turkey, chopped
3 tablespoons catsup
   Onion or garlic salt, and freshly ground pepper to taste
   Oregano or Italian seasoning to taste
1 ounce (1 thin slice) part-skim mozzarella cheese

Split the muffin with a fork and toast lightly. Combine the turkey and catsup and spoon on top of the toasted muffin halves. Season to taste. Put under the broiler briefly or in a toaster-oven, just until turkey is heated. Chop or dice the cheese and put on top of the turkey mixture. Return to the broiler or toaster, just until cheese is melted. *One serving, 365 calories.*

Low-Calorie Sandwiches with a Mexican Accent

If your taste in sandwiches runs to spicy-but-fattening cold cuts, but your diet prescription says lean chicken or turkey, don't despair. If you like zesty fare, try these poultry combinations with a Mexican flair.

Most Americans combine bland chicken or turkey with bland (but fattening) mayonnaise. Instead, I spice up poultry sandwiches with bottled green taco sauce. Made from green tomatoes, it's spicy, but not too hot. There's no fat or sugar added, so taco sauce is even less fattening than catsup or mustard. (You can, of course, use a hot pepper sauce if your taste runs to a little more "heat.")

Here's how they compare (calorie counts approximate):

One Tablespoon	*Calories*
Mayonnaise	100
Catsup	18
Mustard	21
Taco Sauce	3

CHICKEN "TACO" SANDWICHES

2 slices toasted diet high-fiber or high-protein bread
   Crisp lettuce
3 ounces cooked white-meat chicken or turkey
1 tablespoon chopped stuffed green Spanish olives
1 tablespoon, or more, bottled green taco sauce
   Salt and freshly ground pepper

Spread the toast lightly (or liberally) with taco sauce and add remaining ingredients. *One serving, about 275 calories.*

CABALLERO HERO

   Small crisp French or Italian roll
1 tablespoon low-calorie mayonnaise
   Shredded iceberg lettuce
2 ounces white-meat turkey or chicken, thinly sliced
½ ounce sharp cheese, thinly sliced
2 or 3 thin slices ripe tomato
4 stuffed green olives, thinly sliced
   Sprinkle of dried oregano, cumin powder, garlic salt
   Green taco sauce or hot pepper sauce, to taste (optional)

Read the label and choose a brand of rolls made with no added sugar or shortening (fat). If rolls are soggy, crisp briefly in a hot oven. Slice in half lengthwise. Pull out and discard doughy center, leaving only the crisp shell. Spread lightly with low-cal mayonnaise, then fill the cavity with shredded lettuce and remaining ingredients. Add "hot stuff" (taco sauce or pepper sauce) judiciously, to taste. *One serving, about 340 calories.*

MEXICAN CHICKEN-SALAD
SANDWICH SPREAD

2 cups (⅔ pound) chopped cooked white-meat chicken or turkey
3 tablespoons sour half-and-half, sour dressing, or plain yogurt
2 tablespoons low-calorie mayonnaise
2 tablespoons minced onion
2 tablespoons diced red or green bell pepper
¼ teaspoon adobo seasoning (or ¼ teaspoon oregano and ⅛ teaspoon cumin powder)
   Garlic salt and pepper to taste

1 **tablespoon drained chopped green stuffed Spanish olives**
1 **tablespoon olive juice (from jar)**
   Dash of Tabasco or chili powder to taste

Mix all ingredients well, adding hot sauce or chili powder to taste. Chill. Serve as a sandwich filling (or as a salad on a bed of lettuce). *Four luncheon-size servings, 175 calories each (without bread).*

VARIATIONS

Lettuce "Tacos": Crisp large iceberg lettuce leaves in ice water; pat dry with paper toweling. Fill each with a little of the preceding chicken-salad mixture and roll up, taco style.

Unfried Tacos: Use canned or frozen defrosted tortillas. Lay flat on a nonstick cookie sheet in a warm (250-degree) oven for about 10 minutes. Fill with shredded lettuce and Mexican Chicken Salad (see above). Top with green taco sauce, if desired. *Each unfried 5-inch tortilla is about 45 calories.*

Low-Cal Recipe Ideas with High-Fiber Breads

Here are some Slim Gourmet ideas for cooking with the low-calorie high-fiber breads. This recent entry on supermarket shelves has only 50 calories a slice and contains 5 times the fiber of whole-wheat bread. We've experimented extensively with it and found that it can replace regular bread in many recipes. Here are some ideas.

High-Fiber, Low-Cal French Toast: For each serving, lightly beat together 1 egg, ¼ cup skim milk, a few drops vanilla, and a shake of salt. Soak 2 slices high-fiber (white or whole-wheat) bread in the mixture until saturated. Spray a nonstick skillet or electric griddle with cooking spray for no-fat frying. Toast the bread over moderate heat, turning once. Toast is done when golden. (Sprinkle with cinnamon or top with low-sugar jam, diet syrup, or equal parts honey and diet syrup.) *Each slice, 65 calories.*

Hot Turkey or Beef Sandwiches: Make no-fat gravy by thickening well-seasoned fat-skimmed beef or turkey broth with flour. Reheat lean cooked turkey or roast-beef slices in the gravy. Arrange the sliced meat on top of a slice of high-fiber bread on a plate and pour on the hot gravy. Serve with hot cooked vegetables and a salad. *With 3 ounces meat, 1 slice bread, under 250 calories.*

Cheese Croutons: Cut 4 slices stale or toasted high-fiber bread in ½-inch cubes. Shake up in a plastic bag with 1 tablespoon salad oil, 2 tablespoons grated sharp Italian cheese, 1 teaspoon oregano or Italian seasonings, 2 teaspoons garlic salt, ½ teaspoon paprika. Arrange on a nonstick cookie sheet. Bake in a preheated 450-degree oven only until toasted (watch carefully). Cool, then store in a moistureproof container. Use in salads.

High-Fiber Stuffing: High-fiber bread can replace ordinary bread in any favorite combination. Or try this vegetable-rich recipe. Combine 2 finely-chopped large onions, 2 cups minced celery, 1 cup chopped fresh parsley, 8-ounce can mushroom stems and pieces (including liquid), 10 slices of cubed stale (or toasted) high-fiber bread, chopped poultry giblets (optional), 1 teaspoon celery or garlic salt, 1/4 teaspoon pepper, 2 teaspoons poultry seasoning, and 1 beaten egg.

Toss lightly and use to stuff poultry. *About 8 cups. Each 1/2-cup serving is under 50 calories.*

Toasted High-Fiber Breadcrumbs: Several brands of high-fiber bread—both dark and white—are now marketed all over the country. The bread is only 50 calories a slice instead of 65. If you don't have fiber bread, you can use high-protein diet or whole-wheat bread, or leftover French or Italian bread (made without sugar or shortening).

For best results, use dry hard toast; leftover toast is ideal. Otherwise, toast fresh bread lightly, and arrange on a rack, uncovered. Let dry out for a few hours until hard and crisp. Break up each slice and process in a covered blender to make crumbs. Without a blender, put the dry toast in a large plastic bag and roll over the bag with a rolling pin until crushed into fine crumbs. *Two slices make 1/4 cup crumbs (100 calories); 8 slices make 1 cup (400 calories).*

Seasoned Breadcrumbs: Put stale or toasted high-fiber bread in a blender container a slice at a time. Cover and blend to crumbs. Season each cup with 1 teaspoon celery salt, 1 teaspoon onion salt, 1 teaspoon paprika, 1/4 teaspoon pepper, 1/4 teaspoon instant garlic (optional). Use as a coating for oven-fried chicken (no fat added).

16
GRAVIES
AND
SAUCES

If you want to be a Slim Gourmet cook, don't overlook gravies and sauces. Instead of being on the forbidden list, these tasty toppers rightfully belong on your recommended list. Why? Because savory sauces make lean foods more palatable—desirable and delicious, as well! Otherwise the really lean, low-calorie cuts of meat may seem bland and dry. (Ever notice that people who *never* use sauces favor fatty steaks and fried foods?) Vegetables, for want of a more imaginative topping, wind up buried in butter or margarine—and there's nothing more fattening than that!

But don't most diet plans rule out gravies and sauces? Yes, and with good reason. Because conventionally-made gravies usually harbor hidden, unneeded calories in the form of fat and oils. It's the fat, not the thickeners, that thicken waistlines needlessly.

You can skim unneeded calories from gravies simply by skimming the fat from the juices or drippings that serve as their base. You can defat sauces simply by omitting the fat or fatty ingredients unnecessarily called for in conventional recipes. Use this rule to sauce up your holiday turkey with good (nonfattening) gravy.

DEFATTED PAN GRAVY

Your roast (and gravy) will be more flavorful if basted occasionally with a tablespoon of wine. Add a peeled onion, a stalk of celery, and a carrot to the roasting pan.

1. Before making gravy, drain the pan juices into a glass jar or measuring cup. Be sure to scrape up the flavorful residue from the roasting pan (add a little hot water if needed).

2. Wait till the fat rises to the surface, then meticulously siphon off every bit with a squeeze-bulb baster. Or, if you're not in a hurry, chill the jar until the fat hardens on top; then simply lift it off.

3. Measure the stock; add water to make the amount of gravy you want.

4. Reheat in a saucepan.

5. For each cup of gravy wanted, combine 2 tablespoons flour and 4 tablespoons cold water in a small cup. Stir to make a paste; then stir the paste into the simmering liquid.

6. Simmer the gravy until it's the thickness you want. If it's too thick, thin it with a little water.

7. Season to taste or vary the flavor with salt, pepper, herbs, lemon juice, or vinegar. Monosodium glutamate (MSG) will noticeably intensify the flavor of a weak gravy, but some people are allergic to it. For a darker, richly flavored gravy, use a little soy sauce, Worcestershire sauce, or brown gravy flavoring base. Sprinkle with chopped fresh parsley before serving.

VARIATIONS

Gravy Without Drippings: This can be made from canned, condensed chicken or beef broth. (First, skim the globules of fat from the surface.) Combine a 10½-ounce can, undiluted, with 3 tablespoons flour. Cook and stir until thick; then season to taste. Or use homemade fat-skimmed broth simmered from leftover bones. Or a broth reconstituted with boiling water and bouillon cubes or concentrated beef stock.

"Cream" Gravy: Easily made by substituting skim milk (fresh, canned, or reconstituted) for part of the water. Before making the gravy, fat-skim the pan juices and simmer them down to a rich concentrate. Combine cold liquid skim milk with flour. Blend well, then stir into the saucepan. Cook and stir over low heat until thick. Add seasonings and herbs to taste.

Tomato Gravy: This gravy needs no flour thickener. You can make it two ways: with tomato paste or tomato juice. First way: Combine 1½ to 2 cups fat-skimmed meat broth with a 6-ounce can tomato paste. Cook and stir until thick and smooth; dilute with boiling water to sauce consistency and season to taste with oregano or Italian seasonings. Or combine 3 cups tomato juice with fat-skimmed meat drippings and simmer down to sauce consistency. Then season to taste.

LOW-CAL TARTAR SAUCE

Mix equal parts low-calorie, low-fat mayonnaise-type diet dressing with well-drained dill-pickle relish. If desired, stir in a little hot mustard and lemon juice to taste. *About 20 calories per tablespoon.*

SWEET 'N' SOUR PICKLED PINEAPPLE SAUCE

What sounds like a weird combination is actually a very delicious way to add natural sweet 'n' sour tang to a tasty tomato sauce. (The usual way is with sugar and vinegar. But neither has any real nutritional or appetite appeasement value.)

Even if the combination does sound strange, be venturesome and give it a try. The sauce is great over vegetables or meat loaf, and a savory addition to potted meatballs or stuffed cabbage (see pages 101 and 102).

6-ounce can tomato paste
10-ounce can fat-skimmed beef or chicken broth
1 dill pickle, coarsely shredded or finely chopped
1 cup unsweetened crushed pineapple
1 onion, minced
1 clove garlic, minced
Salt and freshly ground pepper

Combine all ingredients in a saucepan. Simmer 15 minutes, stirring occasionally. Serve over lean cooked meat, poultry, or vegetables. *Eight servings, 45 calories each.*

ORIENTAL POULTRY SAUCE

4 ounces dried apricots
1 cup tomato juice
1/3 cup cider vinegar
2 tablespoons honey
1 teaspoon paprika
1/4 cup soy sauce

In a medium-size saucepan, cook apricots in tomato juice over low heat for 30 minutes or until soft (most of juice should be absorbed). Put apricots through a food mill or puree in a food processor or blender. Add rest of ingredients and whir until smooth. Refrigerate until ready to use. *Makes one pint, 16 calories per tablespoon.*

SWISS CHEESE AND WINE SAUCE

2 cups skim milk
½ teaspoon salt (or butter-flavored salt)
  Pinch of grated nutmeg
1 teaspoon prepared mustard
¼ cup dry vermouth
2 tablespoons cornstarch
3 ounces shredded low-fat cheese
1 tablespoon chopped fresh parsley or 1 teaspoon dried parsley

Combine milk, salt, nutmeg, and mustard in a nonstick saucepan over medium heat; stir until just simmering. Lower heat.

Combine vermouth and cornstarch into a paste and stir into milk; simmer until slightly thickened. Gradually stir in shredded cheese until melted. Stir in parsley. *About 15 calories per tablespoon.*

SLIM GOURMET TOMATO SAUCE CONCENTRATE

For 350 days a year you'd trade your teeth for just one tomato—a real tomato, not one of those hard pink tennis balls that pass for tomatoes the rest of the year.

Then one day all the real tomatoes all over the world ripen at once.

Unfortunately there is just no way you can save that fresh ripe texture for winter salads. But you can turn Mother Nature's overstock into a Slim Gourmet tomato-sauce concentrate for your freezer. Then you'll always have a defrost-and-dilute topping for pasta dishes, seafood, meat, poultry, and vegetables.

Make your concentrate unseasoned. Then you can spice it up to suit your mood—oregano, chili, curry, cumin. I even omit salt, because sometimes I like to dilute my tomato concentrate with canned chicken broth or beef bouillon (which tend to be salty).

Since you make this sauce yourself you know it contains no unneeded calorie adders like oil, thickeners, starch, sugar, or syrup. Use chopped olives instead of olive oil for that special flavor.

For each 8 tomatoes, add:

1 cup finely chopped onion
½ cup finely chopped celery
½ cup sliced carrots, fresh or frozen
1 or more cloves minced garlic (optional)
6 chopped green olives
1 cup water

Peel the tomatoes, cut in half, and shake out the seeds. Combine with remaining ingredients in a nonstick saucepan. Cover and simmer 20 minutes. Uncover and simmer, stirring occasionally, until nearly all the liquid evaporates and sauce is very thick and concentrated. If a smooth sauce is desired, strain the sauce or whir it in a covered blender. Pack in 1-cup jars. Label and freeze.

To use, defrost and dilute with equal amounts of water or other liquid (fat-skimmed canned beef broth, chicken bouillon, etc.). Reheat until thick and bubbling. Season to taste. *Each cup of concentrate will make about 2 cups sauce, approximately 35 calories per ¹/₂-cup serving.*

GREEK TOMATO SAUCE FOR VEGETABLES*

6 fresh ripe tomatoes or 28-ounce can of tomatoes
1 bunch scallions, chopped
2 cloves garlic, minced
¼ cup chopped fresh parsley
1 teaspoon dried oregano or Italian seasoning
1 tablespoon crushed fresh mint
2 bay leaves
½ cup dry sherry
Salt and pepper

Peel and chop the tomatoes. Place in a saucepan. Add remaining ingredients and simmer, covered, 20 minutes. *Six servings, 45 calories each.*

Cauliflower: Wash, trim, and cut 1 pound into flowerettes, place in hot tomato sauce, and add water, if needed. Simmer 20 minutes. *65 calories each serving.*

Artichokes: Add 2 boxes frozen artichokes and the juice of 1 lemon to tomato sauce and simmer until tender. *65 calories each.*

Peas: Stir 3 cups frozen peas into tomato sauce and simmer 10 minutes. *70 calories each serving.*

Potatoes: Peel and slice 3 potatoes and simmer in tomato sauce until tender, 25 minutes. *170 calories each serving.*

Zucchini: Slice 6 small zucchini in ¼-inch slices and add to tomato sauce. Simmer until tender, about 10 minutes. *70 calories each serving.*

Green Beans: Parboil 1 pound fresh green beans, whole or cut. Drain and add to tomato sauce. Bring to a boil and simmer till tender, about 10 minutes. *65 calories each serving.*

*Reprinted from *Greek Cooking for the Gods.* Copyright 1970 by Eva Zane. Published by 101 Productions, San Francisco.

Eggplant: Peel and dice 1 pound. Add to tomato sauce, simmer 30 to 40 minutes, adding water when needed. Salt and pepper to taste. *60 calories each serving.* Add grated cheese, if desired.

CHUNKY TOMATO PEPPER SAUCE

   16-ounce can stewed tomatoes
2 bell peppers, seeded and sliced into strips
2 onions, peeled, halved, and sliced
2 or 3 sprigs parsley, chopped
1 clove garlic, minced (optional)
1 or 2 teaspoons oregano or Italian seasoning
½ teaspoon dried (optional)
1 teaspoon bottled beef extract (optional)

Combine all ingredients in a pan, cover, and cook over moderate heat 15 minutes. Uncover and continue to cook until most of liquid evaporates into a thick, chunky sauce. *Four servings, about 60 calories each.*

ITALIAN TOMATO VELVET SAUCE

Pork broth is a delicious addition when making Italian-style tomato sauces.

1 pint pork broth (see page 80) or 10½-ounce can fat-skimmed chicken broth
   6-ounce can tomato paste
1 clove garlic, minced
   Oregano or Italian seasoning to taste

Combine pork broth with a tomato paste. Season with garlic and oregano and simmer until thick. Serve over meat, vegetables, or pasta. *Eight servings, 25 calories each.*

LOW-FAT MEAT SAUCE FOR SPAGHETTI, PRESSURE-COOKER STYLE

1 pound lean, fat-trimmed ground beef round
3 cups water
2 six-ounce cans tomato paste
   16-ounce can tomatoes, broken up
5 onions, sliced
4 cloves garlic, chopped
1 teaspoon salt

¼ teaspoon cayenne pepper (optional)
1 tablespoon oregano or Italian seasoning

In a nonstick pressure cooker over moderate heat, brown the chopped meat in one solid piece. When underside is browned, break up the meat into chunks and continue cooking until chunks are browned. Add 1 cup water, then drain off into a cup. Set aside until all the fat has risen to the surface. Drain and discard the fat, using a bulb-type baster. Return the fat-skimmed liquid to the pressure cooker and add remaining ingredients. Cover and cook under pressure for 20 minutes, following manufacturer's directions.

Reduce pressure, following manufacturer's directions. (If thicker sauce is desired, simmer uncovered until sauce reduces. Serve on hot tender-cooked protein-enriched spaghetti (see page 245). *Six servings, 195 calories each. One cup cooked spaghetti adds 155 calories.*

NOTE: Extra sauce may be frozen.

Here's How to "Decalorize" Your Favorite Spaghetti Sauce

A reader writes:

How can I adapt this recipe to make it slim? It's our favorite spaghetti sauce, and I would like to keep it in my file, but only if it's not fattening.

Betty B.
Florissant, Missouri

Dear Betty: You can easily decalorize this recipe without any drastic change in the ingredients, other than eliminating unneeded fat (olive oil, fatty ground beef, the fat in the sausage). The real flavor makers remain unchanged.

Here's your recipe and my slimmed-down "makeover." The calories are cut in half!

BETTY'S FAVORITE (BUT FATTENING) SPAGHETTI SAUCE

		CALORIES
1	cup chopped onion	65
¼	cup olive oil	477
1	pound hamburger (25 percent fat)	1,300
3	ounces Italian sausage, sliced	423
4	cloves garlic, peeled and chopped	16
3	tablespoons minced parsley	6
1	teaspoon salt	–
⅛	teaspoon freshly ground pepper	–
½	teaspoon crushed red pepper or to taste	–
1	cup canned tomatoes, broken up	51
1	cup tomato puree	89
2	tablespoons tomato paste	70
2	large stalks celery, chopped	14
1	cup shredded carrot	46
	TOTAL	2,557

Sauté onion in olive oil until golden. Add hamburger and sausage, garlic, parsley, salt, pepper, and crushed red pepper. Cook uncovered 10 minutes, stirring frequently. Stir in tomatoes, puree, and paste. Heat to boiling. Add celery and carrot. Cover and cook 1 hour. *Four servings, 639 calories each.*

TO CUT CALORIES IN HALF:

1. Omit olive oil, save 477 calories.

2. For the hamburger, substitute lean beef round, trimmed of fat before grinding. Save 443 calories.

3. Render fat from the sausage as follows: Slice or dice thin. Spray a nonstick skillet with cooking spray for no-fat frying. Combine sausage and 2 tablespoons water over high heat. Cook until steam melts fat and evaporates. Cook until crisp. Drain. Blot sausage on paper towels.

4. Break up ground round in the same skillet. Add 2 tablespoons water. Cook and stir until chunks of meat are well browned. Drain off fat. Blot meat on paper towels. You can eliminate about 5 tablespoons fat from sausage and meat this way . . . save about 500 calories.

5. Put onion, garlic, and 2 tablespoons water into the skillet. Cook and stir over high heat until water evaporates and onion is golden. Stir to prevent sticking.

6. Now combine all ingredients in the skillet. You can add 2 tablespoons sliced black olives (20 calories) to add an olive-oil flavor without olive-oil calories. Simmer, covered, 1 hour or more.

7. One last fat-skimming effort: use a bulb-type baster to remove any globules of fat floating on the surface of the sauce (each tablespoon is worth 100 calories!).

Four servings, only 315 calories each.

Shake-up Baking Sauce for Low-Calorie Basting

Want to slim down? Shake it up!

That's not an exercise prescription. What I'm really talking about is some quick and easy "shake 'n' baste" sauces. They're ideal for low-calorie main courses like tender young chicken, lean beef, or luscious low-cal fish fillets. All three are nonfattening because of their low fat content, but simple baking or broiling tends to leave them dry. That's why these dishes are so often served fried or coated with butter or other fattening sauces. Commercial shake-and-baste baking sauces serve the same purpose, but they're often loaded with fattening ingredients: unnecessary oil, starchy thickeners, corn syrups, or other sugars. Our shake-up sauces are made with low-cal ingredients, mainly natural. And nothing could be easier!

Get yourself a good-size jar with a tight-fitting cover (or a cocktail shaker). Combine ingredients and screw on the lid. Then shake and shake until everything's mixed. Pour the ingredients over the chicken, beef, or seafood and bake uncovered until tender (beef takes longest, fish the least). Baste with the pan juices occasionally while baking. Much of the moisture will evaporate, and by serving time the basting concoction will have thickened itself into a savory sauce.

If the sauce threatens to dry out during the longer cooking time needed for beef or large pieces of chicken, add a little hot water.

Ingredients can also be mixed up quickly in a covered blender, or stirred well in a mixing bowl. The herbs, spices, and seasonings add virtually no calories, and wines added to basting sauces lose their alcohol calories in the cooking.

Here are some to try, then make up your own.

SHAKE 'N' BASTE JAPANESE-STYLE BAKING SAUCE

½ cup canned unsweetened crushed pineapple
¼ cup soy sauce
¼ cup dry sherry or water
2 tablespoons catsup
⅛ teaspoon instant garlic
1 tablespoon dried onion flakes
1 cut-up frying chicken or 1 pound top round steak or fish fillets

Shake up basting-sauce ingredients in a covered jar, then pour over pre-browned chicken, lean round steak, or fish fillets. Use to baste frequently. *Enough for four servings, 40 calories each.*

SHAKE 'N' BASTE BAKING SAUCE MEXICANA

6-ounce can tomato paste
1 cup fat-skimmed fresh or canned chicken or beef broth
1 tablespoon vinegar or lemon juice
1 teaspoon oregano
½ teaspoon cumin seeds
1 teaspoon (or more) chili powder
¼ cup minced fresh bell pepper or 2 tablespoons dried bell pepper flakes
3 pounds cut-up frying chicken or 1½ pounds chicken, round steak, or fish fillets

Stir or shake up basting ingredients. Follow directions in preceding recipe. *Enough for six servings, about 30 calories each.*

Savory Barbecue Sauce, No Oil or Sugar Added

But did you know that many barbecue sauces—homemade or bottled—can calorically sabotage even the slimmest steaks and leanest chickens? Most conventional mixtures are 400 calories a cupful or more, owing to unneeded fat and sugar.

Fat (oil) is the biggest offender at 125 calories a tablespoon (2,000 calories a cup!). Oil adds no flavor, no tenderness, just calories.

The tenderizing ingredients in marinades are the acid liquids: tomato or vinegar; fruit juices like lemon, pineapple, or orange; dry wine (the alcohol calories evaporate in the cooking). The natural fruit sugar found in juices and wines can add a touch of sweetness without refined sugar.

The spices and seasonings in barbecue bastes are the real flavor makers, and they add no calories to speak of. For the most flavorful results, meat, fish, or poultry should be marinated in barbecue sauce mixtures an hour or more beforehand, to soak up flavors and increase tenderness. The reserved marinade should be brushed on while the food cooks.

On rainy days, food can be baked in the oven in barbecue sauce . . . for cookout flavor whatever the weather.

Here are some flavorful combinations, without the usual huge amounts of oil or sugar. Add a generous dash of liquid smoke seasoning to any of these mixtures, if you like.

SUGARLESS BARBECUE BASTE

An unusual combination to try with chicken, steak, or lean pork chops.

    1 cup tomato puree
1½ cups orange juice
    1 tablespoon prepared mustard
    1 teaspoon celery salt

Simmer all ingredients uncovered 5 minutes. Spoon over meat while it broils or barbecues. *About 7 calories per tablespoon.*

NO-SUGAR-ADDED APPLESAUCE BASTE

½ cup soy sauce
½ cup white wine
¾ cup unsweetened applesauce
½ teaspoon garlic powder

Combine all ingredients and use as a marinade or barbecue baste. Particularly good with pork, lamb, or chicken. *About 6 calories per tablespoon.*

SUE'S CHICKEN BBQ BASTE

Here's a favorite developed by my daughter and her college apartment mates:

⅓ **cup vinegar**
2 **tablespoons lemon juice**
½ **cup catsup**
1 **teaspoon Worcestershire sauce**
¼ **teaspoon Tabasco**
½ **teaspoon dry mustard or 2 teaspoons prepared**
2 **tablespoons dried onion flakes**
⅛ **teaspoon instant garlic**
¾ **teaspoon salt**

Combine all ingredients and mix well. Use as a baste in broiling or barbecuing. Or pour over chicken and stir to coat well. Allow to marinate 1 hour at room temperature or several hours in the refrigerator before cooking chicken pieces. Baste chicken with reserved marinade while it cooks. *About 13 calories per tablespoon.*

17 FRUITS AND FRUIT SAUCES, FILLINGS, AND TOPPINGS

Mother Nature's fruits make the ideal dessert. If you could design it yourself, you'd probably make it sweet and delicious but quick and easy, a convenience food with little or no preparation needed. Inexpensive and eye appealing. In a variety of flavors. And, since we're dreaming, why not make it guilt free and nutritious? Something you can eat all you want of—without getting fat!

Good news. Mother Nature has already designed a whole line of luscious low-calorie sweets and treats. They're known as "fresh fruit." In all the most appealing flavors: peach, strawberry, blueberry, pineapple, apricot, melon, and more! Mother Nature sweetens her treats with natural fruit sugar that won't rot your teeth. She packs them with just the right balance of natural vitamins. Even includes moisture and bulking agents, like natural food fiber, to fill you up and prevent overeating.

Just a minute! Didn't I hear somewhere that fruit is fattening?

That idea stems from the now-debunked diet myth that carbohydrate calories make you fat while fat and protein somehow won't—the old carbohydrate-counting notion. Again!

Fresh fruit is always preferred over factory-made desserts. Only cooks, chemists, and canners clutter up fruit with unneeded calories.

Mother Nature's fresh peach is a good example: low in calories and high in vitamin A. But consider what happens when the food processors get hold of it:

Peaches	Calories	Vitamin A
One raw	38	1,330
Canned in juice	45	670
In heavy syrup	78	430
Frozen in sugar	83	650

As the calories go up, the nutrition goes down! For sweet lovers, here's a comparison chart for Mother Nature's seasonal best. The calories for canned fruit refer to those packed in heavy syrup. The counts marked with asterisks (*) refer to frozen fruits in sugar.

FRUIT LOVER'S CALORIE GUIDE

Fruit	Amount	Fresh	Canned
Apricot	1	20	56
Blackberry	1 cup	84	227
Blueberry	1 cup	87	242
Grapefruit	½	41	70
Grapes	1 cup	104	174
Peach	1	38	78
Pear	3 ½ oz.	61	76
Pineapple	1 slice	44	74
Plum	1 cup	120	216
Raspberries	1 cup	82	296*
Stawberries	1 cup	56	224*
Melon	1 cup	48	144*
Cherry	1 cup	108	244*

*Frozen, with sugar

QUICKIE APPLE-CHEESE CASSEROLE

On crisp fall days, one of the most potent perfumes around is Eau de Apple Pie. Never mind all those lemon-scented sprays, the cinnamon-and-spice fragrance of a fresh-baked apple dessert is one of the most effective manbaits around!

Unfortunately, the calories of most apple desserts have just the opposite effect. At 400 or 500 calories a slice—not even including the calories contained in that tempting wedge of sharp Cheddar that makes such a perfect companion —apple pie tends to bury girlish waistlines and manly midriffs in waddles of pot-bellied flab.

To keep both your figures in apple-pie order, tempt your man with this low-calorie dessert. You'll get every bit of the flavor and fragrance—including the cheddar cheese—without all those burdensome calories.

    20-ounce can pie-sliced apples (*not* pie filling)
 3 tablespoons sugar
 1 tablespoon arrowroot or cornstarch
 ½ teaspoon apple-pie spice
    Sprinkling of salt or butter-flavored salt
 ½ cup shredded extra-sharp Cheddar cheese

Stir all ingredients except cheese together in a baking dish. Bake 25 minutes at 350 degrees, uncovered. Sprinkle on cheese and return to oven, just until cheese melts. Serve immediately. *Eight servings, 75 calories each.*

JAMAICAN BAKED BANANAS

Fruits come and go, but bananas—happily—have no season. This hearty appetite-satisfying sweet is with us any time of year.

Somewhere along the line, bananas have gotten the unearned reputation of being fattening. Probably because they taste so rich and sweet, it's hard to believe they're not. But an average banana totals only 100 calories, the same as a fresh pear, canned fruit cup, or 6 tablespoons fruit-flavored sweetened yogurt. And never is a banana so slimming as when you reach for one instead of a chocolate doughnut.

Reach for bananas in your Slim Gourmet kitchen, too. They make a dandy low-calorie ingredient, not only in desserts but in sidedishes to serve with dinner.

 3 large bananas, peeled
 2 tablespoons diet margarine
 1 tablespoon lemon juice
 ¼ cup shredded coconut

Cut peeled bananas in half, then split lengthwise. Place split side down in a shallow baking dish. Spread the surface of each banana lightly with diet margarine. Sprinkle with lemon juice and coconut. Bake in a preheated 375-degree oven for 15 minutes. Serve warm. *Six servings, 95 calories each.*

NECTARINES À LA RUSSE

3 cups sliced fresh nectarines
1 cup low-fat vanilla yogurt
¼ teaspoon grated lemon rind

Place sliced nectarines in 6 sherbet glasses. Combine yogurt and lemon rind and spoon over nectarines. *Six servings, 40 calories each.*

ORANGES GALLIANO

4 sweet eating oranges, peeled, pitted, and cut up
4 teaspoons grated orange peel
¼ cup Galliano liqueur

Combine and chill until serving time. *Four servings, about 70 calories each.*

Peachy Low-Cal Treats with Juice-Packed fruit

Peaches are plainly a nonfattening fruit, only about 38 calories or so, or 32 in a ½-cup serving of slices. Until somebody puts them in a can! Then the calories nearly triple, to about 100 per ½-cup serving.

The calorie culprit, of course, is sugar. Not only in the syrup, but in the slices as well. Calories that simply refuse to be drained or rinsed off.

Luckily for us calorie-cautious types, it's now possible to find peaches canned in fruit juice instead of sugar-laden syrup. By comparison, juice-packed peaches are only about 50 calories a ½-cup serving—more calories than fresh peaches but a lot less fattening than the syrup-packed varieties.

Drained juice-packed peaches make a quick dessert, with a tangy topping of low-fat yogurt. Combined with pineapple or other fruit, peaches make a great garnish for a cottage-cheese lunch. Pureed in the blender with some vinegar and soy sauce, they make a peachy baste for low-cal barbecued chicken. And when you simply must bake a dessert that's fancy but not too fattening, juice-packed peaches can come to the rescue. Here are some ideas to try.

PEACH HALVES MELBA

4 large ripe sweet peaches, chilled
   10-ounce package frozen raspberries, partly thawed
4 teaspoons slivered toasted almonds

Fill a saucepan with water and heat to boiling. Impale each peach in turn on a fork and rotate briefly in water, until skin slips off easily. Remove skin and slice peach in half. Remove pit. Arrange each peach cut side up in a champagne glass.

Puree raspberries in a covered blender until coarsely chopped. Spoon over peach halves. Sprinkle with almonds and serve immediately. *Eight servings, 65 calories each.*

PEACHES CHANTILLY

2 **tablespoons brandy or kirsch**
  16-ounce can juice-packed sliced peaches, drained
2 **eight-ounce containers peach or vanilla yogurt**
1 **cup defrosted whipped topping**
  Grated nutmeg or ground cinnamon

Pour brandy over peach slices; cover and refrigerate several hours or overnight. Fold yogurt and topping together. Spoon into dessert glasses alternately with peach slices; chill thoroughly. To serve, top with nutmeg or cinnamon. *Eight servings, about 125 calories each with peach yogurt, about 90 with vanilla.*

Low-Cal Treats to Make with Fresh Pears

Too many of Mother Nature's sweets are fair-weather friends, abandoning the marketplace when we need winter solace most. Ah, blueberries, peaches, juicy nectarines . . . where are you now?

But not the reliable pear. Midwinter is the best time to enjoy this succulent sweet, a bargain at only 100 calories! There's nothing more delightful than a pear at its moment of perfection.

Trouble is, a pear's "moment of perfection" is just that—a day or so, no more. Pears are often rock hard and unsweet when purchased. They must wait a while, a few days perhaps, before reaching that gently resistant state that signals perfect ripeness. Eat at once, or pears quickly turn mealy-textured.

To use pears imaginatively, consider them as a replacement for apples in any favorite fruit combination. How about a Pear Waldorf Salad with low-cal mayonnaise? Or make homemade chunky "pearsauce," no sugar needed. Or try these:

EASY WINE-POACHED PEARS

  16-ounce can juice-packed pear halves
½ **cup dry white wine**
½ **teaspoon vanilla**
¼ **teaspoon pumpkin-pie spice**

Drain pears. Combine pear juice, wine, vanilla, and spice. Bring to a boil. Simmer 5 minutes. Add pears and let cool in sauce. Chill until ready to serve. *Three servings, 60 calories per serving.*

STOOFPEREN

Dutch Spiced Pears

8 fresh pears
6 tablespoons sugar
⅓ cup water
  3-inch stick cinnamon, halved
½ cup red wine
1 teaspoon coarsely grated orange rind

Pare, halve, and core pears. Combine all ingredients in a deep saucepan; bring to a boil. Cook at a gentle simmer, covered, for 15 minutes, spooning liquid over fruit often. Chill pears in syrup. *Eight servings, 140 calories each.*

PERE RIPIENE

Stuffed Baked Pear Halves

1 cup raisins
1 cup dry white wine
6 large pears
1 cup chopped walnuts
2 tablespoons sugar
1 cup Marsala

Soak raisins in white wine for 30 minutes. Wash and drain pears. Cut in half lengthwise. Core but do not peel. Arrange in a baking dish. Combine raisins and white wine with the walnuts, sugar, and Marsala, and stuff mixture into the centers of the pears. Bake in a preheated 350-degree oven for 30 minutes. Serve warm or chilled. *Twelve servings, 120 calories each.*

PLUMS IN WINE SAUCE

½ orange peel, grated
6 whole cloves
2 pounds fresh plums, each slashed on one side to the pit
2 cups port wine
1 whole cinnamon stick (3 or 4 inches long)

Combine all ingredients in a large heavy saucepan. Simmer, uncovered, until the plums soften (about 10 minutes). Cool.

Transfer plums from saucepan to a storage container and pour port sauce over the fruit. Cover and chill. *Six servings, about 100 calories each.*

BERRY FONDUE

Shake a pint of hulled fresh strawberries in 4 tablespoons brown sugar. Impale each berry on a party toothpick. Fill a small bowl with vanilla yogurt and surround it with berries on picks. *Four servings, 125 calories each.*

POLYNESIAN CROCKED FRUIT

Here's an idea that's as colorful as a summer sunset and just as appealing: a crockful of chilled fresh fruit, marinated in pineapple and their own juices . . . spiked with rum, if you like! You can keep it in the refrigerator and use it as appetizer or dessert, on salads, cottage cheese, yogurt, ice milk, or spongecake. Calorie-wise and convenient!

We like to use a 2-quart clear glass apothecary jar because the mélange is so pretty to see, but a crock or covered cookie jar—or a big glass pickle bottle —will do as well. Simply fill it with bite-size chunks of ripe raw fruit, then pour on undiluted pineapple-juice concentrate. The juices blend deliciously. Rum or rum flavoring is a spirited addition for adult audiences.

You can vary the fruits to suit your whim and what's available. (Bananas, if used, should be added at serving time, not to the refrigerator jar.)

2 eating oranges
5 cups mixed fresh fruit, for example:
1 cup fresh or canned unsweetened pineapple chunks
1 medium mango, peeled and diced, or 2 fresh peaches, or 3 nectarines
1 papaya or small cantaloupe, diced
½ cup pitted dark sweet cherries
½ cup green seedless grapes or diced unpeeled apple or pear
1 cup blueberries
   6-ounce can undiluted unsweetened pineapple or pineapple-orange juice
      concentrate, defrosted
⅔ cup white rum or 1 tablespoon rum flavoring (optional)

Peel the rind from oranges. On a plate (to catch the juice) cut the oranges into slices, then into bite-size chunks. Remove any seeds with a sharp knife. Put the orange chunks and any reserved juice into a crock or large glass jar.

Next, prepare any fruit that tends to darken or turn brown (peaches, nectarines, apples, pears, for example). Add this to the jar and stir well with the orange chunks. (The ascorbic acid in the orange juice will penetrate the fruit and keep it fresh looking.) Prepare and add remaining fruit. Combine defrosted pineapple juice with rum or rum flavoring and pour into the jar.

Cover and chill in refrigerator. Stir before serving. Use as desired; will keep several days refrigerated. *About eighteen half-cup servings, approximately 60 calories each with fruit only or with rum flavoring; 80 calories each with rum.*

SUGGESTIONS FOR USE

South Seas Sundae: Top a scoop of 99 percent fat-free vanilla ice milk with ½ cup Polynesian Crocked Fruit, including juice. Sprinkle with 1 teaspoon toasted coconut flakes, if desired. *About 135 calories with coconut, 130 without.*

Hawaiian Yogurt Sundae: Substitute a scoop of low-fat vanilla or fruit-flavored yogurt, frozen. *Under 140 calories.*

Polynesian Sangría: Combine ¼ cup ice-cold dry red wine with ¼ cup Polynesian Crocked Fruit (including juice) in a tall glass. Fill with chilled club soda. *110 calories.*

Surfside Salad Lunch: Put 2 scoops chilled low-fat cottage cheese into a bowl. Top with ½ cup Polynesian Crocked Fruit. *165 calories.*

Yogurt Shake: In a blender combine ¾ cup Polynesian Crocked Fruit (including juice) with ½ cup plain low-fat yogurt and 5 or 6 ice cubes. Cover and blend on high speed until ice is melted. Serve immediately. *150 calories.*

Banana Compote: Slice a ripe banana into 2 dessert dishes. Top each with ½ cup Polynesian Crocked Fruit, including juice. Sprinkle with cinnamon or apple-pie spice and serve immediately. *Two servings, 100 calories each.*

Yogurt Strata Parfait: In each tall parfait glass, layer ½ cup plain, or fruit-flavored low-fat yogurt, with ½ cup Polynesian Crocked Fruit. *120 calories with plain yogurt, about 180 calories with fruit-flavored yogurt.*

Trader's Shortcake: Top small single-serving spongecake dessert shells (or thin slices of spongecake) with ½ cup Polynesian Crocked Fruit, including juice. *180 calories per serving.* (For an interesting topping, fold plain yogurt into equal parts prepared whipped topping. *About 15 calories per tablespoon.*)

SANGRÍA FRUIT CUPS

Until only a decade ago, Sangría was a cooling summer quencher known only to a limited handful of aficionados. Then the Spanish red-wine-and-fruit-juice combo became a national rage, especially among the post-Pepsi generation. Now sangría has settled into a comfortable niche of year-round popularity, fueled by one of the newer introductions, white sangría. Like the original, white sangría is wine and citrus juice, but with white wine instead of red. A natural innovation, considering the greater popularity of white wine.

Unpeeled red apples, diced
Unpeeled pears, diced
3 tablespoons golden raisins
Fresh tangerines, peeled and sectioned
White sangría

Combine the fruit in a bowl and cover with wine. Chill all day or overnight in the refrigerator. At dessert time use a slotted spoon to apportion the fruit into wine glasses. The wine adds flavor but very few calories to the fruit. *Less than 100 calories per serving.*

BANAMBROSIA

1 banana, peeled and sliced
1 unpeeled red apple, cored and diced
1 eating orange, peeled, seeded, and cut up
1 cup canned unsweetened crushed pineapple, well drained
1 cup green seedless grapes, sliced in half
1 cup vanilla low-fat yogurt or plain low-fat yogurt

Combine banana and apple in a bowl. Cut the orange over the bowl to catch any juice. Add orange chunks and stir well (the juice will delay browning of the apple and banana). Stir in pineapple, grapes, and low-fat yogurt. Chill at least 1 hour before serving. *Six servings, 115 calories each; 105 with unsweetened yogurt.*

CRANBERRY-SAUCED COMPOTE

1 cup whole cranberry sauce
1 tablespoon honey (optional)
Pinch each of ground cinnamon, ginger, allspice
3 pears, peeled, cored, and quartered
3 sweet eating oranges, peeled, seeded, and cut in large chunks

Combine all ingredients in a baking dish. Cover and bake at 350 degrees for 35 to 40 minutes. Serve warm or cold. *Eight servings, 120 calories each.*

BLUSHING POACHED PEARS

8 fresh pears
1 cup port, red sangría, or Concord-grape wine
1 cup water
5 whole cloves
1 teaspoon ground cinnamon
1 tablespoon arrowroot

Cut pears in half lengthwise but don't peel. Remove cores. Put cut side up in a shallow frying pan and pour on the wine and ½ cup water. Add cloves and cinnamon. Cover and simmer gently until just tender, about 8 to 10 minutes. Remove pears with a slotted spoon. Stir arrowroot and ½ cup cold water together and stir into liquid in the skillet; cook and stir until thick. Remove from heat and pour over pears; serve warm or chilled. *Each half with syrup about 60 calories.*

VARIATIONS

Fruited Poached Pears: Substitute unsweetened fruit juice (orange, pineapple, apple, apricot, or grape) for the wine. For extra natural sweetness, add a small box of golden raisins (1½ ounces) to the poaching liquid.

Minted Poached Pears: Substitute ¼ cup green crème de menthe and ¾ cup water for the wine. Garnish with sprigs of fresh mint, if you wish.

CARRIBBEAN FRUIT COMPOTES

1 cup diced fresh or canned (juice-packed) pineapple chunks, undrained
4 fresh sweet peaches or nectarines, peeled (peaches only), pitted, and sliced
1 eating orange, peeled, seeded, and cut up
2 tablespoons Curaçao, or other orange liqueur
1 ripe banana, peeled and sliced

Combine ingredients except banana; cover and chill until serving time. Add sliced banana and spoon into wine glasses. *Six servings, about 95 calories each.*

SPANISH FRUIT

3 eating oranges, peeled, seeded, and cut up
1 pint strawberries, hulled and halved
3 peaches or nectarines, peeled (peaches only), pitted, and sliced
½ cup port wine or unsweetened red grape juice
1 banana, peeled and sliced

Combine prepared fruit, except bananas, with wine or fruit juice. Cover and chill several hours to blend flavors. At serving time add sliced banana and spoon into champagne glasses. *Eight servings, about 95 calories each.*

VARIATION

Try this with any combination of fresh fruits. Diced unpeeled apples would be a nice addition; and the juice from the oranges helps retard browning. Substitute fruit juice for wine if serving children.

MOCK MANGO MACEDOINE

1 cup crushed juice-packed canned pineapple, juice included
4 fresh ripe peaches, peeled, pitted, and finely chopped
1 ripe cantaloupe, halved, seeded, and scooped out with melon baller

Combine ingredients and chill. Serve in stemmed glasses. *Eight servings, 55 calories each.*

Fruit Sauces, Fillings, and Toppings

BEST EVER STRAWBERRY SAUCE

"That is the *best ever* strawberry sauce," exclaimed a friend, finishing her parfait. "What's in it?"
"Strawberries."
"What else?"
"Nothing else."
Proving again that often the simplest things are the best. My strawberriest of strawberry sauces was simply strawberries, whirred until chunky in the blender, then spooned over vanilla ice cream (or, in this case, low-fat ice milk). The sauce was thickened only by berry pulp—no flour, cornstarch, or boiled sugar syrup. The ripeness of the berries provided the bright red hue. The tangy tart sweetness and fresh flavor came from the berries themselves—and the fact

that nothing else had been added to dilute the taste. Nor had anything been taken away by cooking. Not only delicious, but nutritious. Raw fruit sauces keep all their natural vitamin C otherwise lost through cooking.

Wash and hull 1 pint ripe, sweet strawberries. Put them in a blender and cover. Turn blender on and off repeatedly until berries are crushed but chunky. (Don't overblend or you'll have a smooth puree.) Use as a topping for low-fat ice milk, cottage cheese, unsweetened yogurt, spongecake, sugar-free puddings, homemade low-calorie cheesecake, pancakes or French toast, orange ice, crêpes stuffed with cottage cheese, dessert omelets, or other fresh fruit. *Four servings, 25 calories each.*

VARIATIONS

Other "Best Ever" Fruit Sauces: Use 2 cups pitted Bing cherries, sliced ripe peaches or apricots, fresh blueberries, blackberries or raspberries when available. Check your calorie counter. Divide totals by 4 for the single-serving calorie count. *Bing cherries, the most calorific, less than 30 calories per serving.*

For Sweeter Fruit Sauce: Sweeten to taste with sugar, or add one teaspoon honey. *Honey has about 20 calories per level teaspoon, sugar about 18.*

Frozen "Best Ever" Fruit Sauce: Use frozen whole berries (or other loose-packed fruits without sugar may be substituted). Defrost first (retaining juice) a 10-ounce package frozen strawberries (310 calories). *Serves four, 78 calories per single serving.*

"Best Ever" Strawberry Romanoff Sauce: 1 pint fresh ripe strawberries, ¼ cup orange liqueur. *54 calories.*

Wash and hull berries; combine with liqueur in a blender. Cover and blend only till chunky. Use over ice milk or frozen yogurt.

CURRIED FRUIT

Great for "saucing" broiled chicken.

    2 tablespoons chopped onion
    ½ teaspoon garlic salt
    1 teaspoon curry powder
    1 teaspoon ground ginger
      Dash of freshly ground pepper
  1½ tablespoons lemon juice
    2 tablespoons tomato juice
    2 teaspoons sugar
    1 unpeeled red apple
    1 unpeeled ripe pear
    ½ cup green seedless grapes
    3 bananas

Combine first 8 ingredients in a small saucepan, cover, and simmer over very low heat 10 minutes.

Allow to cool while you core and cube the apple and pear, cut the grapes in half, and peel and slice the bananas. Combine fruit, pour cooled mixture over, and serve immediately as a side dish for broiled poultry. *Six servings, 100 calories each.*

ORANGE-PINEAPPLE SAUCE

1 sweet eating orange
16-ounce can unsweetened crushed pineapple, drained
Few drops honey or sugar to taste

Peel and dice the orange; pick out the seeds. Retain about one-quarter of the peel and slice it. Combine in blender with pineapple; cover and blend until chunky. *Six servings, about 65 calories each.*

BRANDIED PEACH SAUCE

Great over low-fat vanilla frozen yogurt or ice milk.

½ cup dried peaches
1 cup water
¼ cup brandy
1 tablespoon raisins (optional)
Ground cinnamon or pumpkin-pie spice to taste (optional)

Combine all the ingredients in a saucepan and simmer until thick and soft. The optional raisins or spice will add a little extra zing. *Six servings, about 40 calories each.*

PLUM WINE SAUCE

6 ripe fresh plums, pitted and diced
1 cup port wine
2 tablespoons cornstarch mixed with ¼ cup water

Combine plums and wine. Simmer until plums are soft. Stir in cornstarch and water. Cook while stirring until mixture bubbles and thickens.

Use hot or cold, over crêpes or other desserts. *Makes about two cups, 10 calories per tablespoon.*

BERRY-ORANGE SAUCE

3 ounces (½ can) undiluted orange-juice concentrate, defrosted
10-ounce package frozen raspberries or strawberries, partly thawed

Combine ingredients in covered blender and puree smooth. *Eight servings, under 60 calories each.*

CHUNKY APPLE 'N' APRICOT SAUCE

8 ounces dried apricots
1 quart water
10 cooking apples

Put apricots and water into a large pot, cover, and let stand 3 hours or more, then simmer 10 to 15 minutes. Meanwhile, peel and slice apples. Add to apricots and cook uncovered another 10 minutes or more, until fruit is tender and thick.

Serve warm or chilled. Store in refrigerator. *Twenty servings, 70 calories each.*

PINEAPPLE FILLING OR TOPPING

20-ounce can unsweetened crushed pineapple, undrained
2 teaspoons arrowroot
Honey to taste (optional)

Cook and stir pineapple and arrowroot until bubbling. Add honey if desired. *Six servings, about 60 calories each without honey; 80 calories with honey.*

PEACH NECTAR FILLING OR TOPPING

1 eating orange, peeled and chopped in chunks
2 large ripe peaches, peeled and thinly sliced
½ cup hulled sliced fresh strawberries
Honey to taste (optional)

Peel orange and dice coarse, retaining juice. Pick out and discard seeds, if any. Stir in remaining ingredients. Cover and store in refrigerator. (Orange juice will keep peaches from browning.) Use as a filling for Oven-Baked

Fat-Free German Pancake (page 341), or as topping on low-cal ice milk or frozen yogurt, or on top of cottage cheese. *Six servings, under 35 calories each without honey; 55 calories with honey.*

HOT RUM-APPLE-RAISIN FILLING OR TOPPINg

3 **large unpeeled apples, cored and diced**
2 **tablespoons raisins**
1 **tablespoon arrowroot or cornstarch**
3 **tablespoons rum or brandy**
¼ **teaspoon salt or butter-flavored salt**
1 **teaspoon apple-pie or pumpkin-pie spice**
2 **tablespoons honey (optional)**

Combine all ingredients and simmer in a saucepan just until sauce is thickened and apples are tender but not mushy. (Or combine ingredients in a baking dish, cover, and bake in oven, separately, while pancake is baking.) Filling may be spooned into pancake, over low-calorie French toast, or on top of vanilla ice milk or frozen yogurt. *Six servings, 60 calories each without honey; 80 calories with honey.*

APPLE-CINNAMON "WHIPPED CREAM"

Whip 1 envelope topping mix in a deep bowl according to package directions, substituting cold apple juice for the water called for. Chill. Spoon over low-calorie dessert and sprinkle with cinnamon or apple-pie spice. *Makes two cups, 9 calories per tablespoon.*

SPICED "WHIPPED CREAM"

Last but not least, a topping that's not made with fruit, but is it ever good with fruit shortcakes or as a topping for plain fresh fruit desserts!

1 **envelope (½ box) regular or low-calorie whipped topping mix**
½ **cup cold skim milk**
⅛ **teaspoon pumpkin-pie spice**
½ **teaspoon freshly grated orange or lemon rind**

In a mixing bowl with an electric mixer, whip topping mix, milk, and spice together until the consistency of whipped cream. Store in refrigerator. *Eight calories per tablespoon (low calorie), 16 with regular.*

18
CAKE
AND
PANCAKE
DESSERTS

CHOCOLATE CAKE WITH CHOCOLATE NEUFCHÂTEL FROSTING

CAKE:
- 4 tablespoons butter or margarine
- 6 tablespoons brown sugar
- 1 egg
- 1⅓ cups all-purpose flour
- 3 tablespoons unsweetened cocoa
- 2 teaspoons baking powder
- ½ teaspoon baking soda
- 1½ teaspoons vanilla
- ½ cup skim milk

CHOCOLATE NEUFCHÂTEL FROSTING:
- 3-ounce package Neufchâtel cheese
- 1 teaspoon vanilla
- Pinch of salt
- 1½ cups confectioner's sugar
- 3 tablespoons unsweetened cocoa
- 1 or 2 teaspoons water

Make the cake batter by combining butter, brown sugar, and egg. Beat 2 minutes at high speed. Add remaining ingredients and beat 2 minutes at low speed. Spread batter in a nonstick 8-inch square or round cake pan. Bake in a preheated 350-degree oven 30 minutes, or until a toothpick inserted in the center comes out clean. Let cool while you prepare the frosting.

Whip all frosting ingredients together until they are of spreading consistency, then spread on the cooled cake. *Nine servings, 210 calories per serving.*

SULTANA CHRISTMAS CAKE

 1 cup graham-cracker crumbs
⅔ cup brown sugar
 1 teaspoon baking powder
¼ teaspoon pumpkin-pie spice
¼ teaspoon ground cinnamon
 2 eggs
¼ cup skim milk
 1 teaspoon brandy or rum flavoring
 7 tablespoons golden raisins

Combine all ingredients, except raisins, in a mixing bowl. Beat smooth with an electric mixer. Stir in raisins. Spoon batter into a nonstick 8- or 9-inch square cake pan. Bake in a preheated 350-degree oven for 30 minutes. Serve warm. *Nine 3-inch square servings, 140 calories each.*

HONEY-APPLESAUCE CAKE

No eggs!

 2 cups sifted cake flour
 1 teaspoon baking soda
½ teaspoon ground cinnamon, ¼ teaspoon grated nutmeg, ¼ teaspoon ground allspice.
½ cup sugar
¼ teaspoon salt or butter-flavored salt
 4 tablespoons polyunsaturated margarine
⅓ cup honey
1¼ cups unsweetened applesauce
 7 tablespoons raisins

Sift flour, soda, pie spice, sugar, and salt together.

Beat margarine and honey until fluffy. Add applesauce and beat well. Beat in sifted ingredients until well blended. Stir in raisins. Pour into an 8- or 9-inch nonstick square cake pan which has been sprayed with vegetable coating for no-fat frying. Bake in a preheated 350-degree oven about 50 minutes. *Twelve servings, about 180 calories each.*

ORANGE PRUNE LOAF

 3/4 cup freshly squeezed orange juice
 1/4 cup water
 1/2 cup chopped pitted uncooked prunes
 1/2 cup sugar
  1 medium egg
  1 tablespoon salad oil
  1 teaspoon vanilla
  2 cups sifted all-purpose flour
2 1/2 teaspoons baking powder
  1 teaspoon soda
 1/2 teaspoon salt

In a saucepan, combine orange juice, water, and prunes; cover and heat just until boiling. Let prunes soften in the covered pan for 5 minutes; drain, reserving juice.

In a large mixing bowl, combine sugar, egg, oil, and vanilla. Blend until smooth.

Sift together flour, baking powder, baking soda, and salt; add to creamed mixture all at once along with orange juice. Stir well until thoroughly blended; add prunes. Batter will be very thick. Spoon into nonstick 9-by-5-by-3-inch loaf pan; bake at 300 degrees for 1 hour, or until loaf tests done. *Twenty 3/8 -inch-thick slices, 85 calories each.*

NOTE: Store in refrigerator, wrapped tightly in aluminum foil.

SPICED APRICOT MUFFINS

Nice for a light dessert or breakfast treat.

  2 cups sifted all-purpose flour
  3 teaspoons baking powder
  1 teaspoon salt
 3/4 teaspoon apple-pie spice
  5 tablespoons sugar
  2 eggs
 2/3 cup skim milk
  2 tablespoons salad oil
  1 cup crushed cornflakes or high-protein cereal flakes
 1/2 cup finely chopped dried apricots

Stir dry ingredients together. Beat eggs, milk, and oil together, then stir into dry ingredients. Mix in cereal flakes and chopped apricots. Spray nonstick muffin tins with cooking spray for grease-free baking. Fill two-thirds full.

Bake in a preheated 400-degree oven for 12 to 15 minutes, until golden. Serve warm (may be lightly "buttered" with diet margarine). *Makes one dozen muffins, 155 calories each.*

APPLE-CHEDDAR CHEESECAKE

Nothing goes with apple pie like Cheddar cheese. Unfortunately, a 1-by-2-inch chunk of cheese is 275 calories, almost as fattening as the pie itself.

If you have to avoid excessive fat calories, you can still enjoy the luscious pairing of tart apples and sharp Cheddar—if you're a Slim Gourmet cook.

The main cheese in this cheesecake is low-fat high-protein diet cream cheese or Neufchâtel cheese; blend in some grated Cheddar for zest. Since namby-pamby mild Cheddar, sharp Cheddar, and super-zippy extra-sharp Cheddar all have the same high calorie count, it makes sense to choose only the sharpest, meanest, nastiest Cheddar you can find! That way you get more cheese flavor for fewer fat calories.

  8 **thin lemon or vanilla wafers**
  3 **apples, peeled and thinly sliced**
  ¼ **teaspoon apple-pie spice**
  ½ **cup low-fat vanilla yogurt**
  2 **eight-ounce packages low-calorie cream cheese or Neufchâtel cheese**
  3 **eggs**
  6 **tablespoons shredded extra-sharp Cheddar cheese**
  ½ **cup sugar**

Arrange the wafers in the bottom of a nonstick 9-inch cake pan in a single layer, edges touching. Arrange the apples on top, and sprinkle with pie spice.

Combine remaining ingredients in a blender, cover, and blend smooth. Spoon over apples.

Bake in a 350-degree oven for 45 minutes, or until set. Serve warm or chilled, straight from the pan. *Ten servings, 205 calories each.*

GERMAN PEACH-FILLED CHEESECAKE

Picture, if you will, a luscious dairy-rich cheesecake filled with fresh, ripe, sweet peach slices, drizzled with glistening fruit glaze.

"Please," you say, "don't tempt me with such thoughts! I'm on a diet."

Well, the delight I've just described is off the forbidden list—thanks to the

Slim Gourmet way of cooking. This German treasure has been translated into a dessert even dieters can enjoy with very little fat or sugar, but rich in dairy protein. A grand finale dessert!

CHEESECAKE:
4 egg whites
Pinch of cream of tartar
1½ cups low-fat cottage cheese
¼ cup vanilla yogurt
3 egg yolks
¼ teaspoon salt or butter-flavored salt
7 tablespoons sugar

PEACH FILLING:
1 cup unsweetened apple juice or white grape juice
½ envelope plain gelatin
2 tablespoons sugar
4 very ripe peaches, peeled and sliced

Put the egg whites and cream of tartar in a nonplastic bowl and set aside. Combine all remaining cheesecake ingredients in a blender. Cover and blend smooth.

Beat the egg whites until stiff peaks form. Pour the cheesecake mixture into the egg whites. Gently but thoroughly fold together—don't overmix. Spoon the mixture into a nonstick 9-inch cake pan.

Bake in a preheated 350-degree oven about 45 minutes, or until thoroughly set. Remove from oven. Cool. Chill in the refrigerator. As the cake cools it will sink down in the middle and form a depression for the filling.

While the cheesecake bakes, put ½ cup (half the amount) unsweetened fruit juice into a small saucepan and sprinkle the gelatin onto it. Add sugar. Wait 1 minute then heat gently over low heat until sugar and gelatin melt. Remove from heat and stir in remaining fruit juice. Chill in the refrigerator until syrupy.

Meanwhile, peel and slice the peaches very thin. When the cake is cold and the gelatin mixture is syrupy but not set, assemble the cake this way: Layer the sliced peaches in the depression of the cake. Then spoon on the glaze, until peaches are covered. Chill in the refrigerator until serving time. *Eight servings, about 165 calories each.*

MOCHA CRÈME CHARLOTTE

Ladyfingers are definitely ladylike when it comes to calories. Of all the snacks and sweets on supermarket shelves, ladyfingers are among the least fattening. They're really a sort of spongecake, with lots of low-calorie air!

Of course, ladyfingers need companionship. Crushed fresh fruit is the quickest topper, and the most figure-wise.

Ladyfingers are also very versatile, the perfect base for all sorts of chill-and serve desserts. Unfortunately, most recipes are fattening . . . but not this one! This mocha dessert is made with skim milk and chocolate drink mix, the kind that comes in single-serving packets. For this recipe you can use either the milkshake type that's meant to be drunk cold, or low-calorie hot cocoa mix. Both work equally well.

This dessert looks and tastes like a fancy torte, the kind you might find in a fancy bakery or elegant restaurant. But the calorie count is 100 or less!

    1   envelope plain gelatin
    2   tablespoons cold water
    1   cup boiling water
        Heaping teaspoon instant coffee
    3   single-serving envelopes low-calorie chocolate-drink mix
    1   tablespoon vanilla
    2   tablespoons sugar
        Pinch of salt
    2   egg whites, stiffly beaten
    1   cup aerosol whipped cream
9½   ladyfingers
    2   chocolate cookies, crushed to crumbs (optional)

Combine gelatin and cold water in a blender; wait 1 minute. Add boiling water and instant coffee (or 1 cup very strong coffee). Cover and blend on high speed until gelatin is dissolved.

Add chocolate-drink mix, vanilla, and sugar. Blend smooth. Put blender container in refrigerator until mixture is chilled and syrupy.

Combine salt and egg whites and beat stiff. Spray aerosol whipped cream into a 1-cup measuring cup. Combine whipped cream and chilled chocolate mixture with beaten egg whites. Fold in gently but thoroughly until mixture is completely blended but light and fluffy. Don't overmix.

Split 7 ladyfingers and stand them up inside a small loaf pan. lining the 2 long sides. Cover the bottom with remaining split ladyfingers. Carefully spoon the chocolate filling into the middle. Sprinkle the top with chocolate crumbs. Refrigerate all day or overnight, until set. Slice to serve. *Eight servings, 100 calories each.*

ENGLISH APPLE-GINGER "COBBLER"

4 apples, peeled and sliced
⅛ teaspoon ground cinnamon
½ package (1¾ cups) dry gingerbread cake mix
½ cup water

Arrange apple slices in a 9-inch nonstick cake pan. Sprinkle with cinnamon. Beat gingerbread mix and water together according to package directions and pour over apples. Bake in a preheated 350-degree oven for 30 to 35 minutes. Cool slightly. Serve warm, from the pan, or chilled. *Nine servings, 120 calories each.*

CHOCOLATE GINGER SPICE SQUARES

1 package dry gingerbread mix
 8-serving package (or two 4-serving packages) regular or low-calorie chocolate pudding mix
¼ teaspoon ground cinnamon
1 cup water

Combine all ingredients in a mixing bowl. Beat with electric mixer 1 minute on medium speed, scraping sides often. Pour into a rectangular 13x9x2-inch nonstick cake pan and bake in a preheated 350-degree oven for 25 to 35 minutes. Allow to cool slightly or chill. Cut into squares. *Sixteen servings, 110 calories each with low-calorie pudding mix; 145 calories with regular.*

These Decalorized Desserts Start with a Mix

You say you like the convenience of cake mixes, but not the calories? Here are two easy desserts you can whip up with packaged gingerbread. By adding low-calorie ingredients, you help str-r-retch the serving to nearly double!

The first is a fresh fruit "cobbler" that makes use of the season's harvest of sweet and juicy apples. However, you could adapt the ideas to any season or time of year. Peeled peaches, nectarines, or apricots could form a friendly alliance with the spicy flavor of the gingerbread cobbler. Canned fruit could also be used (but be sure to choose the unsweetened variety . . . less than half the calories of the syrup-packed kind).

The second treat is a spicy chocolate dessert that makes imaginative use of packaged sugar-free pudding mix, the kind sold on supermarket diet shelves.

Homemade Spongecake for Low-Cal Desserts

If spongecake doesn't turn you on, you're probably thinking of those sticky, soggy packaged powderpuffs they sell at the bread counter. Homemade spongecake is something else—deliciously flavored, light and airy in the middle, and golden on the outside. Spongecake and fruit are a natural, because, as the name implies, spongecake is thirsty for the tangy juices of whatever fruit you choose to use.

A slice of spongecake piled high with strawberries and crowned with just the scantiest squiggle of whipped topping looks and tastes like a million calories. But my Powdered Sugar Spongecake is a skimpy 65 calories a slice, barely a fraction of what you'd "pay" for layer cake or apple pie. Spongecake is one of the lowest-caloried cakes there is—no fat, a minimum of sugar and flour, and lots of protein-rich egg yolks and egg whites to give texture and height.

And, best of all, my spongecake is easy . . . simpler still if you have both a blender and a mixer.

Here are a few tips: The eggs should be at room temperature. Separate the egg yolks into the blender and the whites into your mixing bowl. (For an even higher cake at very few calories more, add 1 or 2 additional egg whites, a maximum of 5.) You may bake this cake in two 8-inch layer-cake pans. Spread the baked layers with crushed sliced strawberries for a 2-layer company shortcake. Or put a layer in your cakebox and the other in your freezer. For a dieter's portion slice 1 layer into 8 wedges. Top with lots of fruit, unsugared or sweetened with sugar substitute. If you're fresh out of fresh fruit, try it with canned peaches packed in juice.

Try these suggestions with the Special Dieter's Sugar-Free Spongecake that follows right after the powdered-sugar version. And do try the Italian Apple Cassata and Zuppa Inglese on pages 337–38.

POWDERED-SUGAR SPONGECAKE

       3 egg yolks
       1 cup confectioner's sugar
     1/4 cup boiling water
    1 1/2 teaspoons vanilla
     1/4 teaspoon grated orange rind
       1 cup sifted cake flour
    1 1/2 teaspoons baking powder
       3 to 5 egg whites
     1/4 teaspoon salt
       1 additional tablespoon confectioner's sugar (optional)

In blender or mixer, beat the egg yolks until lemon-colored. Add the sugar and beat smooth. Add the water, vanilla, and orange rind, and beat. Stir the flour and baking powder together. Uncover the blender and beat in the flour, a little at a time, until smooth.

In mixing bowl, beat the egg whites and salt until stiff peaks form.

Fold the batter into the egg whites, gently but thoroughly, using a rubber scraper or mixer at lowest speed.

Spoon into two 8-inch nonstick cake pans and bake in a preheated 325-degree oven for 25 minutes, until done. Cool thoroughly before removing from pans. When cool, sprinkle with 1 tablespoon confectioner's sugar, if desired. *Sixteen servings (eight each layer), 65 calories each.*

SPECIAL DIETER'S SUGAR-FREE SPONGECAKE

  7 eggs, separated
     Granulated sugar substitute equal to 1 cup
⅔ cup cold water
  1 teaspoon vanilla
  1 teaspoon almond extract
  3 tablespoons lemon juice
1½ cups sifted cake flour, sifted together with ¼ teaspoon salt
¾ teaspoon cream of tartar

In a medium-size bowl, beat egg yolks until thick and lemon-colored, about 5 minutes. Add granulated sugar substitute during the last minute of beating.

Combine water, vanilla, almond extract, lemon juice, and add to egg-yolk mixture. Beat until thick and fluffy, about 10 minutes.

Sift about one quarter of the flour-salt mixture at a time over the egg-yolk mixture, folding in gently until all flour disappears.

In another bowl, beat egg whites until foamy. Add cream of tartar, then beat until stiff. Fold into yolk mixture.

Pour batter into a tube or angel-food cake pan; spread evenly. Bake in a preheated 325-degree oven for 50 to 60 minutes. Allow cake to cool on a rack, or inverted over a funnel 10 to 15 minutes before removing from pan. Store in refrigerator. *Twelve servings, 95 calories each.*

ITALIAN APPLE CASSATA

     Single layer Powdered-Sugar Spongecake (see above)
     15- or 16-ounce container low-fat pot cheese or part-skim ricotta cheese
  1 cup sweetened chunky applesauce
½ teaspoon almond extract
  1 teaspoon vanilla
     Pinch of salt
     1-ounce square unsweetened chocolate
  1 cup Tangy Topping (see below)

With a long sharp bread knife, carefully slice the single spongecake layer to make 2 layers. Set aside.

Combine pot cheese, applesauce, almond and vanilla extracts, and salt in a blender and beat smooth. Grate chocolate and stir into cheese mixture. (Reserve a little for garnish, if you wish.) Carefully spread half of the cheese mixture on a layer of spongecake. Top with second layer and spread remaining cheese mixture. Chill several hours, then spread with whipped topping (sprinkle with a little reserved chocolate, if desired). *Sixteen servings, 135 calories each with pot cheese; 155 calories with ricotta.*

ZUPPA INGLESE

Italian for "English soup," a very moist cake.

¼ **cup rum**
1 **envelope plain gelatin**
1 **cup boiling water**
2 **tablespoons honey**
1½ **cups skim milk**
   Pinch of salt
   4-serving package instant vanilla pudding mix
   Single layer Powdered-Sugar Spongecake (page 336)
1 **pint fresh strawberries, washed, hulled, and sliced**

Combine rum and gelatin in a blender container. Wait 1 minute, then add boiling water. Cover and blend on high speed until gelatin is dissolved. Add honey, milk, salt, and pudding mix. Cover and blend smooth. Refrigerate until mixture is slightly thickened but not set.

With a long sharp bread knife, slice spongecake in half to make 2 layers. Put 1 layer in the bottom of a round casserole. Spoon on half the strawberries and half the pudding mixture. Add second cake layer and remaining berries and pudding. Chill until set. Cut into wedges to serve and garnish with a few whole berries, if desired. *Twelve servings, 175 calories each.*

Tangy Topping: Here's the perfect low-calorie topping for this dessert, as well as for any fresh fruit dessert.

1 **cup plain low-fat yogurt**
½ **teaspoon vanilla**
5 **teaspoons sugar**
1 **envelope (½ package) low-calorie whipped topping mix**

Beat all ingredients at high speed until the consistency of a thick custard sauce. Chill (mixture thickens in the refrigerator). *Makes about 1⅔ cups, 15 calories per tablespoon.*

YOGURT ENGLISH TRIFLE

English Trifle is an easy dessert that can be very trifling about calories if you're a Slim Gourmet cook—or fattening, if you're not. Traditionally, the trifle is simply layered spongecake spiked with wine and topped with fruit (usually raspberries), then slathered with a rich custard, or occasionally "clotted" cream. And perhaps a sprinkling of nuts for crunch. If you're counting calories while I reel off ingredients you can see that a trifle can readily tally up to several hundred calories or more. Hardly a trifle!

This tampered-with trifle begins with packaged spongecake (or try the homemade sugar-free version on page 337.) Then it is topped with sugar-free fruit (whatever's handy or in season) mixed with wine and fruit juice. The "sour-creamy" topping is a tangy mixture of yogurt and whipped topping mix, which leaves enough caloric leeway for a sprinkle of slivered almonds, if you like.

For each serving:

1 small packaged spongecake or 1 slice Special Dieter's Sugar-Free Spongecake (see below)
½ cup unsweetened fresh, canned, or defrosted sliced berries, or other fruit
2 teaspoons dry sherry
1 tablespoon water or fruit juice
¼ cup Tangy Topping (see page 338)
1 teaspoon slivered almonds

Put the spongecake into a small dessert dish. Combine fruit, sherry, and water and spoon onto sponge cake. Chill well. Just before serving, top with Tangy Topping and slivered almonds. *Only 225 calories each, or 190 with the Sugar-Free Spongecake.*

Slim Crêpes for Dessert

STRAWBERRY CRÊPES

Here's how to make 8 delicious strawberry dessert crêpes in a nonstick skillet or omelet pan, using no added fat or oil. (It goes without saying that any fresh fruit can be substituted for the strawberries.)

Basic Egg Crêpes (page 212)
1 pint fresh strawberries
3 tablespoons free-pouring brown sugar
½ cup sour-cream or low-fat sour dressing
½ cup low-fat vanilla yogurt

Prepare crêpes according to the directions on page 212.

TO MAKE FILLING: Wash, hull, and slice the berries and sweeten to taste. In another bowl, stir sour dressing and vanilla yogurt together until well blended. Spoon 3 or 4 tablespoons sliced berries into the center of each crêpe and add some yogurt mixture. Fold up and arrange on plates. Top with additional yogurt cream. *Eight crêpes, 110 calories each.*

COLD CANNOLI CRÊPES

6 Cheese Crêpes (page 213)
1 cup low-fat dry cottage cheese
2 tablespoons white crème de cacao liqueur
1 tablespoon shaved sweet chocolate
1 tablespoon sugar
½ teaspoon vanilla

Cook crêpes and set aside. Combine remaining ingredients and mix well. Spoon onto crêpes and roll up. Chill several hours and serve cold. *Six servings, 120 calories each.*

PINEAPPLE CHEESE BLINTZES

A hearty high-protein dessert or great brunch.

6 Cheese Crêpes (page 213)
1 cup low-fat dry cottage cheese
1 teaspoon vanilla
   Pinch of salt
1 egg
2 tablespoons sugar
1 cup canned juice-packed unsweetened, crushed pineapple

Make crêpes; set aside. Stir cottage cheese, vanilla, salt, egg, and sugar together. Spoon a little of the filling onto each crêpe. Arrange in a nonstick cake pan sprayed with cooking spray. Cover with foil. Bake in a 300-degree oven for 20 minutes. Heat pineapple to boiling and spoon over crêpes to serve. *Each blintz, 220 calories.*

OVEN-BAKED FAT-FREE GERMAN PANCAKE

A puffy German pancake is much too spectacular to face at breakfast. Better at brunch or late at night as a dessert. Despite its dramatic appearance, a German pancake can be low calorie. Our recipe serves 6, yet calls for only ½ cup flour and no fat at all.

In case you're not familiar with it, a German pancake is baked in the oven. If your oven has a window, it's a show worth watching: the batter spreads up the sides of the pan, puffs up, then sinks in the middle to make the ideal "container" for fresh fruit or other nonfattening fillings. You slice it in wedges to serve.

Since the pancake is cooked in the oven at high heat, the ideal thing to cook it in is an all-metal slope-sided skillet or omelet pan with a metal handle—not wood or plastic. A nonstick 9-inch pie pan or other shallow slope-sided oven-proof casserole of a similar size should work as well.

3 **eggs**
½ **cup skim milk**
   Pinch of salt
½ **cup instant-blending flour**
   Filling of your choice (see suggestions on pages 327–28)

Preheat oven to hot (450 degrees). Spray pan well with cooking spray for no-fat frying (or baking, in this case). Use a fork or wire whisk to beat eggs well. Beat in milk and salt. Beat in flour just until blended. Pour into pan. Bake in oven 25 minutes. Remove and fill. Slice into 6 wedges to serve. *Six servings, under 90 calories each (without filling).*

19
PIES,
TARTS,
PASTRIES,
AND
CONFECTIONS

TOPLESS POLYNESIAN PIE

Don't take off your tee-shirt, silly! I'm talking about that redundant upper crust on fattening goodies like home-baked pie.

Since piecrust is the most fattening thing in pie, it only stands to reason that a topless pie is significantly less calorific than a double-crusted one.

> 1 **eating orange, peeled, seeded, and cut up**
> **16-ounce can juice-packed unsweetened crushed pineapple, undrained**
> 1/4 **cup golden raisins**
> 2 **tablespoons granulated tapioca**
> **Pinch of salt**
> **Single 8- or 9-inch piecrust**

Peel and dice the orange; pick out and discard any seeds with the tip of a sharp knife. Combine with the crushed pineapple, including juice. Stir in raisins, tapioca, and salt. Spoon into pie shell. Cover the filling with a smaller cakepan, or cut a round of aluminum foil and lay over the filling, so that the crust will brown but the filling won't dry out.

Bake in a preheated 425-degree (hot) oven for 35 to 45 minutes, until the crust is brown. Serve warm or chilled. *Eight servings, about 150 calories each.*

ALMOND CHOCO-CRÈME PIE

Rich and tangy chocolate cream-cheese pie—piled with whipped cream and sprinkled with slivered almonds. Here's a dessert that looks and tastes like a million . . . calories, that is! Who'd believe you can have it for a skimpy 160 calories a serving? All you have to do is make it.

But make it the Slim Gourmet way, with calorie-saving shortcuts that trim away those unneeded pound provokers! Use low-calorie, low-fat cream cheese or Neufchâtel cheese, the skim-milk taste-twin of fattening cream cheese. In place of a pastry crust, use a base of crushed graham crackers. The frothy "whipped cream" is made with chilled evaporated skim milk, only 176 calories a cup instead of 840! Every step of the way I've eliminated extra fat and sugar while retaining the flavor and tempting texture you love . . . and the protein value as well!

FILLING:
  2 **eggs, separated**
    8-ounce package low-calorie cream cheese or Neufchâtel cheese
¼ **cup skim milk**
  2 **tablespoons unsweetened cocoa**
  7 **tablespoons sugar**
¼ **teaspoon cinnamon**
  2 **teaspoons vanilla**
    Pinch of salt

CRUMB CRUST:
  1 **tablespoon butter or 2 tablespoons diet margarine**
½ **cup graham cracker crumbs or crushed chocolate wafer crumbs**

TOPPING:
  1 **teaspoon vanilla**
  1 **cup evaporated skim milk**
  1 **ounce (about 4 tablespoons) slivered almonds**

Grease the sides and bottom of an 8-inch pie pan with the butter, or diet margarine. Sprinkle with the graham cracker or chocolate wafer and press firmly into place. Set aside while you prepare the filling.

Separate the egg whites into a mixing bowl. Put the yolks, cream cheese, milk, cocoa, sugar, cinnamon, and vanilla into a blender container. Blend on high speed until smooth.

Sprinkle salt on egg whites and beat until stiff. Fold chocolate mixture into egg whites.

Carefully spoon into crumb crust. Bake in a slow (225-degree) oven for 1 hour. Turn off the heat and leave in the oven for 1 more hour. Chill thoroughly before serving.

While the pie is chilling, make the whipped topping.

Mock Whipped Cream: Combine the vanilla and evaporated skim milk in a mixing bowl. Chill the bowl, milk, and beaters in your freezer until ice crystals form around edges. Whip on high speed until peaks form.

At serving time, top each slice with a generous amount of whipped topping and sprinkle on ½ tablespoon almonds, for crunchy texture contrast. *Eight servings, 180 calories each.*

SLIM GOURMET IRISH COFFEE PIE

1 envelope plain gelatin
⅔ cup sugar
2 teaspoons instant coffee powder
¾ cup skim milk
1 egg yolk, slightly beaten
¼ teaspoon salt
1 egg white
1 envelope (½ package) diet whipped topping mix
2 tablespoons Irish whiskey
   Ready-to-fill 8-inch packaged graham-cracker crust

Combine gelatin, sugar, coffee, and milk in a saucepan. Wait 1 minute then cook and stir over low heat until gelatin and sugar are dissolved. Remove from heat and slowly stir a little of the hot mixture into the beaten yolk. Then add mixture to the saucepan and return to the heat. Cook and stir over very low heat about one minute. Do not boil.

Chill in refrigerator until slightly thickened.

Add salt to egg white and beat until stiff.

Prepare topping mix according to package directions. (Two cups defrosted nondairy topping may be substituted.)

Remove the gelatin mixture from the refrigerator. Add the whiskey and beat with an electric mixer until light and foamy. Gently but thoroughly fold in the beaten egg white. Then fold in 1½ cups of the whipped topping (reserve the remaining ½ cup for garnish). Spoon the mixture into the prepared pie shell and chill in the refrigerator all day until set. Garnish with whipped topping at serving time. *Eight servings, about 200 calories each.*

DUTCH CHOCOLATE "CREAM CHEESE" PIE

Chocolate! The first cook who named it "devil's food" knew whereof he or she spoke. At 143 calories an ounce, chocolate is truly the dieter's downfall. Chocolate is bad enough, but then it needs heaps of pound-provoking sugar to sweeten it up to a minimum level of palatability. No wonder chocolate desserts are usually the most fattening of all.

But there are times when a body simply must have something chocolate— rich and sweet and creamy and *chocolate!*

That's the time to head for your Slim Gourmet pantry and whip up a sweet that boasts of "redeeming nutritional value"—a make-room-for dessert creation that seems so filling and fattening you're willing to skimp on dinner. It won't matter if you dine lightly: this Slim Gourmet dessert is so protein rich it's nearly a meal in itself. That's because the unneeded extra fat, sugar, and starch calories have been stripped away while nutrition has been boosted with protein—powdered eggs, milk, and cheese.

  2 **tablespoons diet margarine**
  ½ **cup graham-cracker crumbs or chocolate-wafer crumbs**
      8-ounce package low-calorie cream cheese or Neufchâtel cheese
  1 **cup low-fat cottage cheese**
  ¼ **cup skim milk**
  3 **eggs**
  3 **tablespoons unsweetened cocoa**
  ½ **cup sugar**
  1 **tablespoon vanilla**
  ½ **teaspoon ground cinnamon**

Spread the inside of an 8- or 9-inch pie pan with diet margarine and sprinkle with crumbs. Press firmly into place. Chill, . . . or, if you prefer, quick-bake in a hot oven for 5 or 6 minutes.

Combine remaining ingredients in a blender container and beat smooth. Pour into the crumb crust. Bake in a preheated 225-degree oven for 1 hour. Chill. *Eight servings, 190 calories each.*

CANNOLI PIE

Italian Chocolate Pie

QUESTION: What do you do with chocolate chips, besides make chocolate-chip cookies?

ANSWER: Avoid them if you have to weight-watch.

Wrong!

Despite their high calorie count, there are chocolate-chip treats the calorie-conscious cook can make—desserts relatively light in calories but nutrition rich. Here's my favorite.

    15-ounce container part-skim ricotta cheese
½ cup crème de cacao liqueur
  2 eggs
  2 tablespoons sugar
  3 tablespoons miniature chocolate chips
⅛ teaspoon salt
    Ready-to-fill packaged graham-cracker crust

Combine first 6 ingredients in a blender, cover, and beat smooth. Pour into the pie shell and bake in a preheated 300-degree oven 1 hour. Cool at room temperature, then chill. *Eight servings, about 230 calories each.*

STRAWBERRY ANGEL PIE

2 egg whites
  Pinch of salt
  Pinch of cream of tartar
7 tablespoons sugar
  Double Berry Bavarian (page 371)

Have whites at room temperature. Beat in a nonplastic bowl until frothy. Add salt and cream of tartar and beat until stiff. Gradually beat in the sugar, a tablespoon at a time, until stiff peaks form.

Spread the meringue mixture on the sides and bottom of a 9-inch nonstick pie pan. Bake in a slow (275-degree) oven for 1 hour. Turn off the heat and leave in the oven an additional 30 minutes. Remove from oven and cool.

Meanwhile, prepare the Double Berry Bavarian filling. Spoon filling into cooled pie shell. Chill 3 hours. *Ten servings, 95 calories each, when filling is prepared with diet mix, 130 with regular.*

FRENCH PEAR PIE

  1 9-inch unbaked pie shell
4–6 fresh Bartlett pears (about 5 cups sliced)
  3 tablespoons defrosted orange-juice concentrate, undiluted
½ cup all-purpose flour
  4 tablespoons brown sugar
  1 teaspoon ground cinnamon
    Pinch of salt
  5 tablespoons diet margarine

Peel, core, and thinly slice pears; mix with orange juice and arrange in a pastry-lined pan. Mix together flour, sugar, cinnamon, and salt. Blend in diet margarine until mixture is crumbly; sprinkle over pears. Bake at 400 degrees for 40 minutes. *Twelve servings, 175 calories each.*

SPICY TOPLESS APPLE TART

Single 8- or 9-inch piecrust, homemade or defrosted
20-ounce can unsweetened pie-sliced apples (not pie filling)
½ cup golden raisins
1 sweet eating orange, peeled, seeded, and cut up
1 teaspoon vanilla
1 teaspoon brandy flavoring
Pinch of salt
½ teaspoon ground cinnamon
⅛ teaspoon ground cloves
¼ teaspoon grated nutmeg
¼ teaspoon ground allspice
8-ounce can juice-packed mandarin oranges, drained (optional)

Defrost the frozen pie shell and fold in fourths. Arrange pastry in a straight-sided 8- or 9-inch nonstick layer-cake pan. With the fingers, stretch the pastry to fit up the sides of the cake pan.

Empty the canned apples, including juice, into a bowl and stir in all remaining ingredients, mixing well. Spoon into pieshell.

Cover the top of the filling with a round sheet of foil cut to fit, or invert another pie pan or cake pan to cover the filling so it won't dry out.

Bake in a preheated 425-degree oven for 30 to 40 minutes. Cool. Serve warm or chilled, decorate if you wish with the mandarin orange segments in a circle in the center of the pie. *Serves eight, about 140 calories each without garnish; 150 calories with garnish.*

QUICK HONEY APPLE TART

As a sweetener, honey has more calories than sugar, but it's so much sweeter that you need fewer calories' worth of honey to do the same job sugar would. Honey has a distinctive flavor that really turns on the tangy taste of apples. Here's a decalorized sweet for you to try—without sugar!

Stretch a single piecrust to fit a larger pan; the top "crust" is formed by the low-calorie high-protein cheese mixture.

Frozen 8-inch piecrust, defrosted
20-ounce can unsweetened sliced apples (not pie filling)
⅓ cup honey
2 tablespoons orange liqueur or orange juice
7 tablespoons dried currants or raisins
1 teaspoon apple-pie spice
1 cup low-fat cottage cheese
1 egg
½ cup skim milk
¼ teaspoon salt or butter-flavored salt
1 teaspoon vanilla

Remove the piecrust, still frozen, to a straight-sided 9-inch cake pan and allow it to defrost. With your fingertips, stretch the pastry as thin as possible to cover the inside of the cake pan. Trim off and discard the excess.

Stir apples, honey, orange liqueur, currants, and spice together and pour into the cake pan.

In a blender, beat cottage cheese, egg, milk, salt, and vanilla smooth. Pour over apples. Bake in a 350-degree oven 1 hour. Cool. *Twelve servings, 140 calories each.*

NO-SUGAR-ADDED RAW PEACH TART

1½ teaspoons (½ envelope) plain gelatin
1 cup chilled unsweetened white grape juice
Ready-to-fill 8- or 9-inch packaged graham-cracker crust
4 or more fresh ripe sweet peaches, peeled and sliced

Combine gelatin with ¼ cup grape juice in a small saucepan. Wait 1 minute, then heat and stir gently until gelatin dissolves. Stir in remaining grape juice and chill in freezer or refrigerator until syrupy but not set.

Fill a ready-to-use crust with sliced peaches. Pour the chilled thickened grape syrup over the fruit and chill several hours, until set. *Eight servings, 125 calories each.*

FRESH FRUIT WINDOWPANE TART

2 teaspoons plain gelatin
5 tablespoons sugar (optional)
1 cup chilled unsweetened apple juice
Ready-to-fill 8-inch packaged graham-cracker crust

1 cup sliced fresh strawberries
1 cup sliced fresh peaches
1 cup fresh blueberries

Combine gelatin, sugar, and ½ cup apple juice. Wait until gelatin is softened, then heat gently until dissolved. Stir in remaining cold apple juice. Chill in freezer 8 to 10 minutes, until syrupy. Meanwhile prepare fruit.

Fill the pieshell with the fruit. Don't mix the fruit together, but arrange it in random clumps of color (much prettier!) Gently pack fruit down. When gelatin mixture is syrupy, spoon it over fruit until completely glazed. Chill several hours until set. *Eight servings, 160 calories each; 130 without sugar.*

VARIATION

Mock Mango Pie: Use 3 cups sliced fresh peaches for the fruit and canned unsweetened pineapple juice for the glaze. Follow above directions. *Eight servings, 160 calories each (130 without sugar).*

ARMENIAN PASTRY NESTS

1 apple, peeled, cored, and diced
2 tablespoons chopped almonds (or other nuts)
¼ cup sugar
¼ teaspoon ground cinnamon
1 tablespoon diet margarine
8 sheets phyllo pastry (strudel leaves)
1 tablespoon honey
2 tablespoons water
  Few drops lemon juice

Combine diced apple, chopped nuts, 1 tablespoon of the sugar, and cinnamon. Set aside.

Melt margarine in a small saucepan.

Cut each sheet of pastry in half. Use only one section at a time, keeping the rest covered to prevent them from drying out. (Tightly wrap and refrigerate unused sheets in package; keep for future use.) Spread the half sheet of pastry flat and brush *very* sparingly with margarine.

Use a cooking-spoon handle, or wooden dowel, or similar object which measures approximately 12 inches in length and ⅓ inch in diameter. Starting from a shorter edge, roll the pastry around the handle, leaving a 1-inch flap at the bottom. Slide off the handle, bunching roll together into pleats as you would shir gathers in sewing. Form the roll into a circle with the flap bunched into a fairly flat center. Place on a nonstick cookie tin, sprayed for no-fat baking.

After the pastry nests are formed, divide the apple-nut mixture evenly among them, heaping it in the center of each nest. Bake in a preheated 375-degree oven about 15 minutes, until just golden. Remove from oven.

Mix all remaining ingredients in the margarine pan (no need to wash it). Cook and stir until boiling. Then simmer, uncovered, an additional 5 minutes. Spoon syrup over pastry nests. *Sixteen servings, about 50 calories each.*

LOW-CALORIE ÉCLAIRS

Golden crisp on the outside, sweet and creamy in the middle . . . what more devilish diet breaker is there than a chocolate éclair? If you only could wave a magic wand over the bakery-shop window and make the extra calories vanish from those tempting treats.

If you're a Slim Gourmet cook, you can do the next best thing. Make them yourself, without the extra fat and sugar. Slim Gourmet éclairs are every bit as delicious as the bakery-shop kind, but part of the unneeded sugar and fat have been replaced with extra protein.

Éclairs are admittedly trouble to make, but I think you will find this calorie-saving treat worth the effort. They may be filled with low-fat ice milk and served immediately. Or with prepared diet pudding made according to package directions, or with crushed fruit. Or try the Low-Cal Chocolate Cream filling that follows.

4 tablespoons diet margarine
5 tablespoons water
½ cup all-purpose flour
¼ teaspoon salt
2 eggs

Combine diet margarine and water in a saucepan. Heat until margarine melts and water boils. Over very low heat, add the flour and salt. Beat until mixture leaves the sides of the saucepan. Remove from heat and beat in the eggs, one at a time.

On a nonstick cookie sheet, shape 9 éclairs about 3 inches long. Do this with a spoon, or put the éclair mixture into a pastry bag with a large plain tip and force out the filling in 3-inch lengths. Place the éclairs 3 inches apart.

Bake in a preheated 375-degree oven for 45 minutes. Remove from the oven and cool on a rack before splitting and filling. *Nine éclairs, 65 calories each.*

Low-Cal Chocolate Cream Filling
2 cups skim milk
2 tablespoons cornstarch

¼ teaspoon butter-flavored salt
2 tablespoons unsweetened cocoa
¼ cup sugar
1 egg, beaten
1 teaspoon vanilla

Scald 1½ cups milk in a nonstick saucepan. Combine cornstarch, salt, cocoa, and sugar with remaining milk. Stir into hot milk over low heat until mixture thickens.

Slowly stir some of the hot mixture into the beaten egg. Then gradually stir the egg mixture into the saucepan over low heat, stirring constantly until the mixture is thick and hot. Do not boil.

Remove from heat and stir in vanilla. Chill until thick. Use to fill éclairs. *Each éclair with cream filling, 125 calories.*

Easy Breakfast "Danish" Doubles as Diet Dessert

Danish pastry is what you really want, but cottage cheese is what you should be eating, according to your bathroom scale.

Cottage cheese for breakfast? What an awful way to wake up!

Take heart, would-be skinnies, this pair of nutritious treats tastes like Danish pastry but nourishes like cottage cheese. Because they're made with cottage cheese and other protein-powered dairy goodies like milk and eggs, touched with the sweet taste of fruit.

They're filling but nonfattening, and extra easy to whip up in your blender. And, like Danish pastry, these breakfast treats can double as a dessert or snack —but a filling snack that will keep you safe from hunger for several hours.

APPLE-CHEESE DANISH "PIE"

7 large round milk crackers (such as Royal Lunch)
  20-ounce can unsweetened presliced apples, undrained
7 tablespoons sugar
1 teaspoon cinnamon
7 tablespoons raisins
1 cup low-fat cottage cheese
1 whole egg
½ cup skim milk

Arrange milk crackers in an 8-inch nonstick cake pan, 6 in a circle and one in the center (crackers need not be touching). Stir apples, sugar, cinnamon, and raisins together and spoon over crackers. In a covered blender, beat cottage cheese, egg, and milk smooth. Pour over apples. Bake in a preheated 350-degree oven 1 hour. Serve warm or chilled. *Eight servings, 185 calories each.*

LOW-CALORIE PEACHES 'N' CREAM "TART"

6 large round milk crackers (such as Royal Lunch)
2 cups drained juice-packed peach slices
1 cup low-fat cottage cheese
2 eggs
½ cup juice (from can)
7 tablespoons free-pouring brown sugar
  Pinch of salt or butter-flavored salt
1 teaspoon vanilla
  Ground cinnamon

Arrange the crackers in a single layer in the bottom of an 8-inch round nonstick cake pan (the crackers need not be touching). Drain the peaches and reserve the juice. (If using peach halves, cut in large chunks.) Layer the drained peaches on top of the milk crackers.

In a covered blender, beat smooth the cottage cheese, eggs, juice, sugar, salt, and vanilla. Pour over the peaches. Sprinkle with cinnamon. Bake in a 325-degree oven for 1 hour or longer, until set. (Insert the tip of a knife in the center to check.) Serve warm or chilled. *Eight servings, 150 calories each.*

PINEAPPLE-CHEESE BREAKFAST SQUARES

8 or 9 plain or cinnamon graham crackers
1 cup unsweetened crushed pineapple
1 cup evaporated skim milk
4 eggs
1 teaspoon salt
2 teaspoons vanilla
10 tablespoons sugar
2 tablespoons cornstarch
2 cups low-fat cottage cheese
  Ground cinnamon

Break up graham crackers and arrange to cover the bottom of a nonstick 8-inch square cake pan. It's not necessary that the bottom be completely covered. Cover the crackers with a thin layer of well-drained pineapple. Combine remaining ingredients, except cinnamon, in a blender. Cover blender and beat smooth. Pour mixture over pineapple and sprinkle with cinnamon. Bake in a preheated slow (250-degree) oven for 1 hour, then turn off the heat and let "pastry" cool *in* the oven. Refrigerate. *Eight servings (squares), 185 calories each.*

SLIM PEACH KUCHEN

1 tube bake-and-serve biscuits (10 biscuits)
2 cups drained juice-packed sliced peaches
3 tablespoons honey
  Few drops almond flavoring
½ teaspoon apple-pie spice
1 egg
1 cup vanilla low-fat yogurt

Remove the biscuits from the tube and lay them flat in a nonstick round or square 8-inch baking pan. Press the dough flat, and up the edges, forming a crust. Bake in a preheated 350-degree oven for 5 to 7 minutes.

Drain the peach slices and combine with honey, almond flavoring, and pie spice. Spoon into the biscuit crust. Stir egg and yogurt together and pour over peaches. Return to the oven and bake at 350 degrees for 20 to 30 minutes, until set. Serve warm or chilled. *Eight servings, 175 calories each.*

EASY APPLE KUCHEN

1 tube flaky-style refrigerator biscuits (10 biscuits)
  20-ounce can unsweetened sliced apples (not pie filling)
2 tablespoons honey
½ teaspoon ground cinnamon
1 egg, beaten
1 cup low-fat vanilla yogurt

Flatten biscuits in a regular 9-inch pie pan, sealing edges together. Press biscuit dough around edges of piepan. Bake in a preheated 350-degree oven for 5 minutes.

Combine apple slices, honey, and cinnamon, and spread mixture over biscuit dough.

Combine with beaten egg and yogurt. Pour over fruit. Bake at 350 degrees for 20 minutes. *Eight servings, 180 calories each.*

Try These Low-Cal Confections

CHOCOLATE MERINGUES

  2 ounces unsweetened chocolate
  1 tablespoon hot coffee
½ cup sifted cake flour
  7 tablespoons white sugar
  4 egg whites at room temperature
¼ teaspoon salt
    Pinch of cream of tartar

Combine chocolate and coffee and allow to melt very slowly on a warming tray, or over very low heat.

Meanwhile, sift flour with 3 tablespoons sugar and set aside.

In a glass or metal (not plastic) mixer bowl, combine egg whites, salt, and cream of tartar. Beat with an electric mixer until stiff. Gradually beat in remaining sugar, a tablespoon at a time. Beat in the flour mixture a little at a time. Fold in the melted chocolate.

Spray a nonstick cookie tin with cooking spray for no-stick frying (baking). Drop the meringue mixture by the teaspoon, 1 inch apart.

Bake in a preheated 275-degree (slow) oven for 45 minutes, or until the cookies are dry. Cool before removing. *Two dozen meringues, about 35 calories each.*

HUNGARIAN "NUT" BRITTLES

PASTRY:
  2 cups all-purpose flour
½ cup sugar
¼ teaspoon salt
  4 tablespoons diet margarine
  1 egg
  1 teaspoon vanilla

TOPPING:
  2 eggs
  6 tablespoons sugar
  1 teaspoon maple flavoring
  1 cup high-protein cereal
  1 tablespoon chopped nuts (optional)

Mix flour, sugar, and salt in a bowl. Cut in margarine. Stir in egg and vanilla. (The dough will be dry and crumbly.) Spread evenly in a 10-by-15-inch jelly-roll pan which has been sprayed for nonstick baking. Bake 15 minutes at 375 degrees.

Mix the eggs, sugar, and maple flavoring in a small saucepan. Cook over low heat, stirring constantly, until thickened, about 5 minutes. Stir in the cereal.

Remove pastry from oven. Spread topping over it. Sprinkle with nuts, if desired. Return to oven for 15 minutes more. Cut while still warm into 1½-by-2-inch bars. *Fifty bars, about 40 calories each.*

NEUFCHÂTEL NUT CANDIES

Be sure to pick a brand of cream cheese that's low in calories. The reduced fat content requires it to be labeled "imitation" cream cheese, even though it's higher in protein.

8 ounces low-calorie, low-fat cream cheese or Neufchâtel cheese
  Pinch of salt
5 tablespoons chopped walnuts
½ cup shredded sweetened coconut

Have cream cheese at room temperature so it's soft. Combine it with remaining ingredients and roll into balls. Chill thoroughly. *Two dozen candies, about 35 calories each.*

20
PUDDINGS, CUSTARDS, SOUFFLES, AND FROZEN DESSERTS

LOW-CALORIE STRAWBERRY SWISS-STYLE YOGURT

5 or 6 very ripe strawberries
2 teaspoons sugar
1 cup plain low-fat yogurt
   Few drops of vanilla (optional)

With a fork, crush berries and sugar together, then stir into chilled yogurt, along with a little vanilla if desired. *One serving, only 190 calories instead of the 259 calories in sugar-sweetened "fruit" yogurt.*

DOUBLE STRAWBERRY CRÈME

Strawberries are such a favorite it's easy to forget that they are also one of the least fattening, most nutrition-rich foods there is.

A whole cupful of strawberries is only 55 calories, yet strawberries are high in valuable food fiber and vitamin C. Kids love them for their jewel-bright color and tangy sweet taste.

1½ cups ripe strawberries, hulled
1 cup skim milk, chilled
4-serving package instant strawberry pudding mix

Whir strawberries and milk in a covered blender. Then add pudding mix, cover, and blend smooth. Spoon into 4 parfait glasses and chill until set. Garnish with additional berries if desired. *Four servings, 135 calories each.*

BANANA PARFAITS

Protein-rich!

2 egg yolks
2 tablespoons confectioners' sugar
1 cup low-fat vanilla yogurt
  8-ounce package low-fat cream cheese or Neufchâtel cheese, at room temperature
3 bananas, peeled and sliced
2 tablespoons shredded coconut

In a deep bowl beat egg yolks, sugar, and sugar substitute with an electric mixer until thick and yellow. Gradually beat in vanilla yogurt and softened cream cheese until fluffy. Refrigerate 20 minutes.

Arrange sliced bananas and creamy topping in 6 parfait glasses; top each with 1 teaspoon shredded coconut. *Six servings, 165 calories each.*

NEW-FASHIONED BREAD PUDDING

Peaches, apples, pineapple . . . any favorite fruit can be used.

6 slices stale or toasted high-fiber bread, cubed
2 cups cubed unsweetened fresh or drained canned fruit
¼ cup raisins
2 eggs
1¾ cups skim milk or fruit juice
2 tablespoons honey or ¼ cup sugar
½ teaspoon salt
1 teaspoon vanilla extract
½ teaspoon grated nutmeg, ground cinnamon, or pumpkin-pie spice

Lightly toss the bread cubes with the fruit and raisins. Arrange in a small nonstick baking dish. Beat together the eggs, skim milk or juice, honey, salt, and vanilla and pour over bread-fruit mixture. Sprinkle with nutmeg, cinnamon, or pie spice. Set the pan in a larger pan containing 1 inch hot water. Bake in a preheated 350-degree oven till set, 35 to 45 minutes. *Six servings, under 175 calories each.*

ENGLISH APPLE-BREAD PUDDING

  4 slices white high-fiber or protein bread, toasted
1½ cups skim milk, scalded
  4 eggs
  1 teaspoon apple-pie spice
    Pinch of salt
  1 tablespoon honey
  1 apple, peeled and diced
  ½ cup raisins

Cut toast into cubes and empty into an oven casserole. Add scalded milk; let stand 15 minutes.

Beat together eggs, spice, salt, and honey. Add apple and raisins. Stir into bread mixture.

Bake in a preheated 325-degree oven until custard mixture is set, about 35 minutes. Chill well before serving. *Six servings, about 170 calories each.*

Spirited Rice Puddings Definitely Not for Kids

Image-wise, rice pudding is generally reserved for little old ladies or people with tender tummies. But our X-rated rice puddings are none of the above.

In fact, it's a bit of a quibble even to call these sophisticated desserts rice puddings, since the rice content is very low (only 1 tablespoon per serving) and the texture is dense enough to slice. But, whatever you call it, it's a delicious idea.

One more thing these desserts are *not,* and that's high calorie. More fruit than rice for the most part, there are fewer than 200 calories a serving when they are well spiked with spirits, under 100 calories without. (You can make them kid-safe, and extra low-cal, simply by omitting the booze where it occurs and replacing it with additional fruit juice.)

CURAÇAO RICE SLICES

  2 cups skim milk
  ½ cup instant rice
    Dash of salt

1 **envelope plain gelatin**
3 **tablespoons Curaçao or any orange liqueur (optional)**
  8-ounce can juice-packed peaches or apricots (chopped) *or* **fruit cocktail**
1 **unpeeled red apple, diced**
5 **tablespoons currants or raisins**

Heat milk to a simmer; stir in rice and salt. Cover and set aside 20 minutes. Meanwhile, soften gelatin in liqueur or juice from canned fruit.

When rice is soft, stir in gelatin over very low heat until gelatin is dissolved. Stir in fruits. Spoon into a small loaf pan or square cake pan and chill until set. Cut into slices or squares to serve. *Eight servings, 110 calories each with liqueur; only 90 without.*

VERY WILD RICE PUDDING

We don't call it "wild" because it's made with wild rice! Read on . . .

1¾ **cups unsweetened canned pineapple juice**
½ **cup instant rice**
  Dash of salt
1 **tablespoon sugar (optional)**
1 **envelope plain gelatin**
¼ **cup cold water**
  8-ounce can juice-packed fruit cocktail
1 **eating orange** *or* **2 small tangerines**
1 **teaspoon grated orange peel**
1 **unpeeled small red apple, diced**
1 **small ripe banana, peeled and sliced**
½ **cup gin (optional)**

Combine pineapple juice, rice, salt, and sugar in a heavy saucepan. Heat to boiling. Cover and set aside 20 minutes, until rice is plump and soft. Meanwhile sprinkle gelatin over cold water and allow to soften.

Stir soft gelatin into rice mixture over low heat until gelatin dissolves. Remove from heat. Stir in canned fruit cocktail, including juice.

Peel and seed the orange and cut it into bite-size chunks. Stir it into rice. Stir in grated peel, apple dice, banana slices, and gin. Pour into a small loaf pan and chill several hours until set. Slice and serve. *Eight servings, 175 calories each with sugar and liquor; 165 calories without sugar, only 95 calories without liquor.*

MIDDLE EASTERN RICE PUDDING

Very protein rich!

3 cups skim milk
½ cup long-grain rice
5 tablespoons honey
¼ teaspoon salt or butter-flavored salt
1 cup low-fat cottage cheese
2 teaspoons vanilla
6 tablespoons golden raisins
½ teaspoon grated lemon or orange peel
½ teaspoon ground cinnamon
½ teaspoon ground coriander
   Pinch of mace or grated nutmeg

Combine milk, rice, honey, and salt in a very heavy saucepan over low heat (or in the top of a double boiler over simmering water). Cover and cook slowly for 1 hour, stirring occasionally. Uncover and continue to cook 30 to 45 minutes, until thick.

Meanwhile, beat cottage cheese and vanilla smooth with an electric mixer.

When rice is thick, remove from heat, and stir in cottage cheese, raisins, citrus peel, and spices. Chill until very cold. To serve, spoon into dessert cups and sprinkle with additional cinnamon. *Eight servings, 125 calories each.*

PLANTATION RICE PUDDING

1 quart skim milk
⅓ cup dark molasses
½ cup washed raw rice
½ teaspoon ground cinnamon
½ teaspoon salt
⅔ cup raisins

Combine well in an ovenproof casserole. Bake in a preheated oven at 275 degrees, stirring every 20 minutes for the first hour, every 30 minutes thereafter, until rice is tender (about 2½ hours). Chill. *Eight servings, 150 calories each.*

Low-Cal Noodle Kugel, A Winner Everyone Loves

You don't have to be Jewish to love kugel, a rich and fattening noodle pudding. So my kudos goes to a luscious, protein-rich, decalorized version submitted by Mrs. Theodore Rossman of Portage, Michigan.

"You have taught me so much about cutting calories without giving up favorite foods that I had to save a family favorite. My family has no idea that this is a dieter's delight."

This inspired us to share some other kugel recipe favorites, which follow.

MRS. ROSSMAN'S LOW-CAL KUGEL

8 ounces dry wide egg noodles
2 eggs
¼ cup sugar
¼ teaspoon ground cinnamon
⅓ cup dried currants
1½ cups low-fat cottage cheese
1 cup plain low-fat yogurt
¼ teaspoon salt

Cook noodles according to package directions. Combine with remaining ingredients in an 8- or 9-inch nonstick square baking pan. Bake in a preheated 350-degree oven 45 minutes, or until set and lightly browned. (Recipe can be doubled and baked in a 13- by-9-inch pan. It also freezes beautifully, before or after baking.) Enjoy! *Nine servings, 125 calories each.*

DOT'S BLUEBERRY YOGURT KUGEL

8 ounces dry protein-enriched noodles or spaghetti
2 eggs
1 cup low-fat cottage cheese
1 cup low-fat vanilla yogurt
1½ tablespoons sugar
¼ teaspoon salt
⅓ cup fresh blueberries
  Ground cinnamon

Cook noodles according to package directions; drain. Mix with eggs, cottage cheese, yogurt, sugar, and salt. Gently fold in blueberries. Place in a 9-inch nonstick baking dish. Sprinkle cinnamon over top. Bake at 350 degrees about 45 minutes, until set. *Eight servings at 110 calories each.*

VARIATIONS

Sugar-Free Blueberry Yogurt Kugel: Omit sugar and replace vanilla yogurt with plain unsweetened yogurt and 1 teaspoon vanilla extract. Add sugar substitute equal to ¼ cup sugar, or to taste. *90 calories per serving.*

Heart-Smart Blueberry Yogurt Kugel: Replace 2 whole eggs with 4 egg whites or ½ cup liquid low-cholesterol egg substitute. *About 110 calories per serving.*

HEART-SMART PINEAPPLE KUGEL

8 ounces noodles, cooked and drained
4 egg whites
½ cup low-fat vanilla or pineapple yogurt
    8-ounce can juice-packed crushed pineapple, including juice
¼ teaspoon salt
    Ground cinnamon or grated nutmeg to taste

Into the noodles, stir combined egg whites, yogurt, undrained pineapple, and salt. Spoon into a 9-inch nonstick baking pan. Sprinkle with cinnamon. Bake at 350 degrees for 45 minutes. *Eight servings, under 75 calories each.*

Cutting Calories with Our Slimming Custards . . .

POLYNESIAN PAPAYA CUSTARD

4 cups diced ripe fresh papaya pulp
½ cup shredded coconut
4 cups skim milk
6 eggs
¼ teaspoon salt
2 teaspoons vanilla
3 tablespoons sugar
1 medium-sized eating orange, peeled, seeded, and diced
1 tablespoon grated orange peel

Mix papaya with coconut. Spread in the bottom of a 2-quart nonstick casserole or soufflé dish. Scald milk. Beat eggs with salt, vanilla, and sugar; pour slowly into the hot milk, stirring well. When sugar is dissolved, stir in orange and peel. Pour mixture over papaya and coconut.

Put dish in a shallow pan containing 1 inch of hot water and bake in a 350-degree oven for 35 minutes, or until the blade of a knife inserted in the middle comes out clean. Custard will thicken with cooling. *Ten servings, 160 calories each.*

CURAÇAO CHOCOLATE CUSTARD
WITH TANGERINES

2½ tablespoons unsweetened cocoa
 3 tablespoons cornstarch
 3 cups skim milk
 3 tablespoons sugar
 1 egg plus 2 egg yolks
 2 tangerines
 ¼ cup orange liqueur

Stir the cocoa and cornstarch together. Beat in 1 cup cold milk until smooth. Beat in the sugar, egg and egg yolks. Scald the remaining milk in a saucepan, then slowly stir the hot milk into the chocolate mixture. Return the entire mixture to the saucepan and heat to boiling. Cook and stir for 3 minutes.

Remove from the heat and pour into 6 custard cups. Chill. Arrange tangerine segments in a pinwheel form on top of each custard. Top each with 2 teaspoons orange liqueur just before serving. *Six Servings, 160 calories each.*

Soufflés . . .

CRÈME DE CACAO SOUFFLÉ

4 whole eggs plus 1 egg white
 1 cup low-fat vanilla yogurt
 ¼ cup unsweetened cocoa
 ½ teaspoon vanilla
 2 tablespoons crème de cacao liqueur
   Pinch of salt
 6 tablespoons sugar
 ½ teaspoon butter or margarine

Separate the eggs. Lightly beat the 4 yolks. Mix in the yogurt, cocoa, vanilla, and crème de cacao.

Beat the 5 egg whites and the salt until stiff peaks form. Sprinkle 5 tablespoons of the sugar over the top of the egg whites and beat in thoroughly.

Gently cut and fold the yolk mixture into the whites in several additions.

Lightly grease a deep 2-quart casserole or soufflé dish and sprinkle it with the remaining tablespoon sugar. Spoon the soufflé mixture into the dish and place it in a shallow pan of hot water; bake in a moderate oven (350 degrees) for 45 minutes. Serve warm directly from the oven. (Also good cold, but loses its puffiness.) *Ten servings, 110 calories each.*

SIMPLER SOUFFLÉ

6 eggs, separated
1 cup skim milk
5 tablespooons instant-blending flour
3 ounces (½ can) defrosted orange-juice concentrate
½ cup water
   1 teaspoon grated fresh lemon or orange peel
   Pinch of salt or butter-flavored salt
3 tablespoons sugar

Have eggs at room temperature. Separate the eggs and whites into two separate mixing bowls. Beat the egg yolks until very light; set aside.

Combine milk and flour in a saucepan over low heat. Cook and stir until mixture simmers and thickens. Remove from heat and stir in orange juice, water, and peel.

Slowly beat the milk-orange mixture into the beaten egg yolks.

Wash and dry beater blades. Add a pinch of salt to egg whites and beat until stiff peaks form. Beat in the sugar a tablespoon at a time. Gently fold the first mixture into the egg whites until combined. (Don't overmix.)

Turn into a straight-sided soufflé dish with a paper collar (nice but not necessary) or into a 2-quart or other casserole large enough to contain the mixture. Set the dish in a larger baking pan containing an inch of hot water; put both in a preheated 325-degree oven and bake about 1½ hours, until a knife inserted in the center comes out clean.

Serve immediately. *Eight servings, 130 calories each.*

NOTE: Serve with Berry-Orange Sauce (page 327), if desired.

. . . and Frozen Desserts

ITALIAN LEMON ICE

9 tablespoons sugar
   Pinch of salt
1½ cups water
½ envelope (1½ teaspoons) plain gelatin
⅓ cup fresh lemon juice

Boil sugar, salt, and water for 5 minutes. Meanwhile soften the gelatin by sprinkling it on top of the lemon juice. Stir it into the hot syrup mixture until thoroughly dissolved.

To freeze: Process in an ice-cream freezer according to manufacturer's directions. Or freeze in shallow metal trays until mushy; break up into a mixing bowl and quickly beat with an electric mixer until fluffy; cover and return to freezer. *Nine servings, 50 calories each.*

GREEK MELON ICE

  7 **tablespoons sugar**
1½ **cups water**
  2 **ripe sweet cantaloupes**
⅓ **cup orange juice**
    Mint sprigs (optional)

Boil sugar and water together 5 minutes. Meanwhile, cut melons in half, discard seeds, and scoop pulp into a blender. Add hot syrup and orange juice and blend smooth.

Process in an ice-cream maker according to manufacturer's directions. Or freeze to slushy consistency in shallow metal trays; break up into a mixing bowl and quickly beat until fluffy; cover and freeze. Allow to soften briefly before serving. Garnish with fresh mint sprigs, if desired. *Twelve servings, 50 calories each.*

POLYNESIAN ICE MILK

    13-ounce can evaporated skim milk
3 **bananas**
2 **tablespoons sugar**
6 **tablespoons unsweetened pineapple juice concentrate**

Pour canned milk into a metal mixer bowl and chill in a freezer until ice begins to form around the edges. Freeze beater blades, too. Whip until stiff peaks form.

In another bowl, beat bananas, sugar, and defrosted pineapple concentrate together. Fold into whipped milk. Turn into refrigerator trays and freeze firm. Allow to soften slightly at room temperature before serving. *Eight servings, 110 calories each.*

CHERRIES JUBILEE

10 scoops low-fat vanilla ice milk (about 3⅓ cups)
    16-ounce can unsweetened juice-packed dark cherries, including juice
 1 teaspoon cornstarch
    Pinch of salt
¼ cup brandy

Scoop ice milk into individual dessert dishes and return to freezer.

Combine undrained cherries, cornstarch, and salt in a saucepan. Cook and stir until simmering. Transfer to a heated chafing dish over a flame.

When ready to serve, set out ice milk. Pour brandy over simmering cherries. Carefully ignite the vapors with a long match. Spoon flaming cherries over ice milk. *Ten servings, under 100 calories each.*

BLAZING BANANAS ROYALE

4 scoops vanilla ice milk
2 ripe bananas, peeled and sliced
2 tablespoons water
2 tablespoons rum
1 teaspoon butter
   Dash of ground cinnamon

Scoop the ice milk into 4 serving dishes.

Heat the remaining ingredients in a chafing dish, then ignite with a long match. Spoon, while flaming, over the ice milk and serve immediately. *Four servings, 160 calories each.*

21

MOUSSES, BAVARIANS, AND OTHER GELATIN DESSERTS

QUICK CAPUCCINO MOUSSE

Have some coffee for dessert! You won't feel as if you're missing a sweet if the coffee treat is capuccino. What's capuccino? Dark, sweet espresso, spiked with cinnamon and lightened half and half with warm milk. To make our capuccino calorie safe we lighten it with low-fat milk. Calorically speaking, coffee and cinnamon simply don't count.

CAPUCCINO. To make it, you'll need espresso coffee, the dark Continental blend. But you don't need an espresso maker, or any other special equipment. Brew the espresso in whatever pot or percolator you normally use, but add 2 heaping tablespoons coffee per cup of water instead of 1.

Also add ⅛ teaspoon ground cinnamon per cup of water. At serving time, fill the coffee cups only half full and sweeten to taste. Then "lighten" the coffee by filling the cups with gently-warmed low-fat milk. Delicious!

Spiced espresso coffee is such a dynamite taste you might like to try this combination in a diet-wise dessert.

[continued]

¼ cup cold water
1 envelope plain gelatin
1¼ cups hot espresso coffee
½ teaspoon ground cinnamon
1 pint vanilla ice milk, regular or sugar free
  Whipped low-calorie topping (optional)

Put cold water in a blender container, then sprinkle on gelatin. Wait 1 minute, until gelatin is soft, then add hot coffee and cinnamon. Cover and blend until all gelatin granules are dissolved. Add the ice milk a little at a time. Blend, covered, after each addition. Spoon into 6 dessert cups and chill until set. Serve with whipped low-calorie topping, if desired, and sprinkle with additional cinnamon. *Six servings, about 75 calories each.*

APPLESAUCE MOUSSE

  20-ounce jar unsweetened applesauce
1 envelope plain gelatin
¼ teaspoon apple-pie spice
¼ teaspoon ground cinnamon
2 tablespoons honey
½ teaspoon lemon extract
¼ teaspoon salt
2 egg whites
1 cup defrosted whipped topping
1 tablespoon walnuts
1 large cinnamon graham cracker

Combine ½ cup applesauce and gelatin in a small saucepan. Wait 3 or 4 minutes, until gelatin is softened, then heat over a moderate flame until gelatin granules are completely dissolved. Remove from heat and stir in remaining applesauce, spices, honey and lemon extract. Allow to cool completely.

Combine salt and room-temperature egg whites in a bowl and beat until stiff. Gently but thoroughly fold applesauce mixture into egg whites.

Gently but thoroughly fold whipped topping into apple-egg white mixture.

Spoon into a round bowl or 3-quart gelatin mold and chill several hours until firm. Unmold onto a plate.

Combine walnuts and graham cracker in a blender and blend to a powder. Sprinkle over unmolded apple mixture. *Eight servings, 90 calories each.*

CHOCOLATE MOUSSE

13-ounce can evaporated skim milk
2 tablespoons cornstarch
2 tablespoons unsweetened cocoa
6 tablespoons sugar
1 envelope plain gelatin
3 eggs, separated
Pinch of salt
1 cup defrosted whipped topping

Combine milk, cornstarch, cocoa, sugar, and gelatin in a saucepan. Cook and stir until mixture begins to simmer.

Beat the egg yolks lightly, stir a little of the hot mixture into the egg yolks, then stir the egg-yolk mixture back into the pan. Cook for one minute, but do not boil. Refrigerate until mixture begins to set.

Combine salt and egg whites and whip until stiff.

Remove chocolate mixture from refrigerator and stir smooth. Fold in egg whites and whipped topping. Spoon into a 5-cup mold and chill until firm. *Eight servings, 145 calories each.*

CRÈME DE MENTHE MOUSSE

1 cup boiling water
1 envelope (4 servings) low-calorie or regular lime gelatin dessert mix
¾ cup cold water
3 tablespoons green crème de menthe liqueur
1 envelope whipped topping mix (diet or regular), prepared
1 egg white

Stir boiling water into gelatin mix until dissolved. Stir in cold water and crème de menthe. Chill in refrigerator or freezer until syrupy. Meanwhile, prepare topping mix according to package directions.

Add egg white to syrupy gelatin and beat with electric mixer until fluffy and double in volume. Fold in prepared topping mix. Spoon into 8 footed cocktail glasses and chill until firm. At serving time, top with sliced fruit, if desired. *Eight servings, 50 calories each with diet mixes, 115 with regular.*

POTS DE CRÈME DE CACAO

A doozie of a boozey chocolate mousse!

3 tablespoons crème de cacao liqueur
1 envelope plain gelatin
1 tablespoon sugar (optional)
¾ cup hot black coffee
1 cup chocolate ice milk

Combine liqueur and gelatin in a blender container. Wait 1 minute, then add the sugar and hot coffee. Cover and blend until gelatin granules are dissolved. Add ice milk, cover and blend smooth.

Pour into 4 custard cups and chill until set. *Four servings, about 90 calories each.*

CHOCOLATE POTS DE CRÈME

1 envelope plain gelatin
1 egg
1 cup hot coffee
1 cup cold water
2 tablespoons brown sugar
1 tablespoon unsweetened cocoa
2 cups skim milk
1 envelope (4 servings) instant chocolate-pudding mix

Stir gelatin and egg together in a blender container. Wait 1 minute, until gelatin is soft. Blend on low speed. While blender is running, add hot coffee slowly. Turn speed to high and blend until all gelatin is dissolved. Add remaining ingredients, except pudding mix, and blend smooth. Add pudding mix and blend again. Spoon into 8 dessert cups and chill until set. *Eight servings, about 95 calories each.*

RASPBERRY BAVARIAN

10-ounce package frozen raspberries, defrosted
1 envelope (4 servings) regular or low-calorie strawberry gelatin
1 cup boiling water
Cold water
2 cups defrosted whipped topping

Drain defrosted raspberries, reserving juice. Dissolve gelatin in boiling water. Add cold water to reserved raspberry juice to make 1 cup liquid. Add this to dissolved gelatin. Chill until syrupy.

When partly set, whip gelatin mixture until fluffy. Fold in defrosted topping mix and berries, gently but thoroughly. Turn into a 1-quart bowl or gelatin mold, and chill until set. Unmold onto a platter and garnish with extra fruit, if desired. *Eight servings, under 140 calories each with regular gelatin; under 105 calories each with low-calorie gelatin.*

DOUBLE BERRY BAVARIAN

    2 envelopes (4 servings) low-calorie or regular strawberry gelatin dessert
        mix
      Pinch of salt
1⅓ cups boiling water
  ¼ cup sugar
    1 cup evaporated skim milk
    1 cup thinly sliced fresh strawberries

Dissolve both envelopes gelatin mix in the boiling water. Stir in sugar and salt. Chill in refrigerator until syrupy.

Pour the evaporated milk into a metal mixing bowl. Chill it in the freezer until ice crystals form around the edges. (Chill your beater blades, too.) Beat the chilled milk on high speed until it is the consistency of whipped cream (this may take 8 to 10 minutes).

Gently fold the gelatin mixture and sliced berries into the whipped milk. Chill 3 hours or more, until set. Garnish with additional berries, if desired. *Eight servings, 60 calories each with diet mix, 95 with regular.*

STRAWBERRY COEUR DE LA CRÈME

1 envelope plain gelatin
2 tablespoons water
1 cup skim milk
4 ounces (½ package) low-fat cream cheese
6 tablespoons sugar
1 cup low-fat vanilla yogurt
1 pint fresh strawberries, washed, hulled, and halved

Sprinkle gelatin over water in a blender container. Meanwhile, heat milk gently until hot. Pour over gelatin. Cover and blend on high speed until gelatin is dissolved. Add cream cheese, sugar, and yogurt. Cover and blend smooth. Pour into a heart-shaped mold and chill until set. Unmold and garnish with strawberries. *Six servings, about 135 calories each.*

EASY REAL-FRUIT GELATIN DESSERTS

Want to add new excitement to those so-so gelatin desserts? Make it real!
Real fruit juice—fresh, canned, or frozen—and unflavored gelatin are all
you need to make it yourself. Not much more trouble than dissolving one of
those sugary dessert powders in boiling water, and your homemade "jel-low"
can be as sweet or unsweet as you please.

Simply sprinkle an envelope of gelatin on ½ cup any favorite fruit juice in
a small saucepan. Heat and stir to boiling. Remove from flame and stir in
1½ cups fruit juice. If you like, stir in some sugar or sugar substitute (about
3 or 4 tablespoons' worth, at most!). Pour into 4 dessert cups and chill. *About
60 calories per serving, depending on juice.*

You can use any juice or combination you like. For example, apple, apricot,
blackberry, boysenberry, cherry, cranberry, elderberry, grapefruit, grape,
lemon or lime (¼ cup diluted), nectarine, orange, papaya, peach, prune, pear,
pineapple (canned, not fresh or frozen), plum, raspberry, strawberry, tangelo,
or tangerine. The more exotic non-supermarket juices can generally be found
in gourmet or health-food stores—unsweetened, naturally.

JELLED STRAWBERRIES ROMANOFF

1 **pint fresh ripe strawberries, washed and hulled**
1 **envelope plain gelatin**
¼ **cup Curaçao or other orange liqueur (60 proof) or cold water and a pinch
    of grated orange peel**
1 **cup boiling water**
  6–ounce can unsweetened frozen orange-juice concentrate, partly thawed

Put washed, hulled berries in a round glass bowl. Use small berries, if
available; otherwise slice them in half lengthwise.

Sprinkle gelatin on liqueur or cold water in a mixing bowl or blender
container. Wait 1 minute, then add boiling water. Blend or mix until gelatin
is dissolved. Add orange-juice concentrate and blend smooth. Pour over fruit.
Chill in refrigerator several hours.

Serve from the bowl. Or dip the bowl briefly in warm water, then invert on
a platter to unmold. *Six servings, about 90 calories each with liqueur; 80 calories
without.*

VARIATION

Strawberry-Banana-Orange Jel-low: Follow preceding recipe, but slice a small
ripe banana on top of the strawberries. Use cold water instead of liqueur. *Six
servings, about 90 calories each.*

FANCY FRUIT CHIFFON

Add eggs and skim-milk powder and you've turned your exotic fruit gel into an elegant show-off dessert . . . and a protein powerhouse as well!
Here's how:

1 envelope plain gelatin
  Pinch of salt
2 eggs, separated
⅔ cup dry skim-milk powder
12 ounces (1¾ cups) unsweetened fruit juice
3 tablespoons sugar

Beat gelatin, salt, egg yolks, milk powder, and fruit juice together in a saucepan. Place over very low heat. Cook and stir until gelatin dissolves and mixture thickens slightly, about 5 minutes. Chill in refrigerator until slightly set.

Beat egg whites and sugar until stiff. Fold gelatin mixture into egg whites. Spoon into dessert dishes or a 4–cup mold. Chill until set. *Six servings, 110 calories per serving.*

BLENDER-EASY CHIFFONS

If the recipe above sounds like too much trouble, try this:

2 envelopes plain gelatin
½ cup cold water
1½ cups boiling water
¾ cup dry skim-milk powder
2 whole eggs
5 tablespoons sugar
  Pinch of salt
2 small cans frozen unsweetened juice concentrate (except pineapple)

Sprinkle gelatin on cold water in a blender container. Wait 1 minute. Add boiling water; cover and blend until gelatin granules dissolve. Add milk powder, eggs, sugar, and salt. Cover and blend. Add frozen juice, cover, and blend until dissolved. Chill until set (about ½ hour for individual glasses, or 2 hours in a bowl). *Eight servings, 150 calories per serving.*

LOW-CALORIE HAUPIA

Polynesian Coconut Treat

If you'd like to add an exotic Polynesian touch to a diet dinner, why not finish it off with Haupia, the traditional dessert?

Haupia is a subtly-flavored coconut treat that's creamy like a pudding, but somewhat firmer. It shows up at nearly every luau, generally cut in squares and served on a "plate" of exotic island foliage (those decorator plants that sell for $95 in New York grow like weeds in Hawaii!).

To make authentic Haupia, you'd need taro root, sugar cane, and thick coconut milk—a little tough to find at the local supermarket. However, if you have to count your calories, the genuine article isn't for you anyway.

Our Slim Gourmet adaptation provides a Haupia that's much lower in fat, sugar, and starch, and features the good dairy nutrition of protein-rich milk. Moreover, it's a lot easier to make!

    1 envelope plain gelatin
    1 tablespoon arrowroot or cornstarch
    ½ cup sweetened shredded coconut
      Pinch of salt
    1 tablespoon vanilla
    3 cups cold skim milk

Combine gelatin, arrowroot, coconut, salt, and vanilla in a saucepan. Add half of the milk. Cook and stir constantly over a medium flame until the mixture boils and thickens. Stir in remaining milk. Pour into an 8 or 9-inch square cake pan and chill several hours. Cut in squares to serve. *Nine servings, 65 calories each.*

EGGLESS SLIMMER SABAYON

    1 envelope plain gelatin
    ⅓ cup Marsala
    1 cup boiling water
    2 cups skim milk
    1 envelope (4 servings) instant vanilla-pudding mix
      Shredded orange peel (optional)

Combine gelatin and Marsala in a blender container. Wait 1 minute, until gelatin is soft, then add boiling water. Cover and blend until all gelatin granules are dissolved. Add skim milk, cover, and blend. Add pudding mix, cover, and blend smooth. Spoon into 8 glasses and chill until set. Garnish with peel, if desired. *Eight servings, 90 calories each.*

INDEX